MY SOUL IS RESTED

MY SOUL IS RESTED

MOVEMENT DAYS
IN THE DEEP SOUTH REMEMBERED

HOWELL RAINES

G. P. PUTNAM'S SONS · NEW YORK

Acknowledgments

First, I am grateful to all who granted me interviews, including many whose recollections, through no fault of theirs, are not included in this volume.

I happily thank four New Yorkers who helped bring into being this book about the South: my literary agent, Timothy Seldes; my initial editor, Harvey Ginsberg; Putnam's publisher, Clyde Taylor, and my current editor, Diane Matthews. I am grateful, as well, to a man I've never met, Studs Terkel, for demonstrating the journalistic possibilities of oral-history techniques.

For their assistance in research or other kindnesses, I am indebted to: Bethel Fite and E. Culpepper Clark of the University of Alabama in Tuscaloosa; Fred R. Crawford of Emory University; Tennant S. Mc-Williams of the University of Alabama in Birmingham; Milo Dakin, Rita Jackson Samuels, Page Corsland, Curt Jocoy, Cherie Murdock, Ray Abernathy, Carol Muldawer, and James G. Minter, all of Atlanta; Frank Sikora, Georgia Price, and Mr. and Mrs. W. S. Raines, all of Birmingham; Ann Plott, Charlotte Hayes Woodley, and the late Robert H. Woodley, Sr., all of Tuscaloosa; Paul R. Davis of Auburn, Alabama, and Tom Offenburger of New York.

To these friends, I am grateful for their providing of shelter or companionship during my travels: Judy and Turner Smith of Baltimore; Lee Smith and Jim Seay of Chapel Hill; Joyce and Don Marion of New

Orleans; Penny and Kendal Weaver and Claude Duncan, all of Montgomery; Martha and John Lockett, Father James Robinson, and Bobbie and Dick Morthland, all of Selma; Lucinda Grissom and Marie Jemison, both of Birmingham.

Finally, I offer special thanks to my wife, Susan Woodley Raines, for setting aside her work as a photographer to help transcribe a mountain of tapes, to Hubert A. Grissom, Jr., for his help in so many ways, and to Barbara Harper of Birmingham, fastest and most accurate of typists.

For Susan, Ben, and Jeff, whose love sustained me during the writing of this book, and for John Lewis, whose courage helped make possible the story it tells.

A Chronology of the Civil Rights Movement in the Deep South, 1955–68

THE MONTGOMERY BUS BOYCOTT

December 1, 1955—Mrs. Rosa L. Parks is arrested for violating the bus-segregation ordinance in Montgomery, Alabama.

December 5, 1955—The Montgomery Bus Boycott begins, and Rev. Martin Luther King, Jr., 26, is elected president of the Montgomery Improvement Association.

December 21, 1956—Montgomery's buses are integrated, and the Montgomery Improvement Association calls off its boycott after 381 days.

January 10–11, 1957—The Southern Christian Leadership Conference (SCLC) is founded, with Dr. King as president.

THE STUDENT SIT-INS

February 1, 1960—Four black students sit in at the Woolworth's lunch counter in Greensboro, N.C., starting a wave of student protest that sweeps the Deep South.

April 15, 1960—The Student Nonviolent Coordinating Committee (SNCC) is founded at Shaw University in Raleigh, N.C.

October 19–27, 1960—Dr. King is jailed during a sit-in at Rich's Department Store in Atlanta and subsequently transferred to a maximum security prison. Democratic presidential nominee John F. Kennedy telephones Mrs. King to express his concern.

THE FREEDOM RIDES

May 4, 1961—The Freedom Riders, led by James Farmer of the Congress of Racial Equality (CORE), leave Washington, D.C., by bus.

May 14, 1961—A white mob burns a Freedom Rider bus outside Anniston, Ala. Riders aboard a second bus are beaten by Klansmen in Birmingham.

May 20, 1961—Freedom Riders are beaten at the Montgomery terminal. Whites riot outside a church where Dr. King, Farmer, and the Riders are meeting.

May 21, 1961—The Freedom Riders leave Montgomery under National Guard protection and are imprisoned immediately upon arriving in Jackson, Mississippi.

October 1, 1962—James Meredith becomes the first black man to attend class at the University of Mississippi.

THE BIRMINGHAM DEMONSTRATIONS

April 3, 1963—SCLC launches Project "C" (for confrontation) to protest segregation of lunch counters and rest rooms in downtown Birmingham.

April 12, 1963—Dr. King arrested on Good Friday for defying a state court's injunction against protest marches. While confined over Easter weekend, he writes the "Letter from Birmingham Jail."

May 2–7, 1963—SCLC organizes the "children's crusade," recruiting elementary and high school students for its marches. Police Commissioner Eugene "Bull" Connor retaliates with police dogs, fire hoses, and mass arrests that fill the jails.

May 10, 1963—Dr. King and Rev. Fred L. Shuttlesworth announce that Birmingham's white leaders have agreed to a desegregation plan. That night King's motel is bombed, and blacks riot until dawn.

June 11, 1963—Alabama Gov. George Wallace stages his "Stand in the Schoolhouse Door" in an unsuccessful effort to block integration of the University of Alabama.

June 12, 1963—NAACP leader Medgar Evers is shot to death at his home in Jackson, Mississippi.

September 15, 1963—Four black children die in the bombing of Sixteenth Street Baptist Church in Birmingham.

FREEDOM SUMMER June, 1964—Freedom Summer begins as hundreds of volunteers arrive in Mississippi to work in the Mississippi Summer Project organized by SNCC, CORE, SCLC, and NAACP.

July 2, 1964—President Lyndon B. Johnson signs the 1964 Civil Rights Act outlawing segregation in public accommodations.

August 4, 1964—After a six-week search, the bodies of three missing Summer Project workers are found buried under an earthen dam near Philadelphia, Mississippi.

December 10, 1964—Dr. King receives the Nobel Peace Prize.

THE SELMA MARCH March 7, 1965—"Bloody Sunday." Alabama troopers and Dallas County deputies beat and gas voting-rights marchers in Selma.

March 15, 1965—In his "We Shall Overcome" speech, President Johnson responds to the events in Selma by announcing that he is submitting a Voting Rights Bill to Congress.

March 21–25, 1965—Dr. King leads marchers from Selma to Montgomery. After the march, Mrs. Viola Liuzzo, a marcher from Detroit, is shot to death by nightriders.

August 6, 1965—President Johnson signs the Voting Rights Act.

April 4, 1968—Dr. King is shot to death in Memphis, Tennessee.

TABLE OF CONTENTS

III   FREEDOM RIDERS

INTERLUDE

IV   ALABAMA

The Battleground State

Part One: Birmingham

Part Two: Selma

INTERLUDE

V MISSISSIPPI

SNCC and the Home-Grown Heroes

INTERLUDE

BOOK TWO

I THE DOWN-HOME RESISTANCE

II HIGHER EDUCATION

III LAWYERS AND LAWMEN

INTRODUCTION

This book had its beginning on a gray February day in 1974. From the window of the Atlanta *Constitution*'s pressroom in the Georgia capitol, I watched a chill rain drizzle down on the statue of Tom Watson, my region's failed populist hero. Almost a century earlier, Watson had dreamed of creating a Southern politics that did not pander to racial hatred. As it turned out, the dream was greater than the man, and he betrayed it. But I realized on that cold winter's-end day in 1974 that the fulfillment of Tom Watson's dream was at hand. For a Southerner who had spent most of the previous decade as a reporter in Alabama and Georgia, the signs were too clear to be mistaken or ignored.

A black mayor and a black congressman had won election in Atlanta, the spiritual capital of the Old South. In Tuscaloosa, a diminished George Wallace had crowned a black woman as the University of Alabama's homecoming queen. I had watched from a balcony in the rotunda of the Georgia capitol as Governor Jimmy Carter hung a portrait of Martin Luther King, Jr., in the capitol's pantheon of great Georgians. These events spoke for themselves. But in the sacrifice and unfathomable courage that made such events possible, it seemed to me on that day, lay a story that had not received the telling it deserved. And this story, I was convinced, would be best told by the people who had lived it.

As it happened, my decision to spend my working life in the South had by 1974 delivered me to just the right place to assemble the story of the Civil Rights Movement years in the Deep South. After knocking about with several Alabama newspapers, I was covering the Georgia capitol as political editor of the Atlanta *Constitution*. Julian Bond, a leader of the Atlanta sit-in movement and a founder of the Student Nonviolent Coordinating Committee (SNCC), was in the House of Representatives chamber, down the hall from the pressroom where I sat. Within a few months, Hosea Williams, the firebrand orator who had led the marchers across the bridge at Selma, would join him there. A few blocks uptown was the office of former SNCC president John Lewis, another veteran of Selma's "Bloody Sunday," who was at once the most militant and the gentlest of his organization's "shock troops." Down on Auburn Avenue at the old Southern Christian Leadership Conference (SCLC) headquarters was Rev. Ralph David Abernathy, who had been with King every step of the way from Montgomery to the Lorraine Motel in Memphis. All of us lived within the congressional district then represented by United Nations Ambassador Andrew Young, another of King's associates and the first black congressman elected from the Deep South since Reconstruction. As an Atlanta newspaperman, I had met all of these people and written about most of them. I had learned, too, that this disparate group was united by the conviction that they were Martin Luther King, Jr.'s disciples to the future, obligated to see that the story of the Civil Rights Movement was passed on to the generations who would never know the South as it had been. Hosea Williams, bluntest spoken of the lot, told me one day that whenever he was inclined to refuse an interview he reflected on his experience with a University of Georgia student who wanted to write a thesis on the pioneering voter-registration drive Williams had conducted in Savannah. "First, I said to myself, 'No, I'm not going to tell this white boy all my stuff.' Then I thought about it and decided if I didn't help him tell the story, it might never be told."

Hosea Williams' gruff tone masks a generosity of spirit that is colorblind, and I found him and the other Movement veterans unfailingly willing to "tell the story." And by sharing their memories, they plugged me into a network of people both famous and obscure who had been involved in the Civil Rights Movement. Without their help, particularly that of John Lewis and Julian Bond, I would never have found many of the people whose recollections became important threads in the large fabric of the South's story.

Even with their help, the search for people I needed to interview occupied every spare moment in the nineteen months it took to compile *My Soul Is Rested*. To trace the chain of acquaintances that led from one person to the next, I relied on the suggestions and address files of interviewees, my own alphabetized search lists, luck, and that most fundamental investigative tool of the American journalist—the telephone company's information service. All of these figured, for example, in my progress from Julian Bond to Lawrence Guyot to Hartman Turnbow. Bond, in telling me about the founding of SNCC, mentioned Guyot as one of the first SNCC workers to venture into the Mississippi Delta. Guyot, once I found him, included in his vivid recollections of SNCC's forays a suggestion that I seek out Hartman Turnbow, who was to give me so much more than the exceptional interview contained in this book. On his farm between Mileston and Tchula, I spent a memorable afternoon under the spell of one of the most powerful personalities I expect ever to encounter.

To begin with, that afternoon was part of a week during which I had bounced back and forth between the Delta's two worlds. I started in the upper Delta, talking to Amzie Moore and Fannie Lou Hamer, heroic and unlettered black leaders whose personal courage and vision of the future had so changed Mississippi. Moving on to Jackson, in the middle of the state, I met a white Southerner who seemed untouched by all that had happened in his state in the previous twenty years. Robert Patterson, a former plantation manager in Mrs. Hamer's home county, assured me that he still believed as passionately in segregation in July, 1975, as he had in 1954, when he founded the Citizens Council.

Those reminders of the old and new Mississippi still fresh in my mind, I drove back toward the Delta. As I descended the long ridge that marks the eastern limit of that flat and fertile region, a thunderstorm swept across the fields. I inched northward through white curtains of rain until I reached Holmes County.

Those who know the South know the charged, dustless light that comes when the afternoon sun breaks through after a summer storm. In such light, Hartman Turnbow stood, surveying from his porch his green and glistening farm. He was not at all what I had expected.

Lawrence Guyot had cautioned that even among Movement people who admired his courage, Turnbow had the reputation of being difficult to deal with. He was known as a man who, as the Southern saying has it, covered all the ground he stood on. But where I had expected a big man, Hartman Turnbow was no more than five and a half feet tall. Where I had expected reticence and curt answers, I found the eloquence of a born storyteller. And most remarkably, despite all the troubles related in the Mississippi sequence of this book, I found Hartman Turnbow to be a booster of his native state.

"I tell you, I'm gon' finish up here in Mississippi," he told me as we sat in his living room, where holes from the nightriders' bullets still marked the walls. "I don't care how it gets, I'm gon' stay here till they take me to the cemetery, 'cause I was born here, and I understand the Mississippi way of life. You take a real poor person like I am, he can live in Mississippi better than you can in Detroit, Michigan, and Chicago, Illinois, and New York City. . . . Mississippi is still the best bet for a poor Negro or a poor white man, 'cause they can live here."

Mrs. Turnbow, who was working in the back of the house, called up to us, "Lots of people comin' back."

"Yeah, they comin' back," Hartman Turnbow agreed. "They comin' back. This is the best place. . . . You can spend your whole life in Chicago, Detroit, or New York or any of those major cities and all you'll ever have, the height of your growth, will be maybe a car and a house. . . . It take all the best of your life payin' for it. A car and a house all you wind up with and worked to death. In Mississippi, you can have a car and a house and not work as hard, not work yourself to death. You can have some days to go fishin'. If you like to squirrel hunt, you can have some days to go squirrel huntin'. And you can just enjoy yourself better. It's just a better livin'. A better way of life. And I'm gon' finish it right here."

Hartman Turnbow ended his paean to Mississippi with an observation that has rattled around in my memory ever since. "I'm just sayin' for a poor person," he concluded, "it's just now gittin' right." That sentence explains why I did not find Hartman Turnbow the brusque and difficult man I had expected him to be. He had been difficult when the times demanded it, but the South, by getting right, had at last allowed Hartman Turnbow to be the gentle man it was always his nature to be. The Turnbows' affection for the state they worked to reform explains, too, why the powerful feelings expressed so candidly by Robert Patterson did not in the end prevail. The Turnbows' story, repeated thousands of times, is what transformed the South from a region of despair to the new heartland of American optimism.

People like Mr. and Mrs. Hartman Turnbow don't need a college professor or a visiting journalist or even Jimmy Carter to tell them about the "New South." They've lived its creation, and after a lifetime in the region, I can only marvel at my fellow Southerners' accomplishment. It was in the hope of conveying a sense of the magnitude of their achievement that I included a few voices of Southern resistance in this collection.

No set of interviews presented a more varied set of problems than those collected in the chapter entitled "The Down-home Resistance." Having spent their lifetimes in politics, Roy Harris of Augusta, Georgia, and former Alabama Governor John Patterson were still as willing for me to interview them as they would have been in the fifties, when they were in the mainstream of Southern political thought. Other conservative Southerners were less cooperative. Many had long since adopted a prejudice against journalists, Yankee and Southern alike, every bit as powerful as that once directed toward "civil rights agitators."

My Southern accent—I was born and reared in Birmingham—was sometimes an asset, but it was by no means an infallibly reliable one. Once I drove three hundred miles, thinking I had secured an interview, only to discover that my reluctant subject simply wanted to look me over before deciding if he should talk to me. After what seemed interminable deliberation, he did. In another session, the suspicious interviewee set up his own tape recorder to make sure, so I was informed, that I would not attempt to twist his words. One former intimate of George Wallace, a gentleman of unfailing courtliness, nonetheless refused to tell me anything of consequence about the politician he had come to despise. His wife had made him promise never to criticize Wallace, he later explained, because she was terrified of retaliation by the Wallaceites in their Alabama town. Her fear, unrealistic by the standards of the mid-seventies, was rooted in her very accurate memory of the climate of repression I remembered from my years in Birmingham.

Fortunately, most Southerners part much more willingly with their recollections, for it is true that the South is a region of storytellers. But an interviewer can by no means be lazy about creating the right atmosphere for storytelling. I remember the frustration I felt after two long sessions with Ralph Abernathy, one of the first Movement leaders I interviewed. My frustration stemmed from my own awareness that, although Abernathy had been responsive and generous with his time, I had yet to engage his interest. Finally, near the end of our third session, I brought up the assassination of Martin Luther King, Jr. In those days, Abernathy was being asked at every turn if he thought the investigation into King's death ought to be reopened and about his theories concerning a possible conspiracy. But he had not been asked in a long time, I sensed, about what he and his friend did and said in their last days and hours together. Abernathy's narrative began to move with an energy and emotional force of its own, but to my dismay his secretary stepped into the room and ended the interview by announcing his next appointment. I asked anxiously if he would make room in his schedule for me to return the next afternoon, and he agreed. To my surprise, he picked up his account the next day as if twenty-four hours had not intervened, because, I later decided, he was telling a story he himself wanted to hear. The lesson of that experience served me well in the months ahead.

The interviews in this book were conducted between October, 1974, and April, 1976. Except for the multiple sessions with Ralph Abernathy, John Lewis, and a few others, each interview was done in one sitting. Though I learned that most people are good for sixty to ninety minutes of conversation in a session, I seldom asked for that much time when making appointments with busy people. If an interview was going well, it would run on beyond the forty-five minutes I usually requested.

In transcribing the tapes, my wife Susan and I went over each of them several times to insure the accuracy of the transcription. Later, I edited out, as evenhandedly as I could, many of the repetitious phrases—*well, I mean, and uh,* and the ubiquitous *you know*—that many of us use to punctuate our conversation. About one-third of the people I interviewed wanted to see a transcript of the interview before signing the release required for publication of verbatim remarks. In a few cases I was asked to change my renderings of their pronunciations—substituting *going to* for *gonna,* for instance, or *Negro* for what I had rendered as *nigra*—and I have agreed in order to get permission to publish their remarks. But no one, I hasten to add, asked me to change statements of fact or statements of opinion that the interviewee knew might prove controversial or embarrassing.

The interview with Lawrence Guyot contains material from two sessions in which we covered much of the same material. I have taken the liberty of blending the overlapping parts of the two interviews into one narrative. The same is true of the remarks of Lonnie King. In several cases, I have paired interviews which are related in subject matter—for instance, Lonnie King's and Julian Bond's accounts of the Atlanta sit-ins, and Ben Allen's and Glenn V. Evans' accounts of their police work in Alabama. All these interviews were conducted separately, and there is no connection among these people beyond that which I, as editor, have imposed by presenting their accounts together.

I conducted every interview in the book except the one with Autherine Lucy Foster, the first black person to attend the University of Alabama. Culpepper Clark, a teacher and very able historian at that institution, interviewed Mrs. Foster and helped me secure permission to quote from this, her first extensive interview since she was unjustly expelled from the University.

The Foster interview and that with Rev. Martin Luther King, Sr., are the only interviews included here that were not conducted expressly for this book. I interviewed Rev. King at the request of producer Adam Abram for a program broadcast over Atlanta's educational television station, WETV. I excerpted Rev. King's reflections on the South and his son's death from that twenty-minute broadcast interview.

The South, where for generations black and white have lived in the grip of poverty and injustice, has taught those of us who live here to be cautious in our optimism. But when Movement veteran Albert Turner comes in from the fields of Black Belt Alabama and announces that the South has changed, it is a foolish caution that ignores such powerful witness. In the South today, we are living on the frontier of possibility, and it is my hope that this book will in some measure explain how we got there. I've been over these tapes and transcripts many times now, yet their stories are still as alive for me as they were at the first telling. I believe that is because most of them are stories of commitment and sacrifice, qualities that are neither transient nor tiresome.

Merely saying that the South is a land of storytellers, however, does not fully explain why so many of the people who made the Movement have been able to express their experiences so poetically. Rather, there is a mysterious eloquence in people who have lived with greatness. I think, for instance, of Sheyann Webb. As we talked at her home in Selma the summer before she went off to college at Tuskegee, she asked if I would like to see the scrapbook she kept as a child during the Movement days in Selma. It contained a Kodacolor snapshot showing her as a pigtailed nine-year-old sitting on the lap of a young white man she identified as Jonathan Daniels. A few weeks after the picture was taken, Daniels, an Episcopal seminarian, was shot down on the streets of Hayneville, Alabama, for encouraging blacks to register to vote. Martin Luther King, Jr., had also held her in his lap, and he, too, was shot to death by a white man. Thumbing on through her scrapbook, I came upon her essay, "My Pal Dr. Martin Luther King, Jr." The long-legged printing, the childishly erratic spelling and punctuation, were so at odds with the magnitude of the loss the world had forced upon her at so young an age that I have since kept a copy of her essay as a reminder of the suffering that so many have invested in our region.

"I met Dr. King at the age of 9 [in] 1965 at Brown Chapel Church, . . ." she wrote. "Every time he come to Brown Chapel Church he will ask me to sing some songs for him and I will do that. Me and him have talk together walk together ate together song together and pray together. When ever he get ready to leave he will kiss me and give me an autograph. . . . He died, but I will never forget him, as he said Free at Last Free at Last Thank God of mighty I'm Free at Last."

Free at last. The words which ended Sheyann Webb's tribute to her friend began our new life in the South. Of all the lessons Martin Luther King, Jr., tried to teach us, the hardest for white Southerners to understand was that the Civil Rights Movement would free us, too.

As a newspaperman covering the 1976 campaign, I heard Jimmy

Carter affirm the truth of that teaching many times in many cities. "I could not stand here today as a candidate for president of the United States," he said in Watts and the black wards of Philadelphia, "had it not been for Martin Luther King, Jr." When Jimmy Carter was elected, John Lewis wept for joy and wished aloud that his mentor had lived to see what the Movement had accomplished.

If he had lived, Martin Luther King, Jr., would see a South still burdened with inequities in housing, education, and distribution of wealth. But I believe he would look beyond those problems to see a region changed in a way that millions of us who lacked his vision would have thought impossible twenty years ago. He would see a South where we are all free at last to become what we can.

St. Petersburg, Florida
February 8, 1977

Anybody hada just told me 'fore it happened that conditions would make this much change between the white and the black in Holmes County here where I live, why I'da just said, "You're lyin'. It won't happen." I just wouldn't have believed it. I didn't dream of it. I didn't see no way. But it got to workin' just like the citizenship class teacher told us—that if we would redish to vote and just stick with it. He says it's gon' be some difficults. He told us that when we started. We was looking for it. He said we gon' have difficults, gon' have troubles, folks gon' lose their homes, folks gon' lose their lives, peoples gon' lose all their money, and just like he said, all of that happened. He didn't miss it. He hit it ka-dap on the head, and it's workin' now. It won't never go back where it was.

—Hartman Turnbow

PRELUDE

JAMES FARMER

On Cracking White City

In 1941, fresh out of Howard University's theology school, he hired on as race-relations secretary with the Fellowship of Reconciliation (FOR), a staid, old-line pacifist organization in Chicago.

In the course of my work there, I began studying Gandhi, Gandhi's program, his work in India in nonviolence . . . I sent a memorandum to A.J. Muste, who was executive director of the Fellowship of Reconciliation, proposing that the FOR take the lead in starting an organization which would seek to use Gandhi-like techniques of nonviolent resistance —including civil disobedience, noncooperation, and the whole bit—in the battle against segregation. . . .

. The decision was that the FOR would not sponsor it and assume that measure of responsibility for its outcome, its success or failure, but . . . I was authorized on their payroll to try to set up a local group of the sort I had suggested—in one city—and the FOR would not sponsor it. They would just pay my salary, fifteen dollars a week, while I was doing that.

He convened the first meeting simply by calling together his friends— "most of them graduate students at the University of Chicago . . . pacifists and socialists who were similarly studying Gandhi."

That was an all-night session by the way, deciding what the name was going to be. And one fellow—I have no idea where he is now—name of

Bob Chino, who was half Chinese and half Caucasian, came up with a name during this all-night meeting. He said, "Why don't we call it CORE because it's the core of things. It's the center around which all else is built." Then the problem was, what does C-O-R-E stand for? [Laughs] We then decided that it should be Committee *of* or *on* Racial Equality. A lengthy debate transpired on whether it was to be *on* or *of* Racial Equality. And my side won . . . it became *of.*

Our first project then was a sit-in, or stand-in, I guess you'd call it, at a roller skating rink that was appropriately named White City Roller Skating Rink [laughs], which was at the corner of Sixty-third Street and South Park Avenue in southside Chicago. . . . This was in the ghetto, really, several blocks within the ghetto, but all white. Blacks were not admitted.

I should say that at this same time we met and consulted with an Indian, a Hindu, a Brahmin named Krishnalal Shridharani, who had been a disciple of Gandhi's in India, was with Gandhi on the famous march to the sea, the Salt March.* He at this time was working on his Ph.D. at Columbia in sociology and his dissertation was a book analyzing Gandhi's technique, Gandhi's method. It was entitled *War Without Violence,* and this caught our imagination because that was precisely what we were aimed at. It was not acquiescence, as most people at that time, when they heard of nonviolence, assumed that it was . . . In this book Shridharani had outlined Gandhi's steps of investigation, negotiation, publicity, and then demonstration. And we adopted those steps as our method of action.

At White City we first investigated in order to confirm what we already knew existed by having blacks go in and try to skate and they were stopped, of course, and told, "I'm sorry, we can't sell you tickets. You can't come in." This was done several times to be sure that there was no mistake about the policy. . . . Then we had whites, several

* Gandhi's Salt March of 1930 provided both a spiritual example and a tactical model for the Civil Rights Movement in the South. With the march Gandhi launched the campaign of civil disobedience which broke the power of the British raj in India. First, Gandhi announced that he and a few followers would walk two hundred miles from his Sabarmati ashram to the coastal town of Dandi to protest the British tax on salt, an essential in the peasant diet. Then, on the beach at Dandi Gandhi broke the law guaranteeing the British monopoly in the manufacture of salt by evaporating sea water to make his own untaxed salt crystals. The British arrested Gandhi about thirty days after he arrived on the coast, but by that time it was too late. Gandhi's act of defiance had unified the Indian nationalist movement, and an estimated one hundred thousand Indians followed him into the jails. The protests ended only when the British made the first of the concessions which led eventually to Indian self-government. For comments on the influence of the Salt March on Movement tactics, see Bayard Rustin and Laurie Pritchett.

whites, try to go in, with no apparent connection with the black group, and they were promptly admitted and skated around. Then we had an interracial group go in and seek admission, and this threw White City persons into confusion. Obviously they were part of one group, so what were they going to say?

So finally they had to use the club-night line and they said, "I'm sorry, it's club night, and you can't come in unless you have a club card." And our group said, "Are there no exceptions?" "Absolutely no exceptions, nobody gets in without a club card." "You know, that's strange. Some of our friends are already skating in there, and we know that they have no club card. They are not members of a club." "Well, are you sure of that?" "Yes, we are sure of that. We see them skating right through the door there, and one of them waved at us." So they then consulted with the manager and everything else and said, "I'm just sorry, you can't come in."

We stood in line for a while, . . . then went back every night to do the same thing, and finally tied up the line so that nobody else could get to the gate, and it became pretty rough. A little violence when some of the young tough whites wanted to skate badly. . . . This campaign against White City went on for several months before there was a conclusion, and finally we were victorious. White City admitted everybody after [our] picket lines and standing in line and cutting down on their profit, virtually bringing things to a halt. They began admitting blacks.

. . . during White City—the thing was dragging on for several months—somebody suggested, "Well, why don't we sue? Let's go to court and sue on the basis of century-old civil rights laws." We rejected this because that would be reverting to the old techniques which we knew could work under certain circumstances, but it would not tell us whether nonviolence would work here, direct-action techniques. In the meantime we sat in at restaurants. The first restaurant, which turned out to be the first CORE success, was at a little place in southside Chicago near the University of Chicago at Forty-seventh and Kimbark Avenue called Jack Spratt Coffeehouse or Coffee Shop, and we discovered discrimination there by accident.*

The "accident" occurred one evening after a CORE meeting. He and a white member named Jimmy Robinson stopped by Jack Spratt to continue a discussion of establishing CORE chapters in other cities.

* Portions of interviews set off in this manner—indented and with a hairline rule at left—appear out of sequence. They have been transposed by the author for reasons of clarity and continuity.

* * *

The manager walked over and said, "I can't serve you," to me. And I said, "Why not?" And he said, "I just can't serve you." And I said—here again I was going back to the old legalistic approach—"I suppose you realize you are violating the state law." And he walked away, and I then called and asked him if he would give me his name and his title, his responsibility there. It was the implied threat of a suit, you know. [Laughs, as if at his own innocence] We were not imaginative enough—then.

He then walked back to me and said, "Whaddaya want?" I said, "Coffee and a doughnut." And he said, "The doughnuts will be a dollar apiece." Now this was the day of five-cent doughnuts, or two for five, you know. I said, "That's pretty steep for doughnuts, don't you think?" He said, "That's my price." Robinson said, "I know better. I've gotten doughnuts here many times and it's a nickel for a doughnut and not a dollar." So we went on and ate, and when I paid the bill with a dollar, the man gave me correct change, charging the nickel rather than the dollar for the doughnut.

We decided we owed it to him to return to his place of business, and we went back in a group of about, oh, six or eight and ordered food, and he thought for a while and then had us served. And we said, "Well, I guess there's really no problem here." We put the money on the counter near the cash register and started to go out and he raked the money off the counter, rushed to the door behind us, and hurled our money out into the street, screaming, "Take your money and get out of here. We don't want it."

We left the money there scattered in the street so he couldn't charge legitimately that we had refused to pay our bill and taken the money or had stolen money from him. So we then went into a session, battle session, to decide how we would proceed on Jack Spratt.

"We tried to negotiate then—the Gandhian technique, the Gandhian step." The Jack Spratt management refused all overtures, hanging up when CORE members phoned, ignoring letters. Two members were dispatched "to try to negotiate on the spot, without any appointment." They found in place of the original manager a woman who was apparently his superior. Hers was an argument which twenty years later would be repeated by white businessmen all across the South. "She said, 'Of course, I have no objections to serving you, personally, but it's just a matter of business. We're here to make money; we're not crusaders. We're trying to make a profit and we wouldn't make a profit if we serve you because we'll lose all our white customers.' "

Still clinging to the "Gandhian goodwill bit," the CORE negotiators offered to stand good for any money lost in a one-month trial integration. But finally, the woman said she was sorry, she simply didn't want to talk about it anymore.

We went in with a group of about twenty—this was a small place that seats thirty or thirty-five comfortably at the counter and in the booths—and occupied just about all of the available seats and waited for service. The woman was in charge again. She ordered the waitress to serve the whites who were seated in one booth, and she served them. She ordered the waitress to serve two whites who were seated at the counter, and she served them. Then she told the blacks, "I'm sorry, we can't serve you, you'll have to leave." And they, of course, declined to leave and continued to sit there. By this time the other customers who were in there were aware of what was going on and were watching, and most of these were university people, University of Chicago, who were more or less sympathetic with us. And they stopped eating and the two people at the counter she had served and those whites in the booth she had served were not eating. There was no turnover. People were coming in and standing around for a few minutes and walking out. There were no seats available.

So she walked over to two of the whites at the counter and said, "We served you. Why don't you eat and get out?" They said, "Well, madam, we don't think it would be polite for us to begin eating our food before our friends here have also been served." So a couple of minutes went by and she announced that she would serve the blacks, the Negroes, which was the term used then, in the basement. We, of course, declined and told her we were quite comfortable. She then said, "If all of the Negroes will occupy those two booths in the back we will serve you there." We declined again. She said, "I'll call the police."

Then I said to her, "Fine, I think that might be the appropriate step." By the way, we, still following the Gandhian motif, had called the police in advance, being completely open and above board, everything, in notifying the authorities. We called the police department and told them what we were going to do. In fact, we read the state civil rights law to them. They weren't familiar with that. [Laughs] They assured us that if we followed the pattern which we outlined to them over the phone, there was nothing they could do to arrest us. They'd have no grounds for making an arrest because we were within our rights to insist upon service. And we asked them if they would see that we were served as they were obligated to do by law, but this they would not do. No, they wouldn't do that, but they wouldn't arrest us.

So we said, "Perhaps you should call the police." She did. Two cops came a few minutes later, looked the situation over, said, "Why, lady, what did you call us for? I don't see anybody here disturbing the peace. Everything seems to be peaceful." She said, "Won't you throw these people out on the grounds that we reserve the right to seat our patrons and would serve some of them in the basement?" The cop didn't know. He went to a telephone booth and made a call. I guess he was calling headquarters to see if they could do that. Came out and said, "Nope, sorry lady, there's nothing in the law that allows us to do that. You must either serve them or solve the problem yourself." And the cops then walked out. On the way out they turned around and winked at us. [Laughs]

We stayed there until closing time and then got up and left and went back the next day, a little bit earlier, and stayed until closing time. And so on. Then tried again to negotiate—without success. We went back in, oh, several more times and tied up the whole afternoon, tied up all the seats. They were doing no business at all.

Finally they cracked. The next time we went in, they served everybody. And accepted money. Did not overcharge us. We then sent an interracial group, a smaller group, in the next day. Everyone was served. We then sent an all-black group in and they were served. We waited a week and sent another black group in, and they were all served. We sent individual blacks in and they were all served without any problem. So we then wrote them a letter thanking them for their change in policy. . . .

At this time, this period in history, it was more the rule than the exception that places of public accommodation in Northern cities excluded blacks. It was more the rule. It was quite exceptional to find any restaurant in downtown Chicago that would serve blacks. And we took on some big ones . . . Stoner's Restaurant that seated, oh, five hundred or six hundred people downstairs and upstairs, and we had such experiences as being served garbage sandwiches and having trays of hot food spilled over our heads, and some of the members were kicked in the shin by the owner and such things as that. Finally all the Negro busboys quit their jobs in protest, and they hired Negro busgirls, and they finally quit in protest. Stoner's finally changed, but this took several months of activity, and they began serving everybody. Later they went out of business. I don't think there was any connection, although I couldn't be sure. [Laughs]

Were you having any success in the publicity component that you mentioned?

No, we were not. We'd get a little item, a small item in the Chicago *Defender,* which was a black newspaper . . . a small article, and they would come in and take a picture occasionally. As I recall they never used the pictures really. They were not really interested because this was a rather bizarre technique to them. . . . "They hit you and you are not going to hit them back? . . . What is this nonviolent crap?" They had not warmed up to it, and we had discussions then with a number of the Negro leaders of the time, and they simply could not see nonviolence: "No, no, that is just unrealistic. If they hit you, you've got to do something. Hit them back. It just won't work."

White press displayed no [interest in you].

. . . if we were lucky, we would get a small paragraph on the back page of the Chicago *Tribune* saying in effect that a half-dozen nuts and crackpots sat-in this restaurant—they didn't say "sat-in" because there wasn't such a phrase then—tried to get service in this restaurant and refused to leave and stayed there for two hours or three hours or until closing time or until they were thrown out, whichever came first. That was all, but there was no TV then, no TV coverage, anything. The thing did not spread by itself, but we moved from restaurant to restaurant. We also had stand-ins in cafeterias. We had wade-ins at public beaches, and since there was no owner there to put us out or order us to leave, we had to confront hoodlums who tried to throw us out or tried to drown some people, literally. On some occasions it was difficult to stick with nonviolence, so we did have training sessions. In those days, since we were comparatively small, we had training sessions in the discipline of nonviolence, using sociodrama and so forth. And our members at that time were largely young, largely intellectuals, and I would say more means-oriented than ends-oriented. They were concerned with nonviolence as a technique and proving that it worked. We were not a rank-and-file movement, not a mass movement, and had not begun at that point recruiting from the, quote, lower classes, unquote. We were middle class, all of us, students.

What racial make-up?

Largely white. I would say two-to-one or maybe even three-to-one white, because it was difficult to find blacks who were willing to go through that. In the first place, you had to be some sort of a crusader to go in there and put up with all of this when the focus was on you. *You* were the person being told you couldn't be served. And how many people had skins that thick, to deliberately walk into that kind of situation, especially when they weren't gonna fight back? . . . We found more whites who were cued in to the idealism of the technique and thus willing to do it.

By the following summer, there were three or four CORE chapters, enough to have a "national convention" in Chicago. He was elected president. By the second year there were chapters in New York, Pittsburgh, Philadelphia, Detroit, Los Angeles, Seattle, and San Francisco.

We debated at each of our conventions, annual conventions, whether we were going to move into the South. This was in the forties, the early forties. The term we used was, quote, invade the South, unquote, since we were Northerners. I opposed it at that point, and we did not do it. I opposed it on the grounds that we were new. We did not have the support of the black community or the white liberal community or any masses. We were just a few individuals. I thought the violent reaction we would encounter in the South would be overwhelming, that the movement, the organization—it was not a movement then—would be destroyed and its participants probably killed, if we had begun sitting-in in Birmingham or Montgomery in the early 1940s or sitting-in in waiting rooms or freedom riding then.

I should say that there was a kind of a Freedom Ride that was cosponsored by the FOR and CORE in 1947. This was called the Journey of Reconciliation. . . . This was stimulated, sparked, by the Irene Morgan Supreme Court decision in 1946, where the court ruled that segregated seating on the buses was unconstitutional, should not be allowed. So this group of reconcilers rode the buses with the blacks sitting in the front and the whites sitting in the back through the upper South. They did not venture into the Deep South. They went through Maryland, Virginia, North Carolina, West Virginia. That was it. And there were arrests. In North Carolina, in fact, a number of people spent thirty days on the chain gang for refusing to leave the bus. That was in 1947.

The organization continued to be small. At one point we wondered whether we had to give up the ghost because we weren't growing, and it was hard to keep the chapters alive. We weren't getting any publicity—oh, a little paragraph here and there. There seemed to be no interest in the black community or anyplace else. Nonviolence was still an unknown technique and the word caused adverse reaction. It only began to grow at the time of the Montgomery Bus Boycott of King in 1956. . . .

BOOK ONE

I
THE BEGINNING

MONTGOMERY, 1955–56

E.D. Nixon

"I'm an old man now, but I'm so proud that I had a part in what happened here in Montgomery." He is, in fact, a year older than the century, and although retired from the railroad, he works every day as recreation director of a public housing project in Montgomery. From his office window he can look out over the playground he built. It is teeming with black children who attend the daycare center he founded. He leans back in his chair, props one leg atop his desk to ease an arthritic knee, and recalls the night he was invited to Madison Square Garden to tell the story of the Montgomery Bus Boycott.

There were eighteen thousand people in the Garden that night. He sat between two of his favorite people, Eleanor Roosevelt and A. Philip Randolph, the founder of Nixon's union, the Brotherhood of Sleeping Car Porters. It was past midnight when he was called to speak, and as he approached the lectern, he threw away the speech he had written.

I don't know how, it just came to me all at once. I said, "I'm E.D. Nixon. I'm from Montgomery, Alabama, a city that's known as the Cradle of the Confederacy, that had stood still for more than ninety-three years until Rosa L. Parks was arrested and thrown in jail like a common criminal." [Breaks into a singsong] I said, "Fifty thousand people rose up and caught hold to the Cradle of the Confederacy and began to rock it till the Jim Crow rockers began to reel and the segregated slats began to fall out." Said, "I'm from that city." And man, people just fell out. I coulda sat down then. Right then.

I've known times for years and years I was the only person in Montgomery saying anything about the mistreatment of Negroes—to the end that it got to the place that most people looked on me as a leader, even though I wasn't never designated as such, because I could call a meeting. Say it was necessary that we have a meeting, I bet you I could call forty ministers at that time, at least thirty would be present. And I could appoint a meeting at any church. See, people think because Rev. King was selected and the meetings started at his church, that he done it, but I selected the spot. I called the people together, and I told them we was going to meet at that Dexter Avenue Baptist Church. . . .* If we'da met on the suburbs, insurance mens and doctors and things who were working downtown wouldn't leave the office to go away out. But with it right downtown in the heart there wasn't no question they could walk right around the corner to it, and that's why the meeting was set up there, but a whole lot of people don't know that. They just think Rev. King come in, organized the Montgomery Improvement Association at his church and all. That isn't true. But the question is—we're not arguing the point, I'm just giving you the facts—that the job was done and that's the important thing.

How did the bus boycott get started?

First of all, we'd talked about a bus boycott all the year. We had three other people prior to Mrs. Parks arrested who reported their incidents to us, but you couldn'ta found nobody in Montgomery would agree to have a bus boycott—and I'm not patting myself on the shoulder —unless it was approved by E.D. Nixon. The first one was a minister's daughter. Her name was Mrs. Wayne. After I talked to her I discovered that she would not make a good litigant. Now you are on the outside here. You think that anybody that got arrested would be good. Now you would think that, the average person would think that, but my training with NAACP and the Brotherhood of Sleeping Car Porters taught me different. I've handled so many cases that I know when a man would stand up and when he wouldn't. So after I talked to her, I told the group, "No use in me going to court with this case, we can't win it."

---

* The church near the Alabama capitol where Martin Luther King, Jr., became pastor in 1954.

*"Then we had the second case; she was a young girl, a school girl.
When I got home, two or three carloads were out in front of my door
waiting on me, said, 'We got the right case now.' " He rejected this girl,
too. The same thing happened a third time. One of the girls had personal problems which he knew a clever lawyer could exploit in court.
Another was vetoed when he visited her home and found her father
"sitting there drunk and half-dressed" on the front porch. He believed
that any black who challenged segregation had to be above reproach.*

So then some of the people were getting disgusted with me, see. Some
of them said they didn't know whether I was making the right approach
or not. This was in October when this last case was. Then, on December
one, Rosa L. Parks was arrested. When she was arrested, a friend of
hers called my wife and told my wife they'd arrested Mrs. Parks and
Mrs. Nixon called my office. . . .

She said, "Arrested Mrs. Parks," and I said, "For what?" She said,
"I don't know. Go get her," just like I could go get her. I called down
there and asked them what was the charge against her, and the desk ser-
geant said to me, he said, "None of your so-and-so business." Of
course, no use of me arguing with him, so I called a white lawyer. Our
black lawyer was out of the state at the time, Fred Gray. I called a
white lawyer by the name of Clifford J. Durr.* I said, "Mr. Durr, they
arrested Mrs. Parks." He said, "For what?" and I said, "Something
about on the bus. What I want you to do is to call up down there and
find out the charges against her." So he called up down there, in a few
minutes called me back and said, "The charge is violating the Alabama
segregation law."

* A Federal Communications Commission member in the New Deal, Durr had
resigned from government service during the loyalty-oath probes of the Truman
Administration. Until his death in 1975, he, with his wife Virginia, was among
Alabama's best-known white liberals. The aristocratic Durrs were despised by
segregationists as traitors to their class and admired by progressives for their political courage.

Rosa L. Parks

I had had problems with bus drivers over the years, because I didn't see fit to pay my money into the front and then go around to the back. Sometimes bus drivers wouldn't permit me to get on the bus, and I had been evicted from the bus. But as I say, there had been incidents over the years. One of the things that made this get so much publicity was the fact the police were called in and I was placed under arrest. See, if I had just been evicted from the bus and he hadn't placed me under arrest or had any charges brought against me, it probably could have been just another incident.

I had left my work at the men's alteration shop, a tailor shop in the Montgomery Fair department store, and as I left work, I crossed the street to a drugstore to pick up a few items instead of trying to go directly to the bus stop. And when I had finished this, I came across the street and looked for a Cleveland Avenue bus that apparently had some seats on it. At that time it was a little hard to get a seat on the bus. But when I did get to the entrance to the bus, I got in line with a number of other people who were getting on the same bus.

As I got up on the bus and walked to the seat I saw there was only one vacancy that was just back of where it was considered the white section. So this was the seat that I took, next to the aisle, and a man was sitting next to me. Across the aisle there were two women, and there were a few seats at this point in the very front of the bus that was called the white section. I went on to one stop and I didn't particularly notice who was getting on the bus, didn't particularly notice the other people getting on. And on the third stop there were some people getting on, and at this point all of the front seats were taken. Now in the beginning, at the very first stop I had got on the bus, the back of the bus was filled up with people standing in the aisle and I don't know why this one vacancy that I took was left, because there were quite a few people already standing toward the back of the bus. The third stop is when all the front seats were taken, and this one man was standing and when the driver looked around and saw he was standing, he asked the four of us, the man in the seat with me and the two women across the aisle, to let him have those front seats.

At his first request, didn't any of us move. Then he spoke again and said, "You'd better make it light on yourselves and let me have those seats." At this point, of course, the passenger who would have taken the seat hadn't said anything. In fact, he never did speak to my knowledge. When the three people, the man who was in the seat with me and the two women, stood up and moved into the aisle, I remained where I was. When the driver saw that I was still sitting there, he asked if I was going to stand up. I told him, no, I wasn't. He said, "Well, if you don't stand up, I'm going to have you arrested." I told him to go on and have me arrested.

He got off the bus and came back shortly. A few minutes later, two policemen got on the bus, and they approached me and asked if the driver had asked me to stand up, and I said yes, and they wanted to know why I didn't. I told them I didn't think I should have to stand up. After I had paid my fare and occupied a seat, I didn't think I should have to give it up. They placed me under arrest then and had me to get in the police car, and I was taken to jail and booked on suspicion, I believe. The questions were asked, the usual questions they ask a prisoner or somebody that's under arrest. They had to determine whether or not the driver wanted to press charges or swear out a warrant, which he did. Then they took me to jail and I was placed in a cell. In a little while I was taken from the cell, and my picture was made and fingerprints taken. I went back to the cell then, and a few minutes later I was called back again, and when this happened I found out that Mr. E.D. Nixon and Attorney and Mrs. Clifford Durr had come to make bond for me.

In the meantime before this, of course, . . . I was given permission to make a telephone call after my picture was taken and fingerprints taken. I called my home and spoke to my mother on the telephone and told her what had happened, that I was in jail. She was quite upset and asked me had the police beaten me. I told her, no, I hadn't been physically injured, but I was being held in jail, and I wanted my husband to come and get me out. . . . He didn't have a car at that time, so he had to get someone to bring him down. At the time when he got down, Mr. Nixon and the Durrs had just made bond for me, so we all met at the jail and we went home. . . .

E.D. Nixon

Then we went on up to the house and I said to Mrs. Parks, "Mrs. Parks"—her mother had some coffee made—I said, "Mrs. Parks, this is the case we've been looking for. We can break this situation on the bus with your case."

She said, "Well, I haven't thought of it just like that." So we talked to her mother and her husband, and finally they came 'round, said they'd go along with it.

She said, "All right." She said, "You know, Mr. Nixon, if you say so, I'll go along with it."

I said, "Okay, we can do it."

What was there about Mrs. Parks that made her the right litigant as opposed to these others?

Mrs. Parks was a married woman. She had worked for me for twelve years, and I knew her. She was morally clean, and she had a fairly good academic training. Now, she wasn't afraid and she didn't get excited about anything. If there ever was a person that we woulda been able to break the situation that existed on the Montgomery city line, Rosa L. Parks was the woman to use. And I knew that. I probably woulda examined a dozen more before I got there if Mrs. Parks hadn't come along before I found the right 'un. 'Cause, you see, it's hard for you to see it, it's hard for the average person—it's hard for the black people here in Montgomery to see. It's hard for a whole lot of people far away from here to see it. But when you have set 'cross the table and talked with black people in investigations as long as I have over a period of years, you just know it. . . . Well, I spent years in it and I knew it . . . when I selected Mrs. Parks, that was the person.

E.D. Nixon and Rosa Parks first met when he was president of Montgomery's struggling NAACP chapter. Nixon: "Mrs. Parks came to a NAACP meetin'. When she joined the NAACP, she got to the place she never missed, and I selected her secretary. I ran her for secretary; she was elected. And one year, she didn't run, they elected somebody else, and then I hired her." As Nixon's employee, she ran the office from which he operated as state NAACP president and as a regional officer of the Brotherhood of Sleeping Car Porters. Nixon recalls that on one occasion, without consulting him, Mrs. Parks drafted a letter over his signature protesting an Alabama politician's statement that passage of a federal antilynching law would "destroy the peaceful relations between the two races."

Despite this background, Mrs. Parks has been inaccurately characterized in many accounts as a simple drudge who, though temporarily emboldened by the bus driver's abuse, had no concept of the larger struggle for racial justice. Such characterizations are based on her much-quoted remark that she refused to stand because "my feet hurt."

Actually, "I had almost a life history of being rebellious against being mistreated because of my color," and although no one could have predicted that moment on the bus, Rosa Parks' "life history" had prepared her for it. Only a few months before, in the summer of 1955, she had received through her work in the NAACP an invitation to visit Highlander Folk School, an integrated retreat in the Tennessee hills. (See also Roy Harris and Myles Horton.) "That was the first time in my life I had lived in an atmosphere of complete equality with the members of the other race, and I did enjoy going up there, and I felt it could be done without the signs that said 'White' and 'Colored'—well, without any artificial barriers of racial segregation."

And so after we agreed, oh, I guess we spent a couple of hours discussing this thing. Then I went home and I took a sheet of paper and I drew right in the center of the paper. I used that for the square and then I used Hunter Station, Washington Park, Pickett Springs, all the different areas in Montgomery, and I used a slide rule to get a estimate.

I discovered nowhere in Montgomery at that time a man couldn't walk to work if he wanted to. I said, "We can beat this thing."

I told my wife about it and I said, "You know what?"

She said, "What?"

I said, "We're going to boycott the buses."

She said, "Cold as it is?"

I said, "Yeah."

She said, "I doubt it."

I said, "Well, I'll tell you one thing. If you keep 'em off when it cold, you won't have no trouble keeping 'em off when it get hot."

She shook her head. She said, "My husband! If headaches were selling for a dollar a dozen, my husband would be just the man to walk in the drugstore and say, 'Give me a dozen headaches.'" [Laughs]

So anyhow, I recorded quite a few names, starting off with Rev. Abernathy, Rev. Hubbard, Rev. King, and on down the line, and I called some of the people who represent peoples so that they could get the word out. The first man I called was Reverend Ralph Abernathy. He said, "Yes, Brother Nixon, I'll go along. I think it's a good thing."

The second person I called was the late Reverend H.H. Hubbard. He said, "Yes, I'll go along with you."

And I called Rev. King, was number three, and he said, "Brother Nixon, let me think about it awhile, and call me back."

When I called him back, he was number nineteen, and of course, he agreed to go along. I said, "I'm glad you agreed because I already set the meeting up to meet at your church." 'Course, he didn't even know Mrs. Parks at that time. I couldn't attend the meeting,* and I asked another man, another minister, Methodist minister, to chair the meeting with the understanding that no permanent officers be elected until I come back, and there wasn't any elected.

Why did you make that stipulation?

I wanted to be shore the right people was in office, and I felt that I was, with my work in the community, better prepared to know who the right person would be than anybody else. So nobody was elected. They set up a temporary meeting for Monday evening. So I came back Sunday morning and my wife met me at the station. I got in about nine o'clock. She give me the morning paper. They had an article, a two-column spread wrote by Joe Azbell,** on the front page of the *Adver-*

---

* He was out of town because of his job as a passenger-train porter.

** Joe Azbell, whose reporting so pleased E.D. Nixon, later went to work for Alabama Governor George Wallace. Azbell was publicity director in Wallace's 1976 presidential campaign.

tiser, talking about the bus boycott, a favorable article. The kind of article I'm almost sure that that's what got him fired. But anyhow, he wrote
a good article, kept his promise.

Had you tipped him off?

Oh, yes, I knew him personally.

How did you handle that?

I just called him and told him I had a hot lead, a story. I said, "Now,
if you promise me you would write a good story, I would fill you in on
it. I'll be at the station at two o'clock."* He met me down there and we
talked about it and I made him promise he'd write a good story, and
knowing him like I did, I felt he'd tell me the truth about it. He did
write a good story. He wrote a heck of a good story. . . .

The Advertiser *ran its story as an exposé, quoting from a leaflet
Nixon had circulated in the black neighborhoods: ". . . don't ride the
bus to work, to town, to school, or anyplace, Monday, December
5. . . . Another Negro woman has been arrested and put in jail because she refused to give up her bus seat. . . . Come to a mass meeting
Monday at 7 P.M. at the Holt Street Baptist Church for further instructions." By reprinting the leaflet for the titillation of white Montgomery,
the* Advertiser—as Nixon had anticipated when he tipped off its reporter
—had in effect distributed the leaflet to most of the black households in
Montgomery.*

*Montgomery police, adopting the pattern of overreaction that South-
ern police were to follow for a decade, announced that there would be
"two police behind every bus in the city" to prevent black "goon
squads" from enforcing the boycott against those of either race who
wished to ride. Of course, the police failed to consider what the presence of police escorts signified to black bus riders. "Monday morning,
the black folks come out there and saw two police . . . behind every
bus. They just went the other way, see. Ended up at eight o'clock that
morning, the buses ain't hauled nobody, hadn't hauled nobody, didn't
haul nobody else for the next 381 days."*

Then Mrs. Parks was tried that morning and she was found
guilty. . . . I'd been in court off and on for twenty years, hearing

---

* On Friday afternoon, before E.D. Nixon left on his regular weekend run as a
porter.

different peoples, and very seldom, if ever, there was another black man unless he was being tried. But that particular morning, the morning of December the fifth, 1955, the black man was reborn again. I couldn't believe it when they found her guilty and I had to go through the vestibule down the hall to the clerk's office to sign her appeal bond. . . . People came in that other door, and that door was about ten feet wide, and they was just that crowded in there, people wanting to know what happened. I said, "Well, they found her guilty. Now, I'm gon' have to make another bond for her. As soon as we can get her bond signed, we'll bring her right out." They said, "If you don't hurry and come out, we're coming in there and getchya." I couldn't *believe* it. When we got outside, police were standing outside with sawed-off shotguns, and the people all up and down the streets was from sidewalk to sidewalk out there. I looked around there, and I bet you there was over a thousand black people—black men—on the streets out there.

Did they understand that the guilty verdict was what you were after?

. . . No, they didn't understand that. I didn't tell anybody that. But I know if they'da found her not guilty, we'da had the same thing again. They really did the thing that was best for us when they found her guilty.

He sensed that Montgomery's segregationists had committed a historic tactical blunder. By prosecuting Mrs. Parks under a segregation ordinance rather than on some subterfuge such as disobeying an officer, they were inviting a federal court test of the Jim Crow laws upon which segregation throughout the Deep South depended. Within a few weeks four Montgomery women, spurred by Mrs. Parks' conviction, filed in federal district court in Montgomery what would prove to be a successful challenge of both city and state bus segregation laws.*

However, he was more concerned with the immediate future of the boycott than with the long grind of litigation as he left City Hall that day, December 5, 1955. He fell into step with Rev. Abernathy and Rev. E.N. French, who had also attended the trial. From them, he learned that prior to the rally that night, there was to be a meeting of the city's ministers. In that preliminary meeting the ministers would decide on basic policies for the boycott and pick its leaders. He told Abernathy, "Well, what we need to do, me and you and Rev. French . . . right

---

* For an analysis of the importance of this case, see Judge Elbert P. Tuttle.

now, is agree on a recommendation, agree on a resolution and agree on a name." With such preparation, he sensed, they could dominate the meeting.

I had wrote three mild recommendations. . . . I know one was "Seatin' on the bus, first come, first served," and "Negro bus drivers in predominant Negro neighborhoods." I forgot what the other one was. "More courtesy to Negro patrons," I believe. But anyhow, they agreed on it. Then he and Rev. French wrote the resolution and they read it and I agreed with them. Then we came up with a name for the organization, and I said, "What about the Citizens' Committee?" Rev. Abernathy said, "No, I don't want no Citizens' Committee. Too close to the white Citizens Council." Then he came up and said, "What about the Montgomery Improvement Association?" I said, "I'll go along with it," so we agreed on it.

And Abernathy was sittin' as close as me in here to you, and he leant over. He said, "Brother Nixon, now you gon' serve as president, ain'tchya?" I said, "Naw, not unless'n you all don't accept my man." He said, "Who is your man?" I said, "Martin Luther King." He said, "I'll go along with it." French said, "I'll go along with it." So then we had not only our recommendation, our resolution, our name, we had our president.

Why did you put your finger on King?

In August of 1955 he was the guest speaker for the NAACP, and a professor over at the State Teachers College and I were sitting in the back. His name was J.E. Pierce. When King got through talking, I said, "Pierce, you know that guy made a heck of a speech."

He said, "I agree with you. He sho' did."

I said, "I don't know how I'm going to do it yet, but someday I'm gon' hang him to the stars."

Then the next thing, he had not been here long enough for the city fathers to put their hand on him. Usually, you come to town and you start wantin' to do this and do that, and the city fathers get their hand on you probably and give you a suit of clothes or somethin' of that kind, and it ends up you're on their side. He wasn't the kind ever to accept it, even if they'da tried it.

In that meetin', that evening, everybody was still—all the ministers was still afraid—and if you read Rev. King's book, *Stride Toward Free-*

dom, you'll see my quotation in there.* They would talk about tryin' to do it so the white people wouldn't know about it, and one of 'em said, ". . . well, we'll mimeograph some little pamphlets. Everybody come in the meetin' that night we'll pass 'em one, and nobody will know how it happened."

Well, I was sittin' there boiling over, so mad I didn't know what to do, so I jumped up, and I forgot about we was up in the balcony of the church. I said, "What the hell you people talkin' 'bout?" Just like that, see, and I cussed. I said, "How you gonna have a mass meeting, gonna boycott a city bus line without the white folks knowing it?" [Voice rising] I said, "You guys have went around here and lived off these poor washwomen all your lives and ain't never done nothing for 'em. And now you got a chance to do something for 'em, you talkin' about you don't want the white folks to know it."

I said, "Unless'n this program is accepted and brought into the church like a decent, respectable organization, . . . I'll take the microphone and tell 'em the reason we don't have a program is 'cause you all are too scared to stand on your feet and be counted. You oughta make up your mind right now that you gon' either admit you are a grown man or concede to the fact that you are a bunch of scared boys." And King hollered that he wasn't no coward, that nobody called him a coward.

Once prodded into defending his courage, King, who was then twenty-six years old, had no choice but to accept the presidency of the Montgomery Improvement Association and to make the main address at the MIA's first rally that night. "I said, 'When he's through, I'm gon' come behind him.'"

Rev. King made a *masterpiece* that evenin'. So when he did, then I came behind him, and I never shall forget, I said, "Good evenin', my friends." I said, "I'm so happy to see all of you out here tonight, but I wanna tell you somethin'. If you're scared, you better get your hat and coat and go home. It's gon' be a long drawn-out affair and before it's over with somebody gon' die." I said, "May be me, I don't know. . . . The only request I have is if I'm the one that dies, don't let me die in vain. For twenty-some-odd years I been fighting and saying to myself that I didn't want the children to come along and have to suffer all the insults that I've suffered. Well, hell, I changed my mind tonight." Just

* In *Stride Toward Freedom* (New York: Harper & Row, 1958), an account of the bus boycott, King quotes Nixon as accusing the ministers of "acting like little boys." Angered by the remark, King resolved to prove the older man wrong.

like that. "I decided that I wanted to enjoy some of this freedom my-self." And everybody hollered when I said that.

And anyhow then we took up a collection after that. I served as treas-urer for the first three years. We took up a collection, took up $785 there that night. And I ribbed . . . the commissioner of police that night. He was in the meetin', with two or three police and everything, two of the black police were there. I had my car there and went by there and I told him at the door, I said, "Say, I cain't go home with all this money in the street myself. You got to send me home in the police car." And he turned around and told a policeman named Worthy . . . "You all take Nixon home." He carried me home, 'cause nobody thought the thing gon' last over a week or ten days, then everybody be back on the bus. He carried me home; my wife had to drive my car home by herself. [Laughs]

> I'm called an Uncle Tom now because I can deal with the power structure. For instance, I don't mind telling you, I had an appoint-ment with Governor Wallace day before yesterday evenin'. All the mayor, the commissioners, I can deal with 'em. . . .
>
> You see, I figure now if I'm what you call an Uncle Tom . . . you need ten thousand of 'em here. . . .
>
> I figure it was the best thing that ever happened in Montgomery, and I'm proud that I was part of it, even though . . . so many people got famous out of it and I was still left here. And I'm still here servin' the people and the rest of 'em gone. So I'm gettin' more joy out of it now, knowing that I can touch a telephone or walk into an office and get things done, I'm gettin' more joy out of it now than I imagine them guys did who got in it for a name. And I haven't ever looked for a name. . . .

What do you think the history books ought to say about your role and Mrs. Parks' role?

> I certainly think history books ought to, if you're gonna talk about the boycott, they oughta start from the day Rosa L. Parks was arrested and not just December the fifth when Rev. King was elected president. . . .
>
> I haven't seen anybody yet that wanted to believe anything about the Movement except something what the Reverend King said. I ain't seen nobody yet. Now I've had peoples interviewed me. I betcha I've had a thousand people interview me. Everybody, they'll set and listen at me talk, then they go away and write. Even in the foreign country,

they want to start off with December the fifth. Well, we was doing things before Rev. King had ever finished school, come out of school. We's doing things in this town here. The Movement didn't spring up overnight. It came up that particular night because we found the right person.

'Course, even today, people don't wanna hear the truth about MIA. If you gonna say somethin' that Rev. King didn't do, you're almost spittin' in folks' face. I was on an airplane coming down from New York some time ago, sittin' beside a lady, and she asked me who I was and I told her. She said, "Oh, you're down in Montgomery, Alabama." She said, "Lord, I don't know what'ud happened to the black people if Rev. King hadn't went to town."

I said, "If Mrs. Park had got up and given that white man her seat, you'd never aheard of Rev. King."

When I said that, man, I as well as spit in her face.

BAYARD RUSTIN

He is white-haired, a man of elegant diction, an old lion of the Movement, and he was the first of the Eastern civil-rights professionals to discover the young black preacher in Montgomery. Now, two decades later, he sits for an interview on the carpeted steps of a drafty stairwell of Ebenezer Baptist Church. Cold winds sweep in from Atlanta's Auburn Avenue, where King was born and grew up under his father's stern hand. Rustin has just spoken from King's old pulpit in a service commemorating what would have been the preacher's forty-fourth birthday. The speech marked the end of a long estrangement from his old allies in the Southern Movement. After a decade of the closest cooperation, Rustin in 1966 had opposed as bad strategy King's plan to bring Southern organizing tactics into the big-city ghettos. "I was against his moving into Chicago and I was against the Poor People's Campaign, and only now, because of that, has Coretta* felt she could invite me back to speak. People were very disappointed that I, who had supported every move Martin [pauses, breaking off]—but I honestly couldn't do it."

His affection for King has survived that old disagreement, and it is an affection untainted by the jealousy which so often afflicts gifted men who ally themselves with a man of even greater talents. This was evident when he addressed the Movement veterans gathered in Ebenezer that

---

* King's widow.

day. "Thank God I was in that struggle with him," he said, "for like you, I will now be a footnote to history."

Well, my meeting with Dr. King came about because I at that time worked for an organization called the Fellowship of Reconciliation. It was a pacifist organization. One of the board members of the Fellowship of Reconciliation was Lillian E. Smith,* the writer from Georgia. I got a telegram from her saying that she felt since I had worked with the Gandhi movement in India, that it would be a good idea for me to go to see Dr. King because he was a young man and he had not had great experience in handling nonviolent tactics. I talked to some people in New York and got a leave of absence from my job to be able to shuttle in and out of Montgomery to work with Dr. King.

One of the most amazing things was that when I got there, Dr. King was out of town, and I went to stay with Rev. Abernathy for two days until he returned. And when Rev. Abernathy took me over to the King household to introduce me to Coretta and Martin, I discovered that I'd known Coretta since she was in the 12th grade and I had lectured at the school she went to. And this, of course, immediately made a relationship. Dr. King asked me if I would help, and I did such things as help compose songs, prepare literature, do telephoning for him, and finally discovered that he was very simpatico to discussing the whole question of nonviolence.

Now, quite contrary to what many people think, Dr. King was not a confirmed believer in nonviolence, totally, at the time that the boycott began. On my second visit there the house was still being protected by armed guards. In fact, when I went in, I went in with a chap whose name was Bill Worthy, who became famous because he went to China contrary to the government's desire and they took his passport. He'd been a Nieman fellow at Harvard and was well known. As Bill went to sit down in the King living room, I said, "Hey, Bill, wait!" I said, "There's a gun in that chair." And he might have sat on it. But it was gradually over several weeks that Dr. King continuously deepened his commitment to nonviolence, and within six weeks, he had demanded that there be no armed guards and no effort at associating himself in any form with violence. . . . I take no credit for Dr. King's development, but I think the fact that Dr. King had someone around recommending certain readings and discussing these things with him was helpful to bring up in him what was already obviously there. That's how we met.

* Miss Smith, who died in 1966, wrote the antilynching novel *Strange Fruit* (New York: Harcourt Brace Jovanovich, 1944). She was one of the first Southern whites to support publicly the work of Dr. King.

Did you actually go as a leap of faith, without making the contacts? . . .

Well, what I did was to talk to some people in New York and say, "Now, I'm a Northerner and I have a left-wing political history." And I called in eight people including Jim Farmer and Mr. Randolph* and John Morsell of the N-Double-A-C-P, and I said, "Do you think I will harm the movement?" and they said, "Look, people are going to call names, say miserable things no matter who goes, so you're needed, go."

Now, I didn't contact Martin before I came because I really came to find out whether he could use me, whether he needed me, and the first thing I did when I went there was to tell him all the reasons why I perhaps ought not to come. Martin was never moved by stories and ugliness, so he said, "Look, we need everybody who can come to help us."

Could you give me some detail about your day-to-day work in the boycott?

I was kind of a Jimmy Higgins.** I would help set up the mass meetings. I would do writing chores for him. I would help answer the mail that was piling in. I would have discussions with him. I would help plan what was happening at the meetings. I would telephone key people all over the country urging them to come in, because obviously the fact that important people from all over America were coming to see this was a great psychological boon to the people who had to put up with walking to work, losing jobs, wondering whether they'd ever win. And then, of course, I was a singer and I wrote songs and they were topical about what was happening, and Abernathy would usually introduce them. I discovered also something that many people didn't know. King would very often address the mass meetings using such words as "agape" and "theory," and outline the various forms of love and this sort of thing. Abernathy had a great knack of saying, "Now, let me tell you what that means for tomorrow morning." And then he'd tell them what the plans were for the next morning.

* A. Philip Randolph, who Rustin believes influenced the Montgomery movement from afar: "One of the reasons E.D. Nixon would have taken the initiative in asking people to take some form of direct action is that as far back as 1941 he had been the regional director of Randolph's Southern operation, and consequently, he had been in many marches and demonstrations with Randolph. . . . So that in a sense, Martin Luther King was to some extent a spiritual godchild of Randolph. There was a very, very profound connection, and it was Randolph who raised the funds for me to go down after Lillian Smith sent the telegram."
** An all-purpose aide.

Was there an awareness on the part of Montgomery officialdom of your presence?

There was not only awareness of my presence, but I woke up one morning to find a twelve-by-twelve-inch photograph on the front page, that you might look up sometime in the Montgomery *Advertiser,* in '55, under which it said, "Who is this man? He's wanted for inciting to riot." And I'll never forget that Dr. King whisked me out of town in a car, with a car in front and a car behind, to Birmingham. And then when I returned to Montgomery after that, I actually spent some time not upstairs but downstairs doing certain things that he wanted done just so I wouldn't be taken out of circulation.

You came to Montgomery, or course, as a veteran in the field of civil rights. Can you tell me something about your initial feelings about Dr. King and what was going on there?

It's a very curious thing, and I very seldom would dare to say such a thing, but when I got to know Martin well, I said to him one day, "Martin, I have a feeling that you had better prepare yourself for martyrdom, because I don't see how you can make the challenge that you are making here without a very real possibility of your being murdered, and I wonder if you have made your peace with that." And I also told him that I could feel something in him that was akin to what one felt in the Gandhi circle. There was a—well, I quoted a Negro spiritual and I said, "I have the feeling the Lord has laid his hands on you and that is a dangerous, dangerous thing." And Martin did not take that very seriously at the time. But two years before his death, I think he very profoundly felt that he was going to be killed, and I don't think there was any paranoia in this. If a man is running you down the street with two guns and two knives, you can scarcely be called paranoid.

I remember on some occasions Dr. King and I would cosign letters that were going out for urgent appeals when things were tough, and particularly to keep the money to feed the people who were getting fired and to find transportation for many other people around the city, which required a great deal of upkeep of cars, and petrol and the like. But, of course, the great bulk of the money, in terms of the number of contributions, came from those nightly collections that the people who were walking put on the table. They were not sitting around waiting for someone to support them. This boycott was for them a complete and total proposition.

One of the most fascinating experiences I had after I had been down there about two weeks working. An elderly Negro woman called me and she said, "You seem like a nice young man." I wasn't very young. She said, "And Dr. King is a young man. Perhaps you can really help him see the truth. You know, I've been around a long time. These Negroes in Montgomery are never going to stick together. They're going to run downtown and tell the white folks everything we're doing, and Dr. King is headed for getting a lot of colored people hurt, and I wish you'd tell him so." And I said, "I can understand you saying this, but I don't think that's going to happen. Some of us may get hurt, but you can't do anything without taking that chance." And she shook her head and walked away. Now that woman became one of the most vital people in a couple of weeks.

What Dr. King delivered to blacks there, far more important than whether they got to ride on the bus, was the absence of fear, the ability to be men in the same way that the Jews in the Warsaw ghetto knew that they couldn't win, but, knowing they were going to die, they said, "Let us go down expressing our manhood, which is to fight back." So Dr. King had this tremendous facility for giving people the feeling that they could be bigger and stronger and more courageous and more loving than they thought they could be.

In fact, when the Ku Klux Klan marched into Montgomery and we knew they were coming, Dr. King and I sat down and thought it over. And we said, "Ah! Tell everybody to put on their Sunday clothes, stand on their steps, and when the Ku Kluxers come, applaud 'em." Well, they came, marched three blocks, and unharassed, they left. They could not comprehend the new thing. They were no longer able to engender fear.

In the black community, going to jail had been a badge of dishonor. Martin made going to jail like receiving a Ph.D. But more important, the blacks of Montgomery were basically a religious people, and when Martin would say to them, "As sure as Moses got the children of Israel across the Red Sea, we can stick together and win," he had this ability to communicate victory, and to let everybody know he was prepared to pay for victory.

In this connection Martin did not need to be a strategist or a tactician. His Southern victories were made in part because Southern reaction provided a great dynamism. All right, they used fire hoses. This *draws* people in. [With broad gestures, a dramatic voice] They bombed churches. This *draws* people in. They murdered some kids in Mississippi. This *draws* people in. If the Southerners had been smart and just let Martin alone . . . but Martin had a facility for putting to good use the mistakes of his adversaries. And this is a King ability. It is almost impossible that Daddy King could have gone through what he has gone through and still be a sane man, particularly after seeing your wife murdered in your own church, playing an organ.* But the Kings all have this inner grace, and I'm not adding anything to them that they do not possess. *It's there.* And this inner grace is a part of this religious confidence that if you do the right thing, you must leave the rest to God. So Martin said to me, "It is not for me to say or for you to analyze whether I can win, my obligation is to do the right thing as I am called upon to do it. The rest is in God's hands."

Do you think . . . he retained that fundamentalist's sense of an active, personal God?

Oh, yes, profoundly, and I was always amazed at how it was possible to combine this intense, analytical, philosophical mind with this more or less fundamental—well, I don't like to use the word "fundamentalist"— but this abiding faith. Now, Gandhi had some of this, also. Few men have this. Gandhi, like Martin, was really a spiritual intellectual.

You mentioned your sense of Dr. King's martyrdom or the possibility of it. Rev. King, Sr., during this time, was very concerned about this. . . . Did you ever discuss that with him?

Yes. There was a time when Papa King said to me, "I wonder if Martin should continue in this struggle. His house has been bombed, he has these small children, perhaps he is paying as much a price as he ought." Now dealing with this father-and-son relationship, I had sense enough to let him talk and keep quiet, and I raised some religious questions with him, and he said, "The difference between me and Martin is that Martin perhaps has more faith than I have." This, of course, proved not to be true. Oh, he was deeply concerned about this. I remember once in Montgomery, Martin and his father, Coretta, and I had a prayer session in which his father was deeply concerned to get God's guidance as to how he should advise his son. And Martin, after the prayer meeting, said, "You know, I will have to pray this through myself," and he thanked his father for his concern. And I think this was a very great

---

* In 1974 Mrs. Martin Luther King, Sr., was shot to death by a deranged black man as she played the organ during Sunday services at Ebenezer Baptist Church.

moment in Martin's life because I think to a certain extent he had been up to that point a little too influenced by what his father thought. And I thought that somehow that day I was sitting through a liberating process.

Yancey Martin

In 1972 he was minority affairs adviser to Democratic presidential nominee George McGovern. In 1955 he was a freshman in college.

I came home from college in 1955 in December for Christmas holidays and the boycott had already begun when I got home. I don't remember the exact date that they started, but they were still in the churches and they were still having the meetings in the evening and they were still organizing it. . . .

I talked with an old friend of the family, Ralph Abernathy, who I had been in a play with while Ralph was in college with my brother. We were in a play called *On Whitman Avenue* and I played his grandson. And so I talked with him about what we could do, and he told me the best thing I could do was organize some people to do some driving along the bus stop route and to pick up people. 'Cause what they were doing was they were telling folk just to stand on their regular bus stop route, but as the bus would come by, just to step back. And so all the guys who were on my street . . . and a group of other folk whose parents had cars, we would all get up in the morning as early as we could. I mean, there were some folk out there who had to leave by six o'clock in order to get to the white lady's kitchen, and many times they were just late getting there. We'd all get up in the morning and we'd drive that route, like some would drive the South Jackson route, some would drive the Old Boston bus route, some would drive the Washington Park route, and we'd just mix it around . . . two or three cars per route 'cause you end up with a lot of people. And what we had to do was we had to know the names of everybody in there or else the police would stop and try to charge you with operating an illegal jitney service. And so what we would do is, by knowing everybody's name, we'd just say that these are my cousins or these are friends of mine I'm giving a lift. There's no law against giving anybody a ride. But the police, when they found out what we were doing, they would patrol the bus routes just as much as we would.

After one of the mass meetings . . . I believe it was at Ralph's church, First Baptist Church, it was a decision made that people would not stand at the bus stop, would not get picked up at the bus stop, but either midway the block or just beyond the bus stop, so that police could not get you for picking people up at the bus stop. I don't know what kind of law that was, but for some reason or another that became a key issue as to where you picked people up and where you let them out. And then on Monroe Street just behind a building that was owned by a black doctor, . . . there was a parking lot for the patients he used to see and a taxi stand, black taxi stand. Well, that parking lot became a pick-up point.

But then what would happen . . . the tag numbers would be taken down by policemen, and then for other reasons you'd be harassed. Like, if you were out one night and you were at Gordon's Ice Cream Parlor, which was out on Hall Street, the police would see your car and know that you were one of the cars that were always involved in picking up the people. And then they'd just come in the place and ask who owned that car, and they'd say, "You're not parked close enough to the curb. . . ." They'd find something wrong to harass you about.

He still marvels at the response of black Montgomery during those first days of the boycott.

I had never seen that happen in Montgomery, and I must admit that I have never seen that happen *anywhere* among black people. I mean, they were more unified in Montgomery during the bus boycott than I think may have been the case in Selma during the voters' rights protests or in Birmingham or in any other city. Even the people who were not in attendance at the meetings, who are just sorta like people who don't get involved, decided to abide by the rules. . . .

I remember Mrs. A.W. West. Her husband was a dentist, very prominent dentist in town. . . . She was really Mrs. Middle Class Black America in Montgomery. She was like the chairman of the board, see. And when Mrs. West got involved, even the ladies who were not directly involved and directly participating in meetings were supportive. Like my mother . . . she never attended a mass meeting, but she never rode a bus. She never objected to what I was doing with the car and she knew what I was doing. . . .

By early January, the boycott was going well, but it had become heavily dependent on its cadre of young drivers whose college holidays were ending.

I think that what happened . . . we saw the transportation end really kinda being the backbone of the movement because folks had to work and they had to have that little money. We didn't mind them getting to work late to keep Miss Ann from getting to her job on time, and of course, they was just tellin' Miss Ann, "We not ridin' the bus, and you can come pick me up, or you can find somebody else to get the job done, or you can quit *yo'* job and stay at home and keep your house and baby yourself. . . ."* But we did know that in order for the family to exist they had to have that money . . . they had to get back and forth to work. . . .

So about four or five of us said, "Well, why do we have to go back? It's important that we get a college education, but it's important that we win this thing now that we've gotten into it. . . ." So some of us went home and talked to our parents, who went up in arms, but who allowed us to stay at least till the end of the semester. Fortunately we got credits for it anyway. Most of us had to write a paper on why it was important for us to stay in Montgomery during that period of time.

But I thought it wasn't a symbolic gesture on the parts of the few that I know who stayed. It was just a realization of the fact that there was a need and there was nobody to fill that need. I could not guarantee that my daddy would find somebody who would be able to drive that car every day like I was driving it every day. So I went on and stayed.

And what was really interesting was that the black folk knew that the

* "A lot of white folks were picking up their domestic workers and bringing them to the house and taking 'em home, because they had their job to get to and they needed the money, or else they couldn't keep a domestic worker and all that house they were living in or anything else. But the few who tried to fire or did fire, or release, black folk couldn't find replacements who were going to be any better in terms of time."

movement did not have any money to pay for all this stuff. They were spending enough money on trying to get people out on bail bond if they got arrested. So people started giving you the nickel or the dime or whatever it was that they would give you for the bus, but not let nobody see it, so you could buy some gasoline. At that time, gas was nineteen cents a gallon or so, so you could just about get away without having to spend any of your own money on gasoline. Never asked anybody for anything, but they would just [say], "Here's a dime. . . . Here's a quarter I can give you to help you out with the gasoline." And I used to take that money and put it all back into the gas—well, almost all of it. I mighta saved a little bit of it out for a beer or something. [Laughs]

Do you have any recollections of your responses to Dr. King?

Oh, yeah, everybody was just captivated by the cat, man. He was a very articulate person. He sounded good, and it was just great to see a black person who could get up and move an audience the way he did without talking out of the Bible. I mean, he was talking about what we oughta have, and what we oughta be, and what the situation oughta be in the South, and what kind of country we oughta live in. He was saying the thing and he was saying it so well. You know, Martin was one of your great orators. . . .

I can remember one incident that he wrote about and Ralph talks about a lot. I happened to be in church that day when we had a meeting. That was at Day Street that night. Martin asked this old lady, he said, "Now listen . . . you have been with us all along, so now you go on and start back to ridin' the bus, 'cause you are too old to keep walking. . . ."

She said, "Oh, no." She said, "Oh, no." Said, "I'm gonna walk just as long as everybody else walks. I'm gonna walk till it's over."

So he said, "But aren't your feet tired?"

She said, "Yes, my feets is tired, but my soul is rested." [Laughs] Yes, sir, and that was kind of like a story he used to tell a lot in the Movement throughout the years. As he'd go somewhere and he'd think people would be getting a little tired of marchin', he'd tell that story about the lady who said, "My feets is tired, but my soul is rested."

T.M. ALEXANDER, SR.

He is one of the success stories of "Sweet Auburn" Avenue, the center of black commerce in Atlanta. It is called sweet because even in the era of segregation, many black men became rich there. They gave it the name. His office was two blocks up the street from Ebenezer Baptist Church.

I was born and reared in Montgomery, and my mother and father and all my grandparents were members of Dexter Avenue Baptist Church. I grew up in that church. Then I came here to high school in 1927 and stayed here through my college career. When I came here, M.L.'s father and I were in Morehouse College at the same time. He came back in later years to get his divinity degree. So we became good friends. As a matter of fact, when I graduated he married my wife and myself. Martin King, Jr., came on after I left Morehouse. I was a varsity debater and those of us who were interested and had been varsity debaters were frequently called back to judge the debates or oratorical contests. M.L., Jr., always won his, hands down, no problem.

Then Vernon Johns was in Montgomery as pastor of Dexter Avenue Baptist Church. He left, then Dexter was without a pastor. I called my father and my brother and asked them to have the church to invite King down for a trial sermon, because he was a friend of mine and graduated from Morehouse and just finished at Boston U and was assisting his father. They invited him down and called him. When they called him and got ready to install him, because I was instrumental in getting him down there, they called me down to charge the church, which is the practice in the Baptist Church. So I went down, and without knowing that I was being prophetic—I knew King and being something of a Bible student and Sunday School teacher—I simply said that before Martin Luther King leaves Montgomery, he will put a plumb line on the Cradle of the Confederacy and shake it from center to circumference. Well, I had no idea that I was being prophetic. At the time I was really trying to be oratorical. [Laughs]

But he did. Now during that period . . . I was in the insurance business. I had organized the Southeastern Fidelity Fire and Casualty Insurance Company, and we could write physical damage on automobiles, but at that time we were not qualified to write public liability. We later became a multiple-line company. But I was executive vice president and it was a new fledgling company with less than a half-million dollars in premiums a year because it had just been founded. And the bus boycott started in Montgomery. Well, immediately in the insurance industry the word passed around, "Don't nobody insure Martin Luther King's buses that were given to him." They had nineteen of 'em that were given to him from various churches all over the country.* Because if they couldn't get the public liability and property damage insurance, they couldn't drive the buses. If they couldn't drive the buses, they couldn't take these domestics and these employees to their various jobs. Naturally the people having to work, they woulda had to go back on the buses. . . . So this was one way that they were hoping to break the bus boycott.

Well, King couldn't get any insurance anywhere . . . and he knew that I was writing [insurance on] his father's church and other churches here in Atlanta.** So he called *me* and asked if I could help him get

* Actually, the vehicles were station wagons: "When the people in the Midwest and the North and the East found out what was happening there, different churches gave station wagons . . . and they ended up with practically every church of any consequence in Montgomery having its own station wagon." As the boycott ground on into the fall of 1956, these station wagons, making regularly scheduled runs, bolstered the free-lance transportation system, which had involved as many as three hundred private automobiles driven by volunteers like Yancey Martin.

** His friendship with the elder King had been sorely tested in 1939 when *Gone With the Wind* had its world premiere at a segregated theater in Atlanta. As newly elected president of the NAACP chapter, he publicly criticized King and another minister for allowing their church choirs—clad in Aunt Jemima costumes of "aprons and damn-bannas"—to perform in a sidewalk concert outside the theater. King stalked out of the NAACP meeting, and the next morning the preacher

some liability insurance. . . . I had a strong commitment for what he was doing, and I said, "Hell, I'll just put my reputation on the line."

Well, then I called some of the companies that I was dealin' with here in Atlanta, knowing that I was giving 'em *thousands* of dollars' worth of premiums. I told them what the problem was. They said, "Alexander, we'd do *anything* in the world for you. [Amused, he mimics an exaggerated sincerity.] You give us a lot of business. But the word has been passed 'round throughout the Southeast: Anybody that insures those station wagons in Montgomery will be kicked out of the insurance field." I said, "Well, I got to get some insurance for King. . . ."

The same company that I'm associated with now, the same people who are friends of mine who I share offices with *now,** I called them, asked them about the insurance. They said, "Well, I tell you what we can do for you." I said, "You got to help, as much business as I give you." [They] said, "Now, I'm gonna put you in touch with a man in Chicago that doesn't even look south. He's got contacts with Lloyd's of London." And they called him and told him I was gonna call. When I called him, actually I didn't have the name of the church, I didn't have the make of the station wagons, the motor numbers or nothin'. I just knew how many station wagons there were. I convinced this man to give us a binder, and he cabled Lloyd's and got me a binder on nineteen station wagons, and the policy read like this: "Nineteen Christian churches, nineteen station wagons, Montgomery, Alabama. Signed 'Lloyd's of London.'" And I started those station wagons rollin'. . . .

I had one loss, physical damage loss, that amounted to a little over fifty dollars, which I paid outa my company. Lloyd's didn't have *any* losses during the whole year. The premium was three thousand, two hundred and some odd dollars, something like that. Anyway, they had a banquet at the Ben Moore Hotel on the corner of High and Jackson Street in Montgomery on the top floor, and it was a celebration of the first year of the bus boycott, and it was given for the drivers who had driven under these most adverse circumstances and had very little accidents. And I was guest speaker for 'em. The whites down there poured

---

with the booming voice cornered the feisty young insurance man in the black-owned bank on Auburn Avenue: "Rev. King came in and loud-talked me right in the lobby of the bank. I'm on this side of the bank and he loud-talked me, said 'Young man, you will never succeed in this town if you attack the black pulpit of this city. Ah, blah, blah, blah.' Well, I couldn't lose something I didn't have, see, 'cause I didn't have nothing, see. I say, this is the time for me to establish myself with both barrels. So I say, 'Reverend King, you can take your business and go to hell.'"

* He has since affiliated his agency with a large, white-owned agency in Atlanta.

acid on some of the cars out in front of the Ben Moore Hotel while the banquet was going on.

Subsequently, when things began to tighten up, M.L. came from somewhere here, and Rev. King, Sr., called us out to his house to try to persuade Martin not to go back to Montgomery. That was when they were arresting his assistants and so forth. . . . Rev. King, Sr., called L.D. Milton, Yates, Benny Mays, and one or two others and myself, Walden, up there to try to persuade Martin not to go back to Montgomery.*

And while we were talking Martin came out of the back room and he said, "I know my mother is worried, my father is worried. My mother is subject to a heart attack, and I don't want 'em to worry, but I started this and those are the people that I'm supposed to be leading. And I appreciate you coming up, but I got to go back and I'm going back and I'm going directly to the police station to give myself up." And when he did, his father's—tears lopped on his father's cheek and he said, "Well, if that's my son's decision, I'll go back with him." And that was when he returned and gave himself up.

Now, subsequently, when the pressure got so great that he decided to move the Southern Leadership Conference here, I gave him office space in my building free of charge until he got on his feet. I also introduced him to the bank so they could transfer the money out of the bank down there and get it up here, because they didn't know what was going to happen down there. Those guys didn't care nothing about law and order. [Laughs] They'd do anything to bust the thing up.

* The date was February 22, 1956. After speaking in Nashville, Dr. King had stopped in Atlanta to visit his parents. Word came that he would be arrested as soon as he set foot in Montgomery. A grand jury there had resurrected an all-but-forgotten anti-boycott law, passed thirty-five years earlier to hamper unionization of Birmingham's steel mills, and indicted King and eighty-eight other leaders of the bus protest. Fearful of what might befall his son in an Alabama court, the elder King had invited his closest friends among the city's senior black leaders to meet with his son. The group included Alexander, drugstore owners L.D. Milton and C.R. Yates, Morehouse College President Benjamin Mays, and Attorney A.T. Walden.

JOSEPH E. LOWERY

The Founding of SCLC:
"Practically All Ministers"

When the boycott started in Montgomery he was a Methodist minister in Mobile, 175 miles to the south, where he was a leader in a local civil rights group.

In Montgomery . . . what they first asked for on the bus situation was that black patrons start seating at the back and could fill up the bus if they did, and white would start seating at the front, but that nobody would have to get up. If blacks filled up the bus, it was full. . . . We were critical of that in Mobile [laughing], because we already had that practice. It was already where you didn't have to get up. Blacks boarded the bus and started seating in the rear, but if you filled up the bus, too bad for anybody else who got on and didn't wanna sit down beside a black. . . . And we were dissatisfied with that. We were asking—we weren't boycotting or marching—but we were asking that all forms of discrimination on the bus be eliminated. So when this request came out we were a little critical of it, a little concerned about it. Of course, that didn't last very long because the city of Montgomery rejected that plea. And of course, they went to the boycott, and then the demand was for complete elimination of segregation on the bus.

That was how I got involved . . . We supported the Montgomery boycott. We carried funds to Montgomery. That's where I met Martin. We carried funds to Montgomery to support their efforts, and then later, in Atlanta, Martin called together leaders of various protest movements around the South and we organized the Southern Christian Leadership Conference. . . .

The first meeting was held here in Atlanta and I have forgotten how many came. It must have been at least fifteen or twenty came, practically all ministers. Shuttlesworth from Birmingham, I came from Mobile, Ted Jemison from Baton Rouge, C.K. Steele from Tallahassee, Martin and Ralph from Montgomery, the late Sam Williams of Atlanta was present, and I have that list somewhere but I don't remember. Davis from New Orleans.* And we talked about the need for an organization.

Prior to that, however, Martin, Ralph, Fred Shuttlesworth, and I had been meeting in Alabama. We used to meet in Montgomery. Fred would drive down from Birmingham and I'd come up from Mobile and we'd meet in Montgomery every two or three weeks to try to talk about the Alabama situation. For a while, C.G. Gomillion came from Tuskegee . . . he was the only non-preacher, and I guess we were too preacheristic for him.** Anyhow, he eventually dropped out.

What was the tone of those meetings? Were you thinking of an Alabama movement?

Yes, we were just exchanging ideas, discussing strategies as to how we could support each other in the various movements. Much of our oppression, opposition, resistance came from state level, and so we met to strategize on that. Then the decision was made to call a larger meeting, and the larger meeting was held here in Atlanta at Ebenezer. We agreed that we needed some kind of coordinating force and so we said we ought to organize a "Southern leadership conference." I'm not sure that was the first name suggested, but it was the first one agreed upon. It was later that the word "Christian" was added. But the formal organization was held in New Orleans . . . in the A.L. Davis church, a Baptist church, and that's where the officers were elected. . . .

At that initial meeting in Atlanta on January 10, 1957, the group named itself the Southern Leadership Conference on Transportation and

---

* Rev. A.L. Davis.

** At that time dean of Tuskegee Institute. He later filed a suit against racial gerrymandering which was a precursor of the U.S. Supreme Court's historic one-man, one-vote ruling.

Nonviolent Integration. The New Orleans meeting followed on February 14, 1957, when the name was shortened to Southern Negro Leadership Conference, and King was elected president. At subsequent meetings, the name Southern Christian Leadership Conference (SCLC) was adopted, and Lowery became a vice president.

What was the rationale for Dr. King being elected president?

He had led the Montgomery movement, which had received the most publicity out of all the movements and was the most effective, and he was the much better known of the group . . . he really was the prime convener. And he was nominated to head the organization. I don't think there was much disagreement that he would be the leader, the president of that movement. Those were the very early days, and we didn't have any money, just had the idea, and didn't have any staff. We were mostly the staff. . . .

We had, I think, a very exciting adventure in those early days, as I said, without much staff. Most of us who were board members and officers, we did whatever work there was to be done until we did start getting in funds. No real substantial funds really came in until, well, the Freedom Rides started some funds flowing into the organization. But I guess the Birmingham movement really was the first time we started receiving substantial funds.

Unfortunately money that comes in during a crisis almost always has to be spent in the crisis, so when the crisis is over you are generally back where you have been. Except in those moments of crisis, SCLC has generally been broke all its life, which hadn't been any great problem for black folks, because most black folks have been broke all their lives. While it might be a thing of great interest to some elements of the media, it was never any great concern to us because [laughing] nuthin' from nuthin' leaves nuthin' . . .

You seem to be suggesting the organizational needs were more modest than might have prevailed in other . . .

Right, right. Our commitment, our enthusiasm for the work, the struggle—we'd raise money at local churches. If we had a meeting, we'd ask our churches to pay our fare to the meeting. And if they didn't have it in the treasury, they'd take up an offering. Admittedly, that probably has some advantage over other organizations that didn't have a lot of preachers who had a base from which they could draw resources to help them in the Movement.

Was the dominance of preachers a natural development or an accident?

No, I think there are two or three things in the black community that are not fully understood in the white community as it relates to the preacher. . . . In the black community, historically, it's been the preacher who has been the principal community leader. Now there are several reasons for this. One was, of course, educational. He usually could read and write and had exposure to educational experiences that gave him some advantage. But beneath that was the fact that he was the freest leader in the community. The black congregation supported him, so even though he did solicit a lotta support from the white community for various church causes, actually he was more independent than any other black person in the community. . . .

Aside from that . . . the black preacher in slavery and the spirituals which grew up out of slavery after blacks were introduced to the Christian faith, their exegesis, their interpretation of the Christian faith *always* saw Jesus as a liberator. And when the Christian faith talked about the brotherhood of man, they believed that and they expressed it in songs like "All God's Children Got Shoes." Now, what they were talkin' about was that even though they were barefooted and the white folks, the slave owners, had shoes, they said, "Well, *all* God's children got shoes and when we get to Heaven, we'll put on our shoes."

Now, he wasn't always talkin' about a place after death. Heaven had a dichotomy in its meaning. To some extent, they meant afterlife, but to an equal extent, if not greater, they were talkin' about somewhere outside slavery. When they sang "Steal Away to Jesus," they were singing at night that the Underground Railroad was at work, and Jesus was the symbol of their freedom—try to get up North where there wasn't no slavery. And when they talked about the other song I mentioned, "All God's Children Got Shoes," they'd say, "Heav'n, Heav'n, everybody talkin' 'bout Heav'n, ain't goin' there." They were talking about the white folks were up there singing about the Lord, God, Love, and Peace and then holding them in slavery, see.

So they saw an hypocrisy in the faith, but they saw the fault not with the religion, but with those who were practicing it. And they adopted the religion, and Jesus became a symbol of freedom and liberty. And the gospel to them was a liberating gospel, because when they read about God delivering Moses and the Children of Israel [thumping his desk for emphasis], they saw the parallel between the experience of the Israelites and the black experience. And they figured that God was gonna deliver them. And so, without always articulating it in theological terms, the black church has always seen God as being identified with the downcast and the suffering. Jesus' first text he used when he preached his first sermon was taken from Isaiah, which is, "The Lord has anointed me to preach the gospel to the poor, to deliver the oppressed, to free the captive. . . ."

> In the white community the preacher is pretty much restricted to the responsibilities of his parish.
>
> *And he better not meddle.*
>
> Right. But in the black community . . . freedom of the pulpit has never been a problem. That's always been a white problem. The black preacher's always been free to preach as he felt inspired—by God.

And what was so significant about what SCLC did, because it had a preacher leadership . . . it emphasized in the social struggle the moral aspects. Whereas they were there before, . . . the political and legal aspects overshadowed them. But with the coming of SCLC, the struggle was put in its proper perspective . . . in the moral arena, and that's what got people marching. It opened up people's eyes for the first time to how ugly and immoral segregation was. . . .

You see, what the bus thing did was simply more than withholding patronage from the bus; it was restoring a sense of dignity to the patrons, as best expressed by an oft-quoted black woman in Montgomery who said, "Since I been walking, my feet are tired, but my soul's rested." So that it was also, at the same time and a part of that, the beginning of self-determination. See, self-determination's some new phraseology, but prior to the bus boycotts, the determination of our freedom rested with the courts. With the bus boycott, *we* determined it. It didn't make any difference what the court said. The court could say what it liked, we weren't gon' ride—in the back of the bus. We'd walk.

INTERLUDE

JOHN LEWIS

An Alabama Boyhood

He was born at Dunn's Chapel, a black sharecropper community about forty miles west of Montgomery.

My parents rented land. They tended land that was owned by a very, very wealthy white landowner, who for many years had provided land for my mother's brothers, my mother's father, and other relatives to farm. So I was born on a piece of that land in 1940. In 1944 when I was four years old, my father bought a hundred and ten acres of land for three hundred dollars. I guess the man that he bought it from almost, in my estimation, gave it to him.

In this whole area it was really a black-and-white world. It was just rural Alabama; the land was not that rich; we planted cotton, corn, peanuts. But it was two separate worlds, one black and one white. From time to time when growing up, we would complete our work, and then we would go and work by the day, work in the cotton field pickin' cotton by the pound, particularly to get money for books or clothing for school in August or September.

I guess as a young child, I saw the dual system of segregation and racial discrimination. The grade school that I attended was a little one-room school, from the first through the sixth grade, and it was just a shack really. . . . From the seventh through the twelfth grade, we were bused through Pike County to the Pike County Training School. In many parts of Alabama, the high schools for blacks were considered "training schools," and the county high schools for whites were called just "the county high school." We had the worst buses. We never had a new bus. The white children had new buses. Our school was a run-down school, and all that had an impact on me. . . .

> We didn't have electric lights, we didn't have indoor plumbing, anything like that, until very, very late. I was a teenager, getting ready to go to college, matter of fact, before we got even the highway. We had unpaved roads, and for many years the county refused to pave the major road. They paved it up to where the black section of the county started. . . . Our house was on a hill, a red-clay hill . . . and the road, this highway, came right through our property. And when it would rain—it was a steep hill—people would get stuck in the mud and the ditches and that type of thing. The same thing would happen to the school bus . . . The bus may get stuck; you may be late gettin' to school. Or coming back from school in the evening, the same thing would happen. . . . That area was very, very poor, very, very poor. . . .

Do you remember discussing it much among yourselves?

Not—not really, not really. [A long pause] Not really . . . see . . . we didn't have a subscription to a newspaper. But my grandfather had a subscription to the Montgomery *Advertiser,* and we would get the paper maybe two or three days later—sometime it would be a week later—and we kept up with what was happening in Montgomery or in Alabama or the South by reading the newspaper after he had read it. But we really didn't discuss the whole question of segregation. It was something that existed and that we saw when we went to the town, into Troy, to the dimestore. We saw the sign saying White Only or Colored. When you went to go to the water fountain, you *knew* not to drink out of that fountain that said White Only, that you were directed to drink out of the one saying Colored. You couldn't go to the soda fountain and get a Coke. Somehow we grew up *knowing* that you couldn't cross that line, but there was not that much discussing it within my family, not at all. It was a sense of fear, I guess, on the part of my parents, that we must stay in our place. There was a certain point where then you couldn't—you knew not to go any further.

In 1954, when the school desegregation decision came down, you would have been about fourteen . . .

I was fourteen and I remember that. I do remember the Supreme Court decision of 1954. . . . As I recall, we rejoiced. It was like a day of jubilee . . . that segregation would be ended in the public school system. We thought that we would go to a better school . . . get better transportation, better buses, and that type of thing. But that didn't happen, so I never attended a desegregated public school. Then, a year later was the Montgomery Bus Boycott in 1955, and I think perhaps that incident, what happened in Montgomery, had the greatest impact on me, more than anything else. . . . I grew up with this whole idea of wanting to be a minister. I don't know where it came from. . . . I recall, when I was four years old, I remember baptizing a chicken, and the chicken drowned. I kept it under the water too long. I would preach to the chicken and baptize a particular chicken . . . Then one of my uncles, my mother's brother, had Santa Claus to bring a Bible. So I went through this whole idea, even going through grade school, of becoming a minister, and through grade school and high school, people referred to me as Preacher. . . .

But coming back to 1955, I think the Montgomery Bus Boycott did more than anything else. We didn't have television, but I kept up with what was going on, on radio, in newspaper, everything. In the papers that we got in the public school system in the library, I read *everything* about what was happening there, and it was really one of the most exciting, one of the most moving things to me to see just a few miles away the black folks of Montgomery stickin' together, refusing to ride segregated buses, walking the streets. It was a moving movement.

And I'd heard Dr. King even before the Montgomery Bus Boycott. There's a local radio station in Montgomery . . . a soul station . . . and Dr. King had a sermon. It was called "Paul's Letter to the American Christians," and some of the things that he said sorta stuck with me. As you well know, his message was sort of social-political oriented. It was sort of the social gospel, making religion something real and using the emotionalism within religion to make it do something else for people, and that had an impact.

Do you recall hearing him more or less by chance?

Yeah, that's right, by chance, because I didn't know anything about him. I'd never heard anything about him. Now this was *before*—before the Montgomery Bus Boycott—when he first came to Montgomery and they would have different ministers preaching. And then when he emerged during the bus boycott, I took some particular note.

II
BLACK SURPRISE

THE STUDENT SIT-INS AND
THE BIRTH OF SNCC

FRANKLIN MCCAIN

February 1, 1960: The South's First Sit-in

It was one of those group friendships that spring up among college freshmen. In their first semester at all-black North Carolina A&T College in Greensboro, he and Ezell Blair, Jr., David Richmond, and Joseph McNeil became inseparable. They would study together, eat together, and, "as young freshmen often do in college dormitories late at night, when they finish studying or when they want to cop out from studying . . . resort to the old-fashion type bull session."

Through the fall, their talks continued. He remembers them as "elementary philosophers," young idealists talking about justice and injustice, hypocrisy, how imperfectly their society embodied its own ideals. Slowly their talks swung to a debate as old as philosophy itself: at what point does the moral man act against injustice? ". . . I think the thing that precipitated the sit-in, the idea of the sit-in, more than anything else, was that little bit of incentive and that little bit of courage that each of us instilled within each other."

The planning process was on a Sunday night, I remember it quite well. I think it was Joseph who said, "It's time that we take some action now. We've been getting together, and we've been, up to this point, still like most people we've talked about for the past few weeks or so—that is, people who talk a lot but, in fact, make very little action." After selecting the technique, then we said, "Let's go down and just ask for service." It certainly wasn't titled a "sit-in" or "sit-down" at that time. "Let's just go down to Woolworth's tomorrow and ask for service, and the tactic is going to be simply this: we'll just stay there." We never anticipated being served, certainly, the first day anyway. "We'll stay until we get served." And I think Ezell said, "Well, you know that might be weeks, that might be months, that might be never." And I think it was the consensus of the group, we said, "Well, that's just the chance we'll have to take."

What's likely to happen? Now, I think that that was a question that all of us asked ourselves. . . . What's going to happen once we sit down? Of course, nobody had the answers. Even your wildest imagination couldn't lead you to believe what would, in fact, happen.

Why Woolworth's?

They advertise in public media, newspapers, radios, television, that sort of thing. They tell you to come in: "Yes, buy the toothpaste; yes, come in and buy the notebook paper. . . . No, we don't separate your money in this cash register, but, no, please don't step down to the hot dog stand. . . ." The whole system, of course, was unjust, but that just seemed like insult added to injury. That was just like pouring salt into an open wound. That's inviting you to do something. . . .

Once getting there . . . we did make purchases of school supplies and took the patience and time to get receipts for our purchases, and Joseph and myself went over to the counter and asked to be served coffee and doughnuts. As anticipated, the reply was, "I'm sorry, we don't serve you here." And of course we said, "We just beg to disagree with you. We've in fact already been served; you've served us already and that's just not quite true." The attendant or waitress was a little bit dumbfounded, just didn't know what to say under circumstances like that. And we said, "We wonder why you'd invite us in to serve us at one counter and deny service at another. If this is a private club or private concern, then we believe you ought to sell membership cards and sell only to persons who have a membership card. If we don't have a card, then we'd know pretty well that we shouldn't come in or even attempt to come in." That didn't go over too well, simply because I don't really think she understood what we were talking about, and for the second reason, she had no logical response to a statement like that. And the only thing that an individual in her case or position could do is, of course, call the manager. [Laughs] Well, at this time, I think we were joined by Dave Richmond and Ezell Blair at the counter with us, after that dialogue.

Were you afraid at this point?

Oh, hell yes, no question about that. [Laughs] At that point there was a policeman who had walked in off the street, who was pacing the aisle . . . behind us, where we were seated, with his club in his hand, just sort of knocking it in his hand, and just looking mean and red and a little bit upset and a little bit disgusted. And you had the feeling that he didn't know what the hell to do. You had the feeling that this is the first time that this big bad man with the gun and the club has been pushed in a corner, and he's got absolutely no defense, and the thing that's killing him more than anything else—he doesn't know what he can or what he cannot do. He's defenseless. Usually his defense is offense, and we've provoked him, yes, but we haven't provoked him outwardly enough for him to resort to violence. And I think this is just killing him; you can see it all over him.

People in the store were—we got mixed reactions from people in the store. A couple of old ladies . . . came up to pat us on the back sort of and say, "Ah, you should have done it ten years ago. It's a good thing I think you're doing."

These were black ladies.

No, these are white ladies.

Really?

Yes, and by the same token, we had some white ladies and white men to come up and say to us, "Nasty, dirty niggers, you know you don't belong here at the lunch counter. There's a counter—" There was, in fact, a counter downstairs in the Woolworth store, a stand-up type counter where they sold hot dogs. . . .

But at any rate, there were expressions of support from white people that first day?

Absolutely right. Absolutely. And I think probably that was certainly some incentive for additional courage on the part of us. And the other thing that helped us psychologically quite a lot was seeing the policeman pace the aisle and not be able to do anything. I think that this probably gave us more strength, more encouragement, than anything else on that particular day, on day one.

Unexpected as it was, the well-wishing from the elderly white women was hardly more surprising than the scorn of a middle-aged black dishwasher behind the counter. She said, "That's why we can't get anyplace today, because of people like you, rabble-rousers, trouble-makers. . . . This counter is reserved for white people, it always has been, and you are well aware of that. So why don't you go on out and stop making trouble?"

He has since seen the woman at, of all places, a reunion commemorating the event in which she played so unsupportive a role.

[She said] "Yes, I did say it and I said it because, first of all, I was afraid for what would happen to you as young black boys. Secondly, I was afraid of what would happen to me as an individual who had a job at the Woolworth store. I might have been fired and that's my livelihood. . . ."

It took me a long time to really understand that statement . . . but I know why she said it. She said it out of fear more than anything else. I've come to understand that, and my elders say to me that it's maturity that makes me understand why she said that some fifteen years ago.

But, moved by neither praise nor scorn, he and the others waited for the waitress to return with the manager, a career Woolworth's employee named C. L. Harris.

That was real amusin' as well [laughing] because by then we had the confidence, my goodness, of a Mack truck. And there was virtually nothing that could move us, there was virtually nothing probably at that point that could really frighten us off. . . . If it's possible to know what it means to have your soul cleansed—I felt pretty clean at that time. I probably felt better on that day than I've ever felt in my life. Seems like a lot of feelings of guilt or what-have-you suddenly left me, and I felt as though I had gained my manhood, so to speak, and not only gained it, but had developed quite a lot of respect for it. Not Franklin McCain only as an individual, but I felt as though the manhood of a number of other black persons had been restored and had gotten some respect from just that one day.

But back to Mr. Harris, who was the store manager, he was a fairly nice guy to talk to on that day. I think what he wanted to do more than anything else was to—initially—was to kill us with kindness, to say, "Fellas, you know this is just not the way we do business. Why don't you go on back to your campus? If you're just hungry, go downstairs," and that sort of thing.

We listened to him, paid him the courtesy of listening to what he had to say. We repeated our demands to him, and he ended up by saying, "Well, you know, I don't really set policy for this store. The policy for serving you is set by corporate headquarters." And of course, we found out that that was just a cop out. Corporate headquarters said, "No, it's up to local communities to set standards and set practices and that sort of thing, and whatever they do is all right with us." You know, the usual sort of game of rubber checkers.

The only reason we did leave is the store was closing. We knew, of course, we had to leave when the store was closing. We said to him, "Well, we'll have plenty of time tomorrow, because we'll be back to see you." [Laughs] I don't think that went over too well. But by the time we were leaving, the store was just crowded with people from off the streets and on the streets. . . . As a matter of fact, there were so many people standin' in front of the store, we had to leave from the side entrance.

But back at the campus, there was just a beehive of activity. Word had spread. As a matter of fact, word was back on campus before we ever got back. There were all sorts of phone calls to the administration and to people on the faculty and staff. The mayor's office was aware of it and the governor's office was aware of it. I think it was all over North Carolina within a matter of just an hour or so.

That night they met with about fifty campus leaders to form the Student Executive Committee for Justice.

The movement started out as a movement of nonviolence and as a Christian movement, and we wanted to make that very clear to everybody, that it was a movement that was seeking justice more than anything else and not a movement to start a war. . . . We knew that probably the most powerful and potent weapon that people have literally no defense for is love, kindness. That is, whip the enemy with something that he doesn't understand.

How much was the example of Dr. King and the Montgomery Bus Boycott in your mind in that regard?

Not very much. The individual who had probably most influence on us was Gandhi, more than any single individual. During the time that the Montgomery Bus Boycott was in effect, we were tots for the most part, and we barely heard of Martin Luther King. Yes, Martin Luther King's name was well-known when the sit-in movement was in effect, but to pick out Martin Luther King as a hero. . . . I don't want you to misunderstand what I'm about to say: Yes, Martin Luther King was a hero. . . . No, he was not the individual that we had upmost in mind when we started the sit-in movement. . . .

Most journalists and historians have been quite wrong about the im-
petus for the first sit-in, he insists. Although all of the students had read
extensively on the Montgomery movement, they were not, as has been
widely reported, directly inspired by a Fellowship of Reconciliation
"comic book" entitled "Martin Luther King and the Montgomery
Story." They had not heard of CORE's Chicago sit-in twenty years
earlier. Nor were he and the others persuaded, as one history of the
sit-ins has it, to make their protest by Ralph Johns, an eccentric white
NAACP member who ran a haberdashery near the campus. The subject
irritates him. Dignified even in his light-hearted moments, he now be-
comes even more formal.

Credit for the initiation of the sit-in movement has been granted to one or two ministers, the NAACP, Ralph Johns, CORE, at least a dozen people, and it's rather amusing when you do read some of these articles. I think it's a game. The same type tactic that has been used over and over and over by the white news media and the white press to discredit blacks with particular types of achievement. You don't have to look at the sit-in movement to see that. You can think of things like, well, for instance, the surveying of the laying out of the city of Washington, D.C., or the invention of the traffic signal, or the concept of Labor Day, or even Perry's expedition to the North Pole. These are the kinds of things that come into my mind when I think about the attempt to discredit the people who actually started the sit-in movement.

So what you're saying is . . . the most simple explanation applies?

Four guys met, planned, and went into action. It's just that simple.

On the second day, they were joined by over twenty other A&T stu-
dents, and they kept most of the stools occupied all day. On the fourth
day the first white students joined them from the University of North

Carolina Women's College in Greensboro. By the second week sit-ins had spread to a half-dozen North Carolina towns.

From the Greensboro area there must have been people from six or seven university campuses who wanted to participate, who wanted to help sit-in, who wanted to help picket. We actually got to the point where we had people going down in shifts. It got to the point wherein we took all the seats in the restaurants. We had people there in the mornings as soon as the doors were open to just take every seat in the restaurant or at the lunch counter. . . .

As a manager, you've got to do something. You just can't continue to have people come in and sit around. The cash registers have to ring. What happened is that after we started to take all of the seats in the restaurants, they started to pull the stools up in the restaurants. So we just started to stand around then and take all the standing room. . . . I think at the height of the sit-in movement in Greensboro, we must have had at least, oh, ten or fifteen thousand people downtown who wanted to sit-in, but obviously there weren't that many chairs in downtown Greensboro for people to sit in. . . .

It spread to places like the shopping centers, the drugstores in the shopping centers, the drive-ins. . . . No place was going to be left untouched. The only criteria was that if it did not serve blacks, it was certainly going to be hit. . . .

With such success came attention.

The Congress of Racial Equality offered a funny sort of help, and that kind of help was, in effect, "If you let us control the show, we'll show you how the thing is supposed to be done." And four seventeen-year-old guys were just not in the mood to let someone take their show. That was our position. Our position was, we are probably as much experts about this as anybody else. We were experts because we had had one experience already, and that's more than most people had had.

We got a lot of attention from the Communist party. [Laughs] The Communist party sent representatives down to Greensboro to assist us in any way that we deemed appropriate. If it meant actual participation, they offered to sit in with us. If it meant you needed x number of dollars to do this, or if you needed air fare to go here or there, if you needed anything, they made it known that money was available, assistance was available. Just don't sit down here in Greensboro and want for things that you need. But you know, again, it was a Christian movement, and Christians and Communists just don't mix.

Did you avail yourself of any of that?

No, we didn't need it. Even if we had needed it, there was no reason to affiliate with the Communist party. We were in the driver's seat. . . . Remember, too, you had four guys who were pretty strong-willed, pretty bull-headed, and who were keenly aware that people would rush in and try to take over the Movement, so to speak. And we were quite aware of that, and we felt—not felt—*were* very independent. . . . As a matter of fact, we were criticized on several occasions for being too damned independent. But I still don't regret it.

Did the success that you experienced cause strains among the four of you?

Never. There was enough to go around. [Laughs]

Within a year the students had forced the desegregation of Greensboro's theaters and lunch counters. "The four," however, passed quickly from the Movement scene, Blair to become a teacher in Massachusetts, McNeil a banker in New York. Richmond still lives in Greensboro, and McCain, a chemist, settled in Charlotte, one hundred miles to the south, where he is a development engineer for Celanese Corporation.

His final observation on Greensboro:

I'm told that the chamber of commerce wastes no time in letting prospective industry or businesses know that this is where the sit-in movement originated some fourteen, fifteen years ago, way back in 1960. This is another reason that we can call ourself the Gate City . . . the gateway to the New South. . . .

So, it's rather amusing the way they have . . . used it to their advantage, something that as a matter of fact they were staunchly against at that particular time. But I think that's only smart. It's only good business to do that. I'm sure if I were the chamber of commerce, I'd do the same thing.

Julian Bond
and Lonnie King

An Unmatched Pair

In black Atlanta, they came from opposite sides of the tracks.

Julian Bond was educated in a Pennsylvania prep school, where he was the only black student. His late father, an Atlanta University dean, was one of the nation's preeminent black scholars.

As for Lonnie King, "My mother was a maid and I lived in an alley, grew up in an alley."

They were physical and temperamental opposites, as well.

Julian Bond, slender, light-skinned, fragilely handsome, was a jazz buff and aspiring poet.

Lonnie King, dark, bull-like, a punishing boxer, was four years older than Julian Bond. And madder. He had signed for a four-year navy hitch to escape the South, his poverty, Atlanta—where he had been fired from a YMCA job for whipping the son of a socially prominent black family. Even so, "I told a friend of mine in Hong Kong in '57 that I was coming back to Atlanta when I got out, and this is the corny part. I told him that I believe one thing, that there's going to be a revolution in the South, and I want to be there, be a part of it."

LONNIE KING: First of all, I met Julian Bond when I came back to Atlanta in '57. He was coming to Morehouse, and I was coming back to

Morehouse, and believe it or not, Julian and I were in the line together
to pay our money to the people over there. And they were long lines, so
we talked and talked and talked, and we never really talked any more—
just ever so often, "Hello." But never really anything, and finally in
1960, when that thing broke out in North Carolina, we happened to
have been in the drugstore together, and I went up to him and talked to
him and another guy named Joe Pierce about doing some things in
Atlanta. . . . Julian was reluctant. He probably could explain his reluctance maybe a lot better than I can. All I know is that he *was* reluctant,
and we kept pushing. We pushed him, not because we saw any great
messiah kind of thing where we have to have Julian. It's just that you
need certain kinds of personalities to make things go. Julian had a reputation for being an excellent writer, and my feeling was that the Movement's point of view had to be articulated by young people in as logical
and coherent a fashion as possible. He had been a *Time* magazine intern
and came from a pretty good family and had been around books all of
his life. . . .

JULIAN BOND: On about the third day of February, 1960, I was sitting in what was then Yates and Milton's Drugstore at the corner of
Fair and Chestnut streets which was sort of a student hangout and
served the function of a coffeehouse for Atlanta University Center
students.* Sitting in the back there, just doing nothing, I guess, by myself.
A fellow came over whom I knew to be Lonnie King. I knew him because he was a football player and had just run a touchdown against
someone, a spectacular touchdown. Morehouse didn't have a good
team. And he came up to me and he showed me a copy of the Atlanta
Daily World which at that time was a daily paper. I know it was the
third or fourth of February because the headline said, "Greensboro Student Sit-In, Third Day."

He said, "Have you seen that?" And I was sort of irritated and I said,
"Yeah, you know, I read the papers." And he said, "What do you think
about it?" And I said, "Well, it's all right, pretty good stuff." And he
said, "Don't you think it ought to happen here?" And I said, "It probably will." And he said, "Let's make it happen." And I should have said,
"What do you mean, *let's?*" [Laughs] But I didn't. You know, Lonnie's
a very persuasive guy, and I didn't know him at all except by reputation
as an athlete. And he said, "You take this side of the drugstore and I'll
take the other and we'll call a meeting for Sale Hall Annex [a building

* The Atlanta University Center comprises Morehouse and five other black institutions. The AU schools, as they are called, occupy adjoining campuses near
downtown Atlanta.

on the campus] for noon today to talk about it." So I took half the drugstore, and he took half, and we had a meeting of a small group of people, about twenty people. And the next day enlarged it to more and more, and that began the student movement. . . .

LONNIE KING: Now, let me tell you where I was looking at. In 1959, I believe it was, in Oklahoma or somewhere, some kids down there in the NAACP had been involved in a kind of a sit-in, but it never spread.* And my position was that the situation in Greensboro would again be another isolated incident in black history, if others didn't join in to make it become something that the kids ought to be doing. In really analyzing it, the only people in the black community at that time who were free to take on the Establishment were college kids. . . .

JULIAN BOND: Our original plan was to hit all of the five-and-dimes, Woolworth's and W.T. Grant's and Kresge's and all those places, and we went to the Atlanta University Center presidents . . . and they suggested—Dr. Clement, rather, suggested—what I see in retrospect was a delaying move.** He suggested that if we demonstrated nobody would know why we were demonstrating, which, of course, was foolish. Of course, they would know why. The lunch counters were segregated and we wanted them integrated.

But he said, "Atlanta students are always different; we have to do it better than anyone else." So he suggested that we publish in the paper, in the two daily papers and the *World,* a statement of grievances about what we thought was wrong and how it could be set right. . . .

It was called "An Appeal for Human Rights" and Dr. Clement somehow got the money for that to be published as a full page ad in the *Journal* and *Constitution* and the *World.* Now I say all this to say that what Dr. Clement really wanted to do was just have us put off the initial demonstration, believing that if we ever did begin we couldn't be stopped, and he did succeed in having us delay it until the fifteenth of March. We were ready in the middle of February to do something. He, through this delaying tactic, put us off until the middle of March.

This was the first sign of a rift between the students and their elders. It grew wider in the days ahead. In an ironic reversal of roles, the black educators at one point cast themselves as segregators, forbidding AU

---

* Members of NAACP youth chapters in Oklahoma and Kansas staged little-publicized and short-lived sit-ins in 1958.

** The late Dr. Rufus E. Clement, the first black elected to the Atlanta school board, was chairman of AU's Council of Presidents.

*students to invite sympathetic whites to the campus. More significantly,
they urged on the students a plan which spared the downtown merchants, some of whom were financial supporters of the colleges.*

See, the sit-ins had been going on all over the country at the time and
most of them were at private places like Woolworth's, and there was
some legal question as to what your rights were when you went into a
place that was private property. The businessman's position was that he
had a right to run it the way he wanted to. There was no federal anti-
discrimination law, and so some lawyers and the presidents suggested
that if we wanted to go to some place where we would be on firm footing, to go to cafeterias in public buildings . . . the City Hall cafeteria,
the state cafeteria, the bus station cafeterias, because they are involved
in interstate commerce. . . .

We didn't go to any private places that first day, and I was chosen to
lead the group at City Hall. They had a big sign out in the front at the
time which said "Cafeteria, Public Is Welcome." So we went in, very
neat, neckties, and all the girls looking as sharp as they could, and I was
so goddamn nervous I didn't know what to do. I had told all these kids,
I had about twelve people with me, that we'd be in jail fifteen minutes at
the most. There was a heavyset woman that I guess was the manager,
and she said, "What do you want?" And we said, "We want to eat."
And she said, "Well, we can't serve you here." And I said, "Well, the
sign outside says the public is welcome." She said, "This is just for City
Hall employees." We said, "That's not true, you've got a sign outside
saying the public is welcome and we're the public and we want to eat."
She said, "I'm going to call the police." She did, and a paddy wagon
backed up to that door as you face the City Hall on the right side there,
and we all got in, scared. They took us down to the old big jail, the one
that's been torn down, the one they used to call Big Rock. . . .

And a little later they . . . took us to a hearing before some judge. I
don't remember who it was, but the two lawyers who defended me were
Hollowell and A.T. Walden,* and Walden was in his dotage and liter-
ally fell asleep on his feet. . . . I'm looking at Walden, and I said,
"This guy's my lawyer and he's asleep." [Incredulous] And the judge
said, "Well, how do you plead?" And I looked at Hollowell and I said,
"How do I plead?" [Laughs] And Hollowell said, "Innocent, you fool."
So I said, "Innocent, Your Honor."

And they bound me over to the grand jury and later I was indicted on

---

* Donald Hollowell, a well-known civil rights lawyer, was the younger partner
of A.T. Walden, the pioneering black attorney consulted by Rev. Martin Luther
King, Sr.

nine counts—violation of the anti-trespass law; violation of the anti-mask law, which is an anti-Ku Klux Klan statute; conspiracy in restraint of trade; this enormous collection of charges. I just got them to dead docket it two years ago. . . . I was indicted on enough charges to put me away for ninety-nine years, and you think I wasn't scared? . . .

Then they took us from the courtroom back across to the old jail and time kept passing and these guys kept saying, "Bond, we've been here about six hours. You said we were getting out in about an hour." I said, "Don't worry about it, fellas, we'll be out in a minute." One or two people began to get nervous. None of us had ever been in jail before. Eventually we were bonded out, later that night, and went over to Paschal's,* where Mr. Paschal graciously had a beautiful chicken dinner for us, a free meal. Then we went over to Spelman** where we could be heroes, you know, among the women, and that was it. That was my first and last time in jail.

He recalls the spirit of the times, the happiest of his life.

At one time we had almost fifteen hundred people on a picket line downtown, encircling all of downtown Atlanta. And we had two-way radios. We ran from a little church back over here, Providence Baptist Church, I think it was, a regular shuttle system, cars taking people down and taking them back. We had people coming to spend an hour on their breaks, to spend an hour picketing. [There were] special football coats for the girls, with big hoods, because there were a lot of thugs downtown throwing spitballs and stuff at them. We had special laminated signs that wouldn't wash off in the rain. We were hell. [Laughs]

Even so, downtown Atlanta remained a monolith they could not crack. The merchants figured summer vacation would bring the end of the sit-ins. Lonnie King, who had been in the navy during the era of John Foster Dulles, recalls that he ". . . decided that we ought to employ kind of a domestic domino theory. . . . We would take on Rich's department store as being the kingpin, and if we can topple Rich's, all we have to do is just kind of whisper to the others. . . ."

LONNIE KING: It was good strategy at that point, but we knew that a Rich's charge plate in the black community was like running water.

---

* Paschal's, a black-owned restaurant and motel, subsequently became so popular as a Movement meeting place that Rev. Ralph Abernathy proclaimed, "A new America has been mapped within the walls of Paschal's Motor Hotel."
** The women's college of the AU complex.

There was one in everybody's house, and people didn't want to get rid of it because it wasn't a luxury. They viewed that Rich's charge account as a necessity, easy credit, pretty good terms. So we began a publication called "The Student Movement and You" and we passed them out, thousands, every Sunday in churches, . . . planning and programming them to an economic boycott when the students came back in the fall. We spent three months. We talked to thousands of people telling them what we were going to do in the fall and we wanted your help.

You were working the streets?

Working the streets. Talking to folks about how bad it was to go in Rich's on the fifth floor and spend a thousand dollars for some goods, but if your wife was pregnant, there was no place she could go, except downstairs next door to the honeyroom in a very unkempt restroom. You know, we just showed 'em all parallels. We asked, "How is it you have to drink 'colored' water if you going to spend that kind of money? . . ." And we showed 'em where it wasn't going to hurt them. We showed them where we were going to be the shock troops, we were the ones taking the chances. "All we're asking you to do is just don't buy, just stay at home." And it worked. . . .

> *"Close out your charge account with segregation, open up your ac-count with freedom," became the slogan. The students rented a safety-deposit box to store the Rich's charge cards mailed in by sympa-thetic adults. Once that summer the students staged a brief "test sit-in" at Rich's.*

. . . we went back to our office on Auburn after they closed down the lunch counter, and I got a call from Chief Jenkins,* who asked me to come to the police department for a meeting. So I went down there . . . and when I walked into the chief's office, the chief's con-ference room, here was Dick Rich. Dick Rich said to me that "We didn't arrest you today, but if you come back down to my department store again, I'm going to put you in jail." [Laughs] And I says, "Well, Mr. Rich, we are coming back, so you may as well put us in jail right now."

Anyway, Herschelle** and I . . . decided that in order to dramatize this thing, we really ought to get Martin King arrested, if we could. So we

---

* Atlanta Police Chief Herbert Jenkins.
** Herschelle Sullivan was cochairperson of the student sit-in committee.

called him and asked him would he meet us on the bridge at Rich's*
and go to jail with us. Now this is the part I was telling you about that's
probably never been written before, but we had a big hassle in the committee. A lot of students wanted to go gung ho in September when we
first came back, but we wanted to stage the thing in the middle of October because we wanted to influence, if we could, the presidential election of 1960, believe it or not. We had a tremendous hassle within the
leadership of the Movement. . . . Bernard Lee,** who was down at
SCLC, and A.D. King*** and some others thought we ought to move
forthwith, right now. But our strategy was to get Martin King arrested
with us and do it in the middle of October, so as to influence the election.

Here's what happened. We made our plans and finally got it approved
by the group. The plan was we would send telegrams to Nixon and to
Kennedy and ask them to take a position on the civil rights movement
here. We thought that with Dr. King being involved in it, that would
create enough of a national uproar in the black community and we
would really see where these guys stand.

Now, what was the countervailing argument?

The argument by Bernard and A.D. and others who were with them
was that we should move forward right now. You know, they were im-
patient: "Let's go." Because what it meant was that we had to wait
from the first part of September until the middle of October, and if
you've been priming people all during the summer, there are always
people who want to move faster—and they didn't understand the politics
of it at that point.

Anyway, we asked Herschelle to call Martin about going to Rich's to
get arrested. Herschelle called Martin and asked him about coming. I'm
not sure whether she told him all the ramifications like the national kind
of thing and all, but he said at first that he couldn't come. Wyatt Tee
Walker,† I understand—this was secondhand, what Herschelle told me—
felt that he ought not to go because he had just been arrested with

* An elevated crosswalk connecting portions of the store located on opposite
sides of a downtown street.
** Bernard Lee was stationed at an Air Force base near Montgomery during the
bus boycott. When King moved to Atlanta early in 1960, Lee joined SCLC as his
personal aide and traveling companion.
*** Dr. King's younger brother, then a Morehouse College student. He drowned
in the swimming pool of his Atlanta home in 1970.
† SCLC executive director and a major architect of the organization's policy
and strategy in the early sixties.

Lillian Smith out in DeKalb County. He was on probation in that situation and he did not want to have to go to jail on that kind of an issue.* So Herschelle came back and reported to me. I was talking with a student in the Spelman Library, and she came back and pulled me aside and said, "He won't go."

And so I had her to take over the meeting, and I called him, and he gave me the long story, and I said, "Well, Martin, you've got to go to jail." I went through all the ramifications of it. I said, "You are the spiritual leader of the Movement, and you were born in Atlanta, Georgia, and I think it might add tremendous impetus if you would go."

He said, "Well, where are you going to go tomorrow, L.C.?" He always called me L.C., because I grew up in the church down there.

I said, "I'm going to be on the bridge down at Rich's."

He said, "Well, I'll meet you on the bridge tomorrow at ten o'clock."

So that's what happened. Martin came and we met one another on the bridge and we went to jail together. . . . The rest is almost history. . . .

> *His plan worked to perfection. Dick Rich wept when Martin King sat down in Rich's Magnolia Room. DeKalb County, as expected, revoked King's probation. Under cover of night DeKalb officials whisked him off to the maximum security prison at Reidsville for four months at hard labor—an unheard-of sentence for a first-offense traffic violation which did not involve dangerous driving. The case became a* cause célèbre *when Robert Kennedy appealed to the DeKalb County judge for mercy and John Kennedy called Mrs. King to express his concern—all this two weeks before the November 8, 1960, election.*

> . . . some historians have said that the jailing of Martin King and the intervention of Bobby Kennedy was what swung the election in the black communities in Philadelphia, Cleveland, and all those big cities away from Nixon. If that is, in fact, true, then I think that we had a lot to do with it, because we schemed the whole deal up here

---

* The fear was that DeKalb County would revoke its probation of a ninety-day sentence given King for failing to exchange his Alabama driver's license for a Georgia license after moving back to Atlanta. The arrest took place when King was driving the author Smith to the Emory University Hospital where she was being treated for the cancer which would kill her in 1966. In Fulton County, where King lived, the more enlightened authorities viewed the stiff sentence handed King as a form of harassment intended to discourage him from undertaking any civil rights activities in DeKalb's affluent white suburbs.

during the summer of 1960. I did not have a preference, believe it or not, between Nixon or Kennedy. . . .

The man you ought to talk to on this whole question is John Calhoun.* John Calhoun, as I understand it, used all of his influence to try and get Richard Nixon's people to take a stand and they wouldn't. But nevertheless, John—it's ironic—is such a skillful political organizer till in spite of all the hoopla he was still able to carry the black community in Atlanta for Richard Nixon in 1960 . . . and had the Republicans, in my opinion, listened to Mr. Calhoun, Nixon probably would have been president in 1960. Because I don't think the black community was that committed to John Kennedy. I know Martin King's father, for instance, had already endorsed Richard Nixon. Okay? But switched after Kennedy got involved.**

The boycott ground on into the Christmas shopping season. Lonnie King had learned to read Federal Reserve retail trade statistics; business was bad in Atlanta. He was summoned to the chamber of commerce for "the most important meeting of your life." The city's elders, black and white together now, had made a deal. If the students would halt the boycott, the lunch counters would be desegregated—but not until the following September when schools were to be integrated under a federal court order.

. . . Mr. [A.T.] Walden's position was that we have been segregated every year that I have been born, how come we can't wait ten more months? . . . Daddy King got up and said that he was tired of going through this effort. These white folks had never been willing to do anything like this before, and [he said] I should go on and accept what they were talking about doing. . . .

Anyway, we went back to the campus [that afternoon] and I gave the report to the kids, and Herschelle and I cried, and I resigned and Herschelle resigned. Because the kids did not want to accept it.

They resigned because they felt they had let the students down by not taking a harder line in the negotiations. Although the students rejected their resignations and gave them a vote of confidence, the question of

* A black Republican leader in Fulton County well-known in national party circles as a convention delegate. See page 78 ff.
** Rev. King, Sr., who was thought to have Republican sympathies, was reported to have told his congregation, "I've got a suitcase full of votes, and I'm going to take them to Mr. Kennedy and dump them in his lap."

whether the students would accept the compromise was not decided in the afternoon meeting.

That night there was a mass meeting at Warren Memorial Church. You may have read about it. Martin King made, in my opinion, that night, probably the greatest speech of his life, greater than the one he made at the March on Washington. Okay. His daddy was booed that night on the agreement, and Rev. Borders* and some of them were trying to get Herschelle and me to go up and face the crowd and get them all calm. And Carl Holman, who is now the head of the National Urban Coalition, said, "Hell, no, you all created the problem, so you all resolve it. You are not going to push these kids out there to resolve your problems."

We didn't realize how much we had sold the black community on supporting us until that night. Oh, man, there were about two thousand people down there, and they were ready to lynch some people. They really were. The news media came on with the thing saying that the lunch counters in downtown Atlanta would reopen tomorrow segregated, emphasized that, you know. All that kind of stuff really rubbed some people wrong. I was so disillusioned by the thing . . . I decided to go on off and go to school at Howard, 'cause I had seen people that I had had respect for all my life crumble when faced with an awesome decision. I just didn't think I could take it anymore, to be quite honest with you. You know, I marched across the street from the Klan in the rain. Folks tried to break in my house.

What was the thrust of Dr. King's speech . . . ?

. . . King basically made a kind of speech like the one he made at the March on Washington, except that this time he had tears in his eyes, and he was preaching because his daddy had been humiliated. His daddy got up to make a speech and said that he had been working in this town for thirty years, and before he could say the rest of it, somebody up in the balcony jumped up and said, "That's what's wrong. . . ." And that crushed that man. Okay? And it crushed Martin, seeing his daddy booed down. They all booed him, and there was hissing.

He got up and made the best speech I've ever heard him make, off the cuff, in defense of his father, but at the same time, trying to march

---

* Rev. William Holmes Borders, a well-known black preacher, who led the bus desegregation effort in Atlanta and served as an adviser to the students.

with the hounds who were chasing him. He talked about "the cancerous disease of disunity." That's the first time I ever heard him use that expression. He said it debilitates you, and he talked about unification, and he tried to point out to the audience that older people like his father did make a contribution. On the other hand, it's time now for the younger people to make their contributions.

He was trying to marry [the opposing positions] 'cause the thing was basically a young-versus-old split, and the young folks knew that we had been blackjacked and kind of just bludgeoned in the damn meeting. And the older leaders were fighting for something else, too. They were fighting for survival, because the young people, unlettered and all that kind of stuff, had pulled off the leadership role in Atlanta, and I think they were fighting for that, too.

JULIAN BOND: And another thing is that when the lunch counters finally integrated . . . these guys and women fought to be the first to eat at Woolworth's or Rich's and came to the church in furs.* You know, these were women who go shopping just like every other woman, and they came dressed in furs and all their finery to be the first black person to eat at Rich's. Sad, sad, sad. Elbowing the students aside. In fact, they insisted that we send mixed groups, and by "mixed," I mean adults and students. Because the adults just wanted to be in on it when it happened.

* This was the following September, for Dr. King's speech in defense of his father had tipped the balance in favor of the delayed settlement. By the time the first blacks were served in Rich's, Lonnie King had left Atlanta for law school in Washington, D.C., where he was shortly thereafter hospitalized with a bleeding ulcer.

JOHN CALHOUN

He was director of the Nixon campaign in Atlanta's black precincts. He was also one of the older black leaders meeting with city officials in the sit-in negotiations. At one of those meetings, Mayor William Hartsfield, a Democrat, presented some political news which had yet to hit the papers. Hartsfield proudly announced that his party's presidential nominee had just phoned Mrs. Martin Luther King, Jr., to express his concern over the fact that Dr. King had been imprisoned as a result of his arrest with the students sitting-in at Rich's.

Now, what happened here in Atlanta, I tried to get in touch with Nixon to try to get *him* to make some kinda statement, because Kennedy didn't know King, but Nixon did. Nixon had made a trip to Africa with King.* But Nixon didn't respond.

How far did you get in your efforts?

Well, we got to him. Through some of the white Democrats,** we got to him. He was up in Michigan. He said he would lose some black

* King and Nixon, then Vice-President, met in 1957 when both attended independence ceremonies in Ghana; however, they did not travel together.

** Democrats for Nixon. Throughout the South, many nominal Democrats worked openly for Nixon because of Kennedy's religion and the Democratic party's civil rights platform.

votes, but he'd gain white votes, so he was gonna sit it out, and he wouldn't say anything. . . .

Did you see the political implication of that at the time?

Oh, yes, oh, yes. I saw that. I *knew* what it meant. Oh, yeah, I knew what it meant, and I told Val Washington. . . .* I was called to the phone while the mayor** was in there making that presentation, and it was Val Washington calling me about some other things that I used in the campaign.

And I said, "Val, this is gon' have some terrific repercussions, and you oughta get ahold of Nixon to get him to say something."

He said, "John, I don't know whether I'll be able to do that because Nixon doesn't deal with the Republican committee." Just like he didn't the second time he ran. He didn't deal with the Republican National Committee. "He's got these other organizations he's dealing with, the Democrats for Nixon, and he meets with them every Monday, and I don't know whether I can talk to him or not." But he would try.

But Val wasn't able to get Nixon, so I didn't wait for him. I went on to these new people [the Democrats for Nixon] that he was dealing with. They're the ones that got in touch with him, and they called me and told me what Mr. Nixon had said. . . . He made the decisions then just like he makes them now. Nixon is that kinda person. But I did the best I could.

The Kennedy organization printed a million leaflets describing their candidate's intervention, distributing them at black churches all across America on the Sunday before the election. A half-million were handed out in Chicago alone.

Concluded campaign historian Theodore H. White: "When one reflects that Illinois was carried by only 9,000 votes and that 250,000 Negroes are estimated to have voted for Kennedy; that Michigan was

---

* Vice-chairman of the Republican National Committee.

** The late Mayor Hartsfield may have played a larger role than Calhoun suspected. Eugene Patterson, at that time editor of the Atlanta *Constitution*, says Hartsfield "bragged repeatedly to me, immediately after the 1960 election, that 'I'm the guy who got Kennedy elected president.'" Patterson says that upon learning of King's arrest, "Hartsfield said he got on the phone to Kennedy's people immediately—I don't recall whether he said he called Bobby Kennedy or Bobby Troutman (a Kennedy family friend) in Atlanta, or who—and gave them his urgent advice to make a telephone call to Atlanta in behalf of Dr. King. . . . Nationally, the phone call swung enough black votes to Kennedy to elect him, Hartsfield claimed."

carried by 67,000 votes and that an estimated 250,000 Negroes voted for Kennedy; that South Carolina was carried by 10,000 votes and that an estimated 40,000 Negroes there voted for Kennedy, the candidate's instinctive decision [to phone Mrs. King] must be ranked among the most crucial of the last few weeks" of the campaign.*

Only in the black precincts organized by John Calhoun was the pattern broken. There Nixon got over fifty percent of the vote, but even so, the election marked the end of Republican influence in Atlanta's black community. By 1977 there was but one black Republican officeholder in the city—Councilman John Calhoun.

* Theodore H. White, *The Making of the President* (New York: Atheneum, 1960).

JOHN LEWIS

Leaving Pike County

It was my great desire and dream to come to Morehouse . . . I had
heard that Martin Luther King, Jr., went to Morehouse . . . I was unable to do it. It would have been impossible. There was no way I could
get into Morehouse. My mother had been working as a maid for some
members of the Southern Baptist Church* in Alabama, and she brought
home one day a newspaper, *The Alabama Baptist* . . . and it had an ad
in this paper about the American Baptist Theological Seminary in Nashville, and it said, "For Colored."

It suggested that you could come there and could work. The tuition
was very cheap, so I applied during the spring of 1957 and got accepted. In September of '57 I enrolled in the school and got a job working in the kitchen, washing pots and pans, huge pots, dirty pots and
pans, the biggest pots and pans I ever seen in my life, really heavy. They
were huge things, and this was my first time away from home, seventeen
years old. I did it for two years, but in the meantime I kept up with everything that was going on, on sort of the civil rights front, everything. I
read everything, watched television, and tried to organize a local chapter
of the NAACP on the seminary campus, and the president of the seminary vetoed the idea. He thought it would be bad for the school. It

* An all-white denomination, the most avidly segregationist in the South.

might not continue to get support from the Southern Baptist Convention.

Thus discouraged from NAACP activity, he began attending "nonviolent workshops" run by Jim Lawson, a Vanderbilt theology student. They talked about Jesus, Gandhi, and Montgomery every Tuesday night for two years. Late in 1959 he joined a "test sit-in" at a department store coffee shop in Nashville. This was over two months before the Greensboro sit-ins started—"Very few people know that." But they left politely when refused service, and he remembers that only the Pittsburgh Courier, *a black paper, paid them any attention. In early February came a call from Greensboro: "What can the students in Nashville do to support students in Greensboro?"*

It just so happened that at this particular time that apparently different people, student groups, were studying the whole idea of nonviolent direct action, and so the call from North Carolina really didn't find a vacuum in Nashville, because we were ready, and it was just a matter of days that we were going to be prepared to conduct massive nonviolent sit-ins in the city of Nashville.

Two or three days later, I don't remember the exact date, but a group of us, about five hundred, met on campus, went in to sit-in at a lunch counter. And it was not like the "test sit-in" we had in the fall of 1959. We stayed there. To me, the whole thing was like I had the feeling that we was involved in something like a crusade in a sense. It was a sense of duty, you had an obligation to do it . . . to redeem the city; as Dr. King said so many times, to redeem the soul of America.

A great many of us got caught up in that. Not that we all didn't have a great deal of fear about it. I did, 'cause one thing, growing up in rural Alabama as a child, one thing that was instilled in me . . . you didn't get in trouble with the law. See, my parents and relatives in rural Pike County referred to the sheriff as "the law. . . ." You don't even have any association with any law enforcement group, whether it be the sheriff—as they would call him, the "high sheriff"—or whether it be a policeman. You just stay away from them.

So you had all those things to go up against, the fear of being arrested, of going to jail, and on those first sit-ins, I had a certain amount of fear of what might happen. I'll never forget on February the twenty-ninth, when a group of us went downtown, and it was snow that day in Nashville, and some people had been beaten up, and the local police in Nashville started arresting people. And we went to jail by the hundreds, singing "We Shall Overcome," and it was a fantastic, just a moving thing. I will never forget it. You had the fear, but you had to go on in spite of that, because you felt that you were doing something that *had* to be done, and in the process maybe you would make a contribution toward ending the system of segregation.

The dean informed his parents of his arrest. "My mother sent me a letter—we didn't have a telephone—saying that I should get out of . . . probably she said 'mess.' She didn't say 'movement.' Probably said, 'Get out of that mess, before you get hurt.' " But by that time he had become part of "a cadre . . . a hard-core group . . . true believers."

They believed in the philosophy and discipline of nonviolence, and it was not just a tactic, as a technique to be used, but I think for some of the people it became a philosophy. It became a way of life, a way of doing things, a way of living. When we would go down to sit-in, I think, you had to be prepared not to just go there to sit and be denied service. . . . It was like going to church, I guess. You would put on your church-going clothes, Sunday clothes, and we took books and papers and did our homework at the lunch counter, just quiet and trying to be as dignified as possible.*

I recall I drew up some rules. It was my responsibility to draw up some dos and don'ts on the sit-in movement. I may have some copies of them around some place if I can find them, but Senator Javits used them in a little book he did, and they were used some place else. It was some simple rules, and the whole idea, matter of fact, came from the Montgomery Bus Boycott. This was telling people what to do. Don't talk back. Sit straight up. Don't laugh out. Don't curse. And at the end of the rules, it said something like, "Remember the teachings of Jesus, Gandhi, Martin Luther King. God bless you all."

Once I was fumigated in a Krystal hamburger stand on Church Street in downtown Nashville. I never will forget that. The store manager literally locked us in, and the same thing that you use to fumigate for insects—the man just turned on this machine, and this huge

---

* Even the Richmond *News Leader*—under the editorship of columnist James J. Kilpatrick the most influential and unbending of the segregationist dailies—was impressed by the decorum of the early sit-inners. The newspaper's oft-quoted editorial tribute: "Here were the colored students, in coats, white shirts, ties, and one of them was reading Goethe and one was taking notes from a biology text. And here, on the sidewalk outside, was a gang of white boys come to heckle, a ragtail rabble, slack-jawed, black-jacketed, grinning fit to kill, and some of them, God save the mark, were waving the proud and honored flag of the Southern States in the last war fought by gentlemen. Eheu! It gives one pause."

foam covered the whole place. . . . He refused to let us out. We stayed in there, and finally the Nashville Fire Department came down, and they broke the window of the place.

What would be the reaction when you went into a department store or a dime-store lunch counter?

Well, they said something like, "We cannot serve you here." They closed the counter, put up a sign saying Closed, and we just sat there. I remember once we went to the Trailways Bus Station in Nashville and we stayed all night sitting there. [They] just closed down the counter and closed the restaurant. And we got very sleepy and we would put our heads down and this waitress would walk around with this big knife, hatchetlike, and she said, "This is not a hotel. There will be no sleeping here." [Laughs] And little things came out of that whole effort. Somebody said, "We can't serve you. We don't serve niggers," and somebody said, "Well, we don't eat them."

An afterthought: he recalls that by the time the sit-in movement started, he had already met face to face the preacher of "Paul's Letter to the American Christians." Martin Luther King, Jr., had heard that John Lewis, a young black Alabaman studying in Nashville, had applied for a transfer to Troy State, a white college in Alabama's then totally segregated state university system.

During the summer of '58, when I was home from school, Dr. King and Rev. Abernathy invited me to come to Montgomery one Saturday morning. I didn't have money; they paid my bus fare and everything. I took the bus from Troy to Montgomery and we met. . . . They wanted to know did I really wanna go through with it; it was hard for them to believe, I think, that some crazy boy from rural Pike County, Alabama, wanted to go to Troy State. . . . The whole idea died because my parents refused to sign the suit; I was eighteen years old.

JULIAN BOND

I'll tell you something else that happened. The Student Nonviolent Coordinating Committee (SNCC) was formed Easter weekend of 1960, and it originally was to be exactly what its name said, a coordinating committee. . . .

The Easter meeting of young sit-in veterans was at Shaw University in Raleigh, North Carolina.

Well, there were about three hundred people there from all over the South, as well as, I guess, about another hundred white students—white and black, but predominately white students from Northern schools—who were in support groups. And there were organizational representatives—the meeting was called by SCLC. Ella Baker was the executive director then. She was just being replaced by Wyatt Tee Walker. She was on the way out, and he was on the way in.

But she was very concerned about two things. One, she thought that SCLC *hadn't* been involved in the sit-in movement as much as it should have been, and by that I think she meant Dr. King. And secondly, she felt that the student movement was really directionless, that it had narrow vision and thought the whole world was nothing but lunch counters. And so she called this meeting together, I don't think with any idea that an organization would come out of it, or that may have been her plan.

But there were people there from SCLC, the NAACP, and CORE, and each of them wanted us, the students, to become a part of them. The NAACP wanted us to be NAACP youth chapters, CORE wanted us to become CORE chapters, SCLC wanted us to become the youth wing of SCLC. We finally decided we'd be our own thing and set up what was then called the Temporary Student Nonviolent Coordinating Committee and elected Marion Barry the chairman.*

There was a dynamite, a militant speech given by James Lawson, who was then at Vanderbilt and had been arrested in church while he was preaching one Sunday morning by the Nashville police for conspiracy or something. But there was the feeling among many of us that James Lawson was challenging King for leadership of this group of young people, that he was younger than King, that he was still a student himself at the Vanderbilt Divinity School, that he was in his definition of nonviolence more militant than King. He believed in radical nonviolence, chaining yourself to airplanes and that kind of stuff. Lunch counters were okay, but he was for bigger things. So he made a very aggressive speech, really stirred people up.

Miss Baker made a very thoughtful speech, the theme of which was "more than a hamburger," that we ought to be interested in more than integrating lunch counters, that there was a whole social structure to be changed here. And then King made a speech. Whatever it was, it left no real impression, except that this was Martin Luther King. We used to joke about King. He was a hometown boy . . . so it was hard for us to look at him as *Martin Luther King, Jr.* We used to joke and call him The Lord. But it was hard for us to revere him, I think, the way other people did. You know, no man is a prophet in his own hometown. But there was a lot of pressure for us to join these other groups, and we resisted and set up our own little group.

* John Lewis, in the Nashville contingent at the meeting, remembers: "There was a big conflict between the group from Atlanta and the group from Nashville. This was student politics in a sense, I guess. Campus politics and area politics got involved. Who would be the leader or spokesman of this temporary group and where would the office be based? The compromise was made where Marion Barry, who was a graduate student in Nashville at Fisk in the chemistry department, who had been active in the Nashville Student Movement, became the temporary chairman of the—well, became the chairman of the temporary Student Nonviolent Coordinating Committee, and the office was to be here in Atlanta, sharing offices with SCLC. And that was April 1960. Then in October 1960, there was another meeting here in Atlanta in the AU Center where SNCC became a permanent organization."

CONNIE CURRY

White Girl

She received a proper lady's education at Agnes Scott, a women's college steeped in Atlanta's Old South traditions. The National Student Association (NSA) then hired her to bring together Southern students of both races for seminars on race relations. Financed with sixty thousand dollars from the Field Foundation, she opened an office in Atlanta, where "the idea of holding an integrated conference was still pretty alien."

I came down in December of '59 and set up an office, just myself and a secretary, and we opened the office on January fifteenth, 1960. And, of course, my hometown is Greensboro, North Carolina, and I was up there visiting my sister on February the first, 1960. And it was really funny, because I had never heard of a sit-in. I mean, I had never heard of any of that. [Laughs] And I was driving my car over to my sister's on February the first, and I had the radio on, and it said, "Four students from A&T College were arrested this afternoon"—it was a news report—"for sitting-in at a lunch counter at Woolworth's." And I thought, "Wow, that is really—how bizarre! *What in the world?*"

When I got home that night, Mrs. Grayson,* my next-door neighbor that I had grown up with all my life—uh, she was not exactly a racist,

* A pseudonym.

but she certainly did not believe in integration. And I was the only person she had ever known in her whole life that had been around black people and was involved in this kind of thing. And to this day, she thinks I started the sit-in movement. [Laughs] I got home, she said [arms akimbo here, the accents those of a Southern lady who is "put out"], "Connie, did you do that?"

Really, it was that much of a simplified thing: I was in Greensboro, and I did things with black people, and I—I laughed. She was never hostile about it, but she literally called up and said, "Connie, did you do that?" [She breaks up.]

Anyway, as you can well imagine, that changed the whole tenor of my project, because all of a sudden . . . for white students in particular, going to an interracial meeting and feeling good about it was kind of ridiculous when people were being arrested, beaten. . . . It just wasn't important anymore to hold integrated tea parties or conferences or anything; it was a whole new thing. It was amazing. . . . After February the first, if you remember, the sit-ins sort of spread—Winston-Salem, Orangeburg, Nashville—sort of swept across the South. . . .

She traveled the South from sit-in to sit-in, reporting back to the National Student Association on the situation in each major city. NSA was using this information in directing a Northern student boycott of Woolworth's "that helped break the whole thing in the South." It was a busy time. In 1961 in 100 Southern cities 70,000 students sat-in. There were 3,600 arrests.

So then that spring I went to Raleigh to the meeting where SNCC was formed at Shaw that Easter. . . . Ella Baker and I were elected as the two nonstudent advisors on SNCC. Of course, I was the only white person on the SNCC executive committee at that point in history. When I think back to those days, it's really funny, because I didn't know what the hell I was doin'—everything was just *happenin'*. [Laughs] And Field Foundation and NSA, everybody was really great about it. I thought Field might be a little concerned about the use of their sixty thousand dollars for this weird thing that had sprung up, but they never gave me any problems whatsoever about my role. . . . James Forman* and Julian Bond used to come into the NSA office with phone bills for five hundred dollars from the SNCC office down on Auburn Avenue and say, "This has to be paid." And I used to pull out my checkbook and

---

* SNCC's first full-time executive director. Some years later he commandeered the pulpit of New York's Riverside Church to deliver the "Black Manifesto" demanding $500 million in "reparations" from America's white churches.

just write the check. I mean, that money was used *really* in those early days to support SNCC to a big extent. It was like it was on loan basis, but it was never paid back. . . .

So I got on the SNCC executive committee, and then I have no recall about the chronology. It was just hours and hours spent in the back room of B.B. Beamon's down on Auburn Avenue.* And Bob Moses** and I, everytime he would come back from Mississippi, our relief was to get a chocolate nut sundae at B.B. Beamon's. When it got to be about two o'clock in the morning, and you just thought you could not listen or do one other thing, we would order a chocolate nut sundae. Jane Stembridge came down in the summer of 1960. She was a [white] student at Union Theological Seminary. . . . She came down on volunteer time to be the director of SNCC that summer. . . . That's the summer that Bob Moses went to Mississippi on the bus, and just sorta traveled around by himself and met Amzie Moore*** and met all these people, and he wrote Jane letters about what Mississippi was like in the summer of '60.

She sensed the nature of SNCC slowly changing in those days. Instead of merely coordinating, "At some point, we began to do a strategy thing. . . . I think the theory was that in these places where students on their own did stuff, that SNCC would sort of be the back-up support, whether it was in terms of money or in terms of actual bodies. And then for a long time, the theory was 'fill the jails,' either with students there, or you would bring them in." At Lonnie King's request, she set out to recruit students from Atlanta's white colleges for the sit-ins.

Somehow or other I scraped up a white representative from every college, even Georgia Tech. They only came to one meeting because they

* The soul-food restaurant on "Sweet Auburn" which afforded SNCC temporary meeting space.

** A young black Harvard-educated teacher from New York, he became one of the Movement's most charismatic—and ultimately, one of its most enigmatic—figures. Julian Bond on Moses' arrival in Atlanta during the summer sit-ins: "He came to work for SCLC as a volunteer . . . and SCLC really didn't have anything for him to do except lick envelopes and open letters and take out checks, and he wanted to get into something more. So he began to hang around our office. We thought he was a Communist because he was from New York and wore glasses and was smarter than we were. [Laughs] And he really kept us going, because he would picket all day. Most of us would do it for an hour. It was hot work." Although he had no experience in the rural South, Moses was the first SNCC member to venture into Mississippi.

*** He was Moses' and SNCC's first contact in Mississippi. For that story, see the Mississippi sequence.

were terrified. Oh, it was just hysterical. I thought that I was absolutely brilliant; I thought it was the most marvelous thing in the world because these six white bodies were at the meeting. And my God, they took one look at Lonnie King and all those students and never said a word and went home that night and we never heard of 'em again. [Laughs] But anyway they were there. . . .

I never will forget when I was at Rich's, and they were sitting-in, in the Magnolia Room. I was over at the elevator, and my role was to immediately report to the SNCC office or to SRC* or to the paper or to the police if anything bad happened. And standing right next to me was Calvin Craig.** When the sit-inners were turned down . . . Calvin Craig had just handed me a little leaflet, and he was saying, "Goddamn niggers. . . ." And I was standing there saying, "Dear God, please don't let Lonnie look at me. Please do not let any of them show any recognition when they come out of the Magnolia Room . . . 'cause Calvin Craig will surely kill me. . . ."

In your own life, were you coming under any pressures as a result of being a Southerner . . . and working in the student movement?

Well, not from my family, because my parents were born in Ireland, and of course, I grew up in the South, but I didn't have a lot of roots or stuff. I had a lot of problems. I was evicted twice. And I had a little red-and-white Karman Ghia, which everybody thought was hysterical. . . . Mary King, who was one of the other white women that worked for SNCC a long time after me, said that they used to not be able to understand how I could drive such a conspicuous car. But . . . you don't plan things that are going to happen to you, and I didn't buy my car based on what was gonna be happening. But I came back once from the NSA Congress—this was in August of '60—and the Klan or somebody had come by—Donna, my roommate, said it was the Klan—and it was all painted with blue KKK marks.

And I remember during the spring of '60 we used to get phone calls all the time saying, "Does Lonnie King hold your hand when you go to the bathroom?" That sticks in my mind because it's obviously such a funny thing to say. Of all the possibilities, why that? [Laughs] They said they were gonna—what color of wreaths did Donna and I like? . . . We just changed our phone number.

* Southern Regional Council, a research foundation which kept statistics on the sit-ins.
** Grand Dragon of the Ku Klux Klan in Georgia.

And then . . . we had this strange girl named Sandy* from New York come down. . . . She had a big thing about black guys, and none were safe when Sandy was around. And one time she invited ——— over to my apartment. I was living on Adair Avenue, and again I was at the NSA Congress, and our landlady told Donna and Jane Stembridge, who was there, and Sandy, who was just staying with us temporarily, that they had to be out of the apartment by sunset. You know, it was like the Old West. [Laughs] So when I got back from the NSA Congress, I'd been moved lock, stock, and barrel to another apartment. . . .

"SNCC was in a hurry, because SNCC knew that it had to move fast if it was not to be destroyed by America," wrote a Movement historian.** She, too, remembers that feverish idealism and impatience—and a naïveté which allowed them to believe that "if you were strong and really persevered," victory was inevitable. She heard the old Dixie hands around Atlanta warn that the pace and idealism would result in a lot of burnt-out cases in SNCC's ranks.

Do you think there's any validity to that thesis?

[A long pause] Well, I really do, because I remember watching the changes in Bob Moses. . . . See, we used to have argument after argument of whether or not nonviolence was a technique or a way of life, and that was probably one of the biggest debates in the early days of SNCC. Because I maintained, as did other people, that nonviolence as a way of life was good as an ideal, but it was something that was absolutely alien to all of our backgrounds and the way that we were raised. . . . That's why being beaten and thrown into jail and trying to love everybody while they did it to you . . . was bound to mess you up. So I really do think that the toll that was taken in those early days was just tremendous, much more so than for the people who came after who knew what the stakes were.

Also, those early sit-inners and SNCC people . . . really believed that they were going to win. It was the whole thing of "We Shall Overcome." They really sorta thought there was an end in sight, and when they would sing "God is on our side," I would never sing that verse. . . . I don't think that anybody ever envisioned the long years of struggle and violence and everything—anguish. I don't think they were really aware of it. And as it emerged I think it was just a terrible, terri-

* A pseudonym.
** Pat Watters, *Down to Now: Recollections of the Civil Rights Movement* (New York: Pantheon, 1972).

III
FREEDOM RIDERS

Yes, we are the Freedom Riders
And we ride a long Greyhound;
White or black, we know no difference,
Lord, for we are Glory bound . . .
>—Southern collegiate folk song
of the sixties

JAMES FARMER

He had left CORE to become national program director of the NAACP, and he watched from the sidelines as the sit-inners practiced the direct-action techniques he had tested twenty years earlier. But he would not miss the next great wave of confrontation to sweep the South. Rejoining CORE as national director early in 1961, he started it.

I was impressed by the fact that most of the activity thus far had been of local people working on their local problems—Greensborans sitting-in in Greensboro and Atlantans sitting-in in Atlanta—and the pressure of the opposition against having outsiders come was very, very great. If any outsider came in . . . , "Get that outside agitator." . . . I thought that this was going to limit the growth of the Movement. . . . We somehow had to cut across state lines and establish the position that we were entitled to act any place in the country, no matter where we hung our hat and called home, because it was our country.

We also felt that one of the weaknesses of the student sit-in movement of the South had been that as soon as arrested, the kids bailed out. . . . This was not quite Gandhian and not the best tactic. A better tactic would be to remain in jail and to make the maintenance of segregation so expensive for the state and the city that they would hopefully come to the conclusion that they could no longer afford it. Fill up the jails, as Gandhi did in India, fill them to bursting if we had to. In other words, stay in without bail.

So those were the two things: cutting across state lines, putting the movement on wheels, so to speak, and remaining in jail, not only for its publicity value but for the financial pressure it would put upon the segregators. We decided that a good approach here would be to move away from restaurant lunch counters. That had been the Southern student sit-in movement, and anything we would do on that would be anticlimactic now. We would have to move into another area and so we decided to move into the transportation, interstate transportation. . . .

It would be necessary, he decided, to violate custom and local law to focus attention on the federal laws barring discrimination in interstate transportation. He knew that in 1946 the Supreme Court had ruled against segregated seating on interstate buses, and in 1960, against segregated terminal facilities. The rulings were uniformly ignored throughout the South.

So we, following the Gandhian technique, wrote to Washington. We wrote to the Justice Department, to the FBI, and to the President, and wrote to Greyhound Bus Company and Trailways Bus Company and told them that on May first or May fourth—whatever the date was,* I forget now—we were going to have a Freedom Ride. Blacks and whites were going to leave Washington, D.C., on Greyhound and Trailways, deliberately violating the segregated seating requirements and at each rest stop would violate the segregated use of facilities. And we would be nonviolent, absolutely nonviolent, throughout the campaign, and we would accept the consequences of our actions. This was a deliberate act of civil disobedience. . . .**

Did Justice try to head you off?

No, we got no reply. We got no reply from Justice. Bobby Kennedy, no reply. We got no reply from the FBI. We got no reply from the White House, from President Kennedy. We got no reply from Greyhound or Trailways. *We got no replies.* [Laughs]

He recruited an interracial group of thirteen and brought them to Washington for a week's training.

* May 4.
** Before beginning the Salt March, Gandhi sent a letter of warning to British authorities, although he did not outline the specifics of his strategy.

We had some of the group of thirteen sit at a simulated counter asking for coffee. Somebody else refused them service, and then we'd have others come in as white hoodlums to beat 'em up and knock them off the counter and club 'em around and kick 'em in the ribs and stomp 'em, and they were quite realistic, I must say. I thought they bent over backwards to be realistic. I was aching all over. [Laughs] And then we'd go into a discussion as to how the roles were played, whether there was something that the Freedom Riders did that they shouldn't have done, said that they shouldn't have said, something that they didn't say or do that they should have, and so on. Then we'd reverse roles and play it over and over again and have lengthy discussions of it.

I felt, by the way, that by the time that group left Washington, they were prepared for anything, even death, and this was a possibility, and we knew it, when we got to the Deep South.

Through Virginia we had no problem. In fact they had heard we were coming, Greyhound and Trailways, and they had taken down the For Colored and For Whites signs, and we rode right through. Yep. The same was true in North Carolina. Signs had come down just the previous day, blacks told us. And so the letters in advance did something.

In South Carolina it was a different story. . . . John Lewis started into a white waiting room in some town in South Carolina* . . . and there were several young white hoodlums, leather jackets, ducktail haircuts, standing there smoking, and they blocked the door and said, "Nigger, you can't come in here." He said, "I have every right to enter this waiting room according to the Supreme Court of the United States in the Boynton case."**

They said, "Shit on that." He tried to walk past, and they clubbed him, beat him, and knocked him down. One of the white Freedom Riders . . . Albert Bigelow,*** who had been a Navy captain during World War II, big, tall, strapping fellow, very impressive, from Connecticut—then stepped right between the hoodlums and John Lewis. Lewis had been absorbing more of the punishment. They then clubbed Bigelow and finally knocked him down, and that took some knocking because he was a pretty strapping fellow, and he didn't hit back at all.

* Rock Hill.
** The 1960 Supreme Court case outlawing segregated facilities at bus terminals.
*** Despite his military background, a Quaker pacifist. He was best known for sailing the yacht *Golden Rule* into an atomic testing area in the Pacific as a protest against nuclear warfare.

[They] knocked him down, and at this point police arrived and intervened. They didn't make any arrests. Intervened.

Well, we went through the rest of South Carolina without incident and then to Atlanta, Georgia, and there we met with Dr. King. We called him and told him we were coming, and he had dinner with us and wished us well. Went to Albany first and then Atlanta. And when we were in Atlanta—my father by the way, was in Freedman's Hospital here in Washington with cancer, and I got word just about two hours before the buses left Atlanta that my father had died, and I had to go back and bury him. My mother insisted until her death five years later that my father willed his death at that time, willed the timing of it because he had my schedule. I had talked with him here in Washington during our training session, when he was in the hospital before I left, and told him what we were going to do, and he said, "Well, that's an interesting idea and I hope you survive it." He said, "I think the most dangerous part of it will be through Bama," as he put it, "and Mississippi. There, somebody will probably take a potshot at you, and I just hope they miss." And my mother says that every morning he would take out my itinerary and look at it and say, "Well, now, let's see where Junior is today." And he was relaxed about it until I got to Atlanta, and he says, "Oh, tomorrow he goes through Bama."

He died, and she says that he willed the timing of it to bring me back. It's apocryphal I'm sure. At any rate I had to return then to bury him and informed the Freedom Riders that I would rejoin them as soon as I had gotten this family obligation out of the way. I must confess that while I felt guilty at leaving, there was also a sense of relief at missing this leg of the trip, because all of us were scared. There was one reporter who was one of the Freedom Riders at this stage, and that was Simeon Booker of Johnson publications, *Jet* and *Ebony*. Simeon had come to me just before I got the telegram telling me of my father's death, or the phone call, and he said, "Jim, you know, I've decided that you are the only Freedom Rider I can outrun. So what I'm going to do is to stick with you on this trip, and I figure it's the fellow bringing up the rear who's gonna get caught." [Laughs]

HANK THOMAS

The Freedom Ride didn't really get rough until we got down in the Deep South. Needless to say, Anniston, Alabama, I'm never gonna forget that, when I was on the bus that they threw some kind of incendiary device on.

He was on the first of two buses to cross into "Bama." When it pulled into the depot at Anniston, a Klan hotbed about sixty miles from Birmingham, the bus was surrounded by white men brandishing iron bars. Anniston police held them back long enough for the bus to reach the highway again, but about six miles outside town the pursuing mob caught up.

I got real scared then. You know, I was thinking—I'm looking out the window there, and people are out there yelling and screaming. They just about broke every window out of the bus. . . . I really thought that that was going to be the end of me.

How did the bus get stopped?

They shot the tires out, and the bus driver was forced to stop. . . . He got off, and man, he took off like a rabbit, and might well have. I couldn't very well blame him there. And we were trapped on the bus.

They tried to board. Well, we did have two FBI men aboard the bus. All they were there to do were to observe and gather facts, but the crowd apparently recognized them as FBI men, and they did not try to hurt them.

It wasn't until the thing was shot on the bus and the bus caught afire that everything got out of control, and . . . when the bus was burning, I figured . . . [pauses] . . . panic did get ahold of me. Needless to say, I couldn't survive that burning bus. There was a possibility I could have survived the mob, but I was just so afraid of the mob that I was gonna stay on that bus. I mean, I just got that much afraid. And when we got off the bus . . . first they closed the doors and wouldn't let us off. But then I'm pretty sure they realized, that somebody said, "Hey, the bus is gonna explode," because it had just gassed up, and so they started scattering then, and I guess that's the way we got off the bus.* Otherwise, we probably all would have been succumbed by the smoke, and not being able to get off, probably would have been burned alive or burned on there anyway. That's the only time I was really, really afraid. I got whacked over the head with a rock or I think some kind of a stick as I was coming off the bus.

What happened in Anniston after the bus was attacked?

We were taken to the hospital. The bus started exploding, and a lot of people were cut by flying glass. We were taken to the hospital, most of us, for smoke inhalation.

By whom?

I don't remember. I think I was half out of it, half dazed, as a result of the smoke, and, gosh, I can still smell that stuff down in me now. You got to the point where you started having the dry heaves. Took us to the hospital, and it was incredible. The people at the hospital would not do anything for us. They would not. And I was saying, "You're *doc-*

---

* John Patterson, then governor of Alabama, maintains that he and his public safety director, Floyd Mann, were indirectly responsible for the Freedom Riders' getting off the burning bus: "Floyd recommended that we send a state plainclothes investigator to Atlanta to catch the bus and ride with the Freedom Riders, and we did. Now this has never been reported that I know of in any paper. . . . We sent a man named E.L. Cowling. . . . He went over to Atlanta and caught the bus, and he was on the bus when they came to Anniston. . . . So Cowling walked up to the door of the bus and drew his pistol and backed the crowd away from the bus and told them that if anybody touched anybody he'd kill them. And he got the Freedom Riders off the burning bus. That's true."

tors, you're medical personnel." They wouldn't. Governor Patterson got on statewide radio and said, "Any rioters in this state will not receive police protection." And then the crowd started forming outside the hospital, and the hospital told us to leave. And we said, "No, we're not going out there," and there we were. A caravan from Birmingham, about a fifteen-car caravan led by the Reverend Fred Shuttlesworth, came up from Birmingham to get us out.

Without police escort, I take it?

Without police escort, but every one of those cars had a shotgun in it. And Fred Shuttlesworth had got on the radio and said—you know Fred, he's very dramatic—"I'm going to get my people." [Laughs] He said, "I'm a nonviolent man, but I'm going to get my people." And apparently a hell of a lot of people believed in him. Man, they came there and they were a welcome sight. And each one of 'em got out with their guns and everything and the state police were there, but I think they all realized that this was not a time to say anything because, I'm pretty sure, there would have been a lot of people killed.

The black drivers were openly carrying guns?

Oh, yeah. They had rifles and shotguns. And that's how we got back to Birmingham. . . . I think I was flown to New Orleans for medical treatment, because still they were afraid to let any of us go to the hospitals in Birmingham, and by that time—it was what, two days later—I was fairly all right. I had gotten most of the smoke out of my system.

No one received any attention in the hospital in Anniston?

No, no. Oh, we did have one girl, Genevieve Hughes, a white girl, who had a busted lip. I remember a nurse applying something to that, but other than that, nothing. Now that I look back on it, man, we had some vicious people down there, wouldn't even so much as *treat* you. But that's the way it was. But strangely enough, even those bad things then don't stick in my mind that much. Not that I'm full of love and goodwill for everybody in my heart, but I chalk it off to part of the things that I'm going to be able to sit on my front porch in my rocking chair and tell my young'uns about, my grandchildren about.

Postscript: That same day, Mother's Day, May 14, 1961, the second bus escaped the mob in Anniston and made it to Birmingham. At the

Trailways station there, white men armed with baseball bats and chains beat the Freedom Riders at will for about fifteen minutes before the first police arrived. In 1975 a former Birmingham Klansman, who was a paid informant of the FBI at the time, told the Senate Select Committee on Intelligence that members of the Birmingham police force had promised the Klansmen that no policemen would show up to interfere with the beatings for at least fifteen minutes. In 1976 a Birmingham detective who refused to be interviewed on tape told me that account was correct —as far as it went. The detective said that word was passed in the police department that Public Safety Commissioner Eugene "Bull" Connor had watched from the window of his office in City Hall as the crowd of Klansmen, some brandishing weapons, gathered to await the Freedom Riders. Asked later about the absence of his policemen, Connor said most of them were visiting their mothers.

JOHN LEWIS

He had left the Freedom Ride in South Carolina to keep an appointment for a job interview. Returning to Nashville on May 14, he learned of the attacks in Anniston and Birmingham and that CORE, heeding Attorney General Robert Kennedy's request for a "cooling-off" period, had cancelled the ride altogether. He and a group of sit-in veterans believed that if the Freedom Ride did not continue, segregationists would conclude that they could, indeed, defeat the Movement with violence and intimidation. Using money left over from the sit-in treasury and ignoring the advice of Nashville's SCLC affiliate, they bought tickets for Birmingham and announced that the Freedom Ride was on again.

At the Birmingham city limit, a policeman halted their bus and informed the driver that he was taking charge of the vehicle. When the bus pulled into the station, the "Birmingham police department put up newspapers all around the bus windows so you couldn't see out, and no one could see in." Shielded from inspection, they waited until "Bull" Connor arrived on the scene and ordered them taken into "protective custody." Thus began one of the most bizarre episodes of the Movement.

So they took us all to the jail, the Birmingham city jail. Now this was on a Wednesday. We went to jail and stayed in jail Wednesday night. We didn't eat anything. We went on a hunger strike.

What sort of treatment did you get from the police?

They were very, very nice. They didn't rough us up or anything like that, just very nice, as I recall. They put us in jail, segregated us . . . and that Thursday we stayed in jail all day. That Thursday night around midnight, "Bull" Connor and two reporters . . . and maybe one or two detectives came up to the jail, and "Bull" Connor said they were going to take us back to Nashville, back to the college campus where we belonged. We said, "Well, we don't want to go back. We have a right to be on this Freedom Ride. We have a right to travel. We plan to go to Montgomery, and from Montgomery we're going to Jackson and to New Orleans." And he insisted. And people just sorta went limp, so they had people literally to pick us up and place us into these cars. . . .

Anyway, they drove us on the highway, and "Bull" Connor was really funny. I was in the car that he was in and this young lady, Katherine Burke. He was really funny, he was really joking with us, saying that he was gonna take us back to Nashville, and we told him we would invite him to the campus, and he could have breakfast with us and that type of thing. He said he would like that. It was that type of conversation that we had going with "Bull" Connor.

We got to the Tennessee-Alabama line . . . They dropped us off, saying . . . "You can take the bus back to Nashville." They literally left us there. We didn't know anybody, didn't know any place to go. This is true.

Did it cross your mind that you might be being set up?

Oh, yeah, oh, yeah. We just didn't know what had happened, and it was still dark. It was early morning-like.

The Birmingham police, including the police commissioner, had physically loaded you up in a car and carried you to the state line, a matter of 150 miles.

That's right. That's right. And *left* us, just left us. What we did, we started walking down a road, and we saw a railroad track, and we crossed this railroad track and went to an old house. There was an elderly couple there, must have been in their late sixties, early seventies. We knocked on the door, and they let us in, and they was just really frightened. They'd heard about the Freedom Riders.

This was a black couple?

Black couple. They were just really, really frightened. They didn't know what to do. They didn't really want to let us in, but they did, and we called Nashville and told 'em what had happened. Called Diane Nash on the telephone. She was in the local student movement office there in Nashville, and she wanted to know whether we wanted to continue the ride or whether we wanted a car to pick us up to bring us back to Nashville. We told her to send a car to take us back to Birmingham. We wanted to continue the ride.

In the meantime, we hadn't had anything to eat, and we were very hungry. 'Cause this is now Friday morning, and we hadn't had anything to eat since, I guess, early Wednesday. This man, this elderly man, got in his pickup truck and went around during the early morning to two or three stores and bought something like bologna and bread and cornflakes. Anyway, we had a little meal there, and apparently some of the white people in the community came by, and he told 'em some of his relatives were visiting from Nashville. We waited around till the car from Nashville got there, and this was really something else. It was seven of us and the driver now, eight of us, got in that car on our way back to Birmingham, and we heard a reporter on the radio saying the students had been taken to the state line and apparently they were . . . back in Nashville on their college campuses. . . .

So we drove back to Birmingham, and Rev. Shuttlesworth and several other ministers from the Alabama Christian Movement for Human Rights met us there, and we went directly back to the Greyhound bus station. And we tried to get on the bus around, I recall, three o'clock, on the Greyhound bus from Birmingham to Montgomery, and apparently Greyhound canceled the bus taking off. We were going to try to get on one at five-something, and this bus driver said something that I'll never forget. He said, "I only have one life to give and I'm not going to give it to CORE or the NAACP."

He and his group, along with about twenty fresh volunteers from Nashville, spent the night on the wooden benches of the bus station. Departing from their previous practice, the police repelled a white mob which gathered during the night. Finally a reporter who was covering the story brought a message: "Apparently you all are going to get a chance to go. Attorney General Kennedy has been in contact with Greyhound."

The same bus driver came out to the bus about eight-thirty on Saturday morning, and we got on a bus from Birmingham to Montgomery. And apparently the arrangement was that every so many miles there

would be a state patrol car and there would be a plane. We did see—I
don't know whether it was the arrangement or not—we did see a small
plane flying up above the bus for so many miles and we did have the patrol car. . . .*

It was a nice ride between Birmingham and Montgomery. A few
miles outside of Montgomery you just didn't see anything. You didn't
see the plane, didn't see the state patrol car. It seemed like everything
sort of disappeared, and the moment that we arrived in that station, it
was the strangest feeling to me. It was something strange, that you knew
something. It was really weird. It was an eerie feeling. There was a
funny peace there, a quietness. You didn't see anything happening. Apparently, when you really look back, the mob there must have been so
planned and was so out of sight . . . it just sorta appeared, just appeared on the scene.

You didn't see any sign of it as you went into the bus station?

None. Just didn't see anything. When we drove up, we didn't see anything. . . . We got most of the young ladies in a cab. So they got in a
cab and the black cab driver didn't want to drive, because at that time
there was two white students, young ladies from Peabody or Scarritt,
and in Alabama there was a law that you couldn't have an integrated
cab. So the two young ladies got out, and at that very time, this mob
started all over the place. So everybody, all the young ladies, got away,
and the two young white girls were running down the street trying to get
away. That's when John Siegenthaler got hit.** And at that time, the
rest of us, mostly fellas, just literally standing there because we couldn't
run—no place to go really.***

* In fact, an airplane and sixteen highway patrol cars accompanied the bus, despite Governor Patterson's public statement that "we are not going to escort those
agitators. We stand firm on that position."

** Robert Kennedy's administrative assistant, sent to Alabama as an observer.

*** Freedom Rider William Harbour: "There was nobody there. I didn't see anybody standin' around the bus station. I saw some taxicabs there. That was about it.
So the bus driver opened the bus door up and just walked away from the bus. I
guess in less than fifteen minutes, we had a mob of people, five or six hundred
people with ax handles, chains and everything else. . . . Soon as we walked off
the bus, John Lewis said to me, 'Bill, it doesn't look right. . . .'

"Everything happened so quick. There was a standstill for the first two or three
minutes . . . They were closin' in on us, and we were standin' still tryin' to decide what should we do in order to protect the whites we had with us. But then
you had a middle-aged white female hollerin', 'Git them niggers, git them niggers . . . ,' and that urged the crowd on. From then on, they was constantly movin'
in. I don't think she ever hit anybody or threw anything whatsoever. Just the idea
she started, just kept pushin' and pushin' and pushin' . . . It started just like that."

This was out in the lot?

Just out in the lot. And if you've been at the bus station, there's a rail there. . . . Down below is the entrance to the courthouse, the Post Office building. So when the mob kept coming, several of the people, several of the fellas jumped over and were able to get in the basement of the Post Office, and the postmaster there opened it and made it possible for people to come in and escape the mob. And I said—I remember saying that we shouldn't run, we should just stand there, 'cause the mob was beating people. And the last thing that I recall, I was hit with a crate, a wooden crate what you have soda in, and was left lying in the street. And I remember the Attorney General of Alabama, MacDonald Gallion, serving this injunction that Judge Walter B. Jones had issued saying that it was unlawful for interracial groups to travel. While I was lying there on the ground, he brought this injunction.

JAMES FARMER

After his father's funeral, he flew to Montgomery, where Dr. King and Reverend Abernathy had called a mass meeting at First Baptist Church as a show of support for the Freedom Riders.

Fred Shuttlesworth met me at the airport with a couple of his guys. He said, "Well, gentlemen, it's going to be a touch-and-go as to whether we get to that church. Everybody's at the church; Martin has flown in . . . he's there and so we are under siege. A mob has it surrounded. . . ." And so he drove me back as close as he could, and mobs blocked the way, wouldn't let the car through, began trying to open the door. We backed up and tried another route. . . .

Approaching the church through a nearby graveyard, he and Shuttlesworth could get no closer than three blocks to the church before running into the white toughs again.

And so Fred Shuttlesworth walked into the mob. [Laughs] I must confess I was scared as hell, but Shuttlesworth—[He suddenly leaps from his chair and strides across the room, showing how the preacher shoved his way through the incredulous whites.] These goons were standing there, thousands of them with clubs. "Out of the way. Go on. Out of the way." He didn't have any trouble. They stopped and looked at him: *"That nigger's crazy."* [Laughs] And I was standing right be-

hind him trying to be little. [Still laughing] And we got to the church
and got in. . . .

Obviously, we were going to be there all night. . . . So we were singing, and King and I were consulting, sitting in the office of the church
and talking and mapping alternative plans.

The mob kicked open the door of the church, and they just *poured* in.
And people were screaming, backed up against the wall. I don't know
where they came from or how they did it, but the marshals materialized
in that situation. It seemed almost fictional. *There they were* suddenly,
the marshals confronting the mob. They had arm bands on, U.S. marshals. . . . They didn't draw their guns, but they used their clubs and
forced them into a park and then dispersed those who had come to the
church. Martial law was declared, and we were to stay in the church
under heavy guard all night and not to attempt to leave.*

Then finally, when the mob was more or less permanently dispersed,
we could leave the church. [We] went to homes, ministers' homes, and
we had debates as to what to do, whether we should attempt the rest of
the Freedom Ride, and the conclusion was that we would go on with it.
We decided that we would go on. We had to, although I am sure that
everybody was scared to death at this point. Dr. King declined to go on
the grounds that he was on probation and it would be a violation of
probation. The SNCC people wouldn't accept that though. They said,
"Look, I'm on probation too." "So am I." "Me, too." "Me, too." "Me,
too, and I'm going."

Did you try to prevail on King to go?

No, no, no, no, no. I didn't feel that I should try to urge him to go,
because I was debating whether I was going. [Laughs] I tried to fink
out, I must confess. . . . The two buses were there, and they got on the
buses, and I helped them put their luggage in and get on the bus, and I
said, "Well, bye." [Laughs] And one of the CORE girls, Doris Castle, a
girl from New Orleans, said, "Jim, you're going with us, aren't you?" I
said, "Doris, I've been away from the office now for three weeks, and
mail has piled up and somebody has to mind the store, so I think I've

* Robert Kennedy sent in the U.S. marshals because of Governor John Patterson's reluctance to promise protection for the Freedom Riders. Even so, the white
mob, estimated at several thousand, would probably have overwhelmed the marshals during the night had not Patterson finally relented. He declared martial law
and sent eight hundred national guardsmen to the church. See John Patterson's
account of his battle of wills with Kennedy.

just got to get back to the office in New York to keep this thing going
and raise the necessary money." She said, "Jim, *please.*" I said, "Get
my luggage out of the car and put it on the goddamn bus. I'm going."
How was I going to face her afterwards if something happened, and I
had finked out . . . ?*

> *They rolled out of Montgomery under heavy guard, helicopters*
> *overhead, National Guard riflemen aboard the bus.*

> I don't think any of us thought that we were going to get to Jack-
> son, Mississippi, really. I know I didn't. I was scared and I am sure
> the kids were scared. . . . On the bus, I noticed that they were writ-
> ing notes, many of them, and I walked across the aisle to see what
> they were writing, and they were writing names and addresses of next
> of kin. The girls were shoving them in their bosoms and the men put-
> ting them in pockets or wallets. . . .**

When the bus got to the state line, we saw this famous sign, Welcome
to the Magnolia State. [Laughs] We had to chuckle at that in spite of
the tenseness of the situation. The six Alabama national guardsmen left
the bus, and the Mississippi national guardsmen took their place. The
bus driver left the bus, and another bus driver came on. The state director of public safety came on the bus and whispered something to one of
the reporters. This reporter's eyes bulged, and he passed this whispered
message on to the other reporters on the bus. All except one of them left
the bus and got in cars outside. So when the bus started, I asked this
remaining reporter what the message had been, and he said, "The director of public safety tells us that they have it on excellent authority that
this bus is going to be ambushed and destroyed inside the Mississippi
border." And I said, "And you stayed on it?" He said, "What? Miss a
story like that?" . . . [Laughs]

We had learned that Ross Barnett, who was governor at that time,
had been on radio and TV several times a day for several days telling
people to keep calm. He said, "Those Freedom Riders, so-called Freedom Riders, are coming into Mississippi. They're coming into Jackson,
but don't come into town. Stay at home. Don't come into the city. Let

---

* John Lewis recalls: "That was one of the criticisms that many of the people in
SNCC and CORE had of Dr. King. There's a fantastic picture of a young guy
named Paul—I can't think of his last name—and the other guy was named Matthew
Walker, waving out of a bus in Montgomery to Dr. King. . . . it was a big criticism that he came to the bus station and saw the people off and he refused to go."

** For another account of the tension on this trip, see Dave Dennis.

us handle it according to our Mississippi laws. Anybody who breaks our laws is going to jail. But let us handle it. . . . Don't take the law into your own hands."

He was repeating that over and over and over again. And we passed one place where there were woods, heavy woods, on both sides of the road, and there was a cluster of Mississippi national guardsmen standing there on both sides of the road. I heard one of the officers of the Guard shout over a bullhorn, "Look behind every tree." So I guess that's where the ambush was expected. They had their artillery pointed at the woods on both sides. A military operation, you know.

And when we got to Jackson, "Whew, well, the outskirts of Jackson now." We drove up to the Greyhound bus terminal. A crowd of people there. I said, "Well, this is it. This is where we get it." The door opened and I led the group off the bus. It turned out that the crowd of people were not hoodlums. They were plainclothesmen and reporters. [Laughs] *They* were the crowd. As soon as we walked out of the door, they parted, and they knew precisely where I was going, to the white waiting room and not to the colored waiting room. So they parted and made a path for me leading right to the white waiting room [laughing], and I thought maybe I could have pled entrapment when we got to court, because we couldn't go anyplace else.

He and a veteran of the Nashville sit-ins named Lucretia Collins joined arms and started walking toward the white restrooms. A Captain Ray of the Jackson police was waiting for them.

He blocked the way. He said, "Move on." I said, "Where?" He said, "Move on out." I refused on the grounds of the Supreme Court decision in the Boynton case and gave the date of it. He said, "I said, 'Move on.'" I refused again on the same grounds.

He said, "Do you understand my order?"

I said, "Perfectly."

He said, "Well, I'm going to tell you one more time, move on."

I refused the third time on the same grounds.

He said, "What's your name?"

I said, "James Farmer."

He nodded. He said, "Follow that officer and get in the patrol wagon." So Lucretia and I and the people behind us climbed in the patrol, and we started singing "We Shall Overcome" and rocking that wagon with the song. And so it went. We made a symbol out of Captain Ray's pointed finger when he said, "Follow that patrol wagon." He was like the man who was sticking his finger in the hole in the dyke, trying to hold back the flood waters, but they would overwhelm him.

Jack Young, the only black attorney in Jackson, came to see him in the jailhouse.

I sent word by him to call the CORE office and tell them to keep Freedom Riders coming into Jackson as fast as possible on every bus, every train . . . and recruit madly, and train. Didn't have to do much recruiting because by this time the volunteers were barraging us. CORE was jumping with telegrams coming in, phone calls: "Send me, I'll go." "Need more Freedom Riders? Take me. I'll go."

We had 325 or 326 jailed at one time. We filled up the jails.

We had trouble with some of the Freedom Riders because the training had to be hasty, and many of the people who rushed in, including some of the SNCC people, were not prepared for this sort of thing. "We're gonna stay in 'til hell freezes over." But after two days, "You got money to bail me out?" [Laughs] "No, you're pledged to stay in for forty days." Forty days, it seems, was the maximum that you could stay in and still file an appeal. . . . We wanted to file appeals and get this thing adjudicated before the Supreme Court, if necessary. But we still wanted to stay in jail and make it expensive on Mississippi, and we made it expensive on them. One of the trustees in the jail brought in a newspaper that announced that there was a nuisance tax that they had in Jackson, auto-use tax, that they had planned to eliminate that year. Well, they announced they couldn't eliminate it, because the Freedom Riders were costing too much. . . .

And we were singing the songs, the freedom songs, which they hated. "You gotta stop that singing." You know, "O-o-h, freedom, o-o-o-o-h, free-*dom,* before I'd be a slave, I'd be buried in my grave and go home to my Lord and be free." . . . "Stop that singing!" The other prisoners upstairs began joining in on the singing. . . . They were in for murder, rape, theft, what have you. We developed a communications system by sending a message up a wire. They'd pull it up . . . an old electric wire that wasn't in use. "Stop that singing!" We refused to stop and kept on singing, and they then stopped bringing in the knickknacks. They'd bring in candy bars and chewing gum to sell, and they wouldn't bring that to us. The kids were looking forward to that coming in each day, so we found a way to get it. We would send the money upstairs and have them buy more than they wanted with our money.

One day a black trustee who had the run of the jail came to his cell
with a whispered message: "'They're gonna send you to the prison
farm. That's where they're gonna try to break you. They're gonna try to
whip your ass.' They transferred us there in the dead of night. . . ."
The county prison farm proved to be but a way station on their passage
to the legendary state prison at Parchman. There, black convicts in
striped uniforms trailed mule-drawn plows across the endless vistas of
the state's cotton fields, a tableau from another century. Yet "the sing-
ing went on, and there was still no brutality—physical brutality."

They knew many of us were chain-smokers. They wouldn't allow any
cigarettes in, and the guards would walk down the corridors blowing
cigarette smoke into our cells. We were already climbing the walls for
want of a cigarette. And they knew that most of these were college students. They wouldn't allow any books in, no books whatever. No newspapers . . .

And then psychological brutality—they passed out the clothing for us.
We had to strip, and they then gave us shorts, just a pair of undershorts,
that's all. The big guys got tiny little undershorts, and the little guys had
huge undershorts. The big guys were trying to hold theirs shut, and the
little guys were trying to stay in theirs and keep 'em from falling down.
[Laughs] And they arranged to put two big guys in one cell and two little guys in one cell, so they couldn't swap.

The food was terrible. It was very, very bad. I went on a diet there
and lost about thirty pounds. . . . We wanted to get out, because we
were really suffering in there. It was damp, and it was cold at night, too.
And when they tried to get us to stop singing, we wouldn't stop singing,
so they said, "If you don't stop singing, we'll take away your mattress."
So they yanked those mattresses off those hard metal beds when we
wouldn't stop singing. And we were sleeping on that cold, hard surface,
and then they opened the window and turned on the exhaust fan, which
brought cold air. I didn't know Mississippi could get that cold, but it felt
cold at night. Almost everybody came down with a cold. . . .

I finally—oh, by the way, Ross Barnett came by. Some of the other
Freedom Riders recognized him from a picture. They said, "You know
who that is that just walked in? That's Ross Barnett." Couldn't miss
him. Not only his face, but he's a little man, small-boned man, with an
enormous pot belly. [Laughs] So Ross came in, and he just walked
around the cell block, just looking in, saying nothing. He stopped at my
cell and says, "What's your name?" I said, "James Farmer." He said,
"They treatin' you all right here?" I said, "Well, no violence, no physical brutality." He said, "So they treatin' you all right. No complaints,

huh?" [Laughs] I said, "I didn't say that. We have lots of complaints. The biggest complaint is that we're in here, and we shouldn't be in here." So he nodded and walked off.

I then demanded to see the director of prisons. . . . Two guards came to escort me. Here I was with my tiny little shorts, trying to keep 'em up, couldn't fasten 'em, other than that, naked, walking along and going to meet the director of prisons. And he was seated there, smoking a big cigar, and there was only one chair. That was his. So I could not sit down. I had to stand. It was really quite a humiliating situation. Here he was, well-dressed, Palm Beach suit, smoking his big cigar; me standing, barefoot, too, no shoes or anything else. And I told him that we respectfully requested—the other Freedom Riders had authorized me to request that we be allowed to go outside and work, work on the farm, work in the field. "Naw, we cain't do that, 'cause the other prisoners'll kill you, and we're responsible for keeping you alive." I said, "We'll take our chances on that." He said, "No, ain't gonna do it. And furthermore," he says, "we want you to stay in there and rot. That's what we want you to do. We got to feed you, because the law says we gotta feed you, and the government will see to it we feed you. But we can make that food so damn unpalatable that you can't eat it. We can put so much salt in it that it'll turn your stomach if you swallow it, and that's just what we may do." Then he signaled that the interview was over.

> At the end of forty days, CORE posted a $500 appeal bond for each of the Freedom Riders. Only after they had left the state did Mississippi spring its last surprise. Each of the three-hundred odd cases would have to be tried in the state appeals courts. The matter would not be settled through the arguing of a few selected "test cases."

They agreed to that, yet one week before the arraignment, the state of Mississippi said, "Oh, no, every last one of them Freedom Riders gotta be back here in Jackson, Mississippi, for the arraignment, and anyone who doesn't show will have to forfeit that $500 bond that CORE has put up." And the prosecuting attorney told our lawyer very frankly, "We're gonna bankrupt CORE." . . . They almost did it, too.

> In an ironic final act to the spring's high drama, CORE found itself chartering buses to haul the Freedom Riders back to Mississippi. But this time the riders were under strict orders to stay out of jail, for CORE was now saddled with legal fees, bail bond, and transportation costs of over $300,000.

I called Roy Wilkins and told him of the problem, and Roy said, "Well, Jim, the NAACP will send you a check for a thousand dollars." I said, "Fine, but a thousand dollars won't help." Well, it helped a little bit, I guess. We put down the deposit on the buses that we were chartering. . . .

Thurgood Marshall saved us. I don't know, now that he's a Supreme Court justice, if he would want that known, but he saved us. I was at a cocktail party and Thurgood was there during this period, and he said, "Jim, how you coming along on that Freedom Ride now?"

I said, "Thurgood, Mississippi is gon' knock us out of the box. They're trying to bankrupt us and they don't know it, but they're just about succeeding 'cause we are *really* hard up now."

He said, "What's the problem, bail bond?"

I said, "Yeah. . . ."

He said, "The Inc. Fund* has got a bail bond fund. I don't know just what is in it, maybe $200,000, $250,000. It's not doing nothin'. It's just sitting there, salted away, drawing interest. You might as well use it as long as it lasts."

When he said that, I hugged him. [Laughs]

Postscript: CORE finally won in the Supreme Court and Mississippi had to refund the bond money. At the insistence of Robert Kennedy the Interstate Commerce Commission issued a directive which really did end bus segregation in parts of the South.

But the first phase of the Movement was over. So was James Farmer's moment as its leader, and so was CORE's day as the pacesetter of the Southern Movement. Now the torch would pass to SCLC and its preachers and to SNCC and its students, to these two organizations born in the South and tempered by Southern resistance for the long battle ahead in Alabama and Mississippi. And on the roadside at Anniston, at the terminal in Montgomery, in the drafty corridors of Parchman, the white folks who counted in those states had served notice that it would be a battle.

* The Inc. Fund, the NAACP Legal Defense and Education Fund, Inc., was administered by Marshall independently of the NAACP proper, the parent organization run by Wilkins.

INTERLUDE

RUBY HURLEY

Pioneer

I had a tremendous personal job to do in getting over the trauma of moving from New York to the South. Although born up South in Washington, I had not had the experience of living in a completely segregated society where everything was segregated by law, and this is to me a part of what so few young people really understand about where we came from in the civil rights struggle. I point out always that when I moved to Birmingham in April of 1951, I found that on the statute books were city ordinances which included one that said that Negroes and whites could not play checkers together.

Her office is handsome, but austere, curiously devoid of personal arti-facts. High in a bookcase at the end of the room sits a single object which breaks the pattern. It is a diapered brown doll; from the hairline, rivulets of red paint stream down the bland face.

This setting fits her. She possesses an austere dignity, and yet beneath that, one senses, there is passion. To her the Movement is a chain link-ing the generations of black people. In high school the son of Frederick Douglass taught her. She came to Birmingham and opened the first per-manent NAACP office in the Deep South. To her the Movement is old and its cost has been dear.

The lynchings of the 1950s . . . are not easily forgotten. The Reverend George W. Lee in Belzoni, Mississippi, who pastored two or three churches in Humphries County or in that surrounding area, had been responsible for getting thirty-some people registered to vote, thirty-some Negroes to register in Belzoni. . . .

Then when white people called Rev. Lee down and told him to "get the niggers to take their names off the book," Lee told 'em he wasn't going to do it. They had a right to vote, and he insisted that they use it. And on the eve of Mother's Day in 1955, when he was leaving the tailor shop, having gotten his suit to wear in the pulpit on Sunday morning, he was murdered, ambushed on Church Street. When I went in to investigate that case and saw the place where he had been killed, it was just cold-blooded murder. And then when I saw his body in the casket—I will not be able to forget how the whole lower half of his face had been shot away. A man killed because he, as a minister, said that God's children had rights as God's children and as American citizens. . . .

Lamar Smith was killed on the courthouse lawn on a Saturday afternoon in Brookhaven, Mississippi. . . .* Anybody who knows any Southern town on a Saturday afternoon knows that somebody would see something around a courthouse square. Nobody saw anything surrounding the murder of Lamar Smith, who had been active in registration and voting in that community. This is the kind of thing that was happening all over the South. . . . I, as at that time the only professional civil rights worker in the South, went to all of these communities and sought to get as much information as I could. And [I] did get information in most of these cases and submitted it to the FBI. But . . . they were state cases, and the FBI could only turn over the information they had to the state agencies, and the states did nothing.

In the Emmett Till [murder] case, . . . I went to the trial to see how it was going. It was just like a circus. The defendants were sitting up there eating ice-cream cones and playing with their children in court just

---

* "Brookhaven," she recalls, "was the place where Judge Tom Brady lived. Judge Brady, a state judge, was infamous in the writing of a book called *Black Monday*." (Jackson, Mississippi: Citizens Councils of America, 1955) The title refers to Monday, May 17, 1954, the date of the U.S. Supreme Court decision outlawing segregated schools. Brady's book, which was printed in paperback and distributed throughout the South, is the classic work of segregationist propaganda. Its key argument: "Whenever and wherever the white man has drunk the cup of black hemlock, whenever and wherever his blood has been infused with the blood of the negro, the white man, his intellect and his culture have died." The book depended on frankly racist historical analysis of which this is a sample: "The negro's contribution in our struggle for freedom with England was comparable to that of a well-broken horse." The Citizens Council distributed thousands of copies.

like they were out at a picnic. Everybody was searched going into the courtroom to make sure that none of the Negroes carried any weapons. White folks were not searched. It was again something that I won't forget and that was back twenty years ago. All because Negroes wanted freedom in Mississippi.

> *She investigated the Till case, the most celebrated lynching of the fifties, for the NAACP magazine* Crisis.

The boy was a fourteen-year-old who had infantile paralysis as a child and could not speak clearly. He whistled when he tried to enunciate words, rather than speak clearly. And this was the charge that was made against him, that he had whistled at [a white man's] wife in the store when he went in to get something for his little cousins.* Now I talked with his cousins, and they told me what they thought had happened, and the boys were too young to make up or to fabricate.

There's no question in my mind that [the two white men] . . . decided that they were going to "get a nigger." That's all, and that's the way they behaved, the way they reacted in those days. They took that child out and beat him, and then they tied him up with the chain from a cotton gin and dumped his body in the Tallahatchie River. And I always say, the Lord moves in mysterious ways wonders to perform, because his body was not supposed to come up the way it was weighted down. But it did come up, and a little teenager, white teenager, found the body on a Sunday morning as he was fishing in the Tallahatchie River.

But [they] were acquitted, and there were witnesses to the fact that they had the boy in the pickup truck with them and [that] they went on to the plantation of a brother of [one of the men], and when they left, the boy was not seen, but the tarpaulin was pulled down over the back of the pickup truck. The witnesses who saw this and heard the screaming from the barn where the beatings were taking place, a youngster of sixteen or seventeen and a woman from across the road, sent word that they wanted to talk to me and tell me some information.

I got the information on who saw that. . . . Those persons heard by way of the grapevine that I was investigating the case, and they passed

---

* Two white men were tried and acquitted for the murder of Emmett Till. Later, journalist William Bradford Huie published an account of Till's death, which Huie said was based on information supplied by the two men.

the word back to me that they wouldn't talk to anybody but me. So I had to put on some cotton-pickin' clothes, literal cotton-pickin' clothes for those days, and make my way on to the plantation. . . . I really got a feeling of what the Underground Railroad during the days of slavery was all about—how word would be passed by just the look in an eye, never the exact phraseology being used, never the clear language, always in some form that you have to sorta try to figure out what the people meant. And it was only after going through, as I remember, four different families, going to four different places, did I finally get to the people who had sent word that they wanted to talk to me. You never went directly to a place. You had to go through . . . you were cleared all the way. Protection was there for me all the way and I didn't know it until many years later. There were men around with shotguns standing in various spots to be sure that I got where I was going and got back. . . .

Mississippi's violent summer of 1955, when armed black men stood guard in the piney woods, made even Birmingham seem tranquil by comparison. But that fragile, surface tranquility ended the following winter, when Autherine Lucy,* with the help of Ruby Hurley and the NAACP, became the first black student to enter the University of Alabama.

I could be riding down the street and white men would drive by and say, "We gon' get you." . . . Bombs were thrown at my home, and I've been kept awake all night with threatening telephone calls, finally finding out where some of them came from. The brother of the man who organized the National Association for the Advancement of White People . . . worked for the telephone company, and even though Arthur Shores, the lawyer who was handling the Lucy case, and I had unlisted numbers, he'd get the numbers and still continue to threaten us. Until finally contact was made way upstairs and we were able to get numbers that remained confidential. . . .

Well, come June first of 1956, the state of Alabama got tired of the NAACP, and an injunction was issued against us. It was an injunction obtained by the then Attorney General Patterson, who later became governor, and it was an *ex parte* injunction.** I was talking with the re-

* See Autherine Lucy Foster.

** An *ex parte* order has one feature which made it extremely attractive to the state of Alabama in this case. It can be issued on a temporary basis without the enjoined party, in this case the NAACP, being called to court to present opposing

porter for the Associated Press, who had become a friend of mine and who is here in Atlanta now, and he was calling to tell me that the injunction was being signed in Montgomery. And while I was on the telephone talking to him about this injunction that was being signed, the doorbell rang and I asked him to hold the phone. When I went to the door, and I had on my housecoat and my hair was probably up in rollers at that time, it was two deputy sheriffs—and photographers, newspaper reporters—with the injunction to hand me at my front door. So I said [to the reporter], "That is not the truth you are telling me. The injunction is not being signed, it is being given to me right now at my door."

So they had issued to the press that it was being signed, but it had been done the day before. They could not have come a hundred miles from Montgomery to Birmingham in a matter of minutes. They didn't have any helicopters in those days. So that injunction put us out of business in the state of Alabama, and as the association's agent in the state, that meant that I had to leave. I closed the office that day. I never went back into the office, as a matter of fact.

At that point, I was just about sick of civil rights and sick of fighting the white folks and sick of the South [laughs] and I said, "I've had it." Because every time I picked up the telephone it was a threatening call, and when I'd go home, I never knew whether it was going to be a bomb. I had gotten down in weight; with my height I weighed about one hundred fifteen pounds. I couldn't eat, and days I'd go without food because I *just could not eat* in Jim Crow places. The only way I could get to a lot of places to fight for civil rights was by bus, and the bus stops, the places to eat, were all segregated, and I was not going to eat in a segregated place. So if I ran out of Hershey Bars, then I didn't eat until I got someplace where I could be fed. Many times I'd have to ride all day or

---

arguments. The state of Alabama argued that the NAACP had failed to comply with its laws requiring "foreign corporations" to register with the Secretary of State. Even though the first NAACP chapter in Alabama had been established before 1920, Judge Walter B. Jones of Montgomery apparently agreed that there was good cause to consider the NAACP "foreign," and he enjoined the NAACP from further activity in the state. Equally alarming to the NAACP and Ruby Hurley, however, were the court's efforts to seize its membership rolls. "The judge, who is dead now, bless his soul, had ruled that we would have to pay an exorbitant amount of money for every day that we didn't submit the listing of our members. . . . We knew what would happen to our members if their names were made public." Interestingly, it was Judge Jones who, several years later, issued the injunction against the Freedom Rides which was read over John Lewis as he lay on the pavement outside the Montgomery bus station. For more on the state of Alabama's policy of legal harassment of the NAACP, see John Patterson.

all morning in order to speak in the afternoon and then ride the rest of
the night to get back home because there was no place for me to sleep.
And that would mean ofttimes almost twenty-four hours when I didn't
have anything to eat.

This was segregation. This was what existed in the South. And I listen to young folks nowadays talking about old folks "taking it." They
don't know how we didn't take it. There were those who died rather
than take it, and there were those who suffered much more than I did
who didn't take it, because I could get out every so often and go to New
York and let off steam up there. I could go to Washington and let off
steam up there. But there were people who lived under this hammer all
the time, and who owned property and never knew when their property
was gonna be taken away, or when their lives were going to be taken. So
that was a period when it wasn't easy, and much is said about what happened in the 1960s, but to me the fifties were much worse than the sixties. When I was out there by myself, for instance, there were no TV
cameras with me to give me any protection. There were no reporters
traveling with me to give me protection, because when the eye of the
press or the eye of the camera was on the situation, it was different. It
was different.

A lot of people know about the marching of the sixties and the
dogs of the sixties because television was there, and the cameras were
churning while the dogs were snapping and while "Bull" Connor was
behaving, but we had to deal with "Bull" Connor long before the sixties. "Bull" Connor was police chief when I was in Birmingham, and
"Bull" Connor was the chief of police when the houses were burned
on Dynamite Hill in Birmingham, when I first moved over there.*
The Negroes had moved into a section that had been white before.
What's the girl's name who is alleged to be a Communist from Birmingham?

Angela Davis?

Angela lived on what we called Dynamite Hill. She was a little girl.
I watched the smoke going up from one of those houses that burned
to the ground with a fire department that was less than three miles
away, and it didn't come until after the houses had burned to the
ground. We know that that was arson, and the police department and

* Actually, Connor was police commissioner, the elected superior of the police
chief.

the fire department had to have known what was going on, and they let it happen in Birmingham. I've seen all that. . . .

I had to be very defensive, very careful about what I said, what I did, with whom I was seen. Efforts were made to entrap me sexually. All kinds of tricks were used, but I guess maybe, Scorpio that I am, I have an ingrained ability to defend myself against anything that I think is wrong. So I was able to.

It played havoc physically. As I said, I lost weight and I was sick half the time and didn't know what was wrong. My doctor over there finally said, "There isn't a thing wrong with you physically. It isn't a thing, but these"—the way he put it—"niggers and white folks. That's all that's wrong with you." [Laughs]

But it was a challenge, and I always emphasize, but for the grace of God, I couldn't have done it, because there were days when if I'd had any sense, I'da been scared. But I never let myself. I didn't get scared . . . I was mad. I got mad when we were put out of business and I had time to reflect on what had been going on. I couldn't go into the airport from a trip but what a sheriff wasn't waiting to stick a summons in my hand or a subpoena in my hand for something or other. . . .

And when I'd go downtown to buy clothes, I had to do battle about being recognized. I started a fight in Birmingham—the use of courtesy titles. I refused to spend my money and let some clerk that didn't have an eighth-grade education call me Ruby and she'd never seen me before in my life. Those are the kinds of things that took their toll inwardly, though I was able to, I think, effect at least a climate for some change. I think young people need to know, and some older people need to know, that it didn't all begin in 1960.

Postscript: Eight years to the day after she closed the NAACP office in Birmingham, the U.S. Supreme Court ruled that the organization could operate in Alabama free of harassment. By that time, she had long since returned to the South to open the regional NAACP office in Atlanta. She was still running it in 1977.

IV
ALABAMA

THE BATTLEGROUND STATE

Part One: Birmingham

ED GARDNER

"I Wasn't Saved to Run"

Fourth Avenue North in Birmingham is a dispirited street of black businesses done in by integration. When the racial barriers fell, they lost a captive clientele. On this street of pool halls, barbecue parlors, and vacant theaters is the storefront office of the Alabama Christian Movement for Human Rights, the Alabama arm of SCLC. Once this office was a command post of a movement which stirred America's conscience. Now elderly women have set up a quilting parlor in the back; they pass the days undisturbed, sewing and watching soap operas. Only the old people who remember come this way anymore. The wall above his desk is papered with clippings. On that wall, police dogs still strain at their leashes, fire hoses spin demonstrators into the gutters, and in one of the most famous of the Birmingham photographs, a gang of policemen hold a fat black woman pinned to the ground, nightsticks poised above her. "She disappeared. I don't know where she went. Now all the people got scattered. Some of 'em left the city."

He remains, surrounded by Movement totems, a keeper of the memory of bad days in Birmingham, toughest town in the South.

Everything in Birmingham was segregated. You could go downtown there in one department [of a store] and spend a thousand dollars and go to the lunch counter and be put in jail. Or you go uptown and get on the elevator that was marked White Only, and get put in jail.

Elevators were segregated?

Everything. Everything from top to bottom was segregated. And then the eating places . . . had two doors. They had to have a sign on there, Colored and White, and then the owner had to have a wall inside there seven feet high so the black and white couldn't see each other. . . . [Laughs]

Now at that point in the late fifties . . . the average white person in Birmingham would have said that the blacks here were content except for a few troublemakers.

Yeah, that's right, that's right. "Outside agitators" they called them, like Martin Luther King.

But what was the case with the black community?

Well, the black community was fed up with segregation, and only they were waiting to get a leader to lead out. At that time, any man that attempted to lead out here in Birmingham, well, he was put out of business, see. If he had a business, he couldn't operate, because the city would take his license, and the Ku Klux Klan came in, and the police would harass him. If he was in his car, they would charge him with running a stop sign when there was no stop sign. They would charge him with running a red light when there was no red light. . . . We couldn't hardly get a man in business to lead out in the fight, because he knew that his business was gone when he identified himself with the struggle. So we had to get a man that couldn't lose nothing but his life, and we found Fred Shuttlesworth.

On June 5, 1956, four days after Ruby Hurley was forced to close her NAACP office, he and fellow minister Shuttlesworth called the first meeting of the Alabama Christian Movement for Human Rights.

That night cars were lined up about six blocks long trying to get into the building, because we felt that John Patterson's scheme was to continue to maintain segregation and discrimination. And anything looked like it was pointing to destroy segregation and discrimination, he sought to put it out of business. So he clamped down on the N-Double-A-C-P and put 'em out of business for eight long years. So the Alabama Christian Movement took up where N-Double-A-C-P left off and we carried the fight on. . . . We saw it was going to be a fight to the finish and therefore when we started out, we tried to sit down and talk and to get the whites to voluntarily . . . get these segregation laws off the books. But at that time they refused to talk to us.

> *He remembers those as lonely days. They tested bus segregation in Birmingham and five hundred blacks went to jail, but national attention was focused on the bus protest in Montgomery, one hundred miles away. The reprisals—evictions, firings, bombings—went unnoticed.*

> They came by my place shooting and all like that, so I had two guards to guard my house. Rev. Shuttlesworth had guards guarding his house. We had a lot of laughs about that. I had a Winchester and I told 'em this was a nonviolent Winchester.

The [local] news people wouldn't give us any coverage . . . they played it down. Those five hundred people went to jail; they didn't publicize it. They acted as though nothing was happening, the town was quiet. "Just a few rabble-rousers was agitating and the folks was satisfied and if we can get these few rabble-rousers out of here, there will be good race relations as always been in Birmingham. . . ."

Then we had black informers and we had white informers and people were afraid. They lived under fear, and so our struggle in the fifties was very light, but we kept moving. . . . Then, when we got to the sixties, we decided that these folks wasn't going to give in one inch, and we decided that Birmingham was the Johannesburg of South Africa and that "Bull" Connor was determined whatever scheme he could use, he was gon' use it to maintain segregation. And he says to us, "You all can't fill up my jail. I got enough room for all of you."

So we proved to "Bull" Connor that we could fill his jail up. We gave him a big surprise, the surprise of his life. . . . We invited Dr. Martin Luther King and all his staff into Birmingham and we set up workshops and got these people oriented into what we had in mind and into the doctrine of love and nonviolence. These people were to march, go to jail, and whatever the case might occur in our struggle, they were never to fight back, whatever happened. And those who weren't willing to undertake such an undertaking we eliminated, because at that time the segregationists was armed to the teeth. They were prepared for violence and they could handle violence. But we caught 'em off guard with nonviolence. They didn't know what to do with nonviolence, see.

We went out to test all the segregation laws, because when we went to court, we had to prove that we were segregated and discriminated against. And the only way we could prove it, we had to try and get put in jail. If we hadn't been willing to go to jail, then the segregation laws would have stood. Because if no one had tried it, then you couldn't prove it in court, even if the judge himself knew it himself, see. . . . The weight of responsibility was on us to prove that we were segregated and discriminated against.

He was assigned the task of proving that discrimination existed at the Dobbs House restaurant at the Birmingham airport. The management simply locked the doors when the small group of blacks approached the entrance. Later, thinking the would-be protesters had left the airport, the Dobbs House manager unlocked the front door to admit some white customers. The blacks, who had been hiding nearby, charged the door.

Five of them rushed in. . . . They got a ham sandwich and a glass of iced tea—it was $10.25. They called me here at the office and asked me what to do about it. I told 'em to go on and pay the $10.25 and get a receipt and bring it back to the office. So we paid $51 for five sandwiches. When we went to court the next week, one of the men kept his sandwich. He didn't eat his sandwich. He just wrapped it up and carried it home and put it in the refrigerator and brought that sandwich to court.

They introduced the sandwich as evidence when the Dobbs House manager took the stand in federal court.

[The judge asked:] "Now, do all the persons comes into the Dobbs House pay $10.25 for a sandwich?" The manager said, "Well, naw, sir, Judge." He said, "Well, why did you have to charge these persons $10.25 for a sandwich?" And the manager said, "Well, they were special guests." [The judge said:] "What made 'em special? Because they were black?"

How did the decision to ask SCLC in [to Birmingham] *come about?*

The way it worked at that time—I think I will be very truthful—SCLC had hit a slump, and they were struggling at that time because they had lost out in Augustine, Florida. They had a big setback.

Augustine? In Albany.

Albany. Albany. That's right. Albany. That's right. Albany. They had a big setback, and it was kind of a big slump for 'em, and they were driving in low key because they had run into this slump in Albany.* So coming to Birmingham gave them a shot in the arm. It was the very thing they needed, and it was the very thing we needed. They needed us and we needed them, because King was a national symbol. . . . Then the [local] press had to come out because we had the press coming from other places . . . it forced them out.

When Dr. King came to us, he said, "Now what we're going to have to do, we're going to have to center all our forces here in Birmingham, Alabama, because Birmingham is the testing ground. If we fail here, then we will fail everywhere, because every segregated city and every segregated state is watching which way Birmingham goes. We got to, whatever it takes, break the back of segregation here. We got to do it." He instructed all of us to be ready to pay the price. He said, "Some gon' die, but this is the cost. It'll be another down payment on freedom."

So we had these marches. They were tremendous marches. We would have these mass meetings, and then we would leave these mass meetings and march all through the city, one and two o'clock in the morning. Well, the city couldn't rest. It couldn't rest, because the town was stirred up, and "Bull" tried to put out the fire. Those pictures up there show you where he brought his dogs out. He thought the dogs was going to run 'em in. But the dogs just drawed a bigger crowd for our marches, and every act he would put on would draw a bigger crowd. . . . Everything that Eugene "Bull" Connor attempted to do, it backfired on him.

Another trick he tried was the injunction against the march, wasn't it?

Injunction, yes. You see, they had passed a city ordinance that if three people would gather out there on a sidewalk, he could jail them. Three would constitute a march, even though they was just talking. So when the judge—Judge Jenkins** was the presiding judge—issued the

* In 1961 and 1962, SCLC and SNCC had waged a long, frustrating campaign in Albany, Georgia. See Laurie Pritchett and Andrew Young.

** Circuit Judge William A. Jenkins of Birmingham granted the city's request for an *ex parte* injunction forbidding King and his staff to lead further marches. The writ was served on King on April 11, the Thursday before Easter, and King's biographers agree that the ensuing decision to defy the injunction was a major turning point in his life and career, since it committed him once and for all to the philosophy that one had a positive moral duty to violate unjust laws. King's decision led to a landmark 1967 U. S. Supreme Court decision which held that a state court injunction is temporarily binding even though, on its face, it violates rights guaranteed by the U. S. Constitution. Although King lost this litigation, he had by that time long since won the battle of Birmingham.

order that we couldn't march, Dr. King called a meeting at Room 30 at the Gaston Motel and said, "Now, we got a court order here just served by the deputies that we can't march, but if we obey this order we are out of business. We got to violate it."

The lawyer said, "Well, now, I couldn't tell you to march, I couldn't tell you not to march, because as a lawyer that would be a conflict of interests and my license would be taken away from me. The only thing I can say in regard to the injunction, you can't beat it." Said, "Now, if you are willing to pay the fine and whatever is involved, then that's up to you all."

Dr. King said, "Well, we're gon' to pay the fine and we gon' serve the days. Whatever the judge say, we are going to accept it, 'cause we are gonna violate this injunction."

Was there any opposition sentiment in that meeting?

There was some that wasn't quite ready to go back to jail. But Dr. King said, "Now this is the only alternative we have. If we obey it, then we are out of business . . . Therefore I am going to march if I have to march by myself."

It was on Friday, Friday morning, and Easter was coming. So Abernathy said, "Well, let me call the church and tell the deacons I'll be in jail Easter Sunday."

Dr. King was co-pastor.* His daddy was in the meeting. So his daddy said to him, "Son, I've never interfered with any of your civil rights activities, but I think at this time my advice would be to you to not violate the injunction." He said, "Papa, I got to. I got to. You don't quite understand what's involved." His daddy said, "All right, I won't have no more to say."

> *Dr. King did go to jail and while there he wrote his famous "Letter from the Birmingham Jail." It was addressed to seven Birmingham ministers who had written him a chiding letter, but its purpose was to explain to the nation the morality of civil disobedience. The letter set the tone for the more dramatic demonstrations to come in the next three weeks.*

Altogether, we demonstrated here forty-five days and forty-five nights, and in those forty-five days and forty-five nights, didn't a drop of rain fall. And we had mass meetings seventy-five nights without a

---

* With his father at Ebenezer Baptist Church.

break. That's the way the thing turned out. Not a drop of rain. It was hot and dry. Birmingham was hot.

Were there some black people in Birmingham opposed to Dr. King . . . ?

Oh, yes, yes . . . some he never did get until the big thing came up, and the big thing was when we had the final demonstration that tied up the whole city.* We timed this demonstration about five-thirty in the evening, when the traffic was heavy. And everybody in town couldn't get out; those out of town couldn't get in. But this brought the power structure in. See, they had tried to play as though nothing was happening, but when we marched downtown . . . marched in every department store, every eating joint, and tied up everything, all the traffic, everything was at a standstill. We had forty-five hundred folks in jail, and we had about ten or twenty thousand wanted to get in, and "Bull" Connor had filled up the Bessemer jail, had filled up the county jail—had no place in the city [jail]—filled up the Fair Park. He run out of space, and when he ran out of space, he got the firemen and turned the water on, but the more water he would pour, the more they would come. So then the power structure said something had to be done.

I remember one man, Sid Smyer. Sid Smyer said, "I'm a segregationist from bottom to top, but gentlemen, you see what's happening." He said, "I'm not a damn fool." He said, "Now, we can't win." Said, "We can't win. We gon' have to stop and talk to these folks."

* May 7, 1963.

ANDREW MARRISETT

An SCLC staffer recruited off the streets of Birmingham.

I used to drive the church bus. It was on a Sunday, and I was driving the bus, and I just happened to detour to go down by the park where the demonstrators would always be. What really sticks in my mind then and sticks in my mind now is seeing a K-9 dog being sicced on a six-year-old girl. I went and stood in front of the girl and grabbed her, and the dog jumped on me and I was arrested. That really was the spark. I had an interest all along, but that just took the cake—a big, burly two-hundred-and-eighty-five-pound cop siccing a trained police dog on that little girl, little black girl. And then I got really involved in the Movement.

That changed my whole way of thinking. I was born a great Baptist. All my life I'd been through the Sunday School thing and the Bible School and church on Sunday morning and in the afternoon and at night and prayer meetings and choir rehearsals and traveling around. I was into that Christian thing, like most of my people are now, where they're so blindly engrossed, . . . not really looking at what was going on around them. Like at that time, Birmingham was the most segregated city of its size in the nation.

You grew up in Birmingham. When did you become aware of that?

This is the old cliché, but I'm going to say it because it's true with me. . . . While we were downtown at Kresse's or Pizitz or Loveman's and I had to use the restroom, I would have to be taken out in the alley. That is an old cliché, but that held true in Birmingham. "Bull" Connor ran that city. I mean, he totally ran it. The mayor didn't have no say, the sheriff, the council. . . .

I knew something was wrong, but . . . I didn't have any idea of the value of being able to go to every counter in the store, including the lunch counter. I had read about Greensboro.* I knew about the sit-ins when they started here, but it just didn't ring no bell. So I always tell people that dog incident really rung my bell.

Go ahead. After you got tangled up with the dog . . .

Well, what they did was they drug me away to jail, and I was an unknown . . . When they taken pictures of me and everybody else, I was put down as "civil rights worker." So when the SCLC got folk out of jail, I got out . . . that night I went to the mass meeting, and I met people like Andy Young, Dorothy Cotton, James Bevel. Of course, Ralph Abernathy then was Martin's true aide. . . . I dedicated my life then just to being involved in that movement, life or death, and bringing in other people like James Orange, Elizabeth Hays, and Robert Seals.

> *He and his three friends became totally involved in the Movement, and all eventually joined the SCLC staff.*
>
> What we finally wound up doing, the four of us, was being the kind of teachers, the workshop leaders for tomorrow's demonstration. We would meet at Sixteenth Street Baptist Church . . . that's the one that got bombed . . . we would meet in there and have workshops and make sure that students and people that was involved knew what they were marching for, knew why they were marching, priming them for tonight's mass meeting. . . .

Of course, you know about the three thousand that was sitting on the side of the curbstone, crying to go to jail at the height of that movement, when the compromise was signed.** Well, we were responsible for all that. We would sneak people down . . . we would coordinate, we would do all kinds of tricks. Cops would have all our main trails blocked off, lined up; you know, there was thousands of cops from all over the coun-

* Where he was living in 1975.
** He is talking about the great May 7 demonstration referred to by Rev. Gardner.

try, see.* We would get girls with the big coats and dresses, and they would put their [picket] signs up under there, and we would go down to the Trailways bus station. That's where we would meet. Then we'd all get in there and everybody would orderly break out in twos. You know, that kind of thing, just harass the cops.

The cops did what [in response]?

They would start arresting. Old foolish "Bull" Connor, when he would come, he'd say, "Bust heads," or "Put the water on 'em," or "Carry 'em to jail." So at that last time, "Bull" Connor was going round and round and round and round. "All them niggers, all them niggers, where they coming from?" They used school buses, yeah; three thousand people went to jail *that* day, and then they finally—Now I wasn't in on negotiations. That wasn't my thing. I was action.

He recalls growing up in Birmingham. ". . . where I came from, I had to fight my way through. You know, I had to be mean or else I wouldn't survive." He reflects on my observation that Birmingham represented Dr. King's greatest triumph in teaching nonviolent discipline, because of the high level of suppressed rage among the city's blacks.

If you can say that Birmingham *and* Selma was the most sustained discipline in the nonviolent movement, I can agree. I would have to agree that Birmingham was, because of the kinds of people that were involved. We used to have to run people home, because they would bring their guns and that kind of thing. We'd have to go up and say, "Hey, man, lookie here, you know, if you want to kill cops, you go on over there and form your own little group, but don't kill them in this nonviolent line here. You'll get somebody killed."

And I'd say, "After the meeting tonight, I'll come over here and help you kill some coppers, but don't be throwing a damn garbage can, I mean, like at a tank."

How common was it, people wanting to bring weapons to the demonstrations in Birmingham?

At first, very common, because the syndrome was, "I got a chance to kill me a cracker." That's what they used to call white folks in Birmingham . . . "Honkie" came in later. But anyway, it was that rage

---

* In this case, *all over the country* means "all over the state of Alabama."

that you spoke about, where there were two things that black men wanted to do: one was screw white girls, and two was kill white men. Okay? Because all this stuff had been built up in them all their lives . . . We used to have a little story about the father be done worked down all day. He come home and fusses at the wife because the food ain't ready, she fussed at the oldest kid and then on down the line to the youngest kid. He kicks the cat, the cat chases the dog, and the dog chases the rat, and this go on and on and on through all that frustration. But that was it. What was the question again?

The original question was, how common was it for people to bring weapons?

Oh, yeah, right. I mean at first it was very common until—well, Dr. King, of course, was *the* influence at the mass meetings. And our job was to every time we saw a guy that was really, really enraged and we thought we could at least talk to right then, we would try to get him to the mass meeting and get him involved. We would sit beside him or close around him, a group of us, and get him involved in the spirit, and we would sing the songs and do the chants and freedom-now things, and then we'd hear Dr. King speak, and that would quiet down the angriest lion, because he just had that thing about him, that halo that he would shine.

Abraham Wood

Family Affair

My father was sort of a rough fellow at times when it came to racial situations. I've heard him relate to us on the job how he had gotten into it with a number of white fellows who had given him a beatin' because they called him out of his name or tried to make him fit into the traditional nigger role. . . . Me and, of course, my brother and my children caught the spirit, too. We had three children to be involved in going to jail. My three oldest daughters went to jail, and my baby at the time, my oldest son, cried because he couldn't go. He was about five years old, I believe, and he wanted to go too.

He, his father, and brother were all ministers, all active in the Movement and all supporters of SCLC's decision to recruit school children for the climactic May demonstrations.

Some of the black parents did have some misgivings about it. I remember some of the criticisms which came up. . . . Of course, it reflected the same kind of thing that the officials of the board of education were saying, that some of the white city fathers were saying about the possible harm that could come to these children: "Isn't it a shame using these little children as the cat's paw that reaches in the fire. . . . Dr. King ought to be ashamed of himself. . . ."

Well, here I was seeking to recruit other students to march, and the involvement of my children just came about as a matter of course. . . . There wasn't any asking to come: "Can we be involved?" [Laughs] It's just, "We ought to be in it and we *are* in it. We *want* to be in it."

How old were your three daughters?

I believe . . . eight, nine, and ten, or maybe nine, ten, and eleven. Something like that. . . . When the [school] board sought to handle the children, expel the children, it was my brother's daughter who was a party to one of the suits where they had to get a ruling from a judge to stop them from taking those steps against the children.* So my children's involvement came about as a matter of course. I don't remember telling them to come be involved. They just caught it, you see. When I looked around there they were. . . .

Did you not have any misgivings for their safety?

Well, no, I didn't have any misgivings for their safety. What misgivings I might have had were taken care of by listening to Dr. King. But the question did come up as to subjecting these young people to possible harm, this kind of thing. He said that they had already been subjected to brutality by living in the Southern way of life. Been exploited and abused and misused, you see. And it made a lot of sense. Made a lot of sense. When you get caught up in the Movement, you just lose some of your fear. It's an amazing kind of thing. I can look back now at some of the situations we got involved in and I didn't think about it to be afraid. At the time. But when you look back at some of the situations we were in, you kind of shudder afterwards. But when you are caught up in the emotion of the Movement and you commit yourself, you really don't worry about what's going to happen to you.

What was the turning point of the Birmingham Movement during that time?

Well, I think that with the student involvement, the whites started getting the idea they were going to have to negotiate, but the thing that really broke the camel's back was the selective-buying campaign. At the same time we boycotted the downtown merchants, and I think this was the real concern of men like Sidney Smyer, who was with Birmingham

* See Judge Elbert Tuttle.

Real Estate and head of the chamber. And I had never seen an old white man cry, but at one of the meetings at the chamber of commerce . . . he actually broke down and cried. The merchants were hurting. We had the pressure on them in order that they might pressure the city. . . . This helped move Birmingham to the turning point. . . .

What kind of city is Birmingham for blacks today?

Birmingham has made a lot of progress . . . progress that they just didn't decide to make, but progress that came through agony. Of course, you know the bombings and certainly the Sixteenth Street thing.* During the demonstrations, you remember, lot of people getting shot and killed. Over here in the western section, little boy was shot by whites. Police shot one man, member of my father's church, in the back, shotgun. You know, blacks had started throwing rocks and this sort of thing.

You remember when the motel was bombed** and how the group gathered and turned over taxicabs, set them on fire, and this kind of thing. Now that was the night I was afraid, and I think the Birmingham police were afraid. I saw a black come up behind the Gaston Building with a knife, a long knife in his hand, and he shook it at the policeman, said, "I want that suit you got on. Gimme that suit." I've seen the time when that policeman would have dashed there and got that Negro. Policeman didn't move, just looked at him, and he didn't go. The black man tried to get him to [a soft, beckoning voice]: "You come on back here." Policeman didn't go, you see.

And the policemen had to get us, the black leaders, to get in the cars with them, because in some areas blacks were throwing rocks in the dark, and if a police car would move, they would just bombard it with rocks. And they were trying to get to the alarms—there were fire alarms and stores broken into, those kinds of alarms—and they were trying to maneuver, and every time they'd move, they'd be bombarded. So a

---

* Through the years there had been over fifty racial bombings in Birmingham, culminating with the deaths of four black girls in the explosion at Sixteenth Street Baptist Church on Sunday morning, September 15, 1963.

** On the night of May 11, only one day after SCLC and city officials had agreed to a desegregation plan, a bomb ripped the black-owned motel where SCLC had its command center. Ralph Abernathy: "Dr. King and I shared the same room in the A.G. Gaston Motel. It was a large room on the second floor, corner room, and we held our conference there. The strategy committee met, and within a few minutes after we left that room in order to get a plane to come to Atlanta, the motel was bombed. . . . If he and I had stayed in that room for thirty more minutes, we would have been killed." See Ben Allen.

number of us rode with 'em. I was scared that night, and I put my head out the window: I wanted them to see I was black. [Laughs]

That was a terrible night, when blacks went wild. I knew then that we were not going to be able to long hold this element on check. And then afterwards, when the Sixteenth Street bombings took place and I went to the scene, dashed to that scene, . . . I found a group of young blacks with a pile of rocks, and every car that passed with a white driver in it, they were tearing it up. Of course, I went there and I said, "Brethren, *don't,* don't, don't do this. This isn't the way." Angry mood. "All right, you're one of 'em, you're with 'em." No talking to them . . . not going to be reasoned with, you see. So I had to go away from there. . . . I said to myself, "Not going to be long till this thing is going to take a new turn." You see, that's another element coming in, with "Burn, baby, burn," and this kind of thing.

That was the forerunner. . .

What I saw at Sixteenth Street, what I saw at the motel, was the forerunner of what happened. Later it was "Burn, baby, burn," and Carmichael.* That came later and I saw it coming. I saw it coming.

* Stokely Carmichael, the militant SNCC leader who popularized the Black Power slogan.

FRED L. SHUTTLESWORTH

Feud at the Top

December 25, 1956: I remember preachin' that Sunday about "Wonderful Jesus" over there in Isaiah, sixth chapter: "His name shall be called wonderful." And these were prophetic words. I said, "Any time now, I'm lookin' for somebody to throw a stick of dynamite against my house." Well, that same night, not one stick, but twelve, fifteen, sticks were placed between that house and the church. . . . The floor was blown out from under the bed, and I was blown down into a hole—we never did get the springs—and there I was lying on that mattress. So I understand, and I knew when the bomb went off, I knew exactly what it was. The lights went out at the same time. I knew it was for me, and I knew they were intendin' to kill me, and yet I had the sense enough to know that I wouldn't get hurt, heard somethin' say, "Not yet." I'm still here. Well, now, that's why I got out the next day and led the march on the buses, see. . . .

That house was about fifty years old, all that black dust and stuff, dynamite smoke and stuff, and I came out. On the way from around the back of the house, this Klans—this policeman who *was* a Klansman—said to me, . . . I think it shook him, he said, "I know some people. I know some people in the Klan. They're really after you." He said, "If I was you I'd get outa town as quick as I could."

I said, "Well, you tell them that I'm not going out of town." I said, "You see all this you've come through?" I said, "If God could save me through this, then I'm gon' stay here and clear up this." I said, "I wasn't saved to run. . . ."

Within the Movement, his bravery became legendary. After the bombing his congregation built a new parsonage—with a sentry box on the front porch where the men of the church stood guard every night. In 1957 he and his wife were the first black parents to attempt to enroll their children in a white school. The police stayed far away from Phillips High School that day, allowing a mob of Klansmen to beat him with chains and brass knuckles in the middle of a downtown street. His wife was stabbed in the hip. No inner voice said "not yet" that day. "I began to realize if I didn't get back to the car I would die on that pavement." He lost consciousness as he reached the car and does not remember his companions dragging him into it. In the next year came the second bombing. An old man guarding the parsonage saw a white man plant the dynamite against the side of the church. The guard carried the bomb to the middle of the street, dropped it, and ran. The explosion blew the windows out of the church. The next Sunday, "I had more people on the outside than I had inside. . . . I preached on 'Learning Life's Greatest Lesson: I have learned whatever state I am, therewith be content.'"

I provoked danger and attacks upon my person, and I led others into it, because I knew we had to challenge, and it wasn't just gon' die away. . . . It gradually became into my mind the idea that we needed some different type of confrontation. . . . Here, I thought, with "Bull" Connor being the epitome of segregation and SCLC being organized by us to change it, the two forces should be met . . . so it was at my invitation, my personal invitation, after we discussed it, that Dr. King and Ralph Abernathy and the SCLC boys agreed to come in.

Was there any reluctance on their part to come in, after having had a bad experience in Albany . . . ?

Well, I think the idea of facing "Bull" Connor was the thing . . . we knew that we would have at least the spotlight, I think that. To me, it was a matter of life and death, not only to face "Bull" Connor, but to see if it is true—and it *is* true; I don't think I should say it like that—to really *prove* that where sin did abound, Grace did much more abound, where darkness is, then light can overcome it.

It was September, 1962, when Birmingham's white leaders heard of

*his plan to bring "Grace" and "light" and Martin Luther King, Jr., to
their city.*

I had never met with the power structure. I had never met with the
clergy of this city, which I think is one of the tragic things of this whole
situation, even now. . . . We announced SCLC would come in. Smyer
got a group of businessmen together, and for the first time, all of a sudden, I'm invited [downtown] by A.G. Gaston* . . . the white power
structure wanted to meet with us. A.G. Gaston said to me, "I confessed
to 'em that you have to talk to Fred. Fred's the man that's got the folks.
I got some money, but that's all. Money don't run this thing now. He's
the man with the marbles. You haveta talk to the marbles. . . . I told
them, Fred,"—he told me in front of them—"that they had to talk with
you."

So naturally, I was a "doctor." They shook my hand: "Dr. Shuttlesworth, we're glad to see you." I said, "Well, I don't wanna be a 'doctor.'
Just too bad we haven't shaken all these years. I been here now sufferin'
for five and six or seven years. Church been bombed twice, and nobody
said nothin'."

Old man Smyer, hands shaking, said, "Well, we wanna—we just
wanna know how we can help [keep] Dr. King . . . outa here."

I said, "Well, on your slogan at the airport and elsewhere, 'It's So
Nice to Have You in Birmingham' . . . we think that means King, too.
We think he's nice enough to come in here. He's nice as anybody else,
and there are some things wrong, the mere fact that we have to invite
him in." Then I went on down to relate how I had suffered here without
bein' vindictive, how I had been bombed, hadn't bombed anybody, and
yet these people had never gotten together to bring an outcry. I said,
"So I'm not of a mind that this morning I came to be used by you, and
I'm certain I'm not your darling, and I don't propose to be. I'm nobody's darling, and if you've got some reason for calling me, what can
you offer?" I said, "That's what I'm here for, not to hold a conversation, because I don't think we're that brotherly."

He said, "Well, ah, we—ah, we cain't—ah make promises for the merchants."

I said, "Well, I'm talkin' to the wrong crowd then. Let's go, gentlemen . . . you wastin' my time. I'm busy. I don't waste time, tryin' to
make time. I'm fightin' segregation. . . . You know what it is that we
want. How much of this can you offer?"

. . . Five or six of those big merchants downtown, they were there. I

---

* Millionaire insurance man and property owner. White Birmingham regarded
him as the city's preeminent black leader.

think most of 'em thought I was a great big, bearlike, black-type Negro. They didn't think I was little, spare-made. I was quite calm, you know, because I *knew* where it was. . . .

But Birmingham merchants had a chance to desegregate voluntarily?

Yes, oh yes. Yes, and I believe it was Sears' man said, "Well . . . tell you the truth, that door to my toilet, I can just probably have my janitor paint [over the White Only sign]." He went out then and called him and had him to paint the door. Came back and told me, "He's paintin' the door now." They had to come up with some good-faith thing for us to pledge not to have the demonstrations.* So we came out, and we tried to announce that we had made some progress. But "Bull" Connor began watchin'. The signs that did come down, he made the merchants put 'em back up.

This is the way I woulda rather have had it anyway: Let's fight for it. The merchants tried and couldn't, some of 'em. . . . I beamed my main points at Pizitz.** I said to him, "Mr. Pizitz . . . I'll be happy to be arrested at your store." I said, "Martin Luther King and Ralph and I, we'll be dragged outa your store by 'Bull' Connor's efficient police."

He and King agreed to start the demonstrations immediately after the Birmingham municipal elections of April 2, 1963. By the time those demonstrations brought the same white merchants back to the conference table in early May, Shuttlesworth was in the hospital, a victim of the fire hoses. In his absence, King and his SCLC aides were negotiating with Birmingham's white leaders through federal mediators sent by President Kennedy. When Shuttlesworth was released from the hospital on May 9, he made a startling discovery. President Kennedy and his emissaries, Justice Department officials Burke Marshall and John Doar, had convinced King that the tumultuous demonstrations were hampering negotiations with the whites.

Kennedy was all set to announce in Washington and King in Bir-

---

* In return for delaying demonstrations, he demanded that White and Colored signs be immediately removed from the restrooms and drinking fountains at five downtown stores. However, removing the signs violated city segregation ordinances, as Connor soon noted.

** Louis Pizitz, owner of Birmingham's largest home-owned department store. Despite his large black clientele, Shuttlesworth found him the "most recalcitrant" of the merchants.

mingham that the demonstrations were gon' be called off, but I had to veto that. I said, "Naw, we promised to go on until we got an agreement."* We had a terrific thing, and not to get into details about it, . . . I was strong, and I reminded Dr. King of the fact that when he came in, we promised we were not gon' stop until we won our victory. I said, "That's what people are saying: You go to a point and then you stop.** You won't be stopping here." . . . See, King was a very slow person. He was very deliberate. He wanted to be careful, and it actually hurt him to offend people.

As a historian now, I want to ask you a [question about this] point because I think it's important that it be preserved. . . .

Yeah, one of the points that oughta be said about that is this: I never did agree, and only . . . because I respected Martin Luther King did I agree to allow Burke Marshall, who was assistant attorney general, and John Doar to talk to us on one side and then go talk to the white folks on the other side. I did not believe in that. I thought we should have gotten together face-to-face, 'cause it's never a true negotiation when that's being done. And from what I know about the Justice Department [laughs softly] . . . you know. But this was my concession to Martin, because I really felt . . . that Martin was the man for the hour. But you see, the same Burke Marshall and John Doar . . . had almost sold King on the idea that the merchants cain't negotiate with demonstrations going on. And so when I got outa my hospital . . . doctor told my wife he'd give me three hypos,*** and I resisted 'em. Maybe good now I did. He said, "Well, take him on home. He'll be better at the scene of the action."

So I had just gotten to the motel and tucked into bed, when I had to— Martin had sent for me to come out to John Drew's† house, one of

* At the start of the demonstrations, SCLC put forward four demands: (1) desegregation of lunch counters, restrooms, fitting rooms, and drinking fountains in downtown stores; (2) hiring of blacks in sales and clerical positions; (3) release of jailed demonstrators; (4) establishment of a permanent biracial committee to deal with community problems. Shuttlesworth's position was that not until the four demands were met would the demonstrations be called off. Under the compromise proposed by Kennedy and King, as Shuttlesworth recalls it, the demonstrations would end, with the understanding that white and black leaders would continue to negotiate on the four demands.

** He was reminding King of the criticisms which followed SCLC's less-than-triumphant withdrawal from Albany.

*** Sedative injections.

† An executive in A.G. Gaston's insurance firm. ". . . he was real personally close to Dr. King and Abernathy, even more so than me."

these middle-class people, . . . incidentally, friends of mine. I don't mean to disparage them. When we got out there Martin was lookin' out the window. Ralph was there. Rev. Gardner had me and my wife, and I was reelin' and rockin'. They shoulda come to my room, it seems to me, if there'da been some point [in the meeting]. We had been there for, oh, I guess, three or four minutes before anybody spoke, and I wondered what they wanted. Martin said, "Well, Fred, we've got"—and I really didn't intend for this to get into the books. The King Center has it,* and I will try to shorten it, but the truth is the light, you know.

I think it's important.

It is. It was tremendous pressure from the White House, all around. He said, "Well, Fred, we've got to call the demonstrations off." That shocked me. I said, . . . you know, when you're on them hypos you be doing like this [weaves, as if groggy], I said, "Say that again, Martin." He said, "We've got to call the demonstrations off."

I said, "Well . . ." I guess I'm gonna refuse to say everything, but I'll give you the nutshell. . . . I learned that Kennedy was prepared to make a joint press conference with Martin in Birmingham, callin' 'em off. And I said, "Well, Martin, when you came into Birmingham, you didn't ask President Kennedy. Burke Marshall and John Doar wasn't nowhere around. There were some people here who had confidence in me, 'cause they knew I wasn't gon' lie and wasn't gon' let 'em down."

I said, "And you and I promised that we would *not* stop demonstrating until we *had* the victory. Now, that's it. That's it." I said, "And if you call it off or Mr. Kennedy calls it off, with the last little ounce of strength I got, I'm gonna get back out and lead." We had the kids . . . 'bout three thousand of 'em in church. "I'm gon' lead the last demonstration with what last little ounce I have."

And of course, Ralph tried some of his soothing and grieving words— I love him—he said, "Fred, you know we went to school together." But I wasn't hearing anything like that. Fact, I wasn't—my language probably wasn't as sweet as it shoulda been, disturbed as I was that even they could be pushed to consider this.

Was it your impression that the President had gotten to Dr. King?

I think the President had, and Robert Kennedy. Martin had supreme respect for them, and Burke Marshall is very persuasive. So I said, "I'm

---

* The Martin Luther King, Jr., Center for Social Change in Atlanta, which is administered by King's widow. Its archives, which have not yet been opened, contain taped interviews with most of King's associates.

goin'." I said, "Now, you didn't even come see me at the hospital. I'm goin'." And I got—struggled up. Martin said, "Well, Burke, we just got to have unity."

I said, "Well, we don't have it like this." I said, "Now, you go ahead. You got your press conference." I said, "We wasn't supposed to have press conferences, 'cept joint. But if you got it, you go ahead and have it. I'm goin' back to my bed. I already given you my answer." And Martin said, "Well, wait, Fred, we cain't go like that."

There were some other words which I don't choose to say here. Burke Marshall then spoke up, said, "Well, I made promises to these people." And I asked him point blank, I said, "Burke, who gave you the authority to make any promises to any people without clearing it?" I said, "But if you made promises, you can go back now and tell 'em that the demonstrations'll be on, 'cause you cain't call 'em off, President Kennedy cain't call 'em off, and there's Martin Luther King—he cain't call 'em off." And I got up and left.

So we agreed, as a compromise, to announce limited demonstrations, sumpin' like that. It was a terrific thing, and that was the first time I think I really had seen Martin agonize like that. 'Cause I don't think that the man was a liar, I really don't. I have seen him talk in ways to make people think that he might would have done it another way, but I do not think that Martin Luther King, Jr., was a liar. I don't think that. I don't think that he . . .

[Interrupting] But you stood up to him on that issue?

Oh, yeah. Who, me? Oh man . . . I woulda died right there on that spot. No, sir.

Indeed, he had stuck to his decision so fiercely that before he left the meeting at the Drew residence, a call had been placed to Washington canceling the joint Kennedy-King press announcement. ". . . I heard John Doar. He was telephoning in the other room, sumpin' 'bout, 'We hit a snag—the frail one.' That's me. I was sick. 'The frail one is hanging up. Looks like it won't go through like that.'" Finally, late that night, it was decided that Shuttlesworth and King would announce on the next day, Friday, May 10, that the white merchants had agreed to their four demands in return for the cessation of demonstrations. As part of this compromise, the merchants were allowed ninety days within which to desegregate.

The merchants had agreed, and they had a black person ready for the cash register . . . they were gonna form this biracial committee and so forth. That's right, and I read the agreement. See, I insisted on reading that. You know I read it.

At the press conference. *

Oh, yeah. I was half wavering, but I read it. That's right. But that's the worst thing that happened . . . the most critical one, 'cause if we had ever called 'em off . . . we never could have done anything. And King's name would be mud now instead of immortal.

> *After Birmingham he seemed to drift away from his old comrades in the Southern Movement, perhaps because King's younger aides never quite forgave him for disputing their leader. He took a pastorate in Cincinnati, and although he retained the title of president of the Alabama Christian Movement for Human Rights, he was never again a leader in fact. Of course, the drama of Birmingham—and in particular, "The Letter from the Birmingham Jail"—established King once and for all as the spokesman for the Movement and for black America.*

> My feeling was that the letter should have been jointly signed by all of us . . . simply because we had agreed to do things together, you know. It wouldn't have taken anything for him to let me, but I guess as I look at it now . . . I think King deserves all the credit. . . . He was the spokesman, and he was the one that God had chose to be the charismatic person for that age, and you cain't argue against what God does, you know.

One name has to characterize a movement, a time, a period. That doesn't bother me at all. You see, I think the role that I played was so vital and so basic that King's name never would touch immortality had it not been for Birmingham. . . . Birmingham really made SCLC. In fact, when we went to the White House, Kennedy . . . used these words. If I ever write a book I'm gonna use that: "But for Birmingham, we would not be here today."

"But for Birmingham," I think that oughta be remembered. That's a good title. The only thing is, I'm a lazy writer. I'm not a writer, I'm a fighter.

* Held in the courtyard of the Gaston Motel.

SID SMYER

The stone mansion looks out over a dreaming landscape, the last blue foothills of the Appalachians. Here, just south of Birmingham, he is passing his eighth decade in the kind of retirement reserved for the wealthy. Summer mornings he devotes to puttering around the grounds. For the visitor who would get on with him, a tour of the garden is the mandatory first order of business. In it, laboring over his prized tomatoes, he restored himself from the near-fatal stroke he suffered after Birmingham's "troubles."

In those days, he had been the most influential man in Birmingham, influential enough to lead it into a new age. He did it grudgingly, but he did it, and therein lay the riddle. Why him? There was little in his background to point to the answer. He was, in fact, a Southern type, a gentlemanly segregationist. He had opposed the Klan in the twenties when it took to disrupting black church meetings and flogging Jews. Yet when the Dixiecrats walked out of the Democratic National Convention in 1948, he helped organize the dissident States Rights Convention that nominated Strom Thurmond for President. In the fifties, he sometimes showed up at Citizens Council rallies. He led a laymen's group opposing "radical attempts to break down Southern customs" in the Methodist Church.

Why then was he the one to lead Birmingham to what Dr. King had called "an accord with its conscience"? In the thousands of words writ-

ten about Birmingham, there had not been a satisfactory answer, because he kept to himself the story of his trip to Washington, D.C., in
that stormy spring of 1963.

Yessir, I was up there when Kennedy was President. They asked me
to come up there to tell what was going on. . . .

You went to Washington?

Yeah.

Who did you meet with?

President Kennedy. Just a few minutes though. . . . He wanted to
send troops in there, something like that, and I told him, no, that we
could work it out. And we did. We felt that putting it national would
affect not only Alabama, but it might spread. I don't think that's ever
been known. . . . I didn't want to go. But, of course, when the President sends for you and he wants to do it, you, I think, are under an obligation. . . .

Tell me more about your contact. . . .

President Kennedy had somebody to call me.* We talked on the telephone for some time about what was going on down there, and I told
him, and I'm sure that they reported it back to the President. I was then
asked to come up to the President. . . . I reported to him that we
didn't need any massive federal help. I use "federal help," I don't know
what he was going to send down there. . . .

Did he indicate he was thinking of sending something down?

Yes, in other words, if it was gonna be some more killing and a race
riot—I'm getting the right name now, a "race riot" here—well, he wanted
the government to step in there and prevent, if possible, any such thing
as that. Now, that's why I got mixed up with the Kennedys.

And did you offer him assurances?

Assurances, yeah . . . I was talking with the other fellows, discussed
with them, and we agreed that it would be a black eye to us to have to

* He later identified the caller as Robert Kennedy.

call on the President of the United States to run the city of Birmingham. And it would have been, to send soldiers or officers of a different kind down there.

So you agreed to work it out?

Yeah, well, I didn't agree. I said, "We're working it out. We're gonna work it out. Don't you worry."

What did you think of the man . . . ?

I think he was pretty smart, but he loved himself. Few people can stand the temptation of power or riches.

Did you feel like he was putting the screws on . . . ?

In a way, yes, but I think he had a right to do it, and I don't think we could complain at all about it. I'm gonna give him credit for this. I think he honestly wanted to know the depth of this thing. It really was, "Can you handle the situation?" and we told him, "Yes."

But he was also saying, "If you can't . . ."

"Can't, why we're gonna have to." I mean he told us—you said it—if we couldn't handle it, why, he was going to step in. And we sho' to God didn't want that. That would have been a black eye for us.

It wasn't known at the time the negotiations were going on that you had been up there.

No, no, no. Because that would have made things worse. . . .

It would have made it hard for you to operate?

Yes sir.

A lot of pressure during that time, wasn't there?

God, yeah.

Did you ever consider just walking off from it?

No. I like a good scrap. I've been called a son of a bitch plenty of times. [Laughs] But as long as I can live with myself, why, I'm all right.

After his meeting with the President, he convened the city's business leaders. Many of them who represented national firms had received calls from members of Kennedy's cabinet, urging them to cooperate with him. Out of that meeting came the plan to bypass Connor and the city government and reach a settlement with King.

I guess at that meeting was I expect nearly a hundred of 'em. The leading businessmen of Birmingham met and just talked it out and let it be known . . . that you were hurting Birmingham, you was hurting business, this, that, and the other. I think that was the climax. . . . We had a big meeting, and it wasn't any closed doors,* and person after person just got up and said, "Gentlemen, we've got to get this thing straight." Sidney Smyer didn't have any more to do with it. I mean that was just the feeling. Well, you might say it was a dollar-and-cents thing. [Laughs] If we're going to have a good business in Birmingham, we better change our way of living.

But you were the one that had to step forward as the person whose name was identified.

Well, yes. I don't claim any honor. [A long pause] Listen, I came up the hard way, and I knew what it was to be on the low-down side.

That big meeting was May the seventh and then that night a group of you met privately with King and the others, I believe.

Yeah. [Barely audible] I told him to get out of Birmingham as soon as he could.

You did what?

Told him to get out of Birmingham as soon as he could.

What did he say?

* Here, he is being inaccurate and too modest. The initial meetings were confidential, because most whites would not attend otherwise. He was the first, and for a long while the only, white businessman willing to let his name be used as endorsing the accord with the black leaders.

We didn't say so much. I mean, we didn't say it that way, . . . 'cause if we had, King wouldn't have done right. Gaston* was there and helped. I mean, Gaston wasn't a friend of King. . . . Some of the Negroes did most of the talking to King . . . "We can handle this now."

Only thing we wanted to do was get that shooting and all that—I mean, hate—that was just ruining us. I mean, it got pretty rough. . . . I didn't feel happy about living up here and didn't know when somebody was going to throw a stick of dynamite or something here in my house. I wanted some peace, too [laughs], and that's the honest truth. I suppose I oughtn't to say it.

You were chiefly concerned with business?

Yeah, sure. Hell, damn company that I was with was the company that formed Birmingham. I was very much interested.

And you saw the demonstrations had pretty well ground business to a halt?

Gosh, yeah. We *did* have a depression back in those days.

Postscript: An unexpected revelation: He and the other white leaders made a secret deal with "Bull" Connor. If he would withdraw permanently from city politics, they would help him get elected to the Public Service Commission, which sets utility rates in Alabama. Connor served there until his death in 1973, voting consistently for higher electrical rates for all Alabama consumers, black and white alike.

* Gaston, the black millionaire, was often cited by Birmingham segregationists as living proof that there were no barriers to black success in the city. His stance on civil rights was ambiguous. He was said to have misgivings about SCLC's tactics, but he provided the organization free rooms in his motel. His home, too, was bombed, proving, civil rights leaders said, that even the mildest and most moderate of black men were not safe in Birmingham.

BEN ALLEN
AND GLENN V. EVANS

Two Cops

Ben Allen is big, craggy-faced, a tough cop from Central Casting. He was sent to Birmingham in 1949 by racially moderate Governor "Big Jim" Folsom to investigate the bombings in the black residential neighborhood on "Dynamite Hill."

BEN ALLEN: They was very prevalent up there in that time. It was nothing to blow up a house or blow up a motel, scare people.

Did you ever solve any [bombings]?

After the fact, not during the investigation. Only in later years did I hear about [information] that would have solved 'em had I known about it at that time. . . . I've even solved some of 'em after gettin' out of law enforcement.

Could you give me an example of one you solved?

I had a interview in the state of Georgia since my retirement with the former number-one Klansman in Alabama, who stated that former Commissioner "Bull" Connor had paid five hundred dollars to git Reverend Shuttlesworth's church dynamited in Birmingham. In his statement, he stated that Connor was running for office and wanted to stir up people to have an issue so he could get reelected, which is what happened. So he told me who the man was that did the dynamitin', how much he got paid, and that the man later told *him* about dynamitin' it, along with some places in Clinton, Tennessee, some schoolhouses. Back, if you recall, about that time, there were schoolhouses bein' dynamited in Tennessee.

Did you ever turn up other evidence of Connor being behind the bombings?

Nothin' that was that concrete. There had always been a suspicion on account of several things that happened: his close connection with "Dynamite Bob,"* as he was referred to in Birmingham, a former city employee with the city of Birmingham, who seemed to be a protégé of Connor.

This person that you're talking about, Connor's protégé, were there instances of Connor protecting him?

Yes. Would you like for me to describe 'em the same as I did while ago?

He had insisted on a long preliminary interview without tape recorder. During it, he told of a Klan officer and informant who responded with a riddle when asked to name the man behind the "Dynamite Hill" bombings. The Klansman said, "Find out who Dynamite Bob's friends are." He knew that this was the Klansman's way of answering the question without violating the Klan oath by actually naming the person. The Klansman even told him and his partner how to go about solving the riddle.

We were told by the then number-two Klansman that if we wanted to solve the bombing in Birmingham . . . to arrest Matthews and put him in [the Birmingham] jail and go eat lunch, come back, and see what happened. We did. We came back. We was refused an interview with our prisoner. We went to the chief of police who explained that he'd never done anything like that before, but he could not allow us to see our prisoner we had placed in jail because he was "hired out." In other

---

* To be known here by the pseudonym Robert Matthews.

ords, he was tellin' us that he was under orders from "Bull" Connor
ot to let us interview Robert Matthews at that time and place, which
arried out the point to what the number-two Klansman had told
s. . . .

Is it your theory that Connor incited the Klan . . . ?

There was an instance at one time back when we were fightin' the
lan. I say fightin'. We were tryin' to get to the bottom of it to stop
ome of the violence that was being conducted at that time by the Klan.
here was a bill that Senator Mize,* from Tuscaloosa, was plannin' on
assin' to disrobe the Klan—not disrobe 'em, unmask 'em. They had a
alled meeting behind the slag mill at TCI** for the Klan. We borrowed
robe and attended this meetin'. Commissioner Connor was very much
a evidence at that meeting. He got on top of a car and was makin' a
peech. It seems as though the Klan wanted to go to Tuscaloosa to take
Mize out to whip him. I don't know whether Senator Mize was ever
ware of this or not. But there were hundreds of Klansmen there that
ight, and they were gonna ride to Tuscaloosa and take Senator Mize
ut and either whip or kill him, whatever it took to get the job done.
ut Commissioner Connor prevailed on 'em not to do that. In his favor
ow, I will have to say that he talked 'em out of goin' down to bother
enator Mize, but he was very much evident at that meeting that night.

Was it a standard practice of his to go to Klan meethings?

This is the only time to my knowledge that I know that he was at a
lan meeting.

How did you go about getting information from inside the Klan?

[Laughs] Man, that's a hard one. When Governor Folsom sent us to
irmingham, we were on orders from the governor's office to break up
e Klan in Alabama. This was in 1949. I didn't know a thing in the
orld about the Klan, or neither did the other three state investigators.
/e hit on the idea—I don't know whether they would care to admit it or
ot—so I'll just use my name. I hit on the idea of fightin' fire with fire.
/e kept on 'til we found out who we suspected of bein' a Klan member.

* State Senator Henry Mize, a moderate.
** Tennessee Coal and Iron, the Southern subsidiary of U.S. Steel and Birming-
am's largest employer, supported Connor and other reactionary politicians in both
e city and state governments.

We went to the mule barn, and I don't think this story has ever been told. I know it hadn't been told for publication. [Laughs] We went to White's Mule Barn in Birmingham and got us a horsehide whip. We went to this man's house, got him out, carried him to the woods, handcuffed him around a hickory tree and told him that we was tired of them whippin' on ex-GIs, and we started to administerin' the leather. [Laughs] When we left there we had the password and the robes and the cards, and this man moved to California. [Laughs] So you ought not to ask me how we found out. That's how I got the robe to go to the meetin' to see Connor. [Laughs] I had forgotten about that.

Is that in the police practices handbook?

Oh, no. [Laughs] And I'm sure Governor Folsom wouldn't have approved of it, but we did accomplish our purpose. We found out a little somethin' about the Klan, because thereafter we got to knowin' how to converse with members of the Klan and got to attend several meetings and heard what was fixin' to happen. It wound up that we arrested several folks in the Birmingham area.

If you go right back to it, I was the first man since the early twenties to get convictions outa the Klan or members of the Klan. Since the *twenties*. The first conviction being that "Judge" Aaron case where they emasculated that colored fella in Birmingham.

He recalls the case: On Labor Day of 1957, six white men kidnapped Edward "Judge" Aaron, a thirty-four-year-old black veteran. In a cinderblock cabin on the outskirts of Birmingham, they cut away Aaron's scrotum and testicles with a razor blade, poured turpentine on the wound, hauled him away in a car trunk, and finally threw him out on the side of the road. Only because passing motorists happened to report to police a "bloody Negro" staggering down the road was Aaron taken to a hospital before he bled to death.

Well . . . I suppose I can tell it now. There were several things about the Klan that bein' a Southerner, natural-born—some of their ideas I'd go along with. Others I wouldn't. When that particular thing happened, the "Judge" Aaron thing, I went to the number-two or number-three Klansman in the state, and I explained to him over coffee that I had a gut feeling that they were involved in that, and I was puttin' him on notice that I was gonna investigate that victim. Now I'm being brutally frank. . . . If they had just cause to do somethin' like that, it might be a hard case to crack. But if they didn't have just cause, they'd better find 'em a damn rock to git under, because I was gonna git 'em. . . .

Now what I specifically had in mind . . . I was gonna investigate whether or not this man *had* done anything to instill in them the desire to do this man the way he was done, in other words, rapin' one of their sisters or one of their daughters or sumpin' like this. . . . The subject came from Union Springs, Alabama. I went down there and investigated him for a week and found out that he was a high-type individual that was a good citizen, although he was black and he was poor. . . . N'other words, he was referred to in Union Springs as a "white folks's nigger." They had no reason whatsoever to do this man this way. So I went back and told that Klansman, I said, "Just like I told you, ya'll better find you a damn rock to crawl under because I'm gonna gitchya." And I did.

Four of the Klansmen, convicted on the testimony of two who turned state's evidence, went to prison in 1959 to start twenty-year sentences. The State Board of Pardons and Paroles ruled that they would have to serve one-third of their sentences before being eligible for paroles. In January, 1963, George Wallace took office as governor. In July, 1963, two weeks after Wallace's first appointee joined the parole board, the one-third ruling was set aside. In October, 1963, the first of the four Klansmen walked out of prison.

Glenn V. Evans is a captain of police, a slender, thoughtful man, intensely religious. By 1975 he had been shuffled into a neighborhood precinct to finish out his last year on the force. But in 1963 he was commander of the uniform patrol division of the nation's most notorious police department. His sharpest memory is of a conversation with another captain on one of those tumultuous May days when they "were busily engaged in arresting large numbers of people."

GLENN V. EVANS: We arrested hundreds of school children who were parading in the streets, and we had to transport these people in school buses to the city jail, and to the juvenile courts. My fellow captain made this statement to me, and it has stuck with me ever since. He said, "Evans, ten or fifteen years from now, we will look back on this and we will say, 'How stupid can you be?'"

And sure enough, we looked back on it and we said to ourselves, "How stupid can you be?"

Did you think in 1963 that you'd ever be saying that?

No. Some other things happened to me along about this same time
which caused me to stop and think and to reappraise my own personal
attitude. Not exclusively the attitude of a police officer, but also as a
human being. I was assigned at one time before our demonstration
difficulties . . . on what we call the evening shift, three to eleven. I was
riding the transit bus from my home out here in the eastern part of Birmingham downtown, and at some point between where I got on the bus
and downtown, I saw a Negro woman—young, probably in her twenties,
accompanied by a little boy, as I remember now, probably three or four
years old—get on the bus. At that time, everyone got on the bus at the
same front entrance, but the seating was segregated. The little boy got
on first. His mother helped him up, and then she had to stop and pay
the driver her fare and get her change, and during that interval the little
boy sat down on the seat in front of me. When she got her change and
came back, she grabbed the little boy by the hand and she said
[sharply], "Come on, you can't sit there." Well . . . [His voice breaks.
His eyes fill with tears. After a long pause, he continues with difficulty.]
I ought not to try to repeat this story because I can't do it. I'm sorry.
Well, it did something to me just as a human being, not as a police
officer. I said to myself, "Where are we going with this? What's happening here? How do you explain to a child?"

And I came to the conclusion there wasn't any way to explain
it . . . . What's going to happen later when this child remembers this incident? And children *do* remember. . . . The mother accepted it, I
guess, somewhat philosophically: This is the way of life in Birmingham,
Alabama; this is what you do. But that thing has haunted me ever since.

You see, I had this experience prior to our demonstrations, so I guess
maybe I approached the demonstration difficulties with a somewhat
slightly different attitude from the average police officer. But I was still
under the control of my chief of police and my commissioner of public
safety and the other political leaders of the community, and I was still
under the influence of the community to maintain the status quo. . . .

*Did Connor . . . actively encourage a negative view or brutal treat-
ment of blacks?*

I can't truthfully state that Mr. Connor ever advocated actual brutal
treatment, but, you see, you don't have to enunciate these things. If you
just condone them, if the officer knows that he is not going to be harshly
dealt with, then he has a feeling that this is in effect some kind of, if not

order, permission. So there was brutality. I know that there has been brutality. I have myself participated in brutality. That's one way that I *really* know, and I don't have to take anybody else's word for it, because I have been present and have participated in it myself. God forgive, but the truth is the truth.

Was there any preparation of the force in terms of training sessions or this sort of thing?

Practically none. At that time . . . our management was really a crisis-type management. We waited until we had the situation to try to cope with it. We know that's the worst kind of management. Management by crisis is the worst kind. So that's really what we did.

You were in essence in command of troops who were not prepared psychologically?

They were not prepared psychologically, philosophically. They were . . . quite taken by surprise that this thing would happen, and they were not—well, they were not really prepared fully from a tactical point of view. Our equipment, our riot control equipment was practically nil. We had very little. And I'm pleased—I was pleased later—that we came out of it with as few casualties as we did. It was a kind of surprise to me in a way that we did not have more casualties, more injuries.

On both sides?

Probably on both sides, but my greatest surprise was because of the low casualties on the part of police officers, received by the police officers. I would not have been surprised had there been more casualties in the ranks of the black demonstrators. . . .

How did the decision come about, where did the decision come from to use dogs and later firehoses?

From the top management. From the commissioner of public safety. The dogs, in my opinion, are a useful segment of policing. I think that K-9 corps, where they have been properly established and properly trained and properly supervised, are probably a wonderful adjunct to the police system. But unfortunately, our K-9 corps did not fall in that category. . . .

Would it be up to the superior officer on the scene to decide when to use the hoses and this sort of thing? I'm interested in why this was done and how it was done.

I never personally gave an order to use a firehose. Never. These orders were given by people superior to me, and I believe that they probably were given by the political leaders.

By Commissioner Connor?

Yes . . . On one occasion I recall very vividly, the police were at the intersection of Sixth Avenue and Sixteenth Street . . . where the Sixteenth Street Baptist Church is located. And there had been demonstrations that day and large congregations of black people, and they had assembled back at the Sixteenth Street Baptist Church. They were milling all 'round on the outside, on the sidewalk and on the steps, and the firehoses were brought into play and they were literally washed into the church. At one point, after it seemed that everything was pretty well over, one of the black leaders, and I believe that it was Rev. Fred Shuttlesworth, came out of the church on the Sixth Avenue side and walked around the corner and was walking north on Sixteenth Street, and the firehose was put on him and he was knocked awinding, so to speak.* His feet were knocked out from under him. And I had the thought at that time, what's the purpose of this, why was this done? . . .

I was standing right there beside the firehose, and whether it was a direct order to the fireman manning the hose or not, the firehose was put on him, and his feet were knocked out from under him. And I just, unconsciously I guess, said to myself, "What does this accomplish? What do we *hope* to do here by doing these kind of things?" Now the practical end result was that the fire department went in and pumped every drop of water out of the basement of that church.

That same day?

That same day. So it becomes more and more apparent: How stupid can you be?

You asked me previously about who gave the orders. At the same time that the police were attempting to deal with this situation, the State of Alabama also took an interest in it. The state trooper organization at

* This incident led to the hospitalization described by Shuttlesworth. He suffered chest injuries.

this time was led by—or *headed* by—a man named Al Lingo.* Mr. Lingo, as I recall, was a political appointee of Governor Wallace. Mr. Lingo was a staunch segregationist, as were many of his people, and they on more than one occasion injected themselves into the local troubles without being invited, without being asked. So, you see, the chief of police had more than one worry on his mind. He was not only worried about what was happening to the city. He was worried also about what the state troopers might do under Mr. Lingo's direction.

BEN ALLEN: Oh . . . some of the things Lingo would do none of the career law enforcement officers approved of whatsoever. In fact, it's never been made known to my knowledge, but during the uprisin' or whatever you want to call it at Birmingham there in the park during '63, several meetings were held in which numerous officers threatened to just walk off . . . commanding officers, captains, majors . . . on account of Lingo. It would have been very interesting had all the commandin' officers walked off and left it to Brother Lingo. . . . He came as close to ruinin' the Department of Public Safety in Alabama as anybody ever has, the type persons he would get on. He'd get some out there that couldn't read or write. He would insist that they be placed on.

As patrolmen?

As patrolmen . . . All of the older officers, career officers, knew this, and some of the things that these new people were doin' at Lingo's suggestions was turning the stomachs of these officers. As a result, several meetings were held in which the career officers threatened to walk off, every one of 'em. And there were only one or two that managed to hold 'em together.

What were some of the things that they were rebelling against or upset about?

Well, one thing that flashes to my memory is a preacher, I think he was from Toledo, Ohio. One Sunday morning he was at the park, standin' a block away, takin' a picture with a box camera. Lingo happened to glance down there and see the man. He dispatched a couple of his followers down there to "bring me that SOB." They ran down there and

* The late Al Lingo, a native of George Wallace's home county, piloted Wallace's airplane during the 1961 campaign. When Wallace won, he appointed Lingo the state's chief law enforcement officer. Lingo designated the highway patrolmen "state troopers" and gave himself the title of colonel.

got the man and brought him back up there. The man was frightened to death. Lingo was standin' there with all his scrambled eggs on his cap and probably with a stick in his hand. He wanted to know what the man meant takin' his picture. He said, "I didn't mean any harm, Colonel." He said, "I was comin' through from Florida with my family on the way to Ohio." And said, "This has all been on the radio and television, thought we'd stop by." And said, "This is just a little old box camera. I was just takin' a picture."

Lingo said, "Well, you so and so, you didn't get my permission to take a picture," and he grabbed the thing out of his hand, the camera out of his hand and threw it to the sidewalk and stomped on it. Well, this turned the stomach of all the career law enforcement officers because he violated ever' law in the book by doin' the man this away. . . .

Tell me a little about the caliber of men Lingo brought in.

Sorriest individuals that's ever been employed by the State of Alabama, he brought in. Wasn't fit to be highway patrolmen. He insisted on them bein' made highway patrolmen, and did more to downgrade the highway patrol than anybody ever has or ever will, in my estimation.

How did he get 'em hired?

That's a good question. Just by tellin' folks to put 'em on. How he got by the merit system, I'll never know.

You mentioned in passing that some of them couldn't read and write. Was that literally true or just a manner of speaking?

The major in charge of the Police Academy told me that he had attempted to give an examination to a recruit who could not read nor write. He discharged the student and was told by Lingo to put that man back to work, back in school, and to see that he made passin' grades. You could do a whole book on Lingo.

What sorts of duties would he assign them?

Regular trooper duties. Some of 'em was body guardin' him, carryin' Thompson submachine guns.

Was he paranoid about being—

Oh, was he? Paranoid, period. Paranoid, period. Takin' pills by the handful.

What kind?

Just a whole handful of tranquilizers. I know right at the outset of the outbreak in Birmingham, I was assigned the detail of goin' down there and observin' everything that was happenin' in the park. And at intervals two or three times a day, it was my job to call Lingo to advise him as to what was happenin' at the park. Almost every day or every telephone conversation he'd say, "Well, are you ready for us to come in?" And I'd say, "No, sir, don't think you need to yet. It hasn't got out of hand with the law enforcement officers up here yet. They're doin' a good job of handlin' it." "Well . . . call me in the morning." I'd call him back. "Ready for us to come in?" "No, sir."

Well, he was workin' hisself up to a fever pitch. Finally after a while, he said, "Well, I'm comin' up there anyhow today. I wanna talk to you." I went off up there to his motel room in Birmingham. He said, "What's happening?" I said, "Well, a little incident happened down there today. Somebody threw some plaster or somethin' off of a building at some officers." He jumped out of that bed, and he said, "Well, what would you do? What would you do if somebody threw some stuff like that at you or some of yo' men?" I said, "Well, I'd designate a couple of men to go up and get 'em, put 'em in jail."

"By God, that's what's the matter with this outfit now. I wouldn't." I said, "Well, what would you do, Colonel?" He said, "I'd shoot them goddamn son-bitches, that's what I'd do." I said, "Just for throwin' a little plaster?" "You damn right. That's what I'd do. You damn people just too easy on them people." And that was his attitude. . . .

He watched as Lingo brought in a force of eight hundred troopers. Armed with sawed-off shotguns, they were patrolling the streets when the accord of Friday, May 10, was announced. On Saturday Lingo called a meeting of his staff and announced that he was ordering the troopers back to their home stations unless someone knew of a strong reason for them to remain in Birmingham. Ben Allen spoke up, urging that the troopers be allowed to patrol the city through the weekend.

I had information that the Gaston Motel in Birmingham was gonna be dynamited at a given hour from an informer that had never given me wrong information before. . . . But they didn't take it too seriously, and in fact, that place was dynamited that night, as per my information.

What was Lingo's response?

[Softly] That he could take care of ———.

What inference did you draw from that?

——— was then the head of the Klans in Alabama. Draw your own conclusions.

*The Klan held a rally outside Birmingham on Saturday afternoon.
After nightfall he grew increasingly apprehensive. He went to the home
of a state senator and told him about the warning he had given Lingo.
As they drank coffee in the senator's kitchen, the window rattled in its
frame, as if from a strong gust of wind. "I said, 'There's your bomb.'"
The rioting in the black neighborhoods lasted all night. By daylight the
troopers had been recalled and were once more patrolling the streets
around the Gaston Motel. They had been gone just long enough to
allow for a safe planting of the bomb.*

Chuck Morgan

He is a white lawyer, reared in Birmingham and educated at the University of Alabama. He was practicing in Birmingham in 1963.

Birmingham was a tragedy in the sense that it was like all of history conspired to make Alabama the center of the Civil Rights Movement, which was fine except Alabama could not react in the manner that it should have reacted, there were so many defaults down the line.

I was involved in the University of Alabama desegregation case and, to a degree, in the Birmingham negotiations. I went to one meeting, one of the early [negotiating] sessions just before King violated the court order from the state court judge. I don't want to go into particular names, but I remember the meeting very well. It was at the Church of the Advent. . . . The reason I'd been called and invited to go to the meeting—even though . . . it was a secret meeting—was that some of the white people, one or more of them there, would feel secure if I were present, because they didn't feel like Martin King would disclose me being present in the meeting.* Therefore, my presence in the meeting was helping some of the white people, because they didn't feel like they personally would be exposed for sitting down with "the niggers," as they

---

* On the theory that he and King were friends and King would not want to create problems for him by making it appear he was overly friendly to blacks.

would put it. As I recall, Fred Shuttlesworth was there, Andy Young, and I think Martin's brother was there, too, Smith,* a few others from the Birmingham black community, as well as some whites. And I kind of like air conditioning, I don't get cold easy, and Shuttlesworth was cold, so I took my coat and gave it to him. It was one of those cord coats, and I remember the fellow sitting across the table when I gave Shuttlesworth my coat . . . I didn't want the air conditioning turned down, or rather, turned up. . . . The look on his face! He looked across the table and he says and I quote, "Tell me, what is it that you niggers want?" End quote.

And at that point, I just said, "Well, one thing—probably they don't want to be called niggers."

> *He speaks of his admiration of the black leaders' courage in tackling Birmingham, "a place that was looked upon as like Johannesburg, South Africa, in the black community."*

> It was not a rational movement. Most of the people who were participants now rationalize it. That's what happens with all of history: when historians come they make it rational, looking back at it. . . . The human mind works that way, but it wasn't that rational. There was a split in the Birmingham black community about whether King should come in at all or not, or whether demonstrations should occur there. Martin himself had several great defeats along the way. . . . See, there are always rational reasons not to do these things . . . but Martin was moving forward always.

> *Nor was the opposition to the Movement rational. One of its irrational acts profoundly changed Chuck Morgan's life.*

Birmingham was seen as an extraordinarily tough town, because you had fifty—I guess over a period of years, more than fifty—bombings which had gone unsolved. When you have that many unsolved bombings then you know it's a community rather than a single set of citizens' acts. It's community approval. I mean, all the Bourbons used to talk badly about the Klan, but the Klan was just the shock troopers, the guerilla warriors for preservation of the order. That allowed for the leading citizens who were segregationists to condemn the acts and the others to perform the natural result of their philosophy. . . .

But it is difficult to describe the community in those years. People would call about their phones being tapped, and my ordinary response was that if everybody's got a phone tapped in this town who thinks

* Nelson Smith, a black minister from Birmingham.

they've got a phone tapped, then there's nobody left to talk because they're all out listening. For whites and blacks in the Civil Rights Movement . . . [there were] lawsuits . . . the fear engendered by violence, and then, of course, the [Sixteenth Street] church bombing, and then I left after that. That was the end, that to me was the absolute unthinkable, and the reaction to it was stunned endorsement. . . .

Why did you characterize the reaction to the church bombing as "stunned endorsement"?

Well, I watched television that night, and I thought to myself, "My God, nobody seems to be concerned with anything other than 'it was the act of a lone person.'" Well, of course, it was. I mean, hell, most acts are the acts of a lone person. The Third Army didn't run in and shoot John Kennedy or Robert Kennedy or Martin King. That doesn't mean it's just a lone person.

As I watched television along the way, I thought to myself that that [bombing] was a natural kind of conclusion to what was going on for the fifteen days before that. Wallace had made his schoolhouse-door stand in the summer.* But in the fall, uncontent, Wallace had to move again.**

First, Tuskegee—a decent school superintendent had worked out desegregation in the community. He spoke to the Rotary Club . . . he chatted about it across the board, and he about had things all worked out in the community for peaceful orderly desegregation under a court order. And lo and behold, that morning, as I recall it, in early September, the state troopers walk up to the front door and bang on his house, and they are there to take over. We had a confrontation there.

In Birmingham it's Al Lingo, and a confrontation in Huntsville. The people in Huntsville were saying, "Wallace, stay out." In Birmingham . . . for those fifteen days before the September fifteenth church bombing, you would almost have thought it was like an army coming forward, coming into the community. You find community leaders . . . "Stay out. Stay out."***

* See the Higher Education sequence.
** Wallace's policy, little remembered outside Alabama, was to send state troopers to seize control of school systems in his name if local officials agreed to obey federal court orders to desegregate. After the Tuskegee incident, he threatened to seize control of the schools in Birmingham and Huntsville.
*** After the bombing, Sid Smyer was quoted as laying the blame squarely on Wallace and his policy of intervention in local affairs: "There wouldn't have been any trouble if Wallace had stayed out. Why did he do it? Why didn't he let us alone?"

Each day's headlines were the kind of headlines that set things loose. And then came September fifteenth . . . it wasn't just those four kids in that church. There were three other people killed that day around the state, on bikes or wherever they were.

And beyond that then, came the immediate community reaction. Questions as to whether somebody was going to go to the funeral or not. Or, "What was the mayor's role?" Or, "Where was the leadership?" As I recall watching that night, the sheriff and the police chief were on the air, and it was just like "Let us pray." But we were praying for the wrong things. The reaction was exactly the reaction, of course, that occurs often in a community of, "Oh, God, why did it happen here? It will hurt the community's image."

And that reaction was immediate and instinctive. It operated throughout. At the funeral, they took pictures of everyone attending. The efforts to solve the crime have come to no fruition as of our speaking today. They might later. . . .* I was of the belief then and I am of the belief now that that bombing was as natural an event in the history of that city . . . as any other event in American history. You see, there are times when communities and nations and people are guilty . . . and why I think what I think about the city of Birmingham endorsing it is laid out pretty well in that talk.

*"That talk" changed his life forever. He had grown up in Alabama and dabbled in politics since his law student days in Tuscaloosa. Among his friends, it was taken for granted that he would someday run for governor. He said good-bye to all that on the Monday after the bombing when he spoke before the segregated meeting of the Young Men's Business Club, the city's most "progressive" civic club. His speech.***

Four little girls were killed in Birmingham yesterday. A mad, remorseful, worried community asks, "Who did it? Who threw that bomb? Was it a Negro or a white? . . ."

* This remark may have been prophetic. A few months after this interview the attorney general of Alabama announced the reopening of the investigation into the Sixteenth Street Church bombing. The new investigation was touched off by testimony of a former Klansman during the Senate Intelligence Committee's 1975 inquiry into FBI practices during the Hoover era. The Klansman, a paid FBI informant at the time of the bombing, gave committee investigators the names of Birmingham Klansmen he said had knowledge of the bombing.

** As quoted in *Life* magazine, "Birmingham: An Alabaman's Great Speech Lays the Blame" (September 27, 1963).

But you know the "who" of "Who did it?" is really rather simple. The "who" is every little individual who talks about the "niggers" and spreads the seeds of his hate to his neighbor and his son. The jokester, the crude oaf whose racial jokes rock the party with laughter. The "who" is every governor who ever shouted for lawlessness and became a law violator. . . .

Who is really guilty? Each of us. Each citizen who has not consciously attempted to bring about peaceful compliance with the decisions of the Supreme Court; each citizen who has ever said, "They ought to kill that nigger." Every person in this community who has in any way contributed to the popularity of hatred is at least as guilty, or more so, as the demented fool who threw that bomb.

What's it like living in Birmingham? No one ever really has and no one will until this city becomes part of the United States.

Birmingham is not a dying city. It is dead.

When you decided to make that speech, had you pretty well made up your mind that that would lead to your moving?

I wasn't thinking of any of that, I don't believe. The event itself was of such a nature that I was sitting there that night watching the buffoonery on television of "Let us pray." The next morning in the office, just writing it out and going over things, there wasn't much thought about that. It wasn't conscious anyway. Just wait and see. I mean, there wasn't anybody else saying anything. That's the best example of endorsement I know of. I mean, hell, I'm just a lawyer in town. You had a mayor, a county commission, two newspapers, television stations, a myriad of industrial and business leaders; every damn one of 'em had a better forum or audience than I did, and if that ain't an endorsement by silence, I don't know what is.

After his speech, a member of the Young Men's Business Club moved that the club admit a black member. The motion died on the floor. His speech made the New York Times, Life *magazine. A few weeks later he left Birmingham. He wrote an article for* Look, *"I Watched a City Die," and a book,* A Time to Speak. *He became director of the Atlanta office of the American Civil Liberties Union and in 1973 he moved to Washington as director of the ACLU office there. He resigned that job in 1976 when his superiors in the organization reprimanded him for speaking out in favor of Jimmy Carter's presidential candidacy.*

Chris McNair

Aftermath

He is a professional photographer in Birmingham. His daughter Denise died in the Sixteenth Street Church bombing.

It doesn't hurt me necessarily to talk about it, but I don't talk about it on my own. Number one, I personally would think that people would think that I'm in a roundabout way asking for some sympathy. Number two, you have to be very careful. People will use such things to try to exploit you. I never will forget going to Portland, you know, when I was on the team to help make Birmingham an All-American City.

The All-American City competition was conducted by Look *magazine. In 1971 Birmingham was among the cities invited to send a delegation to Portland, Oregon, to make a presentation before* Look's *jurors.*

One of the persons who approached me about going to Portland to make the presentation said that it would be a "real nice trip." . . . I think that he thought that I accepted it that way, and I also think that the people—the power structure—who were pushing my going thought that I was too naive to know why they wanted me to go.

And I had some real serious thoughts about the thing. But I decided to go, not to satisfy them. I doubt that they realize that till this day. But I decided to because at that time, every time you heard something about Birmingham, it was bad. And I have a crazy philosophy that if you tell a person often enough, forcefully enough, and demeaning enough that he ain't nothin', that somewhere down the line, he kinda begins to believe that he ain't nothin'.

I honestly believed . . . that if I could do something by going out there that would help Birmingham—and when I say Birmingham, I mean the general area—to not be looked down on, but to be looked up to, that then I wouldn't just be pleasing those power magnates who wanted me to go. But that if it made it better for the whole city, then it would be better for all people. . . . I made one or two remarks that weren't in the prepared presentation that they didn't know I was going to make, nobody knew I was going to do so, that I really think may have turned the thing . . . caused Birmingham to be an All-American City.*

What comes to mind when you think of the particular day of the bombing itself?

Hypocrisy.

Why do you say that?

Well, it was on Sunday, wasn't it? It was in a church, wasn't it? They didn't ever indict anybody, not to mention convicting somebody. They never did indict anybody. During that time—I'm not convinced how it really would be even in this time—but during that time, had she at eleven—that's how old she was—had she innocently gone to a church in a white area with the same denominational ties, the chances are almost one hundred percent that she would have been escorted out. . . . There was a lot of hypocrisy involved.

Would you apply that description to the response of the city, white Birmingham, I mean?

I would think so . . . I don't think that the average citizen would want it to happen at anybody's church, but I also think that as long as

---

* Largely on the basis of its improved race relations, Birmingham was designated one of *Look*'s All-American Cities for 1971. Long after the magazine went out of business, the city of Birmingham was still using the appellation on its promotional literature.

the average citizens were condoning the kind of government that we had at that time, then I think they were just as guilty as anybody else.

Postscript: In 1973 he was elected to the Alabama House of Representatives and in 1975 chosen by his colleagues as chairman of the Birmingham-area House delegation.

Part Two: Selma

"Well, Lord, here I am"

ALBERT TURNER

You picked a bad day to try to interview me. I got in bed this morning at five, and I was up at nine and back out again. My routine for the last two or three weeks has been like that. Several days I didn't get to bed at all. We're trying to get the cucumbers sold right now.

A portly man, shiny black, he lowers himself wearily into a swivel chair and unlaces work shoes which are coated with dust from the fields of the Southwest Alabama Farmers' Cooperative Association. SWAFCA, which has its offices and loading sheds midway between Selma and Marion, is one of the success stories of black enterprise in Alabama. He says its very existence is a tribute to the Movement's struggle in the Black Belt.

There has been really a change here. Things ain't what we'd like to see, but let's face it. It ain't ten years ago. I'll be forty my birthday next and I don't need to ask nobody if there has been a change. . . . The mere fact that I'm the manager here is a big thing. There were days when a person with my type of reputation and so forth just couldn't survive in this kind of organization because of the political pressure. . . . They just wouldn't allow it.

He began making his reputation when he returned to Marion, his hometown, in the early sixties.

I was a college graduate, a young fellow who thought I had enough intelligence to at least pass a voter registration test, and they gave us all kind of runarounds, gave us all kinds of tests. . . .

They had tests asking how many words in the Constitution, what side the moon was on, any kind of silliness. I'm serious, it was all kinds of jive. They got so bad once after we started trying to learn how to pass the tests . . . they decided then they'd make up a book of tests with about three or four hundred tests in it. You'd walk up to the desk, and they'd tell you to open the book, and whatever page you opened the book on, that would be your test, and this was fixed where you never would be able to pass the test. You couldn't learn all the tests in the book. . . . We knew exactly what it really was.

And, of course, in the latter part of '64 and early '65, Dr. King and them recognized also the plight of the voter registration movement here in the South, and they came to town. The Student Nonviolent Coordinating Committee came to town out of Mississippi. . . . After they started in Selma, they came to Marion also to help us organize there for a massive voter registration thing. So we recognized that we weren't going to get registered to vote really through the normal procedure of court actions and knocking on the door and trying to pass tests and all that. We recognized that . . . so we decided to go to direct action, and on the first Monday in February, 1965, we organized a mass voter registration drive, and we took about three-hundred people into the courthouse that day to get registered. We decided we were going to stay in there until we registered them, and we marched down there. That was the first march we ever had.

Was that your first march?

Yeah, my first march, too. . . . I was considered at that point as the local leader of the community, so as the local leader of the community I led the line down to the courthouse that day, and we went down and we stayed in the courthouse all day that day, and they didn't register nobody. . . . I guess we went back every day from then on. . . . We met day and night and we marched and we demonstrated—what we called demonstrating—day and night, and it went on for about two weeks.

And of course, the powers that be felt that they had to do something to stop us because they saw our determination, and at that point, they decided that they would organize a bunch of state troopers and send them into Marion to give us all a good whipping. And this happened on the nineteenth, I believe, February eighteenth or nineteenth, something like that. And it was one of those systems where they would beat us up, and we were supposed to stop after the good whipping. That was the theory at that time. So they did.

They sent in maybe a couple of hundred state troopers with nothing in mind but a good whipping, and we had planned a night march. They knew this. They had put James Orange in jail at that time. That was one of the civil rights leaders from SCLC. So they knew we was going to march to the jail that night to protest James' arrest, and their plans were to beat us up that night. They did just that. Probably one of the most vicious situations that was in the whole Civil Rights Movement. Most people don't know that, but it was worse in my opinion than the day on the bridge in Selma. And I was in both of them. But one of the major reasons that thing was so bad that night, they shot the lights out, and nobody was able to report what really happened. They turned all the lights out, shot the lights out, and they beat people at random. They didn't have to be marching. All you had to do was be black. And they hospitaled probably fifteen or twenty folks. And they just was intending to kill somebody as an example, and they did kill Jimmie Jackson. . . . He was shot in the side that night and later died, maybe four or five days after that.

Was he active in the Movement?

Oh, yeah. He was there every night, too. . . . He was not what you would call a leader or nothing of that nature. He was just a person who attended the meetings. His family was much more active than he was. But about this time everybody was active. . . . This was one of the prime reasons for the massacre. Because too many people were getting the message, and a lot of black folks who hadn't never rebelled against the system at all had decided that it was time to rebel against the system. And the white power structure knew that as many people we had sympathizing with us at this point, that it was something had to go one way or the other. And their theory was to try to deter us with force or to brutalize us. This didn't work.

WILLIE BOLDEN

Compact, muscular, a sharp dresser. He looks the part of the Savannah street hustler he was before his admiration for Dr. King led him into SCLC.

I was in Marion, Alabama, the night that Jimmie Lee Jackson was assassinated and that's why when I read these books, I say, "Where do these guys get these stories from?"

Nobody knows much about the whole Jackson episode.

We were in Selma. Dr. King, I believe, was in Montgomery and was scheduled to speak that night in Marion, Alabama. By that time, the relationship between Dr. King and I had developed into the kind of relationship that I wanted it to, where it wasn't just, "Hey, Willie." . . . I must admit that I worked very hard to develop that kind of relationship because with a man as great as he was, I wanted to have that. The reasons my feelings are so close, close and touching, about Martin is because I knew the man, not just heard him speak some place. I marched with him, I ate with him, I talked with him, that kind of thing.

So you had this pretty relaxed relationship by the time the Marion thing came up?

Yeah, and I don't know who was responsible for asking me to go, whether or not it came directly from him or Andy.* But I was asked to go to speak there that night. I took three other people with me, and when I got there, the news media was there. Of course, they were looking for Dr. King. [Laughs] The news media was there, the state patrol was there, the sheriff was there. I drove up, or my co-worker drove up. We went in, and of course, folk were hanging out the rafts. Everybody was looking for Doc. I jotted my speech down on a piece of paper that I found in the car going down, probably one of the best ones I ever made.

I spoke and was not really anticipating a march that night. . . . Most people who speak will say that if you can get to yourself, you know that you are getting to others, and out of the clear blue, at the end of my speech, I asked how many people would like to have a march. Every living soul in that church stood up. So we began to move, the three guys who I brought with me, the preacher from their church, I believe, and some other ladies who participated on the program. I filed out, off the pulpit, down the aisle, and when I got outside, we turned to the right because the courthouse was directly across the street, and we were going to march around there, and I was going to give another little spiel at the courthouse. The cameras were shooting, and all of a sudden, out of nowhere, we heard cameras being broken, newspapermen being hit, and looked around and saw folk trying to run out of the church. And what they had done, they had gone through the side and the back of the church, and the troopers were in there beating folk . . . trying to get 'em out, and troopers were outside along with the local police and sheriff department, beating folk out there. Okay? I'll never forget this night.

A big, white cop—well, a big white fella in a suit—came up to me—I was still in the front of the march—and stuck a double-barrel shotgun, cocked, in my stomach and said, "You're the nigger from Atlanta, aren't you?" And I said, "Yes." He said, "Somebody want to see you across the street." Now, while all of this was going on, people were still getting beaten. Okay? So he took me across the street, and there was a guy standing there who claimed to have been the sheriff, and I think he was because of his badge, with some red suspenders and chewing tobacco and one of those big hats on. Said, "Now, you see what you caused." And I said, "How did I do that?" He said, "Because if you had kept yo' black ass in Atlanta, this would not have happened." I said, "I didn't come here from Atlanta. I came here from Selma, Alabama." He said, "If you had stayed there, this would not have hap-

* Rev. Andrew Young, then SCLC executive director.

pened." I said, "The Constitution gives us the right to peacefully protest whatever grievance we might have." He said, "You don't have any constitutional rights in my town." I said, "Yeah, so I see." At that time, folks were still getting beaten.

He grabbed me by the coat and spin me around, and he said, "I just want you to watch this." Folk were running over each other and trying to protect themselves. So I began to cry, 'cause it was just . . . you had to see it . . . it was just, just . . . you could just see folks grabbing their heads. And one guy was running over toward in our direction, and he saw the polices standin' there by the sheriff, and he tried to make a turn, and when he did, he ran into one of those local cops, and they hit him in the head, and it just bust his head wide open. Blood spewed all over, and he fell. And I tried to get over there to him, and the sheriff pulled me back, and I turned around to say something to him, and when I turned around he stuck a .38 snubnose right in my mouth. [He sticks his index finger into his mouth to show how the barrel was held against his palate. He continues his story, sounding like a man with a mouthful of dental instruments.] He said, "What you gon' say?" I said, "I ain't gon' say nothin'." [He removes the finger.] You know, what the hell you gonna say?

He cocked the hammer back, and he said, "What I really need to do is blow your goddamn brains out, nigger." Of course, I didn't say nothin'. I was *scared to death,* and all I could see was those rounds in that chamber. He said, "Take this nigger over there to the jail." The jail was right up the street from the church and right across the street from the courthouse. So they took me over there, and in taking me over there, the guy just hit me all over the arm, legs, thighs, and the chin, really did me in kind of bad. And when I walked in the door, there was blood on the floor. Just literally puddles of blood leading all the way up the stairs to the jail cell. And when I got up there, folk were hollering, "I need a doctor, I need a doctor, I need a doctor." And nobody paid any attention to 'em. And when the guy opened the cell where I was to push me in, two of 'em caught me at the same time side the head there. The only thing probably saved me a little bit was when the first guy hit me and the other one attempted to hit me, all his billy club did was hit the stick that was already here, so I got a kinda double jog, bip-bip. Had a little hickey up there, and when they pushed me in, my forehead hit the top bunk in the thing, and I had a big knot there.

Shortly after I was in there, that's when we heard the shots. Well, that's when Jimmie Lee Jackson got killed. The cop was beating on his mama, and he was headed toward his mother, and that's when they shot him. 'Course, I never read anything like that in these books and things that I've read about the Civil Rights Movement and why Jimmie Lee Jackson was killed or how he got killed. Much of what I told you, I have never read in a book period about what took place at a particular situation. I am inclined to believe that they got their information either from the paper or tried to analyze some filmstrips on what happened. Even in filming, in many cases, they missed a lot of it because if the shit was gonna *really* go down, those folk tried to get those cameras out of the way first. And many times even after they were able to put the camera back into motion, much of the real *bloody* part of these marches was all over.

ALBERT TURNER

Killing Jimmie Jackson just made things that much worse and made us all just that much more determined. And really when I started that day, I was a bricklayer at the time, and I had no intention of actually going into what we call the Civil Rights Movement. . . . But the way in which we were treated that day gave me no other choice but to go back. And I kept going back and so I never did get back to work, and one thing led to another.

So in a real sense, Jimmie Jackson's murder in Marion was the thing that determined the march on the bridge. . . .* We had to do something else to point out to the nation the evils of the system. So we decided that we would walk all the way to Montgomery to protest, and this is really the forerunner, you might say, of that Edmund Pettus Bridge thing. And after we had started that, then Dr. King and the whole Civil Rights Movement decided that this might be a good thing. Our first plan was to go to Montgomery with Jimmie Jackson, take his body and put it on the steps of the capitol. That was the original plan of drasticness.

Why didn't you follow through with that?

* The "Bloody Sunday" march of March 7, 1965, which marked the real beginning of the Selma movement as a national issue.

Dr. King and everybody else decided that we did need to take a drastic step and go to the capitol, true enough, but it needed to be a much larger and more forceful thing than just a local group of people. They decided to organize a national thing that would bring in all kinds of people that would be involved in a Selma-to-Montgomery march. So we deferred the first Selma-to-Montgomery march that we had talked about and organized a real march.

So what you're saying is that the original notion for the Selma-to-Montgomery march was a local movement thing.

It really was. It originated from Perry County, my home county at that time, to be honest with you.

Why wasn't the idea to march from Marion?

It was at first. That was the original idea, that we gon' walk from Marion to Montgomery, and they decided that was too far and that it would be much more dramatic to go from Selma, instead of Marion. So all the people from Marion was to come to Selma in cars and this is really what did happen. See, people don't know this, but over fifty percent of the people that was in that march that Sunday on that bridge was from Marion . . . and they came with the intentions of going on to Montgomery that Sunday. Now they really didn't know that we wasn't going to be able to go to Montgomery that Sunday, and we had packs on our backs and actually had our camping tools and so forth to go that day. But there was people who knew that we wasn't gon' get to go that day, 'cause Wallace had put the troopers down at the bridge and gave 'em instructions to stop us at all cost. Now the marchers didn't know this, but the leaders knew this.

Did you know it?

I was one of the leaders. . . . [Laughs] After about a month of marching I became a staff member of SCLC's, and I was on the staff when we crossed that bridge. I was walkin' second in line that day. . . . When we got to that bridge, I think everybody know what happened down there that Sunday. That was the second brutalness of the whole thing, brutalness.

Marion being the first.

Marion was the first, yeah.

Why did this one capture the national attention, where Marion, where there was an actual shooting, didn't?

Well, you had the Martin King thing here in Selma . . . plus the fact that you had national television that Sunday. We had television in Marion that night, but the camera was burst, and Valeriani's head was, too. . . .* The story of Marion was never told because the news media was not allowed to picture it . . .

But see, the thing that happened that Sunday—and this is the biggest mistake I think George Wallace and so forth made in the Movement— they allowed the nation to see brutality on the screen nationally, and this irked the whole world. And that was the turning point of the Civil Rights Movement.

* See Richard Valeriani.

WILSON BAKER

"Bloody Sunday": The View from City Hall

He was Selma's director of public safety in 1965. This interview took place on the tenth anniversary of "Bloody Sunday." Visiting in Baker's office that day was John Nixon, who was in Selma in 1965 as the U.S. Justice Department's observer.

When did you first learn that Selma was gon' be the site of a major effort?

I found around the first of October of 1964 that we had obtained through some sources—and I honestly do not know how this thing was obtained—I have heard the story that Dr. King either lost his briefcase or some way it was misplaced in Anniston—a copy of what he called Project Alabama, setting up the whole logistics of it, what they intended, why Selma was chosen and so forth. I think every law enforcement officer in the state had a copy of that thing. . . .

JOHN NIXON: "I believe SCLC mentioned Jim Clark,* also."

They mentioned that it was a ready-made situation here for 'em with the posse that Jim Clark had. He had such a large posse. See, back in

---

* The sheriff of Dallas County. He operated independently of Baker's city police force.

early '63, they had a little trouble at the school at Notasulga, out from Tuskegee over there, and he took his posse over there. He took his posse to Montgomery during the bus-riding days, and he took his posse to Tuscaloosa when the governor stood in the door in Tuscaloosa. He took his posse, volunteered to take them to Birmingham, when Birmingham was having their trouble before we had ours. They mentioned in this Project Alabama they felt that they had a ready-made situation, that if he wanted some of it bad enough to go off, that they would just take it to him, see.

We were determined not to give 'em what they wanted and succeeded for two days that first week that they marched in here. We would try to set him down and talk with him. You got to look at it this way: Jim Clark is an intelligent man . . . but he could be swayed by the last people that talked with him, and that was—

JOHN NIXON [Interrupting]: "Judge Hare."*

That's exactly right, that, and the members of his posse. They were real anxious for action, and we had persuaded him to keep 'em in the courthouse: "Let 'em march. Don't arrest. Meet nonviolence with nonviolence." It went that way for two days . . .

> *After the second day of demonstrations passed without incident, SCLC and the Dallas County Voters' League held a midnight strategy session.*
>
> . . . One of the fellows attending that meeting—ah, let's just say it this way—we had ways of getting to him.** We found out about two-thirty that morning they had decided that there had been too much homework going on in Selma, that they were going to march one mo'

* Judge James A. Hare, now deceased, was Clark's political mentor. He had developed elaborate genealogical theories to support his argument that Selma blacks were descended from inferior African stock and therefore particularly unsuited for social and political equality. See Neil Maxwell.

** When the tape recorder was shut off Baker confided that his informant was an obscure civil rights worker whom the police knew to be homosexual. Baker used the threat of a morals arrest to pry information from the man, whose sexual preference provides the explanation for an incongruous news photograph. It shows Baker arresting King and Abernathy, yet all three are laughing. According to Baker, the civil rights leaders knew of the man's problem and were laughing because at the moment the picture was taken, "I had just asked 'em which one wanted to share a cell with ——."

day, and they were going to make every effort to provoke someone in the posse or Jim Clark into committing some kind of violent arrest. And if they couldn't do it, then Dr. King would make a face-saving out and find another community in Alabama to do it in, and they even mentioned Camden as a possible community. . . . So then we got with the people: "Let's control the posse and Clark one mo' day, and we'll be through."

They were supposed to march at ten o'clock the next morning, and the city attorney, McLean Pitts, and the mayor and some councilmen and some other people came in and said that they could not control Jim, that he was in one of his wild rages. He was with the judge, who's dead now, and that he was gonna arrest every so-and-so that came up here that day.

Pitts, the city attorney, told Baker to arrest the marchers as they filed from the church, thus preventing a confrontation with Clark at the courthouse.

I said, "Arrest 'em and charge 'em with what?"

He said, "Book 'em for investigation. You can book 'em for seventy-two hours and hold 'um, and if you have to, release 'em and then pick 'em up again and book 'em for seventy-two hours."

I said, "No such law as that and you know there's no such law as that."

I remember he shook his finger in my face, and he told me, said, "Your job depends on your doing this, because if they get up there, he's gonna arrest 'em."

I said, "Your job is to go control that man up there, not to tell me to do something illegal. . . . The mayor may be foolish enough to take your damn advice, but I don't want any. . . . If they come out'chere and march lawfully, they gon' go to the courthouse, I guarantee you." And sure enough, they did.

At that time, they would march in small groups, if you remember, John. . . . I say "march," they wouldn't "march." They'd just walk along in groups of maybe four or five, ten feet apart.

JOHN NIXON: "Stop for lights."

I mean, they all tried to control things, just be very careful not to violate a city parade ordinance that we had. So that's the way they came to the courthouse, and when they got'chere Jim Clark started jerkin' 'em around and kicking 'em around.

JOHN NIXON: "It was voter registration day. They were going up to register, to attempt to register."

That's right. Jim he would want 'em to go in *that* door of the courthouse, and they'd want to come in *this* door, and that's really the kind of situation it was. . . . He arrested some several of 'em here that day.

What you're saying, if I understand it, is you were one day away from the Selma movement moving on.

That's exactly right. If he had made no arrests whatsoever that day, they would have moved out.

Was Sheriff Clark aware that if the arrests were bypassed . . .

Oh, yes, oh, yes, he was very much aware of it. They went back to the church that night and voted him an honorary member of SNCC, SCLC, CORE, the N-Double-A-C-P. They voted him an honorary membership in that and openly stated that they could depend on him from now on to do anything foolish they wanted him to. And from then on they played him just like an expert playing a violin.

Sheriff Clark became a favorite topic at the nightly mass meetings at Brown Chapel A.M.E. Church.

Tapes are a bad word to say right now, but we were taping the thing [mass meetings]. It was no secret. . . . They knew we were taping 'em. And he'd get a copy of the tapes just like we'd get a copy of the tapes, and he'd scream bloody murder that he'd never do it again, he wouldn't fall into that trap again and go out the next day and do the same thing.

But after that third march, whenever, as I say, whenever he arrested the people out'chere in front of the courthouse, there was never any question in my mind which way it was going then. I knew we were in for a long spring. . . .

You were talking about the posse. Was it a quasi-professional force?

No, they were not. The posse was made up of some real fine people, a few real fine people, and then a few just run-of-the-mill people, and then a lot of Ku-Klux-Klan type. And Clark's excuse for having them in his posse was that if he had the Klan there he could control them, but he couldn't. They could form his opinion, too, and they would get to him. . . . I have known of Jim to call, with me on one extension and with his lawyer on the other extension, begging Judge Dan Thomas—who at that time was a federal district judge in Mobile—begging him to send up some injunction enjoining the sheriff, so that he would have a face-saving or political out with his posse. And then the minute he'd get the durn thing, he'd hold it up and say, "Look what that damn federal judge has done to me again," see. But I've heard him actually beg for 'em . . . Jim had reached the point that he was beginning to lose control of his posse, and he'd have to have some federal injunction saying, "You must do this." . . . They were beginning to say, "Well, hell, if you're not gonna do it, we're gonna get out and do it."

Fired by Clark's brutality, SCLC workers led protesters to the courthouse every afternoon. The posse grew more restive. Wilson Baker sensed an inexorable progress toward confrontation. The Jimmie Lee Jackson shooting drew older and more prosperous blacks into the Movement in both Marion and Selma. SCLC set Sunday, March 7—one week after Jackson's funeral—as the starting date for a memorial march from Selma to Montgomery. On Saturday Governor Wallace vowed that the march would be turned back because it was "not conducive to the orderly flow of traffic and commerce." When supporters of SCLC and SNCC met Sunday afternoon for a rally at Brown Chapel, the stage was set.

Jim Clark was out of town. He'd been to Washington for some reason, I think to tape a show, *Face the Nation* or *Issues and Answers,* . . . and was flying back into Montgomery that Sunday morning sometime. Ten or eleven o'clock in the morning he was due in, and the governor's office gave specific instructions for Al Lingo, who was the director of the department of public safety, head of the state troopers, not to show up in Selma, not to come to Selma, but to meet the plane and get Jim Clark and detain him in Montgomery until this thing was over with. The governor had made up his mind that he was going to stop the marchers and we had a meeting that morning, and in fact, we had such heated discussion that I resigned as public safety commissioner. Rightly or wrongly, I agreed to meet on Sunday morning with the city council and the mayor and reconsidered and stayed on. They wanted us to have a part of this thing across the river.* They wanted to have a joint situa-

* At the eastern end of the Edmund Pettus Bridge over the Alabama River, where Highway 80 crosses the Selma city limit.

tion of city, state, and county officers stopping them, and they kept assuring us that there would be absolutely no violence. But I didn't feel at that point that there was any way to control the situation. I knew one spark could set it off and that I was not going to have any part of it. I agreed to stay on with the understanding that I was to be in complete charge of the police department, and my answer to that was "Hell, no, there'd be no city police across there."

We were not going to have any part of that thing because I thought at that time that it was time to let them go to Montgomery, if they wanted to go to Montgomery. One reason was I wanted to get them out of Selma. It was selfish, let's be honest about it. And I knew, too, the logistics that had been put into the preparation for the march, that they were not prepared to go. There were people going across that bridge with high heels on. They couldn't have walked, no way in the world.

We met with Major John Cloud who was a commander of the uniform division of the highway patrol of the department of public safety, or the state troopers, as they were then called, and he assured me that he had strict orders from the governor that there would be absolutely no violence. Just stop them, but no violence whatsoever. But for some reason the posse got over there. They had agreed that they would stay around this courthouse, but the mounted posse got over there. They got those horses in behind some of those buildings some way and in force. . . . Anyway, about five minutes before the march was stopped, Lingo showed up with the sheriff at the confrontation line over there. I do not know who threw the first canister. I've been told that Jim threw the first gas canister. I've been told that Lingo threw the first. They had, I guess, made up their minds that they would throw. . . . There must have been five or six hundred of them in that march that day. Once the gas canister explodes, and the gas goes, they go to running and running over state troopers, and the state troopers take that as an excuse to fight back, and all hell broke loose.

But I had a thorough understanding with 'em that whatever happened across that bridge, once the blacks got back into the city limits, no one was to follow them back in here. But the posse did follow 'em back, the mounted posse, and followed 'em back to the church and down in that area. And where it really got scary, there was a lot of anger on the part of the blacks at this point. See, this "civil-rights area" that we refer to—Brown's Chapel Church was the headquarters—but it's right in the midst of a Negro, or black, housing project, which even now is predominantly black. (All those things are integrated now, but it's still predominantly black in this particular one.) People were coming out of those houses with shotguns and rifles and pistols, and the horses were running in there, and they were trying to ride horses up on the steps of the church and everyplace else.

And Congressman Young,* he played such an important part of saving a bloodbath. He was just running wild up and down to these apartment units: "Get back into the house with this weapon. . . . We're not going to have any weapons out." Because I was there with him helping him, but I finally found out that that would not do it, so I went to Jim Clark, the sheriff, and told him, "Now, you get your cowboys, and you get 'em out of here, and you get 'em out of here *now*." . . . I finally told him in such a stern way that he did go get his men and get back out of there. I said, "Now, you are fixin' to cause a bloodbath, and there's gonna be a lot of us killed, too, and I mean get 'em out of here and get 'em out of here now." Because people were beginning to throw bricks and bottles and people were coming out with shotguns and pistols, and we knew things were really fixing to pop.

* SCLC's Andrew Young, who was elected to the U.S. Congress from Atlanta in 1972 and served there until his appointment in 1977 as United States ambassador to the United Nations.

SHEYANN WEBB

In the Lap of "The Lord"

I was in the third grade, and I was walking to school one day, and I saw a whole crowd of people out in front of Brown's Chapel Church. I really didn't know what was going on, so I just stopped and leaned to the fence. I was just looking, and somebody walked up to me and asked me who was I and said, "Don't you supposed to be at school?" And I said, "Yeah, but I wanted to know what was going on." 'Cause it was something that was unusual. So due to the fact that I was small and I had met this person, I began to walk around and meet other people, too. And that day, that particular day, I didn't go to school. I was supposed to have gone, but I didn't.

. . . I became kind of popular with the people that were participating in the Movement. . . . I began singing freedom songs every time that they had a meeting at night and also in the daytime.

She was introduced to Dr. King as "his smallest freedom fighter," and he sought her out whenever he visited the church for a rally.

Every time he came around, I used to sit on his lap in the pulpit and lead a favorite tune of his, "Ain't Gonna Let Nobody Turn Me Around." And everytime he'd come and get ready to leave, he'd say, "Sheyann, what do you want?" I'd say, "Freedom."

Usually when I was at the meetings, I wasn't too interested in all of the speeches . . . But whenever he got up to speak, it just really put something through me. It's like now, when I hear him on a record or something, it just do something to me. . . . I just enjoyed even looking at him, besides listening to him.

JOHN LEWIS

A preliminary meeting with Jim Clark.

I recall the first demonstration of that [Selma] series. . . . I believe it was on January the eighteenth, 1965, when we attempted to march from Brown's Chapel A.M.E. Church to the Dallas County Courthouse, and on our way, near the courthouse, Sheriff Clark approached the line of march, and I remember what he said. . . . I had been in jail there and had some contact with Sheriff Clark in late '63, and he said, "John Lewis, you're an outside agitator, and an agitator is the lowest form of humanity." To me, he was a very strange character.

A great many of the people within SNCC had some real reservations about SCLC coming into Selma, coming into what some people called SNCC territory, SNCC turf. . . . From the very outset, SNCC as an organization sorta played down the idea of a march from Selma to Montgomery.

Why?

There had been some discussion in SNCC that there had been so much violence, so many people been hurt and killed, why have a march from Selma to Montgomery that would only get a lot of people hurt? It was that attitude.

We had a meeting . . . the executive committee of SNCC, we met here in Atlanta on March sixth at Frasier Restaurant over on Hunter Street in the basement of the restaurant. And we met all day, matter of fact, debating whether to support the march or not. Members of the executive committee came in from Mississippi, south Georgia, all over to attend this meeting. The executive committee of SNCC opposed the march from Selma to Montgomery, but said that if any individual staff member wanted to march, they should feel free to participate in the march. Now, during that day we heard that Governor Wallace had said that the march would not be allowed. This was on Saturday. During the meeting, I argued that we should support the march because the people that we had been workin' with in Selma and in other parts of the Black Belt wanted to march. . . . I made a decision that I would go to Selma that Saturday night. . . .

Sunday afternoon, March seventh, we met in the housing project playground . . . a courtyard near the Brown Chapel A.M.E. Church. Andy Young, Hosea Williams,* James Bevel, and local people started gathering, people coming in from Perry County and Wilcox County to participate in the march. By the set time for the march, about six hundred . . . had arrived. I believe SCLC drew lots to determine who would represent SCLC on the line of march. I don't recall whether they threw coins or drew straws or how they did it, but somehow it fell to Hosea's lot to lead the march and be the SCLC representative on the march. I was not there representing SNCC, but it was no question about it, I was national chairman of SNCC, and it was just hard to separate my role as being a participant in the march from my chairmanship of SNCC.

Anyway, Hosea and I, the two of us led the march out of Selma. . . . I don't think most of us that came there that Sunday afternoon, when I look back on it, expected at that point to march all the way from Selma to Montgomery, because we hadn't made the plan. We did have little bags, knapsacks and lunch or somethin' like that, books to read along the way. But we hadn't set up tents along the way; we didn't have any place to stay. Apparently the idea was that we would march outside of Selma that night and then come back, and then the next morning we would continue. But our plan was not to go from Selma to Montgomery straight. That was just impossible.

But it was a beautiful Sunday afternoon. The weather was really good

* Director of the SCLC field staff.

weather . . . a beautiful March day in Selma, in Alabama. We started across the bridge, and on the other side of the bridge—I think we had been singin' freedoms songs—but the moment that we got on the other side of the bridge, a major named Major Cloud, he said, "I am Major Cloud. This is an unlawful march. It will not be allowed to continue. You have three minutes to disperse." . . . What we did, sorta automatically, everybody, every single person, just sorta kneeled, over the Alabama River. Some of the people were still on the bridge, and the front line of the march was across the bridge on the left side comin' outa Selma. Over half of the people were still on the bridge, had not made it across. Then Major Cloud said somethin'—oh, it was much less than three minutes—he said somethin' like "Troopers, advance. . . ."

WILLIE BOLDEN

I remember when they first started throwing the tear gas, I saw several people rolling down the embankment toward the water. There were people who were knocked off the bridge by the horses, 'cause they were standin' up on the side, and the guy just drove the damn horse up on 'em, and rather than get stampeded, they jumped over and fell in that damn water. Then there were others who just rolled down the embankment, and I remember very distinctly seeing seven or eight canisters of tear gas being thrown down there because they were there, not counting the amount that was thrown up on top.

And I went down to help some of the ladies come back up, and I had a little girl about nine or ten on one of my shoulders and had another lady by the hand coming back up the bank toward the highway. When I got them back up . . . the guy came up there with the horse, and the lady was hollerin', and I kind of squeezed her hand very close, with the girl there, and the cop was standing there with the horse, lookin'. He had the stick drawn back, and we just stood there, and I just looked at him. The lady, she was panicking. The little girl, she was almost out. She didn't know what the hell was goin' on. And the cat just turned around and went on.

Then I took the lady, and we walked on down the side. I know when we got down in the downtown area, I stopped and put the girl down to see what I could do with her, 'cause we had sorta gotten out of some of the mass of that tear gas, eyes runnin'. Got her, and another guy stopped to help me, so we finally picked up the girl, and we started back toward the church, and an old man 'bout fifty or sixty years old was running by me, and a cop came by me on a horse and hit him on the head and just bust his head wide open, all over the side. I mean, just laid it open . . . The guy who was with me, who was gonna help me with the girl, grabbed him, and we went on back. And they literally whipped folk all the way back to the church. They even came up in the yard of the church, hittin' on folk. Ladies, men, babies, children—they didn't give a damn who they were. [Pauses] That was one hell of a day.

Do you recall anything about when you peeked over that bridge and could see down the other side?

Uh-mm. When we saw them state troopers? Yeah . . . I guess it was a hundred and fifty, two hundred of 'em, and we didn't see their masks at first. They had 'em hooked on to their side. I remember several people saying, "Well, there ain't gonna be no gas, 'cause these cats are not prepared." 'Cause usually when they gonna throw gas, they already have their masks on. But during the time of the confrontation between us and the guy who was in charge of that thing, when he said we could not go any further . . . that's when we saw them pulling their masks out. Said, "Oh, Lord, this is it." And when they grabbed their sticks, and he said, "All right, disperse the street," and they came in like this, well, you knew then that there was gonna be a whuppin'.

Did y'all have a chance to talk . . . ?

No. You just have to make a decision. Guys like myself, I *knew* what the decision was gonna be. Number one, they were gonna stop us, 'cause if they weren't, they wouldn't have been out there. Number two, they were gonna ask us to disperse. I knew we weren't, because if we had done it, then that march would have *never* gone across that bridge. And there just come a time where you just have to take the stand and say, "Well, Lord, here I am." I *knew,* knowing Hosea like I do, we gon' stay there. So I had maybe a little more on some of the other folk, in terms of being aware and knowing that it was gon' take place. I knew the confrontation was gon' take place because I knew it was no way humanly possible for us to turn around. And that would have happened had anybody been in front. If Martin was there, we would have gotten whupped. You might find some people who would say, "Well, maybe if Dr. King was there . . . Reverend Abernathy . . . they wouldn't have done that." The state troopers didn't care who was there, we were gonna get whupped that day. And we did.

SHEYANN WEBB

Before we went, they had a meetin' at the church, and we were all gettin' spirited up and sayin' we weren't gon' let anybody turn us around. I had led the song, too. You know, that's one of my favorite tunes. Everybody had gotten really spirited up. . . . I got a lotta complaints from people sayin' I was too small, but they didn't bother me 'cause I was gonna do it anyway. When we were marching up, I know I was afraid. But when we got up there, they told us to get back, but we were still singin' and all. At one point, they let the tear gas go, that's when I started runnin'. . . . There were some horses . . . they told us to move back. . . . I can't really express the way it was.

I was up toward the front and everything. I was runnin'. I was afraid, and Hosea picked me up, and I told him to put me down 'cause he was runnin' too slow. . . . Tears was splattered everywhere, and I ran all the way home. . . .* The horses was—like everybody was runnin', you know—horses, they stopped right down on the corner at this street down here. I ran in here. I was callin' my mother and father. Everybody in this community was frightened. My father and mother came to the door.

* She lives in George Washington Carver Homes, the housing project surrounding Brown Chapel.

I was there between 'em with tears in my eyes, because it was . . . it was . . . it's something that I'll never forget. I just didn't think people could really be done certain ways, but now I see just how it is. I saw how it was.

John Lewis

If you've ever been in tear gas, it makes you feel like, you just feel like giving up, you know. I thought it was the end.

Do you remember any details . . . ?

Well, I was hit. I was hit almost in the same spot that I was hit on the Freedom Ride in 1961 by an officer, by a state trooper. This trooper just kept hitting. But it was such a force. They were running . . . over anyone that was standing, so I was literally knocked down and hit. I just felt like it was the beginning of the end. . . . It became very difficult for me to breathe, and you just sorta felt, "Just let me be," in a sense. I recall several people that had been on the march assisted in getting me back down the street. . . .

I did go back to the church and we had a brief—well it was a rally, people comin' in singin', saying what happened, and I remember getting up saying something to the audience, something like, "I don't understand it why President Johnson can send troops to Viet Nam, troops to Africa"—the Congo situation had taken place—"and to the Dominican Republic, and cannot send troops to protect people in Selma, Alabama, who just want to vote."

He was seeing double as he spoke from the Brown Chapel pulpit. He was hospitalized for three days with a brain concussion.

JULIAN BOND

On Professional Jealousy

I don't know if you remember a famous photograph—it was in *Life* magazine and then the New York *Times*—taken at the Selma March. It was a series of pictures in *Life*. The first one shows this crowd of marchers with John Lewis at the head. The second one shows them going toward the police. The next one shows the police beginning to charge, John standing his ground. The third one shows the police among them. They've hit John on the head and he's going down. It shows Hosea just like this, heading for the rear. [He rises from his chair, and demonstrates the pose of retreat caught in the photograph.] That picture appeared in the New York *Times* the day *after* the beating occurred in a full-page [fund-raising] advertisement for SCLC, and that just burned us up [in SNCC], you know. If we had had the ability to do it, the technical ability to quickly have a picture taken, fly it to New York, get it in the *Times,* have the copy all ready, or if we'd even thought in that way, we would have done it ourselves. We had more right to do it. It was *our* chairman who was leading the march.

The Selma campaign aggravated the tensions which had existed for some time between SNCC's young radicals and an increasingly sophisticated SCLC staff.

It wasn't Dr. King. See, we began, most of the times, to separate Dr.

King from SCLC, and our anger was directed at the bureaucrats who were there who were sucking money and our publicity, 'cause publicity was money. If you got your name in the New York *Times,* your organizational name in the New York *Times,* you could reprint that, send it out to your mailing list and they'd send you some dough.

But SCLC was hoggin' all the publicity and all the money and doing very little to deserve it. During the period when we had people working all over Mississippi, throughout most of the Black Belt in Alabama and southwest Georgia, SCLC had Martin Luther King and two or three other staff people and that was it. But they'd piggyback on everything we did—and sometimes at our invitation, you know. We would sometimes ask King to go someplace, because we knew the attention he drew would be helpful to the local scene, even if it wasn't helpful to us. But it was irritation, nonetheless. When King went into Selma . . . we had had five people there for a year beforehand, really softening the community up. And the first big police clash there didn't come across that bridge, but came a year earlier when Forman spoke at a mass meeting in Selma in Brown's Chapel A.M.E. Church, and the police, Jim Clark and his posse, gathered outside the church and wouldn't let anybody leave all night—people had to spend the whole night in the church—and were beating people up as they did sneak away. So we just resented SCLC's ability to capitalize on things we thought we were doing. . . .*

* For a different perspective on SCLC's ability to capitalize on the Selma situation and mobilize national support, see Randolph Blackwell.

WILSON BAKER

After "Bloody Sunday"

I remember asking Mr. [Nicholas] Katzenbach after he got to be attorney general—being in his office once—I asked Mr. Katzenbach what did the Justice Department expect if we had realistically registered blacks as they came in under the existing laws. He pulled a chart out of his desk with Alabama on it and ran down to Dallas County, ran his finger over there, and he said, "About two thousand [black voters], twenty-five hundred."

I said, "What do you expect if the Voter Rights Bill passes?"

He said, "What do you mean *if* it passes. You people passed that on that bridge. You people in Selma passed that on that bridge that Sunday." He said, "You can be sure it will pass, and because of that, if nothing else." And pulled his finger over there a little further, and he said, "About ten thousand." And we wound up with about fifteen thousand.

Postscript: In 1966 he defeated Jim Clark for the office of sheriff. Black voters provided his margin of victory in that election and again in 1970 and 1974. He was still sheriff when he died of heart trouble in the fall of 1975.

MEMORIES OF THE MARCH

STONEY COOKS

I was a student at Anderson College in Anderson, Indiana. . . . A group of us, three or four of us, just decided that we were going to take off and go to Selma. . . . The thought was really just for a weekend, that four of us would just go down, two white students and one professor and myself. . . . All four of us were deeply moved by it. In late '64 you had had the letdown of the Kennedy assassination, the March on Washington. All of those kinds of things had passed, and you found yourself like feeling as though you had missed those things, that you had not in any kind of way identified or supported or worked with it. So here was clearly the build-up of another kind of key movement. . . .

One of the unique things about the Southern Movement, particularly in terms of Dr. King's Movement, was that people like myself show up from no place, express a desire to participate and to work *with,* and readily there was something for you to do or someone to bring you in and to give you a feeling of meaningful participation. And that was what was so important about it . . . it was very open. I could have been an agent like many other people were. I hadn't been there for a day, and I had a job doing something, monitoring something, or people would show up from a seminary in California and in three hours they would be a part of a tent-pitching team. . . .

Postscript: His visit "grew from a day to a month to six months to a year to nine years." He joined the SCLC staff, and when Andrew Young was elected to Congress, he became his administrative assistant. In 1977 he joined Young's staff at the United Nations.

RITA SAMUELS

Even though she was a secretary in SCLC headquarters in Atlanta, she had never been in a march or demonstration. She arrived in Selma with the other SCLC office workers on March 20, the night before the big march was to move out for Montgomery.

And when we got there, it was dark, and I just remember I said, "Oh, my God, . . . I wonder what's gon' happen." I think they had already called in the National Guard, and you could see them on every corner. And it was really frightenin', although for some reason, I just couldn't wait to get to where everybody was, like Dr. King and Hosea and everybody, because you really kind of had a feelin' of bein' safe once you got around them. So we checked into the hotel, and Mary, Paul, and what is it . . . the folk singers . . . they were there that night to entertain us, because people had been in Selma for almost a month. We were late goin'. . . .

I had never seen any celebrities like that before in person, and I remember Tony Bennett was walkin' through the hotel, and I just could not believe it. Rev. Bennette* was standin' there, and he said, "We want you to meet some of Dr. King's staff." And I've got an autograph in one of my schoolbooks now, because I remember I had some schoolbooks with me so I could study, and he autographed one of my books, my history book. I still have that. That was the first time I had ever seen anybody like that in person. I saw Nina Simone that night and . . . kind of got over bein' scared about anything, because I was so fascinated by all these celebrities and seein' Dr. King talk to them and everything.

When that was over, we went back to the hotel and then the next morning, everybody got ready, puttin' on blue jeans and sneakers and everything to go to the march. And we rode—everybody got in cars and went to certain points and then you'd get out. And you know, all durin' the march, I think I personally felt like I was really a part of a big change that was takin' place, and I just didn't feel any better than anybody else. I was so glad to be a part of it, and I remember it was so

* Fred Bennette, an SCLC official.

many people. Like if you looked in the back of you as far as you could see, you couldn't see nothin' but people. So it was like you were almost trapped. It was no way to get out, and as far as you could look ahead, it was nothin' but people.

HARRY ALSTON

He came down from Chicago to represent his union, the Amalgamated Meat Packers. He was among the three thousand marchers who set out for Montgomery on March 21 under the protection of a federal court order and federalized troops.

I was here . . . when the military was here, and I had a lot of mixed emotions. There is still a radical streak somewhere inside, and I think perhaps at times it was foremost in my mind. To think . . . it necessitated a whole fleet of helicopters flying over above, foot personnel from the Army, Army carriers and whatnot to assure that this thing could be done. You were glad to see all of this and said, "Thank God, at least they are seeing to it that we have the right." But on the other hand, you wonder what kind of government forces a group of people into the position where it takes the military, because Selma at that time was just like an invaded [city] or a city under siege. The only thing that was absent was the firing of the howitzers and blockbusters and other things. For all practical purposes, it was a city under siege. . . .

A WHITE WOMAN FROM SELMA

Now all did not see [what went on]. Some people sat back in their houses and watched the TV, and it was not the true picture. . . . The true picture was when you saw the demonstrations, you saw what was goin' on, you saw the filth that came into Selma. The people that sat back in their homes and said about Jim Clark that he was not makin' a good sheriff, all they would have had to have done was to ride downtown some night and see businessmen goin' into their businesses with shotguns because they didn't want somethin' to happen . . . what later has happened in Watts. The same thing could have happened right here in Selma, and it would have happened had it not been that Jim Clark confined them to that area of Selma. I saw that because I rode by. I took food to men [in the posse] who were workin' there, and if you had seen the element that was involved in that [march]. If you had seen the men and women lyin' out on the ground all together. It's something that anyone would have been upset about.

> Because they had their headquarters, and you would see men and women of both races going in and out . . . You can see, now, colored women with a half-breed child. And not only that, businesses were disrupted for six months because of this. You'd say, "Well, they're gonna have a demonstration this afternoon." And I know for myself working near the courthouse in Selma that we were not able to do a lot of work sometimes because of all of this. It was upsetting.

You mentioned that the demonstrators camped near your house.

I live eight miles out of town. They spent their first night in a pasture back of my house, on a hill back of my house. You could hear the noises from that, from their carrying on. And the next morning they came down the hill from my house and stopped for their rest break in front of my house. And we got pictures of them. What they were doing, they had walked for the TV cameras. They had marched as far as that, and then they stopped, and they got on the trucks, they got in the ambulance, and they rode. They changed. They would walk a little ways. The next stop was Southside School, which was just a mile from my house, and they stopped just beyond that. They had rest stops every few miles, and they changed, and they didn't march all the way.

I thought there were some that were supposed to have marched every step?

I know they said so, but I do not believe it because I saw them stopping. . . . Just as they said that that boy with the peg leg did.* But I tell you I have a picture of his getting in an ambulance, and rode off in the ambulance, and then later, he gets out and marches for the TV cameras.

. . . Do you think Selma got a bum rap?

Definitely. If I had set back and watched my TV camera, I would have thought Selma was the worst place in the world. . . . But the ones who were here to see it knows the situation.

* Jim Letherer, an amputee from Michigan, made the march on crutches. As he passed, white hecklers shouted, "Left, left, left."

LEON HALL

I can remember the night the march arrived in Montgomery . . . and a couple of planeloads of entertainers, celebrities, "stars" came. Belafonte. Poitier was there. Sammy Davis. James Baldwin. Eartha Kitt. Slews of them, just slews of them. I think Paul Newman was there. . . . Brando, I'll never forget, probably personified it more than any of the others. These people came, and they blended in. They were so perfectly natural. . . . They tended to come down in almost *awe* of us. . . . I can remember in Selma Brando coming down and "Sunshine"*—Ben Owens, who lost his leg at Dr. King's funeral; a mule pulling Dr. King's casket stepped on him—Brando running with "Sunshine" and some of the older fellows at twelve, one o'clock in the morning in Selma, going to the bootlegger's house. [Laughs] We goin' and drinkin' corn whiskey and he just a regular fella. . . .

J.T. JOHNSON

After we . . . got to Montgomery, Sammy Davis, Jr., Harry Belafonte, everybody was there with us, and we had a great show that night, after sleeping in the mud and what have you. But nobody even complain about that, though. Sometimes the food would get short, but they would never complain. A lot of people came down to participate, a lot of nuns and things. After that "Bloody Sunday," it had picked up a lot of momentum. . . .

We left and got down to Dexter Avenue Church**—that's right there at the capitol—where Dr. King made his speech. I don't know how many peoples we had there. I would say anywhere from thirty to forty thousand. But you know Mrs. Liuzzo, the lady who was killed, I never will forget that. After the march, there was a lot of people who needed transportation back to Selma. She was determined to drive her car. Hosea and I sat with her a long time. . . . We really didn't want her to go alone, being a white lady from the North. We appreciated all her participation and support. She had been great. She really had. She was a

---

* Ben "Sunshine" Owens was much older than most of the SCLC staff members and a popular Movement figure. He led the mule wagon which bore King's body through the streets of Atlanta, and his leg was, indeed, amputated as the result of an injury received from a mule that day.
** On the morning after the big show put on by the visiting celebrities.

very nice lady. But she just wouldn't listen . . . she just had to make that trip [back to Selma]. . . . I stayed and talked with her a long time.

Postscript: Mrs. Viola Liuzzo, a housewife and mother from Detroit, had carried one carload of marchers back to Selma that night and was returning to Montgomery to pick up a second group of marchers when a car carrying four Ku Klux Klansmen from Birmingham pulled alongside. She was shot to death on a lonely stretch of Highway 80 near Hayneville, a sleepy Black Belt town where an all-white jury would later acquit of murder the first of the Klansmen to stand trial. One of the four, an FBI informer who said he had only pretended to fire his pistol at Mrs. Liuzzo's car, was not indicted and testified against his companions. Frustrated by the failure of the Alabama courts to return convictions, federal authorities used the informer's testimony to convict the other three Klansmen under an 1870 statute for conspiring to violate Mrs. Liuzzo's civil rights.

JOSEPH E. LOWERY

As the great crowd of marchers filled the street in front of the capitol, he and Dr. King and the SCLC staff held a hurried meeting on the speakers' platform. Their problem: How to carry out the march's official purpose, which was to deliver a statement of grievances into the governor's hand.

Wallace had said he wasn't going to meet with Martin, and so we had talked it over on the stage, and the decision was made that Martin would name a committee of Alabama people to meet with Wallace, and he named me chairman. . . . When the march dispersed, our committee met right there. The governor had sent word that he wouldn't meet with us. We started up to the state capitol, and the highway patrol stood shoulder to shoulder in front of the capitol, and it seemed like some of them kinda put their hands back toward their things [reaching for an imaginary holster], and the federalized troops gave the order: "Hup-hup. . . ." [Laughing, he demonstrates how the soldiers snapped their bayoneted rifles to present arms.] There I was between the National Guard on the back and the highway patrol on the front. But when the National Guard did that, the patrol opened up and we went on to the door. When we got there, the governor's administrative secretary or administrative assistant came and said the governor would not see us, but we could leave the petition.

We told him, "No thank you." We had marched all this distance to give it to the governor, not to give it to his secretary. So we left. That was the night Mrs. Liuzzo was killed.

Later he did agree to meet with us,* and we met with him for ninety minutes, at which time I was spokesperson. We really challenged the governor that day on a moral basis. I wouldn't let him get in the political arena. I said to him that, "I am speaking to you as a Methodist preacher to a Methodist layman," which he is, and I said, "God has given you great gifts, great gifts of leadership, powers of persuasion, and he will call you to account for how you use them."

And he said, "Well, I don't advocate violence." I said, "You don't in so many words, but you do. You get on television, you rave against people taking the rights of little people and the government coming in and stirring up trouble, and you get your emotions released on TV. But the fella in the dark street, he doesn't have that forum, so he gets a lead pipe to identify with you, and he cracks somebody's skull."

What was Wallace's response?

His response primarily was defensive, of course. He said that he didn't advocate violence and, "You know I've often said that they may do this in Chicago or Philadelphia . . ."

I said, "That's another thing. You are always justifying what's happening in Alabama by what's happening in Philadelphia or Cleveland. That's not the point. The point is what's happening to our people here, and you are responsible for dividing us, and you are responsible for the violence. You can't justify what happened in Alabama by the violence that happened in Philadelphia, Pennsylvania."

Shortly after that, he made a statement, said, "I'm not trying to justify what's happening in Alabama by what's happening in Philadelphia. . . ." And it was right after that he changed his strategy and has very seldom said anything that was directly antiblack. It was sort of antibig government from that time on.

* This meeting took place two weeks after the march, and it was arranged by Kenneth Goodson, the white Methodist bishop of Alabama. There were complex negotiations as to the makeup of the black delegation. Wallace absolutely refused to allow the Reverend Fred L. Shuttlesworth, the firebrand of Birmingham, to attend the meeting, on the grounds that Shuttlesworth had accepted a pastorate in Cincinnati and no longer represented Birmingham's blacks, even though Shuttlesworth was still president of the Alabama Christian Movement for Human Rights. At one point, Wallace sought to bar Lowery, who was then pastoring a Methodist church in Birmingham, because he was also a vice president of SCLC.

Was there any communication that took place that day, do you think?

Yes, I do, and a number of people have felt that. I think for the first time, we put the problem on his sense of morality, on the moral aspects of his conscience. We moralized his conscience that day, I think. It was very interesting, a very interesting confrontation. . . .

That may have been his first meeting with a black civil rights group.

It was. It was. It was . . . and he probably for the first time got to see face to face how the black community felt about him and his leadership. And we weren't bitter, we didn't attack him in any vicious manner, but I did try to impress him with the moral responsibility that was his.

Did you lay the violence and killings that were then going on pretty directly on his doorstep?

Yes, as in the illustration that I gave you. He would get on television, and he would rant, and that's the way he could do his thing. . . . I was sure that people who wanted to identify with him, who did not have a forum on television, got a lead pipe or gun and that he had to assume responsibility for it. [Abruptly, he rips up a sheet of paper with quick, nervous gestures; he points to the scraps.] He tore up little pieces of paper all during the conversations; the entire meeting he was tearing up paper. By the time we ended, he had a nice little pile of paper on his desk. Don't ask me to interpret that. I cain't. I just report it. [Laughs] I just report.

ANDREW DURGAN

A Last Word

He has been a school teacher in Selma for forty years. When the demonstrations started, his classroom emptied. He and the other black teachers stayed behind. "The students were defying us; they were calling us names." Under threat of dismissal, he led the black teachers in a mass march on the Dallas County Courthouse. In the entire history of the Movement, it was the only time black public school teachers—the heart of the black middle class in most Southern towns—demonstrated in force. Later, when the march moved out for Montgomery, he was in the front ranks. "That was the most significant one day in my life."

Has that spirit survived among black people in Selma?

Not as wholeheartedly as it did. I'm afraid that there are people who have forgotten. Young people seem to have the spirit more so than many of the adults, significantly. Let me point out one thing. During that time, while we were meeting at Brown's Chapel Church almost nightly, right around the corner was a store, food market, Gaston's IGA Supermarket. There were so many cars to be parked that there was not enough room on the street, so they parked on his parking lot. I remember one night, notice came to the meeting that cars were being towed away, and so we decided to boycott his store. . . .

Our people wanted to find out where could they get food. . . . We set up a little grocery store. We sold shares for five dollars apiece. You'd be surprised. People gave who were not able to give or contribute more than five dollars . . . [We got] fifty thousand dollars. And we built a supermarket. For the first year or so it was a big success. Blacks from all over the city and county shopped there to buy their groceries. It's on the verge of bankruptcy now. Gradually we left this store and started shopping at the same white stores that were giving us a hard time in the Movement.

It's been almost ten years. . . . How would you assess the amount of change that has occurred?

Oh, I—it's not a hundred percent, but gosh, when I think of the things I had to do prior to this. I never thought I'd live to see it. It has been remarkable. The amount of progress in Selma has been tremendous, and it seems that almost any application for federal aid, urban renewal, for Head Start, Upward Bound, Special Services, the aged, almost anything that is requested, is granted. It's just—it seems that Selma is the adopted child of the nation.

INTERLUDE

TIMOTHY JENKINS AND LONNIE KING

SNCC and Kennedy Justice: A Southern Strategy

Timothy Jenkins was a student at Howard University and vice president of the National Student Association.

In that capacity I had created a project which was intended to be a leadership training school for activist student leaders. It was a project which we were going to hold in Nashville, Tennessee, in the summer of '61. . . . That session was the session when we first raised in a formal way the question of restructuring the priorities of the Student Non-violent Coordinating Committee to comprehend more in the way of political activity and less in the way of activism for . . . the public accommodations aspect.

In the fall Jenkins and several SNCC leaders were invited by Assistant Attorney General Burke Marshall and Harris Wofford, President Kennedy's adviser on civil rights, to meet with representatives of the Taconic Foundation and other liberal foundations. What followed in that and a subsequent meeting was a "hard, cold, matter-of-fact political exchange": How could foundation money be channeled to civil rights groups in such a way as to benefit both President Kennedy and the Southern Movement?

In fact, we had very carefully thought out the politics of our effort, and one of the principal thrusts of our argument was that to the extent that we were successful, it would be in the interest of the Administration for us to be successful. We went through the analysis of the committee structure of the Congress, the nature of the Democratic party of the South, and that any liberalization of the Democratic party across the board required the liberalization of the Southern wing. And that wasn't gonna happen unless you had a viable competition in the state level for the black vote. . . . And if nobody had to compete for it, then the South remained conservative, and if they remained conservative, then the national aspirations of the liberal Washington Democrats were not gonna be served.

So we went through all that and made the connection between our cause and their cause, and it wasn't difficult to make. I mean, we didn't have to sell them very hard on that. The main thing that they wanted to know was that there was the wherewithal, the muscle, the will that was indigenous to the South, to carry the brunt of it. Because as they described it, they couldn't do very much to make things happen unless somebody took the initial risk, and they could take the steps to protect them. And I recall very vividly one of the representations—I believe it was made by Harris Wofford, who was then principal assistant to the President—that if necessary in the course of protecting people's rights to vote, that the Kennedy Administration would fill every jail in the South. [Pause] They proved not to have delivered on that quite as well as we'd have liked. But commitment was made, at least verbally.

There was a follow-on meeting from the Taconic meeting, too, which was held directly with the attorney general himself. This was the session that was attended by all the principals of the Civil Rights Movement. It happened to have come up a time that I was in the hospital undergoing a tonsillectomy, but this was the session at which the commitment was reenforced . . . by the attorney general himself, and that session was held in the office of the attorney general.

LONNIE KING: We met with Bobby Kennedy and a number of other people, but primarily Bobby Kennedy. The thrust of that meeting was to try and get more students to move into Mississippi to deal with voting rights, and Bobby pledged marshals and what have you to help us out.

I was opposed to what I thought they were trying to do, and that's why I quit SNCC and went on to do some other things. I saw John Kennedy as being a little bit concerned about how his national image—I mean, his international image—was being tarnished by all these ragtag black kids wadin'-in and sittin'-in and kneeling-in in churches and what have you, and really talking about the conscience of America and how we had a double standard in terms of democracy. And I felt that what they were trying to do was to kill the Movement, but kill it by rechanneling its energies. And that was my position in that meeting up there. . . .

I may be wrong, but I always will feel that the Administration had some people in our groups who was keeping them informed on what we were doing. Let me tell you what had happened. SNCC's executive council had met in Louisville a few months earlier and had voted to take on AT&T. Okay? And what they were going to do was really to push this employment thing. . . . Let's put dollars into people's pockets so they can afford this equal opportunity. And what we had hoped to do—our national steering committee was gonna negotiate with AT&T nationally. The way we were gonna do it, we would call for a boycott of the telephone company, . . . ask people to cut off their telephones for thirty, sixty days. . . . "Just sacrifice for the Movement thirty to sixty days. We haven't always had telephones." And once we started getting thousands of people to do this on a thirty-day basis or sixty-day basis, can you imagine the impact dollar-wise?

And what we were gonna do was to negotiate, and we were not gonna allow AT&T to say, "Well, we'll desegregate and hire blacks in all these positions in Washington, D.C., and Baltimore, Maryland, and Atlanta, Georgia." We were not gonna call off the boycott until they agreed to do it in Pascagoula, Mississippi . . . just keep it on until they agreed to do it in *every* city in America. And from AT&T, we would go to some others.

We were gettin' ready to really do it. Okay? And within a few months, we're all summoned to Washington. And my position, and I didn't have enough support in that thing, but my position was that we were being duped. I mean, I didn't dislike the Kennedys. That's not what I'm saying. I'm just saying that from their point of view, our moving into voting rights would be more beneficial to them in terms of image than it would be to us. Now, I wasn't opposed to going into voting rights per se. I thought that we could do both of them. . . . There are enough folks around to have somebody down in Mississippi puttin' the pressure on down there while this other pressure continues. Anyway, I lost that particular position, and I said, "Well, SNCC will be dead within three to five years."

Getting foundation money into SNCC's coffers proved to be a problem. The foundations could not directly finance political activity without endangering their tax-exempt status. But they could contribute to a non-

partisan organization devoted to citizenship training and voter registration. With the blessing of the Justice Department and the "Big Five"— SNCC, SCLC, NAACP, CORE, the Urban League—the Voter Education Project (VEP) was established in Atlanta. VEP received grants totaling $870,000 from the Taconic and Field Foundations and from the Edgar Stern Family Fund. It in turn parceled money out to the organization best suited to a particular job and locality.

TIMOTHY JENKINS: This was one of the theories of organizing VEP. Each of the civil rights organizations would take a state. CORE was strong in Louisiana. N-Double-A, I believe, had more chapters in Georgia. . . . SNCC ended up with Alabama and Mississippi, because nobody else wanted 'em. [Laughs] And those two states ended up having more effect on the other states by virtue of the pace and all the horribles took place there. Ultimately the reporters and the media focused there. . . . SNCC ended up with the principal action, the principal attention, and the principal resources for a period.

When the atrocities started occurring in the Deep South—Alabama, Mississippi—did you ever feel any remorse about having helped set the whole thing in motion . . . ?

Well, at a certain point, I became overwhelmed by the emotional impact of it. It's most easily capsulized in my reaction to this day to a telephone call in the night. I give nobody my home number, 'cause I don't want anyone to call me when I go home. And the reason for that is that during that whole period when I was in NSA [National Student Association] and later when I was in law school, *whenever* my phone rang at night, it was tragedy. It always happened. I mean, there was nobody else calling me at eleven and twelve and two and one at night unless it was something terrible had happened. And you know you carry that with you . . . you think many times about the terrible price that was paid.

I guess the thing that was the most terrible thing that we had to do— and we had to do it—was to tell people who believed in us that there was all of this federal support, when we knew how shallow that support *really* was. And we went down and told the people that the U.S. marshals were going to come to support people there.

Well, the pledge had been made for that federal support, hadn't it?

[*Very softly*] Yeah, well, we had had pledges before.

They didn't do what they said they were. . . . You couldn't find those bastards. I am absolutely certain that the FBI knew many of those things that were going to happen before they happened. They had sufficient infiltration of all that Klan so that many of those tragedies could have been avoided, but for the . . . priority that the FBI has, that they must maintain good working relationships with the local police in order to do their job. The close affinity of the FBI agents for the [Southern] police people was something that the FBI and Justice never faced. . . . We told them many times that the FBI was helping the police keep track of us.

I mean, we used to see some of these things going on, and the FBI agents would be sitting around with pads, openly and notoriously looking on, sending back reports to Washington. And we expected them to use their guns to enforce the law. [We said,] "This is a violation of federal law, a crime in your presence. That's not something you have to send a damn report on. If somebody had narcotics out in the open trading them, you wouldn't send a report on it." That's a glaring violating of what they said they were going to do. Our insistence on the use of U.S. marshals to be implementers of the policy of federal will was not delivered on. Our analogy was the use of U.S. marshals in the South like they used U.S. marshals to tame the West. That's what you had. You had a lawless environment as to the federal law when it came to political rights. In order to clean that environment up, you had to use force. . . . They never did deliver. There was never a massive show of feds. . . . All the force, all the demonstrations of force and intimidation, then were on the side of the local authorities who wore badges and suits, and they had the ostensible perquisites of the state. Our part of the state was invisible—the federal state.

Did you ever go back to the people you had talked to?

Oh, sure. As a matter of fact, they had agreed, Burke Marshall had agreed, that the SNCC people in the South could call collect to the Justice Department. . . . When certain key congressmen found out that Justice was receiving [these calls] they raised hell about it, and they stopped receiving collect calls, which was a wipeout. Because here you have these guys with the expectation that at least that one call was going to get them salvation, and they make that one call collect, and it's refused. Can you imagine what that really is? Here's a guy down here surrounded with all these cats about to eat him up with the billy clubs

V
MISSISSIPPI

SNCC AND THE HOME-GROWN HEROES

Nobody never come out into the country and talked to real farmers and things . . . because this is the next thing this country has done: it divided us into classes, and if you hadn't arrived at a certain level, you wasn't treated no better by the blacks than you was by the whites. And it was these kids what broke a lot of this down. They treated us like we were special and we loved 'em. . . . We didn't feel uneasy about our language might not be right or something. We just felt like we could talk to 'em. We trusted 'em, and I can tell the world those kids done their share in Mississippi.

—Fannie Lou Hamer

Amzie Moore

Farewell to the N-Double-A

The U.S. Army made him a man, his own man, when it sent him from the segregated Delta to a segregated unit in the Pacific in World War II. "Here I'm being shipped overseas, and I been segregated from this man whom I might have to save or he save my life. I didn't fail to tell it." He kept on telling it when he got home to the steamy Delta town of Cleveland in 1946.

I had in mind one time to get rich. I thought this was the answer. I built a brick house, and I built a service station, and I had a store, and I worked from early morning 'til late afternoon. I was buying lots and trying to get ahead, and suddenly one day somebody came to see me and asked me if I would go out east of Mount Bayou. They wanted me to look at something, and I went out there, and I went in the house. Mr. Raines, there was a woman there with about fourteen kids, naked from the waist down. Had an old barrel, metal barrel that they were burning cotton stalks in to keep warm. Not a single bed in the house. A few old raggedy quilts were used to wrap the kids up to keep 'em as warm as possible, and *no food*.

Well, don't misunderstand me, I'd been hungry in my life. It was an experience that carried me back to my youth, and I could tell how a hungry child felt, because I knew how I felt. Just looking at that I think really changed my whole outlook on life. I kinda figured it was a sin to think in terms of trying to get rich in view of what I'd seen, and it wasn't over seven miles from me. I guess I could have seen it before then. . . .

When did you get involved in the NAACP?

Well, I came out of the Army in nineteen hundred and forty-six, and in nineteen hundred and fifty-one, somebody held a meeting in a church and elected me president of the NAACP, and I'd never been [to a meeting]. Well, I think at that time they were just passing the buck, getting rid of it as a hot potato. And I decided maybe I wasn't going to serve, and then finally it was kinda forced upon me, and I just went on.

Forced upon you in what way?

Well, by people I suppose. I clearly understood that the individuals who met and had me elected were people who just really didn't wanna fool with it, 'cause they weren't gonna fall out with their white friends on account of it. So they just said, "Well, here's what we'll do. We'll just move it off to him. He's young and able to take it." I think that's how I became involved. Finally enrolled about six hundred members, became vice president-at-large of the state conference of the NAACP branches, and up until SNCC came in, it was a matter of legal maneuvering. Nobody dared move a peg without some lawyer advisin' him.

Were you able to really accomplish much in the Delta through that sort of . . .

I don't think so really, because, you see, the base of operations was too far away. We met in Jackson. That's a hundred and thirty sumpin' miles

from here. We had a nice crowd, but we didn't know about methods
and procedures for demanding things. . . .

Anyway, in nineteen hundred and fifty-five, Emmett Till was found
dead in the Tallahatchie River, and they had newspapers from all
over the continent North America, some from India, and it was the
best advertised lynching that I had ever heard. Personally, I think this
was the beginning of the Civil Rights Movement in Mississippi in the
twentieth century. . . . From that point on, Mississippi began to
move.

Following the Freedom Bus Ride in nineteen hundred and sixty-one,
I was invited to Atlanta by Bob Moses.

How did you meet him?

He came down and spent a while and invited me to the meeting in
Atlanta. It must have been the spring before I went over the following
fall.

Why did he come to you?

Now, that's the sixty-four-thousand-dollar question, and I don't know
until yet why Bob came to me, but he found me and spent most of the
time that summer at my house. In the fall of that year, I went to Atlanta
to the meeting of the Student Nonviolent Coordinating Committee and
invited them to come to Mississippi. So they came, set up their first
office in Jackson, Mississippi, and then kind of spread it out all over the
state. Activities were going on in McComb, Jackson, Indianola, Cleveland, Ruleville. . . . They had more courage than any group of people
I've ever met. . . .

*In that initial meeting that you had with Moses, did y'all discuss
voter-registration tactics?*

Well . . . Moses and I talked about it when he was here visiting
me in the summer. The first thing we had to try to figure out: How
can we expose the conditions in Mississippi with reference to people
voting? How can we uncover what is covered? So then we got together, we went into homes, we persuaded people to go up and register. We had cameras from everywhere, television, the newspapers,
and the whole thing was brought out. . . .

You knew they would be turned away?

Oh, we were well aware of that. . . .

Was it generally known that you were working with SNCC?

I think so. Of course, there was a little jealousy at that time between the N-Double-A-C-P and SNCC. The N-Double-A-C-P at that time seemed to have been a legal organization that required going to court and this type thing.

SNCC was an organization of strong, intelligent, young people who had no fear of death and certainly did not hesitate to get about the business for which they came here. It wasn't a matter of meeting in the Masonic Order or office or at a church to do this. They met anywhere, at any time. One great thing I think was introduced in the South with reference to SNCC's tactics was the business of organizing leadership. If 'leven people went to jail this evening who the power structure considered leaders, tomorrow morning you had 'leven more out there. [Laughs] And the next morning 'leven more.

I found that SNCC was for business, live or die, sink or swim, survive or perish. They were moving, and nobody seemed to worry about whether he was gonna live or die. [Laughs]

. . . Are you gonna sit here and tell me that didn't cross your mind?

Sho' I was scared to death. Now don't misunderstand me. [Laughs] Yeah. . . . It came across my mind because I was constantly threatened. I was called at night and told, "In five minutes, your house gon' blow up." If I'd run out, I coulda been shot, and if I had stayed in, I coulda been blown to pieces. So then, here I am between two opinions. I've got to decide to stay in the house or run out. I mean, What's "safe" . . . ?

Did you get any adverse reaction from your N-Double-A-C-P associates when you . . .

[Laughs] When I went over to SNCC? Well, naturally.

What form did it take?

Well . . . it was like, "Maybe these kids don't know what they're doing. . . . It could get a lotta people hurt." I think what I really did was stayed away from N-Double-A-C-P meetings for years. Now, I didn't join an organization with SNCC. I just worked with 'em. That's more or less how it was. Now, the NAACP certainly has done a lot of great things. Don't misunderstand me. . . . Mr. Wilkins, he's a fine man. He'd fly down and hold our conferences and hold our annual "days" and raise our freedom money and be advised by different people outa New York office. And that was it.

But when an individual stood at a courthouse like the courthouse in Greenwood and in Greenville and watched tiny figures [of the SNCC workers] standing against a huge column . . . [against white] triggermen and drivers and lookout men riding in automobiles with automatic guns . . . *how they stood* . . . how gladly they got in the front of that line, those leaders, and went to jail! It didn't seem to bother 'em. It was an awakening for me. . . .

Why did SCLC never create the kind of impact on Mississippi that it did in other Southern states?

Well, SCLC had a group of preachers following it. Now don't misunderstand me, I think the world and all of ministers. I don't have anything against ministers, but their outlook was entirely different from SNCC's young people. Kids wore blue jeans, and I used to have sleeping in my house six and eight and ten, twelve, who had come. I bought a lots of cheese, and always we'd eat cheese and peaches, and sometimes we would get spaghetti and ground chuck or ground beef and make a huge tub of meatballs and spaghetti to fill everybody up. And this is how we were, and everybody knew they were there, wasn't any secret. They'd eat that without complaining. . . . You *know* they're being really persecuted and pushed to the wall, and they always had a smile and was always ready to try to do something. . . . To me, it was just a new leader. . . .

Not long after he began sponsoring SNCC's work in the Delta, he came to the attention of journalists—and of white Mississippians who read their reports. He received a call from a white man he knew fairly well.

He wanted me to come see him, and he picked up a church maga-

Lawrence Guyot

Inside Agitator

He was born in Pass Christian, Mississippi. In 1957 he entered Tougaloo, a black college near Jackson, which, to the chagrin of Mississippi officials, had white faculty members and welcomed any white students bold enough to attend. The spirit of the Movement was strong there.

Then one weekend I went home with a young lady from Greenwood, Mississippi, who was attending Tougaloo, and I was immediately struck by the county.* Here's a county eighty percent black at that time that had one registered voter, and no one could find him. I went back to Tougaloo and became more and more involved with SNCC. Now my involvement with SNCC was at its earliest in Mississippi. I became involved late in '61. Late '61, early '62, I began becoming more and more involved in traveling with them around the state. Now the people . . . there was Charles McLaurin, Colia Ladelle, James Jones, Lafayette Sur-

* As one approaches from the east, Greenwood is the gateway to the fertile flatlands of the Delta. Both the city of Greenwood and surrounding Leflore County take their names from the same curious historical figure, Greenwood Leflore, a wealthy slave owner who modeled his plantation home after the Empress Josephine's palace, Malmaison. Because of the United States' generosity in granting him title to certain Indian lands, Leflore supported the Union throughout the Civil War. He died on the front porch of his mansion with four grandchildren holding Union flags above him.

ney, Hollis Watkins, Curtis Hayes, myself, Luvaughn Brown, Diane Bevel, Rev. Bevel, Chuck McDew, Marion Barry, who is now a city councilman in Washington, and Bob Moses, who was later to become a legend in Mississippi. While it was clear that Moses was the leader of this group, his style of leadership was by example and directional discussion.

We met in Jackson at 714 Rose Street, and from there we had begun to conduct small workshops, speak in small meetings, attempt to get people to register to vote. And then the decision was made that what we needed was to go to the Delta where there were harsher conditions, where there was a large black population, where there were some counties with no black registration. We needed a person to provide contacts on a local basis, to provide an entree for us into the counties, and that person was Amzie Moore.

We met at his house, we stayed at his house. He had a hell of a network of individuals throughout the state and had had it for years. . . . Whenever anyone was threatened, Amzie Moore was sort of an individual protection agency. He had successfully fought against the Klan, both politically and physically, [was] a noted Bible scholar, a very good stump speaker.

With Moore's home in Cleveland as its base, SNCC opened offices in the two key cities of the northern Delta—Greenwood in the interior and the river town of Greenville. He was assigned to Greenwood, the tougher of the two.

On August the fifteenth, myself and Luvaughn Brown and another guy left Jackson on the bus to go to Greenwood. We were instructed at the time—and we, of course, didn't need to be instructed, but we agreed with the instructions—that there would be no sit-ins on the way. Just go to Greenwood and start working on voter registration. . . . And it was very interesting, because as we were riding on the bus from Jackson, . . . the bus stopped in Yazoo City, and there was a member of the Bahai faith who taught at Jackson who was beaten on the bus because he attempted to use the waiting room. And we, of course, stayed uninvolved in that; we just wrote down what happened.

Now, Greenwood at the time we entered . . . there was a war going on, and the war was a very simple one—surviving and just walkin' around talkin' to [black] people about what *they're* interested in. And it didn't make any difference. If it was fishing, how do you turn that conversation into when are you gonna register to vote? If it was religion, that was an easier one to turn into registering. If it was cotton acreage—

our basic verbal mien was that there's nothin' that's not involved with politics.

How about getting doors slammed in your face?

You learned. You learned very quickly that if you got that door slammed in your face, it just takes a day or two of talking to people to find out whose face the door won't be slammed in. . . . I mean, there are some towns you go into, and you find a man who has none of the characteristics of leadership as we identify them. He is the leader [of the black community] and has been and is unquestioned, and mess with him wrong—forgit it. Don't speed him up too much, dialogue with him, find out what his tempo is, what his objectives are. Then you might alter them a little bit, but don't, don't, don't—be careful. We learned over and over and over again how to find potential leadership, how to groom it, and the most painful lesson for some of us was how to let it go once you've set it into motion. See, I *loved* it, because it was dealing with people, what they could do against large tasks.

What were the no-noes at the grassroots level . . . ?

Well, there's one no-no that you just never walked into a house and you see some kids sittin' around and you say, "Is this your child?" You just don't do it. . . . In a couple of months, it'll all be explained to you once the people know you. So why ask it? Because immediately by the question having to be answered, you're gonna immediately set up a defensive thing, even if it's her child. "Yeah, it's my child. Why? Why would you ask me that?" So we don't do that.

You don't alter the basic format that you walk into. Let's say you're riding past a picnic, and people are cuttin' watermelons. You don't immediately go and say, "Stop the watermelon cuttin', and let's talk about voter registration." You cut some watermelons, or you help somebody else serve 'em.

There were a lot of 'em. The SNCC organizers were no saints. We asked discretion. We were never able to enforce it. And there was a weird kinda thing about, in a town with no heroes, a SNCC organizer who publicly voiced opposition to the status quo and who physically carried that [opposition] out before the police was sought after as a sexual partner. And that varied with individuals. Now there were some clear no-noes. Hartman Turnbow* had a daughter, and it was clearly

* A black farmer who joined the voter-registration drive. See Hartman Turnbow.

understood that if there ever was a no-no, that was *the* no-no. [Laughs]

It's no secret that young people and women led organizationally. When you talk about community mobilization, we not only did community mobilization in Greenwood, but the sociologists, when they were talking about community mobilization, would talk about "like what SNCC is doing in Greenwood." Okay . . . the organizationally hoped-for situation arose. Dewey Green's, a responsible black moderate, home was shot into. We had gathered a couple of hundred people together, so the thirteen of us [SNCC workers] and the couple of hundred people walked down to Chief Curtis Lowery's police force and asked for police protection. No one was arrested but the thirteen of us. The dogs were sent out and an interesting combination of things happened, because some of the highway patrolmen passed and saw me leading the line and the dogs coming at me and Mary Lane, a brave, courageous young lady from Greenwood. We didn't run from the dogs. They didn't bite us, but nevertheless we were arrested and taken to jail. . . .

The jailing of the SNCC workers was calculated to break up the voter registration activity in Greenwood, but it had the opposite effect. SNCC dispatched its entire field staff to the city. The U.S. Justice Department intervened on behalf of the jailed workers, creating the impression of "an alignment between us and the federal government." SNCC had a toehold in the Mississippi Delta.

I guess the reason we got away with what we did in Greenwood was for a couple of reasons. One, we were soundly based in the churches. Two, our objectives were very clear. It was not to desegregate the two or three good local white restaurants. It was simply to register people to vote. One time we led a demonstration down to the courthouse, and we were met by the local Citizens Council and Hardy Locke, a big businessman, really one of the political leaders of that political-social complex, who said, "Look, y'all shouldn't be too worried. Y'all bring in more applicants now than anybody else." And our retort was, "But they're not getting registered." He said, "W-e-e-ll, that's another thing." [Laughs]

See, you have to understand the climate that we were dealing with. When people received a welfare check, there was a letter—a classic letter I'll never forget—stating that people should be very concerned about registering to vote at the request of "radicals" because this may terminate the . . . check.

Those who did attempt to register faced a battery of personal questions.

And then question seventeen, the classic one: "Read and interpret to the satisfaction of the registrar this section of the Constitution." At that time, there were two hundred eighty-two sections of the Mississippi Constitution. . . . Needless to say, we had some Phi Beta Kappas, some Ph.D.'s, and some college and high-school principals failing the literacy test. . . . It got to an extent where we started really marching people down simply to *attempt* to register, fighting for the right to take the damn unconstitutional literacy test.

The county decided that what it would do was it would cut off all welfare supplies. So it did just that. All food was cut off.

Then what we did was, with the assistance of Dick Gregory . . . he provided the money and the food, we set up our alternative service, which caused more people to register to vote. . . .

Where did you get the food?

You name it. Gregory spearheaded it and actually physically flew some of the food down. It came in truckloads . . . and we made it very clear, while we were concerned about feeding everyone, we were primarily concerned about feeding those who attempted to register to vote.

We did this in Greenwood, then we moved into other counties, picking up the beginning of a fledgling state apparatus: an individual here, someone who stood up to white folks here. But we were very, very conscious about one thing. Our objective was *simply* voter registration and political mobilization. We were *not* concerned about sit-ins. We were *not* concerned about desegregation.

He talks of trumped-up arrests of SNCC workers, the firing of community people who befriended them, the grinding psychological pressure. "The whole uncertainty of the thing . . . you would be taking someone down to register, and you would simply be trailed by two cars of whites. Maybe they would do nothing, but you would never know. Maybe they would get out and whip you. Maybe they wouldn't." He believes white oppression proved to blacks the truth of SNCC's constant theme: "There is a relationship between your not being able to feed your children and your not registering to vote. . . ."

See, the simplicity of the political apparatus in Greenwood was made much clearer than if our enemies would have simply said: "All right, we're not gonna cut off the food. We're not gonna fire people. We're gonna even register a couple. We'll register ten percent of the ones y'all bring down." But more and more, the black people would see that the board of supervisors* controlled everything. What they didn't control, they left to the chief of police. It's easy to sell political involvement when you have that kind of activity by an identifiable political apparatus.

* County commissioners.

CHARLES COBB

Outside Agitator

In 1962 after his freshman year at Howard University, he made his first trip into the Deep South. His destination was a CORE seminar on sit-in tactics in Houston. Earlier in the year, intrigued by a New York Times *story about Bob Moses' work in Mississippi, he had twice written SNCC headquarters in Atlanta, asking if they needed field workers. The letters had gone unanswered.*

I had heard somewhere in the meantime that SNCC also had an office in Jackson, Mississippi, and when the bus finally did get to Jackson, Mississippi, I got off, called up the N-Double-A-C-P and asked if there was a SNCC office in Jackson, Mississippi. And I was told it was right up the street. . . . I went up there, and I never did get to Texas. Larry Guyot, almost from the moment I got to Jackson, was adamant about the fact that I didn't need to go to Texas to participate in some talk about what to do in the South, since I was already in the South. Larry, Sam Block, Willie Peacock, were on the way up to Greenwood, Mississippi, which was more or less the first SNCC project in the Mississippi Delta, and they were leaving a day after I got there. . . .

We were staying in this house [in Jackson], and one night the phone rang with Guyot on the phone [from Greenwood] saying the Ku Klux

Klan was breaking down the door *right then*.* They had called the FBI who had told them, "If anything happens, call us." [Laughs] . . .

What did you do?

We went up. Bob Moses, Charlie McLaurin, myself, and Landy McNair . . . we all went up. A trip was planned anyway, because in addition to the Greenwood project, the plans were pretty definite to open up a project in Sunflower County, the reason being Jim Eastland's home county.** And I was in the midst of trying to decide whether I would stay and go up to the Delta or not, and this kinda settled it.

They visited the shaken group in Greenwood and then pressed on across the Delta to Cleveland. He met Amzie Moore, "who was central to SNCC's ability to work in the Delta. . . . It was a place you could stay. It was a telephone number you could leave messages at in the Delta, and it was he who identified the people throughout the Delta who would be sympathetic."

Moses then drove him, McNair, and McLaurin to Ruleville, the heart of Sunflower County, and dropped them off at the home of Joe McDonald, one of three black voters in the county. "Ruleville . . . Jim East-

---

* Lawrence Guyot: ". . . We saw the chief of police, Curtis Lowery, drive up, park right below the office, and get out of his car and use the radio. That looked very strange. . . . Then we saw two cars loaded with people and with shotguns sticking out of the window, so then we decided to leave. So we got out a window, across another building, onto a house, and we came down a television antenna. At that time I weighed about two hundred sixty pounds, and when I hit the ground there was a hell of a loud noise. . . . I ripped my hand apart. But it was just . . . you just had to; if you weren't prepared to think that quickly and move that quickly, I don't think any of us would have survived." They were taken in by a black woman who lived nearby and used her telephone to report their escape. Shortly, the telephone rang. "The operator called the lady and said, 'There's some trouble makers in your house. When are you going to get them out?'"

** Eastland, the senior Democrat in the U.S. Senate, owned a 5,400-acre Sunflower County plantation on which blacks labored for as little as 30¢ an hour. Although a fierce critic of government spending for welfare and social services, he each year accepted federal crop subsidies of over $100,000 from the U.S. Department of Agriculture, and as a member of the Senate Agriculture Committee, he was able to work to perpetuate the subsidy program. An advocate of open defiance of federal court desegregation rulings, he did much to set the violent tone of Mississippi's political rhetoric. A typical outpouring: "The choice is between victory and defeat. Defeat means death, the death of Southern culture and our aspirations as an Anglo-Saxon people. We of the South have seen the tides rise before. We know what it is to fight. We will carry the fight to victory." As President Pro Tem of the Senate, he for many years stood fourth in line of succession to the presidency.

land's home county . . . the birthplace of the white Citizens Coun-
cil."* McNair and McLaurin were from Mississippi. Cobb was from
Massachusetts and thus became the first Northern student permanently
stationed in the Delta. "It was quick. I got to Mississippi, and within
three days, I was in Ruleville in the midst of a voter registration
project."

I think eleven hundred people lived in the town, so it was literally twenty-four hours before everybody knew in the town, white and black, that, quote, "Freedom Riders" were in town. The Freedom Rides really had an impact over the state, and anybody doing anything with civil rights—especially if they were from out of state *or* from Jackson, which was seen in some respects as remote in terms of the Delta—were viewed [as] and termed Freedom Riders.

It's important to understand also the state was very, very tense, because James Meredith was trying to get into Ole Miss at the exact same period. . . . If it's possible to feel violence and tension in the air, you could certainly feel it in the Delta of Mississippi in the late summer and fall of 1962. Within a few weeks we had gotten our first people to make an effort to register to vote in the county seat, Indianola, something like, oh, fifteen or twenty people, which had a dramatic effect. The white people were stunned . . . it triggered violence.

Right after the first attempt to register people to vote, nightriders came through the black community and shot up three houses, wounding the daughter of a neighbor of the person we were staying with. The Mc-Donalds jumped in the bathtub when the shooting began and just laid low in the bathtub. . . .

I was across the town. We heard the shots and weren't sure. By the time I got back, it was clear. I saw the police. I was arrested for the shooting. [Laughs] . . . I saw the people and the police around the [neighbor's] house and burst in the door, and I remember sliding on the blood, which was in a pool on the floor near the door, and realizing at that moment, as my foot slipped in the blood, that somebody had been hurt. . . .

The mayor of Ruleville was in the house. He was also the justice of the peace, the only judge in town, and he also ran the major store in the town. . . . Well, he looked at me and recognized me as a voter-registration worker and ordered the deputy to place me under arrest. I asked what the charges were, and he never said. . . . He said, "Hold him. Put him under arrest."

* The Citizens Council was founded in Indianola, county seat of Sunflower County.

Another interesting aside is this deputy. . . . His brother was involved in the Emmett Till killing. . . . This was the brother of the guy who wrote the article about how they did the Emmett Till killing.* And I was put in the car, and it was there that they ran down their line about, "You people are looking for publicity, and that's why you shot here to make it seem like you're meeting with all this violence." . . .

I was released the next day. No charges. No reason given really for the arrest. But it paralyzed the town. It really did. The fear just froze all efforts, and it was months before we were able to get anybody else to try and register to vote, because that specific act of violence dovetailed with major economic harassment. That's where Mrs. Fannie Lou Hamer comes into the picture. . . .**

Our decision was that we couldn't really tell people that we had a way of protecting them, either from economic harassment or from physical violence. . . . So, given that reality, our decision was basically just to be physically present in the county, just to show people. Even more important than bringing people down to the county courthouse, it was important for people to know that despite the physical violence—which increasingly became less directed at us and more directed at the people in the county—that we were prepared to stay and stick it out. And that's basically what we did for months, just were there talking on porches, holding some meetings, small, in the one church that let us meet. . . .

That winter of '63 the whole state was being swept by this wave of violence against blacks, and it was directly related to the voter-registration effort. Southwest Mississippi to the Delta, churches were being bombed, economic reprisals were being effected, killings were happening. Most of those killings, we couldn't even get out the information about 'em. Because it was clear, unless you were somebody famous, no paper or TV station was very interested that x person like Lewis Allen was killed down in Amite that winter.***

What happens in these small towns . . . you get funny kinds of assistance. The major thing that people can do is register to vote. Most people aren't going to do that for sound reasons, the physical and eco-

---

* See William Bradford Huie.

** See Mrs. Hamer's account of the economic pressures brought to bear on her and her family.

*** Lewis Allen's was the second of two little-publicized killings in Amite County. In 1961 Herbert Lee, a black farmer who had befriended SNCC workers, was shot to death outside the cotton gin in Liberty, Mississippi, by a white state legislator. Lewis Allen, an eyewitness, was later shot to death in the front yard of his home. No one was ever charged or prosecuted in either killing.

nomic harassment. However, most people are sympathetic, so they tend to point out to you the people that they think are strong enough to stand the heat . . . Also people, I found, pointed out who to watch out for. The key white people, of course, were pointed out to us. Also blacks. . . . For instance, Jim Eastland, on his plantation, at the time anyway, had a considerable amount of prison labor. People coming out of Parchman. They weren't confined, so obviously their loyalty was to Jim Eastland and all things that attached to that. And those people were pointed out to us. I mean, they had the run of the town. They were "Jim Eastland's niggers," and that's how they were described, and that's how they behaved. It's often been believed in terms of the shooting that I just described that the houses . . . all of which were pretty key in terms of support for us . . . were pointed out by a particular black person who also lived in that section of the black community in Ruleville. So those people were pointed out to you, and you were told to watch out for them. People did a lot of things. They wouldn't go to the courthouse with you; they would bring you some food. They knew that the McDonalds' having the three young students who ate a lot . . . was a burden on them, and one of the levels of assistance was getting food, helping with just the feeding of us.

The interview takes place in a broadcast studio at WHUR, the Howard University radio station in Washington, D.C. He is a newsman there. The air conditioning is uncomfortably cool. He rubs his arms against the chill. Those first summer days in the choking heat of the Delta seem far away, a remote experience in a strange land. He ponders the question of fear. "There were moments . . . like driving from Greenville to Meridian . . . the middle of the night, knowing that your car is known . . . seeing a truck with a white farmer and a shotgun or a rifle, and it tailgates you for thirty miles across flat, flat country owned by white farmers." But the SNCC worker, although black, had an advantage simply because he was an alien. ". . . The attitude of the authorities was they shouldn't really push you too hard, because you knew the number of the Justice Department or you had an office in Atlanta or parents in Massachusetts, so that you could stand up to them, one-on-one."

But the effect of that. You sometimes had the nagging worry that the effect of that was for that guy to take it out on some other black guy. I remember being stopped by a state trooper on a highway in the Delta, hassling us about something. I mean, he knew the car; he just hassled us. But everything was in order, and we went on our way. And reading

FANNIE LOU HAMER

Well, we were living on a plantation about four and a half miles east of here. . . . Pap had been out there thirty years, and I had been out there eighteen years, 'cause we had been married at that time eighteen years. And you know, things were just rough. . . . I don't think that I ever remember working for as much as four dollars a day. Yes, one year I remember working for four dollars a day, and I was gettin' as much as the men, 'cause I kept up with the time. . . . But anyway, I just knowed things wasn't right.

So then that was in 1962 when the civil rights workers came into this county. Now, I didn't know anything about voter registration or nothin' like that, 'cause people had never been told that they could register to vote. And livin' out in the country, if you had a little radio, by the time you got in at night, you'd be too tired to listen at what was goin' on. . . . So they had a rally. I had gone to church that Sunday, and the minister announced that they were gon' have a mass meeting that Monday night. Well, I didn't know what a mass meeting was, and I was just curious to go to a mass meeting. So I did . . . and they was talkin' about how blacks had a right to register and how they had a right to *vote*. . . . Just listenin' at 'em, I could just see myself votin' people outa office that I know was wrong and didn't do nothin' to help the poor. I said, you know, that's sumpin' I really wanna be involved in, and finally at the end of that rally, I had made up my mind that I was gonna come out there when they said you could go down that Friday to try to register.

> *She remembers the date precisely: August 31, 1962. She and seventeen others climbed aboard an old bus owned by a black man from neighboring Bolivar County. SNCC had chartered it for the thirty-mile ride to the county seat in Indianola. Once there, she was the first into the registrar's office.*

> . . . He brought a big old book out there, and he gave me the sixteenth section of the Constitution of Mississippi, and that was dealing with de facto laws, and I didn't know nothin' about no de facto laws, didn't know nothin' about any of 'em. I could copy it like it was in the book . . . but after I got through copying it, he told me to give a reasonable interpretation and tell the meaning of that section that I had copied. Well, I flunked out. . . .

So then we started back to Ruleville and on our way back to Ruleville, this same highway patrolman that I had seen steady cruisin' around this bus stopped us. We had crossed that bridge, coming over from Indianola. They got out the cars, flagged the bus down. When they flagged the bus down, they told all of us to get off of the bus. So at this time, we just started singing "Have a Little Talk with Jesus," and we got off the bus, and all they wanted then was for us to get back on the bus. They arrested Bob* and told the bus driver he was under arrest. So we went back then to Indianola. The bus driver was fined one hundred dollars for driving a bus with too much yellow in it. Now ain't that ridiculous?

For what?

Too much yellow. Said the bus looked too much like a school bus. That's funny, but it's the truth. But you see, it was to frighten us to death. This same bus had been used year after year hauling cotton choppers and cotton pickers to Florida to try to make a livin' that winter, and he had never been arrested before. But the day he tried . . . to carry us to Indianola, they fined him a hundred dollars, and I guess it was so ridiculous that they finally cut the fine down to thirty dollars, and all of us *together*—not one, but all us together—had enough to pay the

---
* Bob Moses, who had come back to Ruleville to accompany the group to the courthouse.

fine. So we paid the fine, and then we got back on the bus and come on to Ruleville.

So Rev. Jeff Summers, who live on Charles Street, just the next street over, he carried me out there on the Marlowe Plantation where I had worked for eighteen years. And when I got out there, my little girl—she's dead now, Dorothy—she met me and one of Pap's cousins, and said that man [who owned the plantation] had been raising a lot of Cain ever since we left, that he had been in the field more times than he usually come a day, because I had gone to the courthouse. See, the people at the courthouse would call and tell it. So they was kinda scared, and quite natural I began to feel nervous, but I knowed I hadn't done nothin' wrong. So after my little girl told me, wasn't too long 'fore Pap got off, and he was tellin' me the same thing that the other kids had told me.

I went on in the house, and I sat down on a little old bed that belonged to the little girl, and when I sat down on the bed, this man [who owned the plantation] he come up and he asked Pap, "Did you tell Fannie Lou what I said?" And Pap said, "Yessir, I sho' did." And I got up and walked to the door, and then he asked me, "Did Pap tell you what I said?" I said, "He told me." And he said, "I mean that. You'll have to go back to Indianola and withdraw, or you have to leave this place." So I said, "Mr. Dee, I didn't go down there to register for you. I went down there to register for myself." And that made him madder, you know.

So he told me, "I want your answer now, yea or nay." And he said, "They gon' "—now, I don't know who the *they* were, whether it was the white Citizens Council or the Ku Klux Klan, 'cause I don't think one is no worse than the other—"they gon' worry me tonight. They gon' worry the hell outa me, and I'm gon' worry hell outa you. You got 'til in the mornin' to tell me. But if you don't go back there and withdraw, you got to leave the plantation."

So I knowed I wasn't goin' back to withdraw, so wasn't nothin' for me to do but leave the plantation. So Pap brought me out that same night and I come to Mrs. Tucker's, a lady live over on Byron Street. I went to her house, and I stayed, and Pap began to feel nervous when he went to the shop* and saw some buckshot shells. And they don't have buckshot shells to *play* with in August and September, because you ain't huntin' or nothin' like that.

On September tenth—again she recalls the date precisely—came the nightrider attack described by Charles Cobb. The riders shot into the

---

* The maintenance shop on the plantation.

McDonald home, where the SNCC workers were staying, and into the Tucker home, where Mrs. Hamer had been given shelter. "They shot in that house sixteen times, tryin' to kill me," she remembers. She fled to the home of a niece in Tallahatchie County when the nighttime terrorism continued on into the fall.

I stayed away, 'cause things then—you could see 'em at night. They would have fires in the middle of the road. . . . You wouldn't see no Klan signs, but just make a fire in the middle of the road. And it was *so dangerous,* I stayed in Tallahatchie County all of September and then October, and then November I come back to Ruleville. I was comin', I didn't know why I was comin', but I was just sick of runnin' and hadn't done nothin'. . . . I started tryin' to find a place to stay, 'cause we didn't have nothin'.

The woman who had been her sixth-grade school teacher put her in touch with a black woman who had a three-room house for rent "for eighteen dollars a month and that was a lotta money." She and her family moved in on December 3.

That was on a Sunday, and that Monday, the fourth of December, I went back to Indianola to the circuit clerk's office and I told him who I was and I was there to take that literacy test again.

I said, "Now, you cain't have me fired 'cause I'm already fired, and I won't have to move now, because I'm not livin' in no white man's house." I said, "I'll be here every thirty days until I become a registered voter." 'Cause that's what you would have to do: go every thirty days and see had you passed the literacy test. . . . I went back then the tenth of January in 1963, and I had become registered. . . . I passed the second one, because at the second time I went back, I had been studying sections of the Mississippi Constitution, so I would know if I got one that was simple enough that I might could pass it.

I passed that second test, but it made us become like criminals. We would have to have our lights out before dark. It was cars passing that house all times of the night, driving real slow with guns, and pickups with white mens in it, and they'd pass that house just as slow as they could pass it . . . three guns lined up in the back. All of that. This was the kind of stuff. Pap couldn't get nothin' to do. . . .

So I started teachin' citizenship class,* and I became the supervisor of the citizenship class in this county. So I moved around the county to do

---

* In a voter-education program administered by SCLC.

citizenship education, and later on I become a field secretary for SNCC
—I guess being about one of the oldest people at that time that was a
field secretary, 'cause they was real young.

*Once more the classic Southern story was repeated. White oppression
created a Movement heroine. She became a leader in the Mississippi
Freedom Democratic Party and, at the 1964 Democratic Convention, a
national celebrity with her televised testimony before the Credentials
Committee about that "woesome time for us when we was arrested in
Winona." That time came in the summer of 1963. She was with a group
returning from a voter-registration workshop in South Carolina. Their
bus stopped in Winona, a central Mississippi town which had not bowed
to the ICC's bus-depot ruling. "Some of the folks got off to go in to get
food, and some of 'em got off to go in the washroom. Well, they went in
what at that time was called the white side, and you just didn't go in the
white side of a restaurant." She was one of seven arrested.*

They carried us on to the county jail. It wasn't the city jail. The
county jail, so we could be far enough out, they didn't care how loud we
hollered, wasn't nobody gon' hear us. . . . I was put in the cell with
. . . I cain't think of this child's name . . . Evester Simpson. She's Mrs.
Morris now. But anyway, I was in the cell with her, and they left Miss
Ponder* and somebody else out, and I started hearing screaming like I
had never heard. And I could hear the sounds of the licks, but I
couldn't see nobody. And I hear somebody when they say, "Cain't you
say yessir, nigger? Cain't you say yessir, bitch?"

And I could understand Miss Ponder's voice. She said, "Yes, I can
say yessir." He said, "Well, say it." She said, "I don't know you well
enough." She never would say yessir, and I could hear when she would
hit the flo', and then I could hear them licks just soundin'. [Softly] That
was somethin'. That's a experience—that's a experience that I wouldn't
want to go through again. But anyway, she kept screamin', and they
kept beatin' on her, and finally she started prayin' for 'em, and she
asked God to have mercy on 'em, because they didn't know what they
was doin'.

And after then . . . I heard some real *keen* screams, and that's when
they passed my cell with a girl, she was fifteen years old, Miss Johnson.
June Johnson. They passed my cell, and the blood was runnin' down in
her face, and they put her in another cell.

---

* Annelle Ponder, one of two SCLC voter-education teachers permanently stationed in Mississippi.

And then finally they come to my room, and one of them men told me, "Get up from there, fatso," and he carried me outa that cell. They first asked me, when they first come to the cell, they asked me where I was from, and I told 'em. And they said, "We gon' check that out," and I reckon they was callin' the white folks here. Well, the white folks here knowed I had tried to register, so they was gon' give me as much trouble as possible, 'cause when they come back, the man say, "You from Ruleville, all right." Said, "You, bitch, you, we gon' make you wish you was dead." And let me tell you, before they stopped beatin' me, I wish they would have hit me one lick that could have ended the misery that they had me in. They had me to lay down on this bunk bed with my face down, and they had two black prisoners. You know, a lot of folks would say, "Well, I woulda died before I'd done that." But nobody know the condition that those prisoners was in, before they were s'posed to beat me. And I heard that highway patrolman tell that black man, said, "If you don't beat her, you *know* what we'll do to you." And he didn't have no other choice.

So they had me lay down on my face, and they beat with a thick leather thing that was wide. And it had sumpin' in it *heavy*. I don't know what that was, rocks or lead. But everytime they hit me, I got just as hard, and I put my hands behind my back, and they beat me in my hands 'til my hands . . . my hands was as navy blue as anything you ever seen . . . that blood, I guess, and then beatin' it 'til it just turned black.

And then after the first one beat, they ordered the second one to beat me, and when the second one started beatin', it was just—it was just too much. I started wiggling . . . you know, kickin' my feet back there. The highway patrolman walked over there and had that first one had beat, told him to sit on my feet . . . while the second one beat. . . . But anyway, they finally told me to get up, and I just couldn't hardly get up, and they kept on tellin' me to get up. I finally could get up, but when I got back to my cell bed, I couldn't set down. I would *scream*. It hurted me to set down.

After I got beat, I didn't hardly see my family in 'bout a month, 'cause I went on to Atlanta, from Atlanta to Washington, and from Washington to New York, because they didn't want my family to see me in the shape I was in. I had been beat 'til I was real hard, just hard like a piece of wood or somethin'. A person don't know what can happen to they body if they beat with something like I was beat with.

Less than four years after she failed that first literacy test at the Sunflower County Courthouse, less than three years after that devastating beating in Winona, Mississippi *magazine named her as one of six "Women of Influence" in the state. The magazine carried her picture next to that of another woman of influence—an aristocratic Delta matron who wrote a newspaper column entitled "Dis an' Dat." Within ten years Ruleville had held Fannie Lou Hamer Day. The white mayor who had once clapped her husband in jail for an overdue water bill said she would go down in history as a champion of her people.*

On this midsummer day in 1975—a campaign year in Mississippi—she sits in a kitchen chair in the shade of a pecan tree. Her husband, Pap, a big, loose-jointed man who "rule well his house," is watering his tomato plants. Here, in the backyard of her brick bungalow in Ruleville, Mrs. Hamer receives political callers. A sharply dressed black man driving a shiny Pontiac has just pled the case of the white candidate who has hired him.

It's really sumpin' now to see this same Fannie Lou that they talked about. . . . It used to be where if you had come up here in yo' car, them white folks woulda been by here a hundred-and-sumpin' times, and then you woulda been picked up when you left. That's the way it was. But today them same white folks will come down here askin' for support, too.

When you decided to go down and register, was that like a bolt out of the blue?

No, I would get out in the fields and I was always talkin' to folks about conditions. And I was one that they said sometimes didn't have real good sense. . . .

Do you think through all the years leading up to the Movement days, did white people in Mississippi know they were wrong?

Some of 'em really didn't, 'cause I don't think they really saw us as human beings. We would smile and that would just fool 'em, that would just trap 'em. Now we have been some of the greatest actors on earth, 'cause we could smile when we would see 'em coming and they'd get about ten feet and we would say—you know it wouldn't be right to put it in the book what we would say. . . .

I always believed some cared and some I don't think saw us as people. This same plantation I was on, we moved in a house that white folks had lived, and there was a bathroom there, and we had to go outdoors to outside toilet, 'cause this one wasn't working in the house, and I asked that man to fix it, and he told me we didn't need it. And several weeks after that I was over to they house cleaning up a bathroom, and his daughter told me—she was a little girl then—she told me I didn't have to take too much pains in that room, because that was old Honey's bathroom, and that was they dog.

I was mad enough to boil when I left that house, but she ain't never knowed it, and I went home and I told Pap, I said, "Now they got they dog higher'n us. We workin' and got them settin' down. They settin' down off what we've done for them."

Yeah, I knowed a long time ago. It wasn't no bolt out of the blue. . . .

Postscript: In the winter of 1975, a few months after this interview, her health began failing. Although ill, she worked through the winter and on into 1976 to unite the black and the white factions of the Mississippi Democratic party so that a single integrated delegation could represent the state at the 1976 Democratic Convention in New York. She died of cancer on March 15, 1977, in the hospital at Mount Bayou, Mississippi, a black-governed town thirty miles north of her home in Ruleville. She was sixty years old. A few weeks after her death, the Mississippi legislature passed unanimously a resolution praising her service to the state.

Ivanhoe Donaldson

The District of Columbia Building in Washington, D.C. He works there as chief aide to an old SNCC comrade, Councilman Marion Barry. He is an engaging, sophisticated conversationalist, a natty dresser. It is almost impossible to imagine him as a dungareed member of SNCC's Delta cadre.

What happened was, in the Mississippi Delta, a number of people were being pushed off the plantation who were trying either to go down and register to vote or who were organizing other people to go down and register to vote. And it was coming into the fall, and winter was due, and the plantation owners were not only being hostile in terms of pushing people off the plantation, but were economically isolating people from credit at stores or from banks. . . .

SNCC organized and sent out an appeal in the fall of '62 across the country for food, and of course, I had a base up at Michigan State. . . .* I and another guy organized a "Freedom Run" which went from Ann Arbor, Michigan, to Clarksdale, Mississippi, and we stopped off all along the way to pick up food or clothes or medical goods, whatever we could get. We warehoused all this stuff in Louisville, which was sort of halfway there . . . until we had enough for maybe four or five trips into Clarksdale. . . . Though the food was for Greenwood, it was

* Where he was a student.

Clarksdale where we based out of. And Dr. Aaron Henry—"doctor" was the popular term; he's a pharmacist who is president of the Mississippi state N-Double-A-C-P—was our contact, and he was sort of in charge of the process.*

On a run in December he and his partner, fellow Michigan State student Ben Taylor, rolled into Clarksdale well after midnight.

We got in about two hours after when we were supposed to have been there. Doc had closed up about an hour before. So we said the smartest thing was to sit in the truck, crack the windows and just go to sleep, which is what we proceeded to do. And I don't know, I was fast asleep, and someone banged on the window. . . . It was a policeman, and they asked us what we were doing there. And we said that we were delivering some food and clothes and things to Doc Henry, and we showed them our ID and established the fact that the truck was legal. . . . Anyway, they arrested us for whatever cause. No cause, we were just arrested. Didn't ask a lot of questions at three o'clock in the morning anyway. The man says, "You are under arrest," and you say, "Yessir." So we went off to jail. To be frank about it, we never thought much about it. We went to sleep. We were tired. Ben, I think, was paralyzed by the whole thing. I was too tired to really be concerned about what was happening.

So I woke up in the morning, and then things started dawning on me. . . . We wanted to call someone, and they told us we couldn't make any calls, and they called us a bunch of niggers, this, and niggers, that. And what were we doing down here? We weren't from Mississippi; we were disrupting; we were Commies. . . .

This went on about three or four days, and I was getting nervous. Ben, I know, was getting nervous. We asked what the charges were. They didn't say anything to us. Finally, we were informed that we were being charged with crossing the border with illegal drugs. Well, we didn't have any drugs to our knowledge in the truck. We did get some materials from a doctor in Louisville to deliver to Doc Henry. As it turned out, these things were bandages, band aids, aspirin, and things which anybody can buy over the counter. But I didn't even know they were in the truck. We collected whatever we collected.

And so a couple of times we were close enough to the front in the cell that we were in that we could hear. . . . We knew someone had called

---

* Despite the general contempt in SNCC ranks for NAACP "conservatives," Aaron Henry enjoyed a personal respect like that accorded Amzie Moore, and Henry's drugstore in Clarksdale was an important SNCC way station in the Delta.

to inquire. . . . I could tell, because I have an unusual first name in the sense of Ivanhoe, and they would make a lot of mockery of it. "Ivanhoe? Ain't no nigger named Ivanhoe here." . . .

Anyway, typical of Southern jails, the people in Clarksdale City Jail . . . collected money in the parking meters during the day, and I gave one of the guys a note. Jails were segregated, so we were on the black side. I gave one of them a note to slip to Doc Henry, because I knew the guy was going down Fourth Street, and he said he would drop it at Doc Henry's store. And I just wrote a simple note: "Doc, we are in jail. Get us out. Ivanhoe." And that was the first time that Doc Henry knew, in fact, that we were there. And Doc came down and that relieved our tensions a little bit and told us that SNCC was singing songs about us in Atlanta, that he was glad to know we were okay, and of course, we would be out the next day. So Ben and I said, "Great."

Their relief did not survive the bail bond hearing the next day before a local magistrate. ". . . I thought it was going to be like five hundred dollars. When the guy said 'Fifteen thousand,' I mean my whole stomach went out. It was more money than SNCC had in its annual budget. . . . I said, 'I'm going to be in here forever.' " Later, Justice Department and NAACP Inc. Fund attorneys entered the case, and he was released, but not before receiving a final jailhouse beating which broke several ribs. He and Ben Taylor toured the country, telling their story and raising money for SNCC.

Eventually, I went up to Holly Springs, north of Greenwood . . . there you really learned about the stark terror of day-to-day living . . . wondering whether someone was going to sneak in and dynamite you or firebomb your home. Always checking your car before you got in it, because you were worrying about whether someone stuck a piece of dynamite under it. Always making sure your tires were in good condition, because you never know, you may have to race up the road at night. At night you just didn't stop for anybody, not on the open highway. You know, if it was cops, you just race into the city and let 'em stop you in the open downtown area and throw you in jail, and maybe somebody would see you. . . .

On Mississippi cops:

You had to be careful to never show fear. If they thought you were frightened of them, they took total advantage of the situation. . . . The key was not whether you were frightened or not, but how much you exhibited that fear. . . . I mean, there were a number of times when I was just paralyzed in a situation, but you took the aggressive action: "I'm going to sue you. . . . I'm going to call the FBI, the President. . . . I'll have a thousand people in this city tomorrow. . . ."

Once, he was thrown into a cop car at the airport in Jackson.

. . . the guy pulled a gun and cocked it and put it right up in front of my nose, and he said he was going to blow me away, and I thought he was. . . . Then some other cop put his head in and said, "You can't kill that nigger out here. . . ."

It wiped out half the people who got involved. I think you kind of had to be a little philosophical about life to survive. . . . I think the people who believed change was possible, but expected it to happen the next day, burnt out first. They just got frustrated. They freaked out. Some people freaked out from the violence. Some people were battle-weary, you know, battle fatigue. They went into shock. SNCC had an elaborate community of friends across the country . . . many of them were doctors and stuff, and people with SNCC would go and visit psychiatrists, psychoanalysts, and try and get their heads back together. Once you've had a bad experience physically, where you've been mauled or beaten or brutalized or hit with a bullet or had some broken bones, that fear is always in you. . . . I think there was a heavy toll in that generation, people who were active. It's not to be romantic. I think the evidence is just there. Even today, when you look around for what happened to SNCC people, I mean some of them are just barely functioning . . .

He describes the symptoms of SNCC's burnt-out cases.

. . . you kind of drift from job to job . . . a total cynic about anything and everything . . . you're just out there. Maybe you become a cab driver in San Diego, an all-white community, or you become an airplane mechanic. Anything which keeps you away from anything which deals with social commentary of any sort, because it's just too much. Some people ended up in homes, institutions. . . .

HARTMAN TURNBOW

From his house you can see back in the east the long green ridge marking the rim of the Delta. Here, just south of Tchula, he owns seventy acres of land as flat as a table and as rich as any in America. In the year he was seventy years old he made twenty bales of cotton on this farm, his land long since bought and paid for, where he made his stand.

How I first got interested in the Movement was a fella come in here talkin' 'bout redish and vote to become a first-class citizen, and he come down here in Holmes County outa Leflore County several times before we got interested in redishin' and votin'. Nobody in Holmes County or nowhere in Mississippi hadn't never redished and hadn't never voted, and I was quite a ageable man at that time, and I hadn't never did it and hadn't never heard anything 'bout it, so I just wasn't too interested in it. I thought maybe I had all life had in store for me, but he made several trips. . . . He said, "Now at this time the Negro don't vote. . . . Who the white peoples want to put in office, they just have a meetin' 'mong theirselves, and they 'point Miz So-and-So or Mister So-and-So." The people then was just mostly 'pointed to the local office in these little village-towns like Tchula and Lexington. I guess they voted in them days for the big office like governor, lieutenant governor, and all like that, but in these little ones, why, they just 'pointed the most of 'em.

So when I heard the story about redishin' and votin', how you'd be a first-class citizen and make your livin' standard better, then I was interested in becoming a redished voter to be a first-class citizen. So he talked it at the school, at the church, at my church down there at Mileston, so the people all got interested in it all 'round Mileston. In the Mileston community, everybody got interested in it, so we commenced to havin' meetin's then ever Wednesday night, talkin' 'bout redishin' and votin'. And at the same time it was another lady come in here, and they set up what you call citizenship classes, teachin' us what redishin' meant to us, and everybody oughta be a redished voter. So we got sho'nuff interested in it then, after we commenced to havin' the classes. So after we had the classes about a couple of weeks or maybe a little longer, twelve of us decided we'd go to Lexington and try it out.

The next morning we set, we all met, and we got in our cars, and we went to Lexington, where we discussed it well. We said, "Now we ain't gon' drive our cars up in town to give 'em no kinda excuse. We gon' park 'em out on the outer edge, on side the road." So we did, and we got out. We said, "Now, we not gon' walk in a big drove. They'll say we're huddlin', we're takin' up all the streets and crowdin' 'em out. We gon' walk by twos, and we gon' walk a distance apart, and we gon' give everybody the street we meet." So we did that. We went on 'round to the south courthouse door, and there we met Mr. Andrew P. Smith, the sheriff of Holmes County. Oh, he commenced to hollerin' and cursin'. We had a leader leadin' us, John Ball, that'uz a Negro from Leflore County. They had that thing goin' on up there. And Mr. Smith he snatched his club and slapped his hand on his pistol to hit John Ball 'cross the head with that billy club. So right at that time, I stepped out the line. I told him, I said, "Mr. Smith, we only come to vote . . . to *redish*. We only come to redish *to* vote." He said, "Well, Turnbow, y'all go one by one around on the north side and huddle under that tree."

We went 'round there. We huddled under that tree, all of us. So we got there, he came 'round there. He looked at us, looked at all of us 'fore he said anything. Then when he did say anything, he said, "All right now, who will be first? Who will be first?" And the Negroes, they commenced to lookin' at one another. Right fast, I said to myself, "Now, these Negroes gon' run, that's what they gon' do. They gon' run." [Laughs] That's what I had in my mind. I stepped out the line. I said, "Me, Hartman Turnbow, will be first."

He said, "All right, Turnbow, go right down the edge of the curb to the sidewalk, to the walk, and then go in the courthouse and take the first door to the left and do what you got to do." I told him, "Yessir." I went on down side the curb, got on the sidewalk, went in the first door on the left. I walked in. There was a lady in there. Mr. Henry McClellan was the circuit clerk, but he wasn't in there at that time, so the lady, she'uz mighty friendly. She say, "Well, what can I do for you?" I say, "I come to redish to vote." She say, *"Redish to vote?"* I say, "Yes, ma'am. Redish to vote." She say, "Well, Mr. McClellan is not in here. He'll be back after while." I said, "May I wait for him? May I have a seat and wait?" She say, "Yes. You welcome. Just have a seat over there and wait 'til he come."

I sat in there till twelve o'clock. It was 'bout eleven. That was a full hour I set there. He didn't show up. She said, "Well, it's noon now, I'm going to dinner." I said, "Well, I'm goin' out and after dinner, I'll be back." She say, "All right." I went on out and told 'em wasn't nobody in there to redish me. They all wanted to know, they was waitin' to hear the story, what happened. Told 'em I didn't get redished, wasn't nobody in there.

I waited till one o'clock. I went back in there and there was Mr. Henry McClellan. He said, "What can I do for you?" I say, "I wants to redish to vote." He say, *"Redish to vote?"* I say, "Yessir, that's what I want. Want to redish to vote." Well, he didn't do nothin', but just went over there and got the books, and he brought it to me and give me the questionnaire. They was mighty hard, the questions, but I filled 'em, I filled 'em, I filled 'em correct at that time, those he give me. So then I went on out. I met my crowd and they asked me, "Well, what happened?" I say, "He give me the books and I redished. He had a lotsa hard questions there, and I filled 'em out to the best of my knowledge and give 'em back to him and signed it and that 'uz all." Well that got the rest of 'em interested in gwine. Said, "We'll go and see can we fill 'em." Then they commenced to goin', one by one. It was about twelve of us and took 'em all that half-a-day to get us redished up. And at that time, while it was goin' on, peoples all out in the street was climbin' up on cars and lookin' at us just like we'uz somethin' out the zoo. And white and colored knowed everyone of us, 'cause we was born and raised right here at Tchula and Lexington. And they well knowed us, white and black. But white and black was climbin' up on cars and things lookin' at us. And we had a newsman here from Jackson, and he met us and talked and asked a lot of questions, so we answered them to the best of our knowledge. So that ended up for that day and that was all happened the first day.

Was anything done . . . against the people that went down to register?

Well, certainly it was. I was the first one that said I want to redish to vote, and I'uz the first one got my house bombed. Oh, I redished like today, and about four or five days from then, they done come to my house and firebombed the living room, the back bedroom, and shot all in it. Made 'bout five shots right in the living room here. That big forty-five hole right there at the corner of that picture, that's one of the holes. That bullet bedded in that wall. They got it. Another 'un come right through the window and went through a couch we had settin' there. Not that one. That one burned up what was settin' there. . . . 'Bout three of 'em hit up over the ceiling and bedded. FBIs found 'em all and got 'em. So they come down one night 'bout one o'clock and they firebombed this house and shot all in it.

Were you in the house?

Myself, wife, and fourteen-year-old daughter was in the house, and my wife and daughter jumped up and run out, and the first thing they met was two white fellas in the backyard. And I didn't go out till I got my rifle, and when I got my rifle, I pushed the safety off, I got it in shootin' position, and then I run out. The first thing I met was those two white fellas. They start to shootin' at me, and I start to shootin' at them. So they run off, and then we come back and put the fire out.

It didn't destroy your house?

No, it didn't destroy it. It burnt up that couch and just messed up all the ceiling. We repainted, but it's still rough. And burnt the curtains all off the wall and burnt that couch up there. In the back bedroom, it burnt up all of my wife's bed linens. She had did 'em up and had 'em piled on that bed 'cause it was summer, and all of that burnt up—the mattress, all of her quilts, blankets, sheets, and everything. So after we got them away, we start to fightin' fire, and we put it out.

You say the FBI came. Did the local law?

Oh, they come, they come arrest me. They come the next day. But that happened about one o'clock that night, and no sooner was day come, we called the Justice Department in Washington, D.C., and told 'em about the incident, how they had firebombed the house and shot all in it, and we would certainly 'preciate it if they'd send some FBIs from the Justice Department. They told me by eight o'clock they'd have some here. So 'fore Mr. Andrew Smith* and them got here, the Justice De-

* The sheriff of Holmes County.

partment [representative] had done flew from Washington to Memphis and got him a car and had drove here. He'us right here writin' up the story when Mr. Andrew Smith come. So, he told Mr. Smith he was busy then, right then, and Mr. Smith he left and went on back to Lexington.

But later that evenin', Mr. Smith come back and 'rested me for arsony. Said I'uz tellin' a lie. Said no white peoples hadn't been here, and they didn't bomb that house and they didn't shoot in it. Said . . . I bombed my own house and I shot it full of holes.

I told him, "Why, I ain't never owned a forty-five in my life. Them forty-five bullets and forty-five holes, and I never owned nary'un." I told him three of those forty-five hulls where they'uz shootin' in the back-yard at me was still there.

He said, "That's a lie." Said I put 'em there. So they tried me in a lit-tle preliminary trial up here at Tchula, and they convicted me for ar-sony.

On what evidence?

Just said I was a liar . . . that's the onliest evidence they had. So the FBI from Washington, they was still there, and they had a secretary, had a lady there that writes everything you say. Other words, she had one of them little machines. She just beat it, and at the end of the court, everything everybody said, she got it.

So since she was there, they didn't say everything they wanted to say. But they just say I was watchin' the TV, wanna say I got that story from the TV of what was did here. And then they convicted me.

So them FBIs, they 'pealed it, they 'pealed it right then to a federal court in Jackson that fall in the Post Office building. So we had another trial. So when that time come and we went to Jackson for trial . . . they said they had done dropped the charges, said they didn't have no charges against me, said they had done dropped 'em.

And the reason they dropped the charges, they know what they had and how they tried me here and Tchula—they know that wasn't gon' stand up in federal court. Mr. John Doar was my lawyer from Washing-ton, D.C. . . . They knew it wasn't gon' stand up, not with Mr. John Doar. So they just dropped the charges, and that was the end of that.

Mrs. Turnbow joins in, calling from the kitchen, "No, it wasn't."

Huh?

Mrs. Turnbow: "They come by here and shot all in my kitchen."

That was another year, sweet.

Mrs. Turnbow: "That was the same year."

Naw, it wasn't, sweet. That was another year. They shot in here and bombed the house in '63, and that was '64, they rode by on the highway and shot all in the house with a thirty rifle . . . hit the house four times. And t'was a white lady stayin' with us from New York, workin' down here, and if they hada shot six inches higher, why that bullet woulda hit her right in the head. . . . She got scared. She left. [Laughs] She didn't stay nary another night here.

Is that right?

That's right, and I couldn't blame her. Then the next year, I shot back. When they shot over here, I got a automatic shotgun, Remington, twelve gauge, them high-velocity buckshot. So I jumped up and run out and turn it loose a time or two. . . .
I reported it to the FBI in Jackson and told 'em, "Now, y'all come up here, 'cause there's gonna be some trouble, and I'm gonna give y'all the first chance to stop it. And they come right away. I was out there workin' on my plows, fixin' to go to the field. They introduced theirself to me, and they come tellin' me, first words they said to me was "Don't kill nobody. Don't kill nobody."
I said, "Now here y'all two Mississippi FBIs comin', jumpin' straddle of my neck, talkin' 'bout 'Don't kill nobody.' How do you think I feel and they just shootin' all through my house and I got a wife and a fourteen-year-old daughter? They could shoot any one of 'em or even me. . . . I want this to be the last time. If you don't, it's gonna be some trouble. 'Cause I'm gonna git my gun and git busy and see who can I shoot." So I ain't heard no more from it since then. It cooled off.

Did any of the civil rights people ever try to talk you out of shootin' back . . . ?

Never did. Ain't but one. Ain't but one. He used to git on me a whole lot 'bout it, and that was Martin Lufus King. I went to a meetin' in Frogmore, South Carolina, and he were there, and he'uz against that shootin' back. He believed in nonviolent. I told him, "Well, I never, never make a nonviolent man."

He and Martin Luther King were to meet one more time. In 1964 he was in the Mississippi Freedom Democratic party (MFDP) delegation to the Democratic National Convention. He was among those chosen to testify about segregation in Mississippi, to support the MFDP contention that the official, all-white Mississippi delegation should not be seated.

In Atlantic City, New Jersey, in the national politician meeting . . . I got to talkin' about the incident happened at my house, how they fire-bombed and shoot all in it and I had a fourteen-year-old daughter and a wife and ary one of them coulda got hit or even me, and I talked about how I got my gun and went out and shot with 'em, and they runned off.

And then he said to me, Dr. Martin Lufus King said to me right there in the politician meetin', said he was nonviolent and he'd never 'prove of violence. And then I replied to him, I said, "This nonviolent stuff ain't no good. It'll get ya killed."

I said, "If you follow it long enough, it's gon' get *you* killed."

And right at that time when I said that, it was a nice-lookin', young Negro lady in there and she said, "Mr. Turnbow, well what is some good, what's good? If nonviolent ain't no good, what's good?"

I said, "It ain't but one thing that is good." I said, "Every what the Mississippi white man pose with, he got to be met with."

I said, "Meet him with ever what he pose with. If he pose with a smile, meet him with a smile, and if he pose with a gun, meet him with a gun."

At that time, all the peoples in there, white and the colored, they 'greed with me. They said that was the answer, the only answer for that question, said, "Meet 'em with ever what they pose with." So he was the only one in that national politician meetin' that believed and agreed on nonviolent.

Did he make any response when you told him that it would get him killed?

He said that was it, said that's just his way, say he gon' finish up with nonviolent. I told him, "Well you finish up in a cemetery you just keep a followin' it." Them was my words to him, and for a witness, Mrs. Fannie Lou Hamer, she heard it.

Had you been a rebellious person before against the system of segregation . . . ?

Never, never, never. I don't know where all that there braveness come from. I just found myself, I just found myself with it. Other words, the shootin' in my house: I had a wife, and I had a daughter, and I loved my wife just like a white man loves his'n, and I loved my baby daughter just like a white man loves his'n, and a white man will die for his'n, and I say I'll die for mine. Say if I catch anybody shootin' in my house, they gon' have to kill me or I'm gon' kill them. One of us got to go. They cain't do that and I know it and both of us stay here. And since that time, near about every Negro done got the same thought. It won't work no more. It'd be a war. It'd be a big riot between the whites and the blacks if it started again. It's gone bye-bye. The Negroes just won't go for it no more. So it's better. It's better. A whole lot better. . . .

Julian Bond

There was a big debate in SNCC once about carrying guns, whether or not we should carry guns, and two or three of the guys from Mississippi said, "This is all academic. We been carrying guns. I got mine here."

The rest of us were shocked: "We can't carry guns. We're non-violent."

Guy said, "Don't tell me I can't carry my gun. I been carrying this for a year or more." Guy had a little automatic.

Almost everybody with whom we stayed in Mississippi had guns, as a matter of course, hunting guns. But, you know, they were there for other purposes, too.

This old guy, Hartman Turnbow, I remember him. He used to carry an army automatic in a briefcase, and it's funny to see a man who looks like a farmer and is dressed like a farmer in coveralls and boots and, let's say, an old hat, with a briefcase. And he opens the briefcase and nothing's in it but an automatic.

Lawrence Guyot

There was such an interrelationship between Greenwood and the surrounding towns. . . . I remember distinctly when the two highway patrolmen drove past, and I was leading the line with Mary Lane, and we wouldn't run from the dogs. The dogs were snapping at us, and we just moved ahead. . . . But the highway patrolmen saw that I wasn't afraid of the dogs. When Fannie Lou Hamer and Annelle Ponder and June Jackson and other people were arrested in Winona and I went over there to see about them, they said, "Oh, you the nigger who wasn't afraid of the dogs."

You were involved in the Winona incident?

Someone called and said, "We've been arrested in Winona," and I called the jail, and the sheriff answered the phone, and I said, "Do you have"—I gave the names—"arrested?" He said, "Yeah, we got the niggers." I said, "What's their bail?" He said, "Well, if you are so interested, you come on down here and find out."

So I did, and what they did was they had nine policemen, and they took turns punching me with the butts of guns and this sort of thing. And they took all my clothes, forced me to take all my clothes off, then they threatened burning my genitals with fire and a sharp stick. My whole thing was not to go unconscious, you know, so I took that for about four hours, and then they called in a doctor, and they said, "Well, can he take anymore?" And he said, "Well, I'm not going to be responsible if you do."

When he did not return from Winona, SNCC resorted to a tactic it had found effective in similar situations. SNCC allies from Chicago, New York, California, Detroit, were asked to flood Winona jail with long-distance phone calls. They were to say, "Do you have Lawrence Guyot? I want to speak to Lawrence Guyot."

Once the calls started they then started moving me from different jails, Vaiden, back to Winona, then to another small town, and they got very cute. They had beaten almost—I don't think I could have taken much more. . . . The doctor said, "Well now, I understand that you were in an automobile accident . . . you came to Winona, and you got to drinking a little bit, and you had an accident."

I had never driven a car, didn't have a driver's license, but I wasn't at that time about to argue the facts. So anyway, he treated me. . . . It was quite a beating. That was about it.

When you went into the jail, did they take you to a cell?

No . . . I remember very clearly, because this [case] was tried, and I had to testify in the trial. We parked in front of the courthouse, and I walked around the back. Front door was closed. It was on a Sunday, and I walked in and I said, "I'd like to see the sheriff," and the guy said, "He's right in that room." The room was quite full. I said, "Sheriff, I come to see about these people," I gave their names. . . . He said, "I got 'em. What you gon' do about it?" I said, "All I want to do is find out what the charges are so we can raise the money to get them out. . . ." He said, "You get the fuck out of here." So I decided to do that—just that.

So I got to the car, and the sheriff walked out there and said, "Nigger, what you causing all these problems for?" and hit me in the mouth. And then reached for his gun, and I, of course, immediately put my hands in my pocket. I didn't want no mistakes to be made. And then he just beat on me till he got me in the jail and just kept beating on me. One guy was a prize fighter, and he just stood me up to the wall and just beat on me, and then they used guns.

One constable came to me and showed me a little gold badge and said, "I'm from the FBI. Tell me all about what happened." Well, I knew that that wasn't the identification of the FBI; we had had enough experience with them. So I said, [casually], "Oh, I don't have anything to say. Talk to the sheriff." So he said, "You smart mother-fucker," and walked away.

I've decided that the best thing for me to do is to inform the other prisoners who I am, 'cause I didn't expect to come outa there. At least they would know that I *was* there, and if they were not too afraid, they might talk. . . . I played like I was out, okay? So they left the cell open, they left a knife right outside, and there were two guys with shotguns standing right outside the hall waiting for me to act a goddamn fool and try to come on outa there. I didn't fall for that one.

You know what they charged me with? Attempted murder . . . because I had a note in my pocket that said someone had been killed, someone had been stabbed in a car. So they took that note and said, "Oh, ho, you killed somebody, didn't you?" So they charged me with all of that, and then the Department of Justice became involved and became very interested in the trial and this sort of thing. And Andy Young, who was then with SCLC, came down to Winona and paid the bond and I was out and that was it. While I was in the jail, after having been beaten, they cut off the radio. That was when Medgar Evers was killed. They didn't want that known in the jail.

Postscript: "The case was tried by the federal government. . . . We identified them, we told them exactly what had happened, told them how it had happened and when it had happened. The jury didn't convict 'em."

RUBY HURLEY

Many times when Medgar and I would be driving together, Medgar would tell about carrying his gun. I said, "Medgar, it's not gon' do any good to carry a gun." He used to sit on it, under his pillow. Said, "Medgar, that's not gon' do any good. If they're gon' get us, they're gon' get us. Because the way they behave, they're cowards. They're not gonna come and tell you, 'I'm gonna shoot you.'" And sure enough, that's the way he died: A sniper got him. . . . Medgar they didn't get until 1963, but that was a buildup from the time he came on the staff in December of 1954.

She last saw Medgar Evers alive in Greenwood on the night before he died.

Lena Horne was down, and she spoke. What's the comedian's name? Dick Gregory was there. That place was jammed. I was to introduce Lena, and Medgar sent a note to me asking me to tell some men who were smoking that they shouldn't smoke in that auditorium. He pointed in the direction of where they were sitting, and when I saw them, I recognized one of them as having—two of them, as a matter of fact—had been hanging around our office. . . . I'd seen these two fellows in there. One of them was a policeman.

These were white men?

Uh-mm. [Speaks very slowly, reflectively] And the other one was Byron de la Beckwith in that auditorium that night. When I called attention to the fact that there should be no smoking in there, they got up and left, and that's when I could see them clearly.

I had to leave town . . . to speak over in South Carolina, an engagement I had had for a long time. When I got back in here, back into Atlanta—we had moved to Atlanta by that time, of course—I got a telephone call that he'd been shot. I knew he was dead, even at that moment he had not died. But he died while they were talking to me, and I got the first thing flying back over there, and everybody was in such a state of shock that nobody had done anything about getting the blood cleaned up off the driveway or off his car or anything. So that was the first thing I did—get that blood up—before his wife sees it and before the children come back home. And get the blood off their car.

Byron de la ("DeLay") Beckwith, a Greenwood fertilizer salesman and scion of an old Delta family, was tried twice for the murder of Medgar Evers. He was not convicted. In 1975 Beckwith was convicted in federal court of illegally transporting a dynamite bomb to New Orleans. He testified he had not known the bomb was in his car. New Orleans police were said to suspect that he was on his way to blow up the home of a Jewish leader in New Orleans.

Dave Dennis

Freedom Summer

He has a handsomely appointed law office in downtown New Orleans. From the street far below, the roar of afternoon rush-hour traffic drifts up—muted, somehow soothing. He speaks softly, recalling his years in Mississippi. Finally the state had worn him out, and he had gone up to the University of Michigan to take a law degree. But there was no escaping reminders of Mississippi and the Movement. At the checkout desk in the law library was a young woman he recognized as a veteran of Mississippi, too, a white girl he remembered as having survived an ugly incident with the Natchez police. "They had held a pistol to her head and played Russian roulette." It was some time before he learned that her library job was part of her therapy at the hospital she had entered immediately after the Natchez incident. ". . . she's still in a mental institution. That's around eleven years now."

He had helped bring that girl and others like her to Mississippi. In 1961 at the age of twenty-one he became CORE's field director for Mississippi. When CORE, NAACP, SCLC, and SNCC joined forces to form a state-wide organization named COFO (Council of Federated Organizations), he became a field director second in rank only to Bob Moses. Together, he and Moses planned COFO's 1964 Summer Project, which brought hundreds of white college students to Mississippi for Freedom Summer. In planning the summer-long assault on segregation

the two of them decided to ignore the conventional warnings that large
numbers of white civil rights workers could not survive in Mississippi.

It's sorta cold, so I'm gonna just tell you what my feeling was about
it. We knew that if we had brought in a thousand blacks, the country
would have watched them slaughtered without doing anything about it.
Bring a thousand whites and the country is going to react to that in two
ways. First of all is to protect. We made sure that we had the children,
sons and daughters, of some very powerful people in this country over
there, including Jerry Brown, who's now governor of California, for instance . . . we made sure of that. . . . The idea was not only to begin
to organize for the Democratic Convention, but also to get the country
to begin to respond to what was going on there. They were not gonna
respond to a thousand blacks working in that area. They would respond
to a thousand young white college students, and white college females
who were down there. All right? And that's the reason why, and if there
were gonna take some deaths to do it, the death of a white college student would bring on more attention to what was going on than for a
black college student getting it. That's cold, but that was also in another
sense speaking the language of this country. What we were trying to do
was get a message over to the country, so we spoke their language. And
that had more to do with that decision to bring 'em in by the two of us
at the top than anything else.

You [and Bob Moses] discussed it that clearly?

Uh-mm, the two of us did. The two of us discussed it. That was not
opened up to the staff and everything else in the meetings, because the
fact is that we didn't know who was working for the press or whatever,
and most things that happened in staff meetings always got out. And
that's something we didn't want to. Now I guess it can be told. . . . We
didn't plan anything that happened, for it to happen. That's what the
Klan and the rest of 'em did, you know. We didn't plan any of the violence. [Pauses] But we just wanted the country to respond to what was
going on.

What sorts of problems, if any, did that decision cause you and
Moses?

Well, I can't speak for Bob. It caused problems—I mean, psychologically—for me in terms of the fact that you felt responsible for what happened to people, you know, and I still do. I mean, it's the price that I

had to pay and the price that I still pay for the decision. [Pauses] But it was something that had to be done. You see, one of the things is that we were in a war, and it wasn't very romantic for those people involved in it.* You look at that as an era of our time when there were things happening and you look back on it—some people wishing they were involved, those who were involved happy about it . . . they might have demonstrated a couple of times . . . [and can claim] "I was a part of that thing." But the people who were down there staying, that was a real war. We weren't being slapped on the wrist. Every time people got up the next morning, you didn't know whether you were going to see 'em again or not as they went out on different assignments, you see. Everything was a risk. We didn't have much fun. We made our fun. We didn't have many parties. It was work. Work seven days a week. We didn't take off for vacations and things of that nature. We worked. Seven days a week. And a lot of people were making twenty-five dollars per week. . . . It wasn't fun. [Very softly] It was twenty-five dollars per week. That's what George Raymer made.

He had spoken earlier of George Raymer, a co-worker in CORE. He leaves the room to take a telephone call, and when he returns, he brings a newspaper clipping permanently encased in plastic. There is a photograph of a young black man and below it the funeral notice of George Raymer.

At that time, we didn't spend that much time thinking about death. I mean, it was right there. Very seldom did I think about it until something happened . . . then you'd say, "Wow, you know that was close!" Most of my thinking or reflecting on death being that close . . . came after I left Mississippi, and more after I got out of the Movement completely, because it was something you just didn't dwell upon.

There was a shock-fear kinda thing that went through me for several weeks after Chaney and Goodman** were missing in terms of closeness

* The metaphor of Mississippi as a war zone appears over and over again in these interviews. In June of 1964 Mrs. Fannie Lou Hamer went to Oxford, Ohio, to address the Freedom Summer volunteers assembled there for orientation. "Number one, I told 'em what had happened to me in 1963, and I told 'em the same thing could happen to them in 1964. We didn't tell 'em no lies. We prepared 'em for exactly what it was like, and it was like you going into combat. You know, I've heard of combat, but that's exactly what we was having here."

** James Chaney, Andrew Goodman, and Michael Schwerner were the victims in the Movement's most celebrated murder case. On the night of June 21, 1964, after being released from jail by Neshoba County Deputy Sheriff Cecil Price, they were executed by Klansmen on a lonely road outside Philadelphia, Mississippi. However,

to that. And then one night . . . I said, "I can't deal with this." So I walked out of the COFO office, got in the car and drove into Philadelphia, Mississippi, one night and just drove around, went to the COFO headquarters that we had, talked to people, got in my car, and drove around the city and drove back out. And I had to do that just for myself to basically get that out of my head, which was quite successful and after that it didn't bother me. But I had to do it, and I had to do it by myself.

Schwerner, Goodman, and Chaney . . . that bothers me all the time, because as it's come to me from FBI agents who investigated and also the fact of actual statements by the people who did it . . . they didn't want Goodman. At the time that they stopped the car, they thought that I was in that car. The car belonged to me anyway, you know. It was a car assigned to me by CORE. . . . Mickey Schwerner was over there, Chaney was involved in that, because the fact is that I assigned Schwerner to the Meridian and Philadelphia, Mississippi, areas. I can't help but think quite often . . . maybe, if I had done something differently. You can't help but blame yourself to some extent.

Take . . . George Raymer who died two years ago of a heart attack. He dropped out of high school and came into Mississippi with me and wanted to stay, and he worked day and night, worked hard. And he died of a cardiac condition. . . . According to the doctors he had a heart of a seventy-year-old man. That is, that his heart was just that overworked. It was a old man's heart. That's just like somebody pulling a gun and shooting a man . . . George wasn't even thirty years old when he died of a heart attack. I've had problems with that, too, because I can't but say, well, when I left Mississippi, maybe I should have used my influence to get George outa Mississippi. . . . That's not something easy to deal with.

He ponders a question about chance, living on the edge.

It just seems that through that whole Movement . . . for some reason, I wasn't there at the time, and they were all by chance. All by

their fates were not known until six weeks later, when their bodies were discovered under an earthen dam on a farm outside Philadelphia. Goodman, a twenty-one-year-old white college student from New York, was a Summer Project volunteer. Chaney, also twenty-one and a black Mississippian, was a volunteer worker for CORE. Schwerner, twenty-four and white, was a New York social worker who had come South some months earlier to run CORE's office in Meridian. See William Bradford Huie and Dick Gregory.

chance. When Medgar was killed, I had his car all day. I had gone to Canton, Mississippi, came back in, met him at the church, gave him his car, and he told me that why don't I come have a drink. I told him, "Naw, you're a bad risk for me to go with you to have a drink." So we laughed about that. I told him I wasn't going with him; we just laughed. He got in his car and went home, and I got a ride with somebody else that took me home. And a little while later, there was a phone call saying Medgar Evers had just been shot. During that period of time, very seldom I ever, you know, missed a chance to have a drink, because you didn't get it too often in Mississippi at that period of time. But I said no. . . .

But it just seems as if I was—I was just never there, and that weighs heavy, too, because a lot of things that happened that caused a lot of people to become physically hurt, I started. All right? And I came out of it ninety-nine percent of the time without even getting a scratch . . . when people around me would get it. So that became a problem with me, because I always began to feel as if maybe some way . . . this sounds crazy, but like as if I've been cheated.* I mean, nothing ever happened. You begin to find that you feel guilty about it, because you want to know why him, or why her, not me?

These feelings that you've been talking about, was that the emotional energy behind your speaking at the James Chaney memorial service?

Yeah, you see for a long time in the Movement . . . one of the problems I had was the problem of nonviolence. I had tried it, and I was going around to areas in the backwoods talking to people who were saying, "If they come after me, I'm going to shoot 'em." And I would go through the "love-thy-neighbor" bit: "Put your gun down." And they would get beaten, and again people getting killed. I don't know. When I got up there and I looked at all those faces, everything seemed so useless. I knew the power of the government to do whatever they wanted to

---

* He first observed this fatalism—a readiness for death bordering on the perverse —in the Freedom Rides: "When the group left Montgomery, the first busload to go into Jackson, Mississippi, everyone on that bus was prepared to die. Now what happened there was a very strange scene. . . . We were just arrested and put in jail. Well, everybody was prepared to die. One girl in particular just started pulling hands full of hair out. She just started screaming. Nothing happened, and there was the cold shock. I mean, people just were doing strange things. One guy was beating his head up against the wall. *We didn't die.* . . . It was just that right then and there everybody wanted to die. They had been willing to give up their lives. . . . Now what that means and what it meant then and what does it mean to the individuals now, I don't know. But I know what I saw."

do, whenever they wanted to do it. . . . They all told us the same thing: "There's nothing that we can do. It's up to the states to prosecute because there are no laws."

The memorial service was in a small Baptist church in Meridian in August of 1964. James Chaney had been buried that afternoon—or rather, reburied. For forty-four days Chaney lay with Schwerner and Goodman under the dam in Neshoba County.

"I'm sick and tired of going to the funerals of black men who have been murdered by white men . . . ," he was quoted as saying in newspaper accounts of the service. "I've got vengeance in my heart tonight. . . . If you go back home and sit down and take what these white men in Mississippi are doing to us . . . if you take it and don't do something about it . . . then God damn your souls. . . ." He began crying as he spoke that day and finally broke off, sobbing.

And the other thing that I thought about was, during the time that Chaney and Goodman and Schwerner were missing . . . it would be interesting to find out how many bodies did they find. It was almost a daily thing. A body was found here. Two bodies were found floating in the river. . . . Most people I talked to were saying the same thing: "Whew, that wasn't them either." *They were finding people,* black people, floating in rivers and every place else, and nothing was being done about it.* And I just began to think about what was going on, and to me it was just—I really got tired, mentally tired of the whole scene.

I felt then that there was only one solution. If we're gonna have a war, let's have it. And that people ought not to say, "Let's leave it up to the government to take care of this. . . ." Let's do it ourselves, let's go on and get it over with, one way or the other. That's the emotion I felt. I was just tired of going to funerals. I'm still tired of going to funerals. That's what that was all about. I never did . . . try to deal with anybody on nonviolence again. I would never do it.

* There was an abundant supply of black bodies in Mississippi that summer. In searching for the bodies of the Philadelphia victims federal agents found several unidentified corpses. One of these, the body of a fourteen-year-old boy wearing a CORE T-shirt, was found floating in the Big Black River.

MARY DORA JONES

She is a tall, handsome black woman with a mouth full of gold-rimmed teeth. Her home in Cleveland, Mississippi, is comfortably furnished and spotlessly clean. On the living room wall is a tapestry of the Last Supper. Grouped around the tapestry are photographs of John F. Kennedy, Martin Luther King, Jr., and Robert Kennedy. Robert Kennedy's photograph is in the center and higher than the others, because once, on a tour of the Delta, he visited the home of her friend Amzie Moore. Atop the television set is a giant plastic replica of an I.W. Harper bottle. There is also a half-gallon Gordon's Gin bottle filled with red water.

She loves to smoke Winston cigarettes and talk about the day the Freedom Summer volunteers came to Marks, Mississippi, where she used to live.

I had about seven blacks and four whites in my house, wouldn't nobody else take 'em.

In Marks?

Right . . . they really move. They comes in, they mean business. They didn't mind dyin', and as I see they really mean business, I just love that for 'em, because they was there to help us. And since they was there to help us, I was there to help them.

Did that cause you any problems in the community . . . opening your home up?

Oh, really, because they talkin' 'bout burnin' my house down. . . . Some of the black folks got the news that they were gonna burn it down. . . . My neighbors was afraid of gettin' killed. People standin' behind buildin's, peepin' out behind the buildin's, to see what's goin' on. So I just told 'em, "Dyin' is all right. Ain't but one thing 'bout dyin'. That's make sho' you right, 'cause you gon' die anyway." . . . If they had burnt it down, it was just a house burned down. . . .

That's the attitude that changed the South.

So that's the way I thought about it. So those kids, some of 'em from California, some of 'em from Iowa, some of 'em from Cincinnati, they worked, and they sho' had them white people up there shook up.

. . . youngsters that came in, particularly the white ones from outside the South, did they have a hard time adjusting . . . ?

They had a hard time adjustin' because most all of the blacks up there didn't want to see 'em comin' . . . said they ain't lettin' no damn civil rights come. "If they come up here to my house, I'm gon' shoot 'em."

See, this is what the black folks were sayin', and those kids had went to the preachers' houses, they had done went to the deacons' houses, they had done went to the teachers' houses, all tryin' to get in. Some of 'em come in around five o'clock that evenin', landed in my house. I give 'em my house. "My house is yo' house." I was workin' for a man, he was workin' at the Post Office, and he and his wife was beggin' me everyday, "Don't fool with them Communists."

The white people?

That's what they was tellin' me, those kids was Communists. I said, "Well, I tell you what. I don't think they no more Communists than right here where I am, because if they Communists, then you Communists. They cain't hurt me no mo' than I already been hurt." Anything that helped the peoples, then I'm right there. So I didn't stop, although I got him scared to fire me. He would have fired me, but I got him scared to fire me. . . .

This was your white boss?

This was my white boss I was working for. His wife was sick, and every day she would talk to me about those people, askin' me where they lived. I said, "Well, they ain't livin' at yo' house. Why you want to know where they live?" So she said, "They ain't livin' with you?" And I said, "Well, I'm payin' the last note on that house," just like that. And I never did tell her.

Finally one day she brought me home, and it was a car sittin' there in my driveway, and two white men was in there, and there were some sittin' on the porch. She put me out and she went on back. When I went to work the next morning, she say, "Mary, was them, ah, civil rights peoples at yo' house?" I said, "Now when you turned around and stopped and they were sittin' there, you oughta been askin' 'em what they was. They'da told you."

And I never did tell 'em anything. So it went on some, she said, "Ain't but one thing I hate about it, this intermarriage." And I said, "Well, ain't no need in worryin' about that, because if you wanna worry about that, you oughta been talkin' to your granddaddy. . . ."

HARRY BOWIE

A black Episcopal priest from New Jersey who came down for Freedom Summer.

Curtis Hayes* and myself were going out to the country to get a key to an apartment in the projects in McComb. . . . We were going to have to house some people, and we didn't have enough room in the Freedom House. . . . I guess it was the silliness that kind of makes it stick out. Curtis was kidding me about my Northern accent and not knowing the "survival kit" and my inability to say "yassuh." And so I'd say, "Oh, is this the way you say 'yes, sir?'" And he'd say, "No, no."

We were just laughing and joking about that kind of silly thing, and all of a sudden—we're on this dirt road—a car passed us. . . . There's a car in front of us, then a second car in front of us, and a car behind us. Curtis said, "Hey, something's wrong. There shouldn't be this much traffic on this road." Wheels out to try and pass the two cars, and just as he wheels out, the first car . . . peels off also. So they got both sides of the road blocked, and they are kind of slowing down, and Curtis had enough sense not to slow down. Okay?

He said, "Harry, I'm worried." At that point, we broke into laughter because I said, *"Yas-suh."* [Laughs] And as we were laughing, I'll

---

* A veteran SNCC worker in McComb, Mississippi.

never forget, he or myself—I don't know who said it—said, "I'll bet Schwerner and Chaney and Goodman were laughing when they were being chased, too." And the laughter was hysterical . . . we couldn't do anything but laugh. Okay? . . . Curtis was a hell of a good driver. A lot of those cats were. Curtis pulled out one time . . . and told me to hold on, and when the other car started back in, he spun right back out, went down on the shoulder of the road, got around and took his ass off on that road about seventy. We don't know who they were. Hell, they might have been cops that wanted to question us. We don't know, but we weren't going to stop to find out, not on that road.

MARION BARRY

Now a Washington, D.C., councilman, he was SNCC's first chairman. After stepping down as chairman, he was in charge of the Friends of SNCC fund-raising apparatus.

We did a number of things. One is that after the killings in Mississippi of Goodman, Chaney, and Schwerner, we got, I think it might have been James Baldwin to write a letter. We did a massive mail appeal. We had Harry Belafonte to send out letters. We used to get mailing lists from various sources, *Progressive* magazine or from *The Nation.* They sell those mailing lists. . . . During the summer and fall of '64, we must have raised out of New York alone at least six hundred thousand dollars. I remember we had at least occasions where there were ten banks we had fifty thousand dollars in. . . . I think SNCC's budget was about a million dollars a year, and so New York was the primary source. Sixty percent of the total money the organization raised was out of the New York area.

We had these fund-raising parties where we would get movie actors. Sidney Poitier, Diahann Carroll, or Robert Ryan or Shelley Winters or Theo Bikel and others would come to somebody's house, and we would get somebody to have a party, and we would raise thirteen or fourteen thousand dollars at those kinds of things. . . . We would send it to Atlanta, and they would spend it, simple as that. . . .

A lot of this money came from the Jewish community, too, because most of our parties were at these Jewish families' homes, and we'd bring somebody up from the South, and we'd say, "Here is a living example of how tough it is down there," and the person would speak. Some of them were very dramatic. Mrs. Hamer came one time, and when she finished describing her situation, people were crying and all upset. . . . That was easy to do then because the whole question of racism and segregation had not reached the North.

LAWRENCE GUYOT

Summer's End

In the spring of '64 he attended the meeting during which the Freedom Summer plan was first presented to the entire COFO staff. "First of all, there was a decision in Mississippi by the Mississippi staff not to have this Freedom Summer. The staff voted not to do it."

This part of the staff meeting was held at a little Catholic conference in Greenville. This was the part chaired by Dave Dennis in Moses' absence. Moses returned on the second day and said, "We're gonna have it."

Why did the Mississippi staff initially vote against the project?

Very clear . . . a large number of people on the staff at the time had not excelled in intellectual rigors. Some of 'em couldn't read and write, but my God, they could do anything else . . . and did. They could get people to register to vote. They could speak well at mass meetings. They could mobilize a community. Any three people in that room could do that to any community anywhere. And here they were faced with competing in this newly found constituency that had developed respect for them . . . with these white, competent people. *Why they might even be able to type.* That was, as far as I'm concerned, the friction. . . .*

_____
* Charles Cobb, a "vociferous" opponent of calling in white helpers, provides a

Moses came on the second day and said, "Look, I'm not gonna be a part of anything all-black. We're gonna have the Summer Project. We need it. We need it for these reasons." And suddenly, there was a reconsideration of the vote. And that's the way it happened. Moses put himself and his political credibility with the staff on the line and won. See, had Moses not wanted it to happen, it wouldn'ta happened.

He sided with Moses because of something he had observed the previous summer, when a few Yale students visited the SNCC office in Hattiesburg, Mississippi.

Wherever those white volunteers went, FBI agents followed. It was really a problem to count the number of FBI agents who were there to protect the students. It was just that gross.

So then we said, "Well, now, why don't we invite a lot of whites"—we attempted to recruit blacks but that was unsuccessful—"to come and serve as volunteers in the state of Mississippi?" We thought it would bring federal protection. It didn't bring federal protection early enough for Schwerner, Chaney, and Goodman.

What was the impact of the murders on the Summer Project?

It made us face what all of us knew. I mean, we never made any claim about being able to prevent anyone from being killed, not to one volunteer. Okay? . . . The bodies were not to be discovered for some two months, and you had reports in the Mississippi newspaper that they'd been spotted. The sheriff of Houganush County* "saw" the three of them. There had been five or six reports of them being reported in the newspaper. We didn't accept any of those. During the next day, when Rita** couldn't get in touch with him . . . then we had no question that they were dead. All right?

---

different interpretation of the opponents' motives. They objected to inviting white volunteers because "it was a concession. You're conceding that you're not able to deal with the situation. I mean, the reason for the 1964 Summer Project was simply that we weren't able to cope with the violence in the state." But the opponents never had a real chance of stopping the project. ". . . you are victims of your own rhetoric, because at the same time, we were arguing desegregation, integration . . . the necessity for a society in which black and white did not make a difference. So you couldn't argue that you were opposed to white people coming down."

* A name he made up, parodying such Mississippi place-names as Yalobusha.

** Rita Schwerner was at the Summer Project orientation session in Oxford, Ohio, when her husband Mickey disappeared. She telephoned all around the state trying to locate him and his companions.

And it just made us a *bit* more cautious in getting the names and addresses of everyone, making sure that they got on the buses that traveled from Ohio to Mississippi, and there was definite people to pick them up, when they were to be picked up and this sorta thing. We never tried to hide the fact that there had been killings. We didn't glorify in it. That was simply the way it was.

> *He ponders a question about whether there would have been an intense national reaction if all three of the Philadelphia victims had been black.*
>
> The question answers itself. We'd had hundreds of killings. We had some sixty-three people killed around the question of the vote before '64. Any other question on that subject? None of them were white. Lord knows how many people were run out of homes, run out of the state. In Yazoo City, at this period of time, it was unthinkable to hold a membership card in the NAACP, absolutely unthinkable. And register to vote—good God, man, you're talkin' death. Why don't I just shoot myself? It'd be quicker.

Why weren't . . .

More people killed?

More people killed. I was trying to think of a different way to say it. . . .

No, no, you're right, you're right, you're right. The only reason more people weren't killed was because of the timing of the Schwerner, Chaney, and Goodman killings, the involvement of the President in the search, and his denunciation of the act by having the search conducted. . . .*

What would have happened to those of you in the project if the federal government had not pushed for solution . . . ?

You would be conducting this interview with someone else.

You really believe that?

* At President Johnson's order, 210 Navy men came in to search for the bodies, and the largest local FBI office in the nation was set up in Jackson.

Oh, man, look . . . [claps his hands for emphasis] . . . we were an open book. The phones were tapped, people knew where we were going, people knew where we bought our gas, where we lived . . . you name it. Fortunately, we didn't operate internally as though we had something to hide. I mean, our protection was the black community. We never doubted that and we knew it and we acted like it. I have no doubt that the twenty-five people who really made decisions in that state politically at that time could have been wiped out in a day—*and would have been.* I mean, what's to prevent it?

I don't know, you may think I'm overstating my case, because I was individually involved, but I have no doubt about it. Logically that's the way the state deals with that kinda situation; that's the way it woulda been dealt with. But the national attention, the involvement of the President, the concern of the CIA. Allen Dulles came to Mississippi.* The FBI then began its infiltrating of the Klan and the Civil Rights Movement. I'm sure this was when the surveillance and tapping of King was stepped up.

> The only time that I really have opposition to the role of the federal government in Mississippi was when Allen Dulles came to Mississippi and met with myself, Aaron Henry, Bob Moses, Dave Dennis, a couple of other people, and said, "Look, I'm going to meet with the governor in an hour"—this was when they were looking for the bodies of Schwerner, Chaney, and Goodman—"and we want this mess cleaned up."
>
> And Aaron Henry stood up and said, "What do you mean?"
>
> Dulles said, "Well, these civil rights demonstrations are causin' this kind of friction, and we're just not gonna have it, even if we have to bring troops in here."
>
> Fortunately, Aaron Henry took the right position, 'cause he said, "You talkin' to the wrong people. . . . Everything we're trying to do is constitutionally protected and we oughta be having more help from the federal government rather than you, as an agent of the federal government, come and tell us to be quiet." *Now that happened.*

•

You told me that Moses saved the Summer Project on the basis that he thought it ought to be integrated. I have read that he wound up several years later refusing to speak to white people.

That is a fact.

* As a special emissary for President Johnson. Dulles had retired as CIA director in 1961.

What happened?

That is a fact. Moses was at one time the most ardent integrationist and later after, oh, about '65, '66, took the position that [pauses] whites weren't serious about their apparently positive relationships to blacks, that the blacks should cut off their relationship with whites, and he did so. He's now teaching school in Africa, and I don't think he plans to communicate with anyone white or return to the United States.

Tell me about battle fatigue.

It takes different forms with different people. I came out of a meeting of the Freedom Democratic party, its organizational meeting in the Masonic Temple, and I got against the wall, and I couldn't move the left side of my body—just, just couldn't move it. A couple of people picked me up . . . a doctor came to see me, and he said, "You're just exhausted. Just get some rest." Some people would drink. Some people would knock down doors. Just—that's it.

Just as a consequence of the daily pressure?

Which could sometimes be most excruciating. It had to do with the very personalness of the operation. . . . If *you* stayed at someone's house and then that house was blown up or burned because of that. Take a couple of months of that and it begins to wear you down, and it happened. Some people simply retreated. They were still in SNCC, they were still involved in a project, but you'd never hear too much of 'em. And you didn't pressure 'em. If possible, you'd get 'em to go to Dorchester, come to Atlanta, or what have you.

How did you come to leave Mississippi?

The only reason I left Mississippi in '68 was because of health. I was a delegate to the '68 Democratic Convention. I went to a doctor [in Chicago] who was one of the top internists in the country. . . . He said, "Yes, if you go back to Mississippi you have about two months to live."

I had high blood pressure. I had heart trouble. I was and still am overweight, and I'd had enough.

How old were you?

Oh, let's see. In '68, oh, I guess I must have been twenty-nine. [A long pause] Why?

INTERLUDE

DICK GREGORY

End of a Funnyman

He was one of the hottest nightclub comics in America in 1963 and an unlikely ally for the black preachers leading the Movement in the South. He had grown up a streetwise kid in St. Louis and, after years of struggle, was just beginning to enjoy the high life in Chicago. Yet when Martin Luther King's call for help came during the critical last days of the Birmingham campaign, he did more than just send money.

They had a stalemate down there, and he called me, and after he called, the President called and asked me not to go down, and I really loved that. Oh, man.

This would have been . . .

President Kennedy. Yeah. I come home, my wife was upset. She said, "The President been tryin' to get you all day." I said, "I ain't thinkin' 'bout him. I goin' to bed." She said, "You not goin' to bed in this house till you call the President."

So I called him. He said, "Hi, Greg. Jack." I said, "Yeah." He said, "*Please* don't go down to Birmingham. We've got it all solved. Dr. King is wrong, what he's doing."

"Man, I will be there in the morning," and I went down.

Was he offended?

I didn't know. Presidents, you know, you can't tell what it is on the phone. I might not even been talkin' to him, mighta been a recording. He liable to have left a message on the box for me. [Laughs]

He was beaten in the Birmingham jail for fighting back when a jailer struck him with a billy club. His press conference about what he called "the first real professional beating I ever had" added to the city government's woes during the tumultuous final week of demonstrations. After Birmingham he began working closely with the SNCC organizers in Greenwood, Mississippi, where his audacious bad-mouthing of white cops quickly established him as a hero with both SNCC and the resident blacks.

I did somethin' else, too. I would wear a big white cowboy hat . . . because I felt that the mentality that I was dealing with was a cowboy mentality, and the big white cowboy hat could make me the good guy, and it would scare 'em. As a consequence I never went to jail in Mississippi. That's unreal. . . . They have arrested everybody but me. They arrested three and four hundred people. I have *never, ever* been arrested in Mississippi . . .

What is your explanation for that?

My cowboy hat, and talkin' to 'em in the way I talked to 'em. They became the boy and I became the man. They became the nigger, I became the white man. . . . I'd have a guy tell me, say "Here come that nigger." I'd say, "Your momma's a nigger. . . ."

How did the Mississippi police and sheriffs react to that?

Oh, they would go crazy. You know, they would get upset and uptight. But . . . I always had federal agents around me, and I was still Dick Gregory, and they'd have to be careful about what they were gonna do. Those three kids got killed in Mississippi, I was in Washington that day. I got on the plane that night, and that *night* I was down there . . . saying, "We know you killed 'em, and I'm gonna prove it." So I borrowed twenty-five thousand dollars and put it up for a reward. Things started falling. Things started falling.

Did anybody get your twenty-five thousand?

No, what happened was, the FBI put up thirty-thousand-dollar reward. First time in the history of this government the FBI put up a reward. But the guy double-crossed 'em. He brought it to them and me. Had he just brought it to them, they still wouldn'ta found them bodies.

Tell me about that.

First, tell me what you mean, tell you about it.

The information that you received.

I got some information. The guy said, "Here's where you can reach me to pay me." I called Robert Kennedy. He had 'em send an FBI agent to my room . . . I had the tapes of the people that did it and where the bodies were. He said, "Well, just give me the tapes, Dick." I said, "Nooooo."

See, I *knew* the FBI, and I didn't trust none of 'em, includin' Bobby, as far as this was concerned. And so he sent the FBI agent in. I gave him the information . . . I waited three weeks for them. Nothing happened. I held a press conference and said, "The FBI know where the bodies are 'cause I gave 'em the information." Then Hoover went around talkin' about I was a liar and I didn't know what I was talkin' about, so I . . . held another press conference. Said, "If the bodies ain't up in eighteen hours, I will *lead* the press down there." And they found 'em that day, where my information said they were.

Postscript: New Year's Day, 1976, a cold, drizzly day in Atlanta. He has just returned from a brisk morning jog to celebrate the end of a seven-day "air fast" to call attention to world hunger. He is extremely thin, but healthy looking, and he seems possessed of a deep inner contentment. The snappy comebacks and putdowns have been replaced by "Peace and love, my brother." He has long since shelved his show-business career, save for campus lectures which support his various crusades. As soon as he regains his strength from the fast, he is to leave on a Los Angeles-to-New York run which, like the fast, is intended to alert the world to the global food crisis he believes is bound to come.

"I have to thank Martin Luther King for where I am now, Abernathy and that whole Movement, because in playing games with nonviolence, I had to either say that I was nonviolent or I wasn't . . ."

BOOK TWO

I
THE DOWN-HOME RESISTANCE

ROBERT PATTERSON

The General's Grandson

If I had ill will toward the black people, I surely wouldn't have lived in Sunflower County, Mississippi, with a sixty-eight percent black population. I surely wouldn't have been out operating a plantation with sixty-five black families and mine the only white family, if I had disliked Negroes.

I was the manager of a plantation there of fifteen hundred and eighty-five acres, and I was conscious of the fact that our Negro-white ratio was about seven-to-three, roughly, in our county. We had always had our white school system and our black school system . . . and in the last few years prior to '54, we had equalized the school system. We had built new schools, and at that time, the Negro schools in Sunflower County were actually newer and there were more of them and they were better buildings than the ones that the white children were going to.

Our representative in the Mississippi legislature, Mrs. Wilma Sledge, was a lady, and she called a meeting prior to the Supreme Court decision, one Sunday afternoon. And she told those of us there—just a cross section of the county, any people who were interested—that they anticipated an adverse ruling by the Supreme Court on the question of segregated schools. And she said there was nothing we could do about it, that we were going to have to accept it and that our schools would be integrated at the rate of seven-to-one, seven blacks for every white child.

I didn't say anything at the meeting. I just went on home like everybody else, but I got to thinking about it. And I had a little daughter who would start school immediately . . . she would enter the first grade in '55, I believe. And I just knew that if that was done, that if the Supreme Court and federal government did force integration, that it would completely destroy our school system, and it would create an environment for our children that was just utterly unacceptable. I had the same reaction then as these people in Boston and Detroit and other cities of the North are having when they're talking about busing their children. . . . I remember I was lying awake at night.

He was then thirty-one, a former Mississippi State football hero and World War II paratroop officer—and up to that time almost completely apolitical. He got out of bed that night and, sitting at the kitchen table, drafted a protest letter. He had it printed up for distribution to newspaper editors, congressmen, "just about everybody I knew."

"I, for one, would gladly lay down my life to prevent mongrelization," he wrote.* "There is no greater cause." But buried in the letter was the germ of a more practical idea conceived on the day of his meeting with the state legislator: "On the way home the solution, so simple I hadn't thought of it, came to me. I gathered my children and promised them that they would never have to go to school with children of other races against their will. . . . If every Southerner who feels as I do, and they are in the vast majority, will make this vow, we will defeat this Communistic disease that is being thrust upon us. Of course, we must work out the details, but if we all stand together, this can be accomplished."

The details were worked out on July 11, 1954. He and thirteen of Indianola's leading businessmen and politicians met at the home of the manager of the cotton compress. "We elected the banker president. I was the secretary . . . and in the space of a few months, it spread. The organization spread all over the Deep South and into other states." Critics called their new organization the white-collar Klan. They named it the Citizens Council, and by late 1956 the Council had 85,000 members in Mississippi, 60,000 in Alabama, and was a political force throughout the Deep South.

Only in Mississippi does the Council still prosper, however. Off the plantation for twenty years now, he administers its affairs from the Council's handsome headquarters building near the state capitol in

* John Bartlow Martin, *The Deep South Says Never* (New York: Ballantine Books, 1957).

Jackson. In an office dominated by a portrait of Robert E. Lee, he ob-
serves that he has grown "gun-shy" about granting interviews.

Over the years, we've felt that we have been mistreated by the nation's news media. They've come down here in swarms for years. I think
it all started probably with a case of a young Negro boy named Emmett
Till getting killed in Mississippi for offending some white woman . . .
that made every newspaper on the face of the earth. And following that
there were other incidents that happened in the South, and whenever
something happened to a Negro in the South, it was made a national
issue against the South.

Now at this same time the crime rate in the North was going up,
jumping by leaps and bounds. . . . I remember about the time Emmett
Till was killed, there was a little thirteen-year-old white Girl Scout, I
think in Chicago, that was killed, raped by something like thirteen Negroes. A horrible crime. It was on page thirty-three by the used-car ads
and never got out. And then, of course, you remember how *Life* magazine wrote this tear-jerking article about Emmett Till and how Emmett
Till was this young man whose father had died a hero's death in Europe.
And that, oh, would just make you cry just to read it, see. And then
they found out that Emmett Till's soldier-hero father was hanged in
Italy by Dwight D. Eisenhower for the crime of double murder and rape.
But the people of this country never found that out . . . and those are
examples of what I am talking about. I could just list hundreds of them,
how they have done that.

How about personally, after you emerged as a spokesman?

Well, I've had people come and interview me, and I thought I was
raised as a gentleman, and I've tried to be courteous and polite to everybody until they gave me reason to be otherwise. And I've had people
come into my home, like you're doing now, and I greeted them. I'd give
them an interview, and there wouldn't be any witnesses present, and
they'd go off and say I made the most outlandish statements you ever
heard. Had one fellow named Bigart, I think it was Homer Bigart,* if I
remember correctly. This was eighteen or twenty years ago. He came in
my house, and I was courteous and polite to him, and he went off and
said that I said that "This is not the United States of America. This is
Mississippi." And I didn't say any such thing. . . .

I've been accused of being anti-Semitic, anti-everything. I've been ac-

* A reporter for the New York *Herald Tribune.* The contested quote was used
by the NAACP in a pamphlet of the time, *M Is for Mississippi and Murder.*

cused of being a racist, a hate monger, and well, you finally get kind of used to it and immune to it. That's the reason we established the *Citizen* magazine. . . . We've always had competent people working on our magazine. Now, we have a Yale Ph.D. in English who has been with our *Citizen* magazine for many years.* Its present editor is George Shannon, who for eighteen years was editor of the Shreveport *Journal,* which is one of the South's leading daily newspapers. . . . The magazine now goes into every state in the nation, to libraries all over the nation, and if anybody wants information about our position, we'll send it to them free.

What about if the New York Times *or* Time *magazine called you for an interview today . . . ?*

Well, if I had any reason to believe they'd quote me properly, I wouldn't mind giving them one. I'm not bitter, because I know that some of them just thought they were doing their job. They were sent to do a hatchet job on the South and they did it. That was their job. Whether it was fair or not, I don't worry about that.

Judge Brady . . . wrote that Southern whites would never accept social integration, yet today I see integrated motels and restaurants in the Delta. . . .

[Interrupting] That's not social integration, that's *forced* integration under the might of the federal government. . . . To be subjected to integration is one thing, but to submit to it is something else entirely. We are being subjected to integration; we're not submitting to it. And you'll find that the white people do not frequent places where there are a whole lot of Negroes through choice. And I think gradually . . . things will resegregate themselves.

You don't think your side has lost the fight over integration in public facilities?

* Despite their Old South chauvinism, Council members have always been quick to boast of members possessing an Eastern background or education. For instance, much is made of the fact that Judge Thomas Brady, author of *Black Monday* and Patterson's intellectual mentor, was a graduate of the Lawrenceville School in New Jersey and Yale. By showcasing such members the Council apparently hoped to put distance between its members and their supposed social and economic inferiors in the Klan.

Well, we haven't won it. We've been overwhelmed, but that doesn't mean we've lost it. This country's been overwhelmed before. This country was overwhelmed by the British one time. The South has been overwhelmed several times by the North, but we've always come back. We're going to come back again. Just because you've been overcome by physical might doesn't mean that you've lost. No, I don't think we've lost. In fact, Judge Brady's statement is true. I don't think we have social integration in Jackson, Mississippi, or in Detroit, Michigan, or in Atlanta, Georgia. Now you've got a certain class of white people that like to mingle with Negroes for various reasons. Down here in the South, we used to have riffraff white people that would cohabitate with Negroes . . . but the general run of white people and the better class Negroes do not want to integrate. I've had Negroes tell me, they said, "Decent Negroes don't want to integrate with white people and decent white people don't want to integrate with Negroes."

What would you say to this observation . . .

[Interrupting] Or force themselves on each other. Who wants to force himself where he's not wanted and he knows he's not wanted?

What would you say to this observation? That the great majority of Southern white people no longer care as deeply as you do about this whole area.

I don't believe that. If they do, why do they all live in the suburbs, and why do they move out of the neighborhood when Negroes move in? And why do they send their children to private schools? And why do they manipulate and move to go out to an area that doesn't have many Negroes in it so they can send their child to a virtually all-white school? Why have the white people in Washington, D.C., moved out of Washington and left it virtually an all-black city? They haven't accepted integration. They've run from it.

In other words, if you're going to be a segregationist, you got to do so in secret, just like the Kennedys. The Kennedys don't integrate. They've sent all their children to private schools, and they're seen with the right Negroes . . . in front of the right cameras. But they don't integrate with Negroes any more than they need to for political purposes.

See, the philosophy of the average American: Integration is a wonderful thing as long as no Negroes are involved or just a few Negroes are involved. But when you really have to integrate, they don't do it. They try it and they get out of it just as quick as they can.

In the early fifties . . . the prospect of any sort of integration was seen as deadly to the Southern way of life. Is life in the Delta of Mississippi where you've lived all your life that much different today from what it was twenty years ago?

The change is almost indiscernible. We have private schools all over the Delta.* We have our public schools where white children that are not able to afford the private schools are forced to go to school with the Negroes. . . .

The Negro in the Delta doesn't overwhelm the white restaurants and so forth. Many restaurants have never had a black in them, or they may have one come in there just to show he can go in there. Some white civil rights person will bring him in there, but he doesn't come back. He doesn't want to go where he's not wanted. Decent Negroes have pride just like white people do. They don't want to integrate with white trash.

Your grandfather was a Confederate general. I take it you still identify strongly with that heritage.

Yeah, I sure do. I think they were a noble people.

What future do you see . . .

[Interrupting] And I respect my grandparents just like I think everybody should respect their grandparents, if they know who they were.

You really don't see an erosion in that old Confederate spirit?

Well, it all depends on what you talkin' about by erosion. Now, you take thirty-thousand bayonets and you can do a lot of eroding. In other words the South is living under a system of force. In other words we're integrating because we're *forced* to integrate. They hire Negroes down here because they're *forced* to do it. We send Negroes to medical school 'cause we're forced to do it. That's why we do it. That doesn't make it right, and it doesn't make it accepted. In other words, we're being subjected to something. We're not submitting to it. We'll never submit anymore than the Jews and the Arabs will ever submit to each other. . . .

* The operation of all-white private schools is now the Citizens Council's major activity in Mississippi. Over five thousand elementary and secondary students attend Council schools in Jackson.

You know, you can raise a lion and a tiger together as cubs, and they'll breed and produce young. Did you know that? But it's not natural. You have to force it on them. That's what the federal government is trying to do to the white and the black, trying to force them together to make one race out of them. And I believe the black man resists it subconsciously, and I believe the white man resists it. You cannot teach racial pride to the blacks and then teach them that they need to be in the presence of a white man before they can get an education.

If what you say about black people's attitudes in the South is true, why were the civil rights organizations able to mobilize and organize hundreds and thousands of Southern blacks?

They didn't organize and mobilize hundreds of thousands of Southern blacks. They organized and mobilized hundreds of thousands of white newspapermen [laughing] and Freedom Riders and politicians. That is what they organized. The Southern black is virtually unmoved in many cases. . . . The federal government has undone everything the Mississippi legislature has done for the last twenty years, trying to elect blacks, and they still can't elect them.

But when you go into. . . .

[Interrupting] No, they never did mobilize the black South.

But when you go into a black home in Mississippi, don't you see pictures of Martin Luther King and the Kennedys on the wall?

Well, I don't go into black homes in Mississippi, but I imagine there are. But that's all right. If they want to put Martin Luther King and Senator Kennedy on the wall, that's a good place for both of them. [Pauses] In their homes there. That's fine. Nothing wrong with that. [A longer pause] I'm not against black people, and I don't think any of us are, but we believe that white people have rights.

John Patterson*

A Political Odyssey

I had an opportunity probably at one stage to play some role in national politics, but I was denied this because of the race issue . . . which I could not help, which I didn't create. I couldn't get rid of it; I was stuck with it. . . . It has been a millstone around our necks, and we've had to live with it. That's right, and whatever chances I might have had to play a part in national affairs was diminished as a result of the race issue and because of a stand that I had to take to even be on the scene at all in the South, you see. This is true.

He took office in 1954 as Alabama's crime-fighting attorney general. He completed the "Phenix City Cleanup" begun by his father, a district attorney who had been assassinated for attacking the gambling and prostitution rackets in that Army-base town. The U.S. Junior Chamber of Commerce named him one of America's Ten Outstanding Young Men. His eye fixed on the governor's race of '58, he met with other Southern attorneys general to plan a legal strategy of "massive resistance" to integration. He did his part by getting the Alabama courts to boot the NAACP and Ruby Hurley out of the state.

It helped maintain segregation in public facilities for a number of years, and I received a great deal of publicity in Alabama as a result of

* He and the Citizens Council's Robert Patterson are not related.

that. . . . So it wasn't long before the key issue in the governor's race became the race issue, and if I had not been a strong supporter of segregation in public facilities, then I would not have been elected governor [in 1958]. And I saw this and, of course, used the issue to get elected governor. . . . I would have preferred not to have the issue at all, frankly. I wished we didn't have a problem, but we did, and to be governor and to do the things you wanted to do, you had to be right on that question as far as a majority of the people were concerned at that time. Otherwise, you couldn't have made it. George Wallace was considered soft on the issue in the '58 race, and that's one of the things that beat him.

Did you know you had the upper hand on him there?

Absolutely, no question about it. I came from an area of the state in which we had always gotten along well with the black race. I had no feeling that I was any better than any of them. Really, I don't believe that I am a racist at all.

Did you have any misgivings about using that issue in a political way?

No . . . I had no misgivings about it. That was it. You either were well grounded on that issue or you might as well forget it. . . . I had no misgivings about it. I knew full well what I was doing.

In the '58 race against Wallace he had the support of the Ku Klux Klan; he resisted pressure from the newspapers to repudiate the endorsement of Grand Dragon Bobby Shelton.

I said, "Now look, I'm not denouncing anybody. I want anybody's vote who's qualified to vote in Alabama, regardless of who he is." . . . The Klan at that time in Alabama probably, if you got 'em all together, would number about five thousand people, and they're interesting people—in a way. They'll work in an election. . . . They'll work all night nailing up signs, puttin' out literature. . . . And not only can they nail your signs up all over Alabama in one night, they can also tear 'em down in one night, too, and they're a factor to consider. . . . They can do you great harm; they can do you great good. I'm talkin' about a political campaign now. An average guy, he won't get out and get involved like that, but they will. And of course, I wasn't about to run 'em off. And it's interesting that later on, George had their support. [Laughs] That's right.

So you were elected in '58 and inaugurated in '59 . . .

That's right . . . January nineteenth, 1959.

A segregationist and also a loyal Democrat.

That's right.

So then comes John Kennedy. Tell me about that.

Well, I knew Mr. Kennedy personally. I knew him before he ever announced that he was going to run for president. I had gotten acquainted with him when I was attorney general, primarily because of my law enforcement background. . . . He had expressed an interest in me to some people, and they made arrangements for us to meet. . . . He invited me to visit him in Washington. I'd been to his office several times, had breakfast over at his home in Georgetown several times, and met his family. So we became, I thought, fairly personal friends. I liked the fellow. So when he began to talk about running for president, they let me know that he was going to do this, he was going to seek the nomination, and that they were interested in having support in the South. And so I threw in with him early because I liked him first, and secondly, I thought that he would probably be more understanding of our situation down here than any of the other candidates. Now, of course, I knew, and of course, he knew well that you couldn't be elected president of the United States if you were a segregationist. We knew that, you understand. What I hoped was that they would concentrate in making their record in civil rights in equal voting opportunities and equal job opportunities and to go a little easy—that's not the best word—to take on the school situation in a more deliberative fashion, since the schools are so bound up in the neighborhoods and are a part of the social activities of a community. . . .

He never promised me anything, you understand. I never asked him to do anything like that. I never had any agreements with him. I supported him because I liked him, and I thought that he would make a good president, and I thought that he was a man that was sensitive and who I thought understood some of the problems that we are confronted with down here. This was the reason. Now of course when I got involved in it, right away I had tremendous opposition in Alabama from the Dixiecrats and the conservatives . . . and from the churches, the Baptist and Methodist churches in Alabama. They fought me bitterly on this question. They didn't want a Catholic for president. You know, I didn't

really believe that they would feel that strongly against a fellow because of his religion, but I had a real fuss with my own pastor at my
own church here. . . . It hurt me politically, no question about that.

*Even so, he led the Kennedy forces at the state Democratic conven-
tion in 1960, turning his back on his old allies, "the white Citizens
Council people, the Kluxers, the Dixiecrats." They were supporting Senator Lyndon B. Johnson of Texas. The fight over election of the seventy-two delegates who would cast Alabama's thirty-six votes at the
national convention in Los Angeles was bitter, the "old politics" at its
most devious.*

We had a rather popular ex-governor at that time named Frank M.
Dixon of Birmingham, a very popular lawyer-businessman. We found a
twenty-three-year-old truck driver for an asphalt company up here in
Gadsden named Frank M. Dixon, and we qualified him and ran him as
a delegate, and he got elected. People didn't know which one to vote
for, and they voted for both of them. He got elected. We did all kinds of
things to try to get delegates for Kennedy. We had guys running as
pledged to Faubus when they really were gonna vote for Kennedy when
they got there. It was a very interesting campaign.

*He was able to elect a handful of Kennedy delegates and to handpick
the delegation's chairman. ". . . I had to use the powers of the governor's office to do it . . . but I did it."*

But anyway, when we went to California . . . all the time we were
there the Johnson folks and the Adlai Stevenson people and everybody
was trying to woo these delegates. Some of 'em, being just young fellows, inexperienced and everything, they were putting the starlets on
'em and wining and dining 'em, and it was something, I'll tell you. You
could go to bed at night, thinking you had so many votes, and you'd
wake up the next morning, and you wouldn't have that many anymore,
and you'd have to go back and get 'em again. And they were getting
long wires, three and four feet long, from folks back home, saying, "If
you vote for a Catholic for president, don't come home," and there'd be
every prominent person in town signed the telegram. . . . It was hard
to hold 'em in line, I'll tell you.

Anyway, when the time came to vote, Steve Smith, who was a
brother-in-law of John Kennedy and who was one of the floor managers
and the finance chairman, came over to me in the Alabama delegation
. . . and said, "How many you got?" And I said, "I got fourteen."

He said, "Well, now we want you to vote six." That's twelve people, see. "So if we don't get the nomination and have to start over and roll call again, I want you to go to fourteen . . ." to show a bandwagon thing to start right off with, you see.

And I said, "Look, you shoulda told me about this earlier. You can't realize how hard it has been to get fourteen of 'em here. . . . That's twenty-eight people. And now, here just before they are gonna vote, I'm gonna tell 'em to vote for somebody else. They're never gonna understand that."

"Do it."

So we held a quick caucus in a stairwell in which I told 'em what I wanted 'em to do, and you've never heard folks so mad in their lives, having to put up with all of this harassment and then being asked not to vote for him. But anyway, they were all concerned that if they voted for somebody else and it didn't go all the way through and they didn't get a chance to switch, would Mr. Kennedy know about it? I said, "Don't worry, we'll tell him. Everything will be all right." [Laughs] Of course, that never happened . . . he got the nomination on Wyoming and these guys never got a chance to vote again. Some of 'em are mad to this day at me for that.

I came on back home, and then things rocked along, and I was up there two or three times. Went up there on the Appalachian bill one time, when the President was considering this Appalachian program, and had lunch at the White House and entertained by them, and I enjoyed it, and we had a very good relationship. Then suddenly the Freedom Riders arrived. Worst situation you've ever seen. It was not a civil rights thing. It was a law enforcement problem from the very start, and these people weren't bona fide interstate travelers. They were buying tickets from town to town in Alabama, and they were getting off the buses and going into restaurants and places that were traditionally white establishments, and they were mixed groups. There were black boys and white girls. Just infuriated the local people and it culminated in two or three riots.

And Robert showed no knowledge whatsoever of the problem, and he ran the whole affair from his command post in the Justice Department, and making telephone calls at two or three o'clock here in the morning, telling us we didn't have enough policemen on a certain corner. Just a terrible, terrible situation. . . . In the meantime, he'd prevailed on the White House to send about six hundred federal marshals in here, who were patrolling the streets in the city of Montgomery. Not needed, and of course, it was unconstitutional as it could be. They had no right to do that. But anyway, he and I fell out. I'm talking about Robert now. We had some awful arguments during that period of time. . . . Robert and I were never friendly after that, and my relations with the White House cooled considerably after that. It was quite obvious from that time on, that if I ever wanted to serve in any political office here in the future, that I had to separate myself politically from them because they made me look mighty bad. I had supported them and had worked with them, and they just rammed this Freedom Rider thing down my throat publicly, and it hurt me politically. . . . And it was embarrassing.

You mentioned heated discussions with the Attorney General on the phone . . .

Four-letter words. Yeah. Terrible. Well, one thing, he called up down here one night, and he demanded that the bus company run that bus, and he wanted to know how to get ahold of "Mr. Greyhound." There were several people lost their jobs in the bus company as a result of that.* He didn't understand, really didn't understand the problem. He didn't understand who these people were. . . . They were known Communists, some of 'em. . . .

He and Robert Kennedy engaged in a celebrated shouting match by long-distance telephone. He told Kennedy that he and Alabama National Guard General Henry Graham could not guarantee Martin Luther King's safety when King came to Montgomery after the Freedom Riders were beaten at the bus terminal. "You understand, when you've got a man rambling all over this town that will not do what you say, and people all over town wanting to kill him, how can you personally guarantee that man's protection? . . . I did not believe that I could deliver on that unless he agreed to abide by the instructions of our police."

Kennedy retorted: "I don't believe that. Have General Graham call me. I want to hear a general of the United States Army say he can't protect Martin Luther King."

Fifty marshals met King at the airport and escorted him through town to that church** just like he was the president of the United

---

* This incident occurred when Greyhound officials in Birmingham refused to carry the Freedom Riders to Montgomery. Kennedy went over their heads and pressured Greyhound executives into running the bus.

** Rev. Ralph Abernathy's First Baptist Church, where King met with James Farmer and the Freedom Riders. This is the rally described by James Farmer in which Farmer and Rev. Fred Shuttlesworth reached the church by marching through the mob of angry whites.

States. Infuriated people, just infuriated people. And of course, as soon as it got dark, they had an awful riot at the church. If it hadn't been for our state police and our National Guard, then somebody would have got hurt. The marshals undertook to defend the church. . . . They were process servers. They were not trained for riot duty. . . . Some of the rioters got their courage up when it got dark, so they attacked the marshals. And we had to move in real quick, break it up because the marshals broke their ranks and began to cover their heads, and when they did, the crowd just ran over 'em. So we had to feed in the squads of infantry . . . took us about ten minutes to restore order. Nobody got killed. Nobody got hurt real bad, and I called out a whole combat team that night and just shut the whole town down. That was the end of it. They got their marshals out next morning, and I never heard from Robert again.

No Southern governor . . . had ever had to deal with that sort of federal leverage.

That's right. . . . Right at the height of that thing they sent "Whizzer" White* down here, you know, Justice White, who I like very much. . . . White didn't wanna stay in a hotel. I don't know whether they'd give him a room or not, but they put him out here at Maxwell Field.** So he came up, we had a conference . . . in the governor's office, at which time I told him that we did not want any federal assistance, that we were fully capable of enforcing the law ourselves . . . and we wanted the federal people and the federal marshals and *him* to leave Alabama and go back to Washington and to leave us alone. I recorded that. . . . I made it as plain and as blunt as I could, because I felt like that under the circumstances that the sovereignty of the state of Alabama required that. I mean we could not abandon our duty to maintain order and submit to the federal government maintaining a farce. . . . They were playing it from their point of view for political gain at our expense, you see. This is exactly the way I saw it, and they were making a record in civil rights for their Administration at the expense of the state of Alabama. . . . I tried to make that as plain to Mr. White as I could.

Well, he went out that night to Maxwell Field, and he called the White House, and he told the President that he thought we meant what we said and that there was no reason to have federal forces here. . . .

* Supreme Court Justice Byron "Whizzer" White, at that time a Justice Department official.
** An Air Force installation near Montgomery.

And he recommended to the White House that they pull all their men out of here and leave us alone. That's true. The reason I know that is because one of the girls that worked the switchboard out there at that time is the wife of a state trooper who worked for me, and we monitored his phone call. We know what he said, you see. We know exactly what he said. . . . I've always liked him as a result of that. They told him no and told him to stay down here and he did.

> Our whole reaction to this whole thing—even the Freedom Rider thing—was a complete mistake. I learned the hard way. . . . I'd handle it completely different. I would operate as if I were a one-term governor. I'd never think about reelection, and if you do that and do the best job you can and try to mediate all the problems that you should try to mediate, the chances are you'll get reelected.

Of course, after I left office, George Wallace preempted that issue as far as I was concerned. I ran again in '66 . . . and these dyed-in-the-wool segregationists didn't even remember me. This is right. People's memories are very short. I kid old Shelton, Bobby Shelton, the grand dragon, about that every time I see him. [Laughs] Even they are trying to change their image. This is true. They want to be a respectable outfit, too . . . like a civic club. In fact, I think they are now taking in Catholics and Jews. The Klan is. Pretty soon, I guess, they'll be taking in blacks.

SOL TEPPER

He is a prosperous landlord in Selma and an unrepentant segregationist. He helped organize the Dallas County Citizens Council and later joined the sheriff's posse which battled civil rights marchers during the 1965 demonstrations.

Why would a man like yourself get involved in Sheriff Jim Clark's posse?

I felt what I was doin' was right. That's what one old guy said: "Sol, I ain't got a damn thing. . . . I ain't gettin' nothin' out of it, but somehow or another, I feel like what I'm doin' is right, and I just cain't stand to get run over." . . .

Hell, I came up there [to the courthouse] with a army rifle on a sling on my shoulder, a M-1 that I'd purchased long time ago. And Crocker, the chief deputy [whispering], "Put that rifle up!" I said, "What are you talkin' about? You think I'm gonna get out there in front of a mob unarmed?" "You just put that rifle up. Now I don't mind you carryin' a side arm."

It kinda floored me a little. I thought we was gon' have a riot right off the hand. I thought, "Here's a riot right here," and I said, "I asked for it. I volunteered for it. . . ." I thought I was gon' get killed, really.

Were you prepared to shoot back?

If they shot at me, I was prepared to shoot back. . . .

We had the hotheads in the posse and that's the way we controlled 'em. If they hadn't been in there, we mighta had trouble. . . .

He was ready for trouble the night he and fifteen posse men were dispatched to a prison camp outside town where young demonstrators were being held. A crowd of angry blacks had gathered at the gates. The white posse men left their vehicle some distance from the camp and crept up through the darkness.

I was thinking, "Hell, we're liable to get killed," and I had a garbage can top I was holdin' in front of me, thought I would ward off a brick. [Laughs] I remember one of the guys just then comin' around, "What's the matter, Tepper, you scared?" I said, "Yeah, I am." And we walked out under the searchlights. Before we got under the searchlights, "Motherfucker. Bastards." We heard that. Time we showed ourselves, "Let's go back to Selma, ain't nothin' out here. . . ." Folded up just like a crowd dispersin' from a football game.

That's one thing the press helped us on, by tellin' how brutal we were. Two of us could walk down the street, blacks would get off the street and walk to the other side. That was the advertisement we got. I know, I was walkin' down the street one day with this guy that was a truck driver, a very mild fella. He said, "See those three nigras comin' down the street? They haven't looked up. Watch 'em when they look up." Sure 'nuff, they looked up. They were about two hundred yards off. They cut across the street, just automatic. Then I started thinking, "That's what the news media has done."

Were there not in your opinion any legitimate grievances on the parts of blacks in Selma at that time?

I'm tryin' to think of one. If you can name one, I'll be glad to give my opinion. I don't know right offhand of any.

What about the white Citizens Council?

There's no such thing as a "white" Citizens Council.

Okay.

It was composed of strictly white people, but that's not the name of it. That's just a technicality. It's called the Citizens Council. This was known as the Dallas County Citizens Council.* Now what do you want to know about it? I believe I can answer any questions you want.

Okay. How did it come into being . . . ?

The main purpose of it was to maintain segregation, maintain law when segregation was legal. . . . Every businessman in Selma at one time belonged to the Citizens Council, includin' the bankers, the merchants, Jews, Catholics, and Protestants, every white man. . . . You couldn't get in if you were black. It wasn't for black people, 'cause it was to maintain white—you might say, white supremacy—at least in social things. Not anything in economics, nothin' in economics.

What kinda power did you have? You said you had everybody in town.

Yeah, we were pretty influential with local politicians. In fact, our power at one time was probably rated beyond its capability. . . . "Can't do nothin' without the white Citizens Council okayin' it." I think that's what one school down here said. We considered that a compliment. We didn't know we were that powerful. It was just a group of businessmen that would meet. . . .

I was a member of it. I was invited. I'm Jewish, by the way. And one time, one guy came up there with a paper called *The Thunderbolt.*** You know that one? . . . George Tate, who is a friend of mine, said, "Sol, did you see that?" He was as upset about it as I was. I said, "Yes, I'll say somethin' about it just a minute." I let 'em get through with their business, and I stood up and I said, "I'm just as staunch a segregationist as anybody in this room. I don't appreciate this paper comin' in here. It ain't nothin' but a Jew-hatin' paper. Anybody wants to step outside with me, I'll take 'em on one by one or two by two." And you know, everybody in there shook my hand. The guy that brought it in said, "I didn't

* The Dallas County Citizens Council, organized with the aid of proselytizers from Mississippi, was started in October, 1954, only four months after the Council's founding in Indianola. It was the first and most active council in Alabama.

** The official publication of the National States Rights party. It is both antiblack and anti-Semitic, a favorite theme being that blacks are the pawns in a subversive movement directed and financed by Jews.

mean nothin' by it." I said, "What ya mean, you didn't mean nothin' by it? You can read, cain't ya?" Well, it wasn't brought in there after that. It started gettin' around town, "Tepper challenged the whole gang to a fight." I said, "Well, they could whip my ass, but it just made me mad." . . .

Do you never see any analogy between the discrimination against the Jews and the discrimination against blacks?

I cain't see one particle of discrimination. Jews in New York like to see it. I cain't see it. . . . I think the Jews are segregated in New York more than they are in Selma. They are in big cities, but the Jews in Selma were pretty well looked up to. I think their reputation was injured a little bit when some of these rabbis came down here to have fun. That's all it was, comin' down here to join in the fun, persecute the white business people of Selma. They thought they might miss a little nigra women or somethin' that joined in the fun, at our expense. . . . Maybe you explain it to me. I cain't see any analogy. . . . Nobody let me vote 'cause I was white or didn't prevent me from votin' because I was Jewish. In fact, I never even thought about it much. It might have been some that I don't know about. Maybe some of the other Jewish people are aware of it. I'm not. I reckon that's why it made me so mad when I saw that *Thunderbolt*. It was a surprise to me.

Bobby Shelton

He emerged in the early sixties as the Deep South's best-known Klan spokesman, but his involvement with the Klan started years earlier.

What really got me interested was being in the service, being overseas and seeing a proud race of people, the German people, in the agony of defeat, being conquered, and seeing the black soldiers that were taking advantage of starvation, movin' in on the German people, to where you had kids on the street . . . they would do anything to get food, even to the point of selling their sisters and things of this nature. Then Harry "Solomon" Truman comin' along with his integration order in the Armed Forces. . . . I just realized that we was in for some trouble.

Back home, he became the Invisible Empire's rising star. Imperial Wizard E.L. Edwards of Atlanta declared him Grand Dragon of Alabama. Then, claiming that Edwards was skimming the Klektokens (Klan dues), he led dissidents into the United Klans of America, Inc. (U.K.A.), became its Imperial Wizard, and quit his job at B.F. Goodrich's Tuscaloosa plant. (Goodrich, following the example of U.S. Steel in Birmingham, had judiciously ignored the feverish Klan organizational activity within its plant. Goodrich workers were the shock troops in the riots which drove Autherine Lucy from the University of Alabama campus.)

In 1966 he served nine months in federal prison for refusing to turn over U.K.A. membership lists to the U.S. House Un-American Activities Committee. He claims the imprisonment was only part of a long campaign of government harassment directed by the FBI.

It was not unusual to look out the window of your house and to see a car sitting there with two men in it for periods of two and three and four hours at a time. It wasn't unusual for these individuals to follow you around. I've had 'em to follow me all over the country, everywhere I've been. If you come to a hotel, we'd have our conventions, it wasn't unusual for the FBI to come in, flash an identification to the clerk and say, "I wanna see all your registration forms." Naturally the big-boy FBI scares a lotta people, and even without exercising the right of protecting his records, the hotel clerk would voluntarily turn 'em over to 'em.

Were you wiretapped?

Oh, very definitely, I've been one of the forty-eight that has been wiretapped for the past fifteen years.

One of the forty-eight . . . ?

I understand there were forty-eight people that there was a continuous monitor on their telephone. I had one of the congressmen himself to verify to me before I went to prison that my phone had been under constant surveillance.

Ironically, that's one thing that you and Martin Luther King did have in common. . . .

Well, I would imagine that I was under as much observation as King, if not more, because I could go into an area, say, out in Texas. I remember one time I had leased a piece of property from Lyndon Johnson's cousin that was joining the Johnson ranch. We were going to have a big public speaking, and Johnson himself personally got involved. He sent the Secret Service agents down and threatened his cousin. . . . "You've gotta remember you've gotta live here the rest of your life," and therefore his cousin canceled out. Well, I want out to make arrangements for other property. I had sixteen cars that stayed with me for a period of two weeks that I was in Texas.

Did this cousin of Johnson's know who you were when you leased the property?

Oh, absolutely. He was kinda down on Johnson himself, but this was a Big-Brother stick that was thrown against him. . . . "If you gonna live in Texas and be at peace, you better cancel out."

"The 'Cointelpro' part of the FBI was designed for the United Klans of America. . . . It had unlimited sources of money. . . ." However, he dismisses as exaggerated the FBI claim that "Cointelpro," a surveillance program instituted by Hoover in 1956, brought six percent of his membership under FBI sway as informants.

To me there's a difference in a paid pimp and an informant, and this is what the agency had in most cases . . . just plain-out paid pimps. They ever' one was receiving money, and it was paid to them through the "blue chit" system that the FBI used, where they had the cash, and the agent would be sent a check. Then the agent would cash that check and pay the pimp in cash, and he would tell him, "Now, you know, nobody has to know anything about this but you and I. You don't have to report it on your tax. . . ."

Well, a year and a half later, Internal Revenue would come to this pimp and say, "Look, we understand you received x number of dollars." Well, the pimp would get excited and he'd call his agent and say, "Look, I thought nobody was going to know anything about this but you and I, but all of a sudden, the Internal Revenue is threatening to get me on perjury and failing to file. . . ."

Then the agent would say, "Well, I don't know what I can do, but I'll see about it." So he'd come back a few days later and say, "Look, I think I'm gonna be able to hold this off of you, but you have to understand we're not gonna be able to pay you anymore." In essence, what he's doing is holding a hammer over his head . . . and this is what was transpiring in a lot of cases.

. . . I have been offered a large sum of money by the FBI through a contact of a person, a friend of mine in Birmingham, that brought the head of the FBI department at that time in Birmingham to Tuscaloosa. He didn't actually offer me the money. He put it to me in these terms: "We have unlimited sources of funds we don't have to account for and that I have eight names that I would like for you to identify as Klansmen. Now we don't care whether you put the money in your pocket, or you split it up with the man that's brought me down here. . . . All you have to do is identify x number of men." I've forgotten what number it was. It was in regards to this so-called church bombing in Birmingham, and I believe the sum was fifty thousand dollars or something of that nature. But I just told him right off the bat that I didn't have any knowledge, wasn't interested in it—certainly not for the money.*

There's nobody got the guts to speak up for the Southerner and the white man. If you will check the record you would find that ninety percent of the harassment has been on us, not on King and the other people. I don't care what they say, whether they say it's the FBI discreditin' King, you cain't make nothin' black turn white. And King had certain involvements and certain things that they cain't smut out and try to put him back on that pedestal. They're tryin' now to get King back on the pedestal of martyrdom.

In other words, you don't buy the proposition that King and the other civil rights organizations were harassed as much as . . .

Not to the extent that we were, absolutely not. There's no way possible. . . . Well, this was back in '65, I believe. I was on the way to Washington. We was gon' up to film and observe the march that Martin Luther King and them were preparing on Washington. We crashed in a national park outa Seneca, South Carolina.

In the process of the lawsuits involved afterwards, my attorneys had an injunction against the federal government aeronautical agency and forced them to turn the instruments over to the court. In turn the court sent the instruments to a laboratory in Florida, and the report came back that definitely the instrument had been tampered with, that there was pitted marks on the bead of the altimeter. And this was the problem we felt like, the reason of the crash . . . by the altimeter, we were flyin' in the neighborhood of some six thousand feet at the time we hit the high peak of twenty-six hundred feet. . . .

You're saying your plane was sabotaged.

Well, somebody had to have tampered with the instruments, and it was a leased plane. And incidentally . . . the owner of the plane from here at the airport in Tuscaloosa, "Doc" Carr . . . before he died, he wanted me to come down and meet him at his yacht down here on the

---

* His theory is that the explosion which killed the four children at Sixteenth Street Baptist Church was caused by a leaking natural gas line. The FBI attempted to blame it on the Klan to create sympathy for the Movement, he claims. ". . . I was one of the first to go to Birmingham and to lay a thousand dollar reward down when they started building this reward fund."

river, that he had a story he wanted to tell. Then he told me about the whole thing. His insurance company was notified by the federal government, the FBI, and told that they didn't want this case to go to court, and if the insurance company would settle it outa court, the government would refund them and it wouldn't cost them anything. This was the information that "Doc" himself gave to me. The FBI was sitting out there the morning we left, photographing and filming the takeoff. . . .

J.B. Stoner

"I've been fighting Jews and niggers full time more or less since start-ing in 1942." His small, close-set eyes flick upward to check the impact of what he has said. "Nigger" is one of his favorite words. In 1974 he went to court to establish his right to use it in television ads for his cam-paign as the "white racist candidate" for lieutenant governor of Georgia. He is, indeed, the white racist nonpareil, the ultimate human expression of the Southern aberration. Former Archleader of the Christian Knights of the Ku Klux Klan, founder and still chairman of the National States Rights party, he has been a perennial suspect in race bombings through-out the Deep South for the past twenty years. Birmingham police claimed he lectured Klansmen at a rally outside Birmingham on con-struction of delay-fuse dynamite bombs shortly before such a device blew up the Sixteenth Street Church. But he has never been charged in that or any other bombing.

From a squat brick building in the Atlanta suburb of Marietta, he conducts his quixotic legal and political career and oversees publication of the Thunderbolt tabloid. Tacked to the wall behind his desk is a red banner which reflects his admiration for Nazi Germany. At its center, in place of the swastika, a black lightning bolt breaks across a crimson field. "The only trouble with Hitler, he was too moderate," is his favor-ite shocker for visiting journalists. That sort of talk brought him a burst of national notoriety when he served briefly as the lawyer for James

Earl Ray, who he contends was set up by the "Federal Bureau of Integration" to take the rap for the Martin Luther King killing.

In fact, I think the FBI had Martin Lucifer Coon assassinated through undercover agents. They've offered me money, twenty-five thousand dollars, to have him killed several years before he was killed.

How did that come about?

Well, one of their undercover agents approached me. That was at a time when King still lived in Montgomery, just before he moved to Atlanta, and an undercover agent for the FBI approached me and offered twenty-five thousand dollars. He wanted me to get a good marksman who would use a rifle and then to come by his house afterwards, and he would call and have the people who were going to pay the money to come over and pay the twenty-five thousand dollars. I started checking up on him and finding out more about him, and he was a pimp for the FBI.

You say an "undercover agent." You mean a full-fledged agent?

No, sir, I'm talking about a pimp type, informer type.

Paid informer?

What they call informers. Informant.

How did you read that situation . . . ?

Well, I figured that they wanted to get rid of King and me, too. I came to the conclusion they wanted to kill King and then convict me, send me to the electric chair and call the case solved.

You're convinced it was a bona fide offer?

Yessir, same agent made an offer to Ace Carter.* His name's Asa, but everybody calls him Ace.

* Asa "Ace" Carter was Birmingham's most prominent segregationist spokesman in the mid-fifties. He got his start as a Citizens-Council-sponsored radio commentator denouncing "be-bop" as part of a Communist plot to bring about integration. He proved too much the activist for the council's Rotarian leadership, however, and split off to form the Original Ku Klux Klan of the Confederacy. (Members of this group were convicted in the "Judge" Aaron castration, although

A similar offer?

Yessir. Twenty-five thousand dollars.

Can you name the man?

I can or I could, but I don't want to right now.

Did you ever, in your representation of James Earl Ray, did you ever turn up any evidence of similar . . .

I've had people to contact me at the time I represented him . . . that told me that federal agents approached them at a nearer time to King's killing in regard to killing him. These other people I don't know so well, but I know Ace fairly well. He and I both know the same pimp. The same pimp offered both of us twenty-five thousand dollars but I think they wanted to get rid of Ace and King at the same time [laughing] or get rid of me and King at the same time. [Pauses] And they finally got rid of King.

> I was real happy [about King's death]. I thought it was a occasion for celebration. I was makin' a speech at the time in Meridian, Mississippi, when the news came he'd been killed. That meeting was being spied upon by the FBI and the political squad of the Meridian Police Department. I told the people that "Martin Lucifer Coon is a good nigger now."

Carter himself was not implicated.) In Alabama political circles Carter is generally credited with writing the "segregation now, segregation forever" speech delivered by George Wallace at his inauguration as governor in 1962.

II
HIGHER EDUCATION

AUTHERINE LUCY FOSTER

On February 3, 1956, she became the first black student to sit in a University of Alabama classroom. She took a desk in the front row.

. . . I cannot help but remember this particular teacher. . . . I had not been accustomed to seeing professors sit on the desk. He sat on the desk, and he took his cigarettes out, and he smoked during class, and the students could do the same. Everyone was so relaxed. Of course, I wasn't as relaxed as I could have been. He talked, and he looked at the members of the class, and it didn't seem that he ever noticed I was in the class. He might have, but I didn't find him noticing that I was in his class. I said, "He acts just like I'm not here." That's the thought that went through my mind, "He acts just as if I'm not in his class."

As it turned out, the professor's indifference was benign. In the days ahead he would be one of the few to speak out for her right to attend the university. On the following Monday after the Klan and its student sympathizers had a weekend to do their work on the campus, she returned to a different greeting. There had been a riot on Saturday night, and the ugly mood had persisted.

I went on around to Smith Hall, and as we drove up there, we could not get the car up close to the building, because the policemen were all around there. I saw a crowd . . . but I just didn't feel it would affect me one way or another. So I just walked through and thought in my mind that I was to hold my head high and walk tall. I just walked through and smiled and said, "Excuse me, please," and I walked in the building. I took my seat on the front seat again.

> . . . the door was slightly ajar, and I could see Mrs. Healy* standing out there looking directly at me . . . and the only thought that would come to my mind—why, I don't know—was that she must have been waiting to tell me that there had been a change of plans and that I would be given a room in the dormitory. This is what ran through my mind, that she must have decided that they were going to let me stay on campus after all.
>
> So after I came out she told me, "Autherine, I think we are going to have to carry you down the back way here, because the crowd out there is waiting for you, so we're going to have to leave from the back." And she went on to tell me that Mr. Bennett** was out there with the car to take me to my next class . . . and just about the time he was about to drive off, the windshield was shattered slightly. No glass blew in our faces or anything, but it was just glass shattered, and we kept driving though, he did, and he drove around to my next class. . . .

So, anyway, I jumped out of the car and ran for the building, and I got to the door and felt that I had made it, and just then I felt something hitting me on my shoulder. At the time I didn't know what it was. I didn't take time to stop and see . . . it really didn't hurt, so I kept going. I ran up the steps and to the door and got inside the door, and someone locked it . . . to keep the crowd from following me, but they were right behind me, because I could hear them say, "Let's kill her, let's kill her," and following me up those steps. So you might know that I was very much afraid at this time. I sat there and tried to compose myself, and naturally the next thing that I thought of doing was saying a prayer. And I can remember, not the exact words, but I can remember in this prayer that I asked to be able to see the time when I would be able to complete my work on the campus, but that if it was not the will of God that I do this, that he give me the courage to accept the fact that I would lose my life there, and to help me to accept it, because this was a time when I felt then that I might not get out of it really alive. Of

---

* Dean of Women Sarah Healy, who had earlier denied her dormitory space.
** Jeff Bennett, an assistant to the president of the University.

course, I wanted to, but I wanted the courage to accept death at that point if it had to be that way.

. . . I want to ask you particularly what you heard from the mob outside . . . ?

Well, I was sitting in the library; naturally I could hear the mob shouting, and there were two statements in particular that I recall hearing them chant. One was, "Hey, hey, ho, where in the world did Autherine go?" No, let me go back. That wasn't the way. . . . "Hey, hey, ho, where in the hell did Autherine go? Hey, hey, ho, where in the hell did that nigger go?"

Postscript: The riots continued until the university suspended her—for her own safety, it was said. Her Inc. Fund attorney, Arthur Shores of Birmingham, issued a statement in her name accusing university officials of conspiring to bar her from classes. Citing that statement as evidence of insubordination, they expelled her permanently. In the two weeks following her first day in class the Citizens Council enrolled forty thousand new members in Alabama. She left Alabama, married a minister, and lived for many years in Louisiana and Texas.

In 1975 she moved back to Birmingham and in the spring of that year made her first return visit to Tuscaloosa. She came back to the University of Alabama at the invitation of Howard Jones and Culpepper Clark, faculty members who wanted her to address their history students. Her speech was reported in the Tuscaloosa newspaper, but otherwise her day on campus made no news.

BEN ALLEN

George Wallace and the "Stand in the Schoolhouse Door,"
1963

His job as an Alabama state detective led to a strange new assign-
ment in the spring of 1963.

Well, at that time, it was my job to go around and interview all the
black applicants that made application for admission to colleges at Auburn, University of Alabama . . . to run a background investigation,
and to find out, if at all possible, if there was anything in the backgrounds of these people to prevent 'em from, as they said, associatin'
with white people in the schools. And I had investigated and turned
down several from their past. Some of 'em had been arrested for various
crimes, and their application was immediately taken out of file. Then for
various and sundry reasons, others were dismissed until I hit this Vivian
Malone application. . . .

What happened with her?

Well, there was nothin' in her background. I interviewed Vivian at
the Alabama A&M College at Huntsville, where she was employed as a
switchboard operator. Vivian was good people. She had made good
grades. She wasn't the type to try to lord it over people, so to speak. She
didn't give you the impression that somebody was pushin' her to break

the barrier to go to school or somethin'. . . . I'm sure she didn't realize that she was bein' questioned or interrogated about what her desires were. She convinced me that A&M didn't have the facilities to further her education and that the only one that did have it in Alabama was the University of Alabama. . . . And there was nothin' in her background to prevent her from goin', and I had a gut feelin' that here was the first person to break the color barrier in the state of Alabama. . . .

What was the reaction of the state officials when you reported that?

They was very much upset. [Laughs] They were very much upset when they, too, realized that she was to be the first 'un to enter the University of Alabama. . . .

Weren't the state officials really interested in having you find some grounds that they could bump these people off on?

Oh, yes. As I said, that was my job. One amusin' note: We had an applicant in Mobile that they reported as bein' black, and when I went down there, it was very confusin' because the girl was a blond. [Laughs] She was very much blond. She was a white girl. I spent two days tryin' to find a black girl with the same name. Whoever put on the application "black," they was mistaken, 'cause she was white. [Laughs] That tickled the hell outa me.

Wasn't that sort of an unusual thing for the Department of Public Safety to be involved in?

Not in the state of Alabama at that time. That ain't never been told either.

Who did you give the bad news to that Vivian was going to pass muster?

Colonel Al Lingo.

What did he tell you?

He was a little perturbed. [Laughs] Yeah, Vivian oughta get a kick outa that.

You remember what he said?

Some of it wouldn't be fit to print. [Laughs]

How about some of it that was?

Let's just say he was very much upset, because I think his intentions were to keep them all out. He thought all of 'em's backgrounds would prevent any of 'em from attendin' college.

Did you ever hear of a white student bein' investigated?

Let's say that I've never investigated one.

Did you follow Vivian on through the stand in the door then?

Um-mm. Yeah, I was down there at the stand-in-the-door day, watched her when the marshals brought her in.*

What happened there?

There's a lot about this that hadn't been told. What's the general's name that was at Vietnam?

He searches his memory for the name. He is apparently referring to General Creighton Abrams, later commander of American forces in Vietnam. Abrams had been dispatched to Alabama by Army Chief of Staff Earle Wheeler to prepare for any military action required. Three thousand Regular Army troops were being held on stand-by in case trouble broke out on the campus.

They were headquartered at an abandoned school at Vance, Alabama.** [Laughing] I'm tellin' you stuff that ain't never been told before. . . . [These Regular Army troops] were headquartered at the school, and whichever one of the generals it was, he was tough. He wanted to put Wallace in jail. [Laughs] Graham*** talked him out of it.

---

* At the "Stand in the Schoolhouse Door," Alabama Gov. George Wallace attempted to block the enrollments of Vivian Malone and James Hood, a young black man from Huntsville. Hood, who won in federal court the right to enroll, dropped out of the university two months later. He became a police officer in Detroit.

** A small town near Tuscaloosa.

*** General Henry Graham, the veteran of the Freedom Rider riots, was commanding the federalized Alabama national guardsmen stationed on the campus.

But he had a bunch trained. They had been practicin' at the school how to snatch Wallace up *and walk off* with him . . . grab him by the wrist with one hand and up under the armpits with another and forcibly walk him off. And this is what the [Regular Army] general wanted to do, and what he was *determined* to do, because his men done been trained. They'd done been gone through these dry runs there in the schoolhouse [at Vance] with a man about Wallace's size, and they were gonna pick Wallace up and move him off. I don't know whether George Wallace even knows this or not. But this is exactly from our information what happened right there at that schoolhouse. . . . But General Graham handled it, and it wasn't necessary to call on the Regular Army.*

What was Wallace like that day?

He was highly nervous, highly nervous wonderin' if they were, in fact, gonna arrest him.** Wonderin' if the federal authorities were gonna put him in jail. And I know it was awfully hot. We had men stationed on top of these buildings in this hundred-degree weather, stationed up there with rifles, and I don't see how they stood the heat.

Toward what end were they stationed . . . ?

I think Governor Wallace . . . had promised the President that there would be no trouble, and I think their job was to see that there wasn't any trouble.

[Laughing] How does a man with a rifle on a rooftop prevent trouble?

[Laughs] By seein' that none breaks out, I suppose. It was my job prior to Vivian gettin' down there to go down and talk to Robert Shelton and talk him out of doin' anything, to pull all his Klansmen off the street, because they were sittin' around with *KKK* written on the cars and with the Confederate flags flyin', in groups. You could tell who they

* Because, at the last moment, Wallace stepped aside. For an account of this confrontation, see Nicholas Katzenbach.
** He waited with Wallace in an anteroom for the arrival of Deputy Attorney General Nicholas Katzenbach and the actual confrontation in the doorway of Denny Auditorium, where the students were to register for classes. He recalled that Wallace asked him repeatedly, "Ben, do you think they'll actually arrest me?"

VIVIAN MALONE JONES

I have been described by some reporters as being introverted or shy, and I guess this is true to some extent. . . . I think one reason why I was able to survive the university is that I didn't feel that I really needed to have a lot of people around me at all times. . . . I felt secure in terms of the few people who had expressed some kind of warmth and friendliness. Now for the bulk of the people, I had no more desire to fraternize with everybody on that campus than they had any desire to fraternize with me. So I think we kind of went our own separate ways. Now I've been in classes at times where people have gotten up and moved, changed their seats. It didn't hurt me personally. . . . I really felt more sorry for the people who were doing that than I did for myself, because I didn't personally care one way or the other whether or not they sat next to me.

You see, I really went there for the express purpose of getting a degree in personnel management, which was what I really wanted at that time. I had gone to Alabama A&M, where I had to major in business education because A&M did not offer personnel management. I had one hundred and one semester hours when I transferred. I was very close to getting a degree from that school in an area that I had absolutely no desire to work in. This was my situation: Because of limited finances, I couldn't afford to go to an out-of-state school that offered personnel management.

But the University of Alabama had a reasonable fee, it had the major that I was interested in, and here they were telling me, a citizen of Alabama, that the only reason that I couldn't attend was because I happened to be black. It was just absolutely ridiculous. . . . A person can get very emotional about a thing like that when you really sit down and think about it. . . .

From what you say, I get the feeling that it was not the sort of overt harassment . . .

That's not exactly right. I was called "nigger." I would walk across the campus to the Commerce Department, and some of the students would say, "Here comes our nigger," and they'd laugh. But I was never physically hurt. I didn't have the kind of harassment that went on at some of the schools. One of the marshals told me that at one school, white students would bounce basketballs all night in the dorm to keep the black student on the floor below from sleeping. . . . I didn't really have that kind of harassment. Of course, I did have twenty-four-hour protection. . . .

How long were you actually at Alabama?

From June, '63 to May, '65.

Was the development of the situation such that you made any friendships that have become valuable to you?

Well . . . I guess my basic character or personality didn't really require me to go out and do an awful lot of meeting and greeting and that kind of thing. But I can count at least one friend other than a professor that I have kept in pretty close contact with since school. . . . She's in California now, but whenever I'm out there, I always call her, and I spent a night with her when I was out there recently. But she's not from Alabama. She was a graduate student from Germany.

Postscript: She is married to a physician and lives in Atlanta, where at the time of the interview she directed the civil-rights-compliance division of the U.S. Environmental Protection Agency's regional office. In 1972 she returned to Tuscaloosa for a ceremony dedicating the new Afro-American Cultural Center in her honor as the University's first black graduate.

Through it all, she "never had the pleasure or displeasure, whatever," of meeting the man who tried to bar her enrollment at Alabama. But each morning when she steps from the elevator in the EPA building in Atlanta, she finds herself facing a group of portraits of the governors of states in the EPA's Deep South region. There, smiling down on a successful graduate of his state's university, is George Corley Wallace.

HAMILTON HOLMES

In 1959 he and Charlayne Hunter,* Atlanta high school seniors, wrote the University of Georgia for application forms. None came, so they drove up to Athens one Saturday morning and went to the registrar's office. "That was the first time I think they realized that we were black, when we walked in the office and said, 'We want an application.' You should have seen their faces. Never will forget that."

The state of Georgia fought them doggedly. At one point the legislature convened to debate—in all seriousness—whether the university ought to be closed. Only after an eighteen-month court battle were they admitted. By that time he was in his sophomore year at Morehouse, a starting halfback on the football team and "just to be honest, I wouldn't have been that disappointed if the court decision had gone against us. But after we won the decision, I felt that I would be letting down myself and also a lot of other people if I did not accept the challenge. But I tell you, I almost didn't go. I almost didn't leave.

"I did not stay in Athens a single weekend that I was in school. I looked forward to the weekends. During the week I would go to school, come back home, and study. . . ."

I was going to the German lab, and the German lab was in a building that faced the back of one of the fraternity houses. I think it was

---

* Charlayne Hunter-Gault, who became a reporter for the New York *Times*.

KA—guys that always had a big Rebel flag on their house. . . .* This one particular day when I went in, I was parked near the driveway to the KA house, but I was not blocking the driveway. I went to the language lab the way I usually did and returned, and when I returned, I noticed they had parked a car behind the one in front of me, which was blocking their driveway. Also, they had a car that was double-parked, and I was jammed in. . . . I looked around, and I just happened to glance up at the house, and there were two or three of the windows up there filled with bodies that were just enjoying themselves, really enjoying themselves. And I surveyed the situation, and I noticed one thing . . . they really woulda had me, but they left all the doors open . . . unlocked. So I got into the car on the side of me, and I rolled it down the street and I stopped it, and I got in the one in front of me that was blocking the driveway, and I rolled that one down the street. . . . I guess that was a little too much for the guys inside, so by the time that I was rolling down the second car, these fellows came out. Gosh, musta been about fifteen or twenty of 'em, and the ringleader was a little guy, really a little guy, but obviously he was the leader. This little fellow walked up, backed up by the other guys, and he said, "Say, boy, is that your car?"

And I said, "No." So he says, "Well, what're you doing in it, if it's not your car?" I was trying—trying to be calm; that's all I was doing. I said, "The car was blockin' me, and I think that it was illegally parked, so I was moving it." He said, "That's my car, and I don't think you have any right to be in it." And I said, "Man, it was obvious that you were tryin' to block me. . . . I don't want any trouble. I just wanna leave."

And he said, "Well, I think you got trouble, boy, 'cause you were in my car and you didn't have any business bein' there." And I said, "If you want to get the police, I think that we probably can settle this . . . I think you mighta dented my car." He said, "We don't need the police to settle this." So by then, I was beginning to get a little rankled. . . . He just kept on, and he walked up on me, and I said, "Man, look, I don't want any trouble, but if that's what you want, I'm ready." He turned around, and he said, talking to the boys, "He sure is talking big, ain't he?"

I never kept a weapon . . . but I figured that this was a time for me to make a show of strength and that if they got the better of me, then I'd be in trouble from then on on the campus. So I had a flashlight in

---

* Kappa Alpha Order, a Southern fraternity which venerates the memory of Robert E. Lee and all things Confederate, flies the Confederate battle flag outside all its houses.

III
LAWYERS AND LAWMEN

Nicholas Katzenbach

He was Lyndon Johnson's attorney general during the Selma crisis. He drafted the 1965 Voting Rights Act.

Johnson's instructions as far as [drafting] that act was concerned, he said, "I want you to write the goddamnedest toughest voting rights act that you can devise." . . . He was pressing me, as the civil rights groups all the time were, to have him sign a resolution and get the troops down there,* and I was the person who was hanging tough on that. . . . He was more responsive to them in lots of ways than I was. I don't think because he had any greater commitment, at least I hope not. I think I was more conscious of, one, the constitutional issues and, secondly, the philosophy that Bob Kennedy had had and that I had, and that was that you didn't solve all the South's problems for it. There's nothing local law enforcement likes better than not being given the job of protection, and I was always very reluctant on taking that away from them.

Why?

Because they *had to do it.* Eventually, they had to do this. You didn't want an occupation of the South, and the constant pressure was to say,

---

* To protect the marchers in Selma by taking over law enforcement from the Alabama authorities.

"Look, you're the people that maintain law and order. *Do it*—and don't do it one way. . . ."

Why then did the Selma march finally go forward under federalized troops?

Wallace asked for 'em. Made him do it. Made him say he couldn't maintain law and order without 'em. Now, that's a little phony because what he said was that he couldn't do it because he didn't have the money in the budget . . . and he couldn't do it with his ordinary forces. So we just made him *ask* for the federal troops.

. . . There was a meeting between the two [Johnson and Wallace]?

He asked for 'em in a telegram which I happen to remember . . . it's very funny. I was down testifying before Manny Celler's committee* in the House on the Voting Rights Act, and had finished a rather long statement all about Selma, and Burke Marshall was with me, and a lady, a clerk there, came over. The microphone was on, and the room was crowded. She says [a stage whisper], "The President wants you." [Laughs] This was heard all over the room. Celler said, "Would you like to be excused?" I said, "Yes." So I went, and he says, "I got this telegram from George Wallace. I just read about it on the ticker." He had a ticker tape in his office.** He said, "What should I do?" I said, "Well, Mr. President, why don't you wait until you get the telegram so that you know that you've got it accurately, then we'll reply to it." And he said, "All right."

Back I go, and twenty minutes later [the same stage whisper]: "The President wants you." [Laughs] "All right," he says, "I got the telegram now." And I said, "Well, let's answer it." So he said, "All right, I'll put a secretary on." So he put a secretary on, and I dictated an answer, and he said, "Fine, okay, go back and testify." So back I went, and twenty minutes later the President wants me again. Off I go. He said, "Ya gotta dictate that telegram again. That girl didn't take shorthand." [A long laugh]

So we wrote it again, and that was where we made George Wallace pretty much swallow that. He had been up the week before to see the President on Saturday morning, and immediately following that was

* The House Judiciary Committee chaired by New York Congressman Emanuel Celler.

** A wire-service news teletype, not a stock market ticker.

when the press got backgrounded on the Voting Rights Act, and it was sent up the following Monday.

What was the view of Wallace?

The view of Wallace? The view of Wallace was the President oughta turn off all those demonstrations.

No, I mean what was the view from the federal standpoint of Wallace's behavior?

That he was being very political about it, I think more political than principled . . . He was trying to take advantage of the demonstrations and trying to tell the President that it was his responsibility to turn off those demonstrations. President Johnson's response was, "You know, George, you can turn those off in a minute." He said, "Why don'tcha— why don'tcha just desegregate all your schools?" He said, "You and I go out there in front of those television cameras right now, and you announce you've decided to desegregate every school in Alabama." Wallace said, "Oh, Mr. President, I can't do that, you know. The schools have got school boards, they're locally run. I haven't got the political power to do that." Johnson said, *"Don't you shit me, George Wallace."* [Laughs]

This was not his first brush with Southern segregationists. He got his baptism in 1962 when Attorney General Robert Kennedy dispatched him to enroll James Meredith in the University of Mississippi.

I do remember—it sounds terribly cynical, but it was funny at the time—when I went down to Ole Miss, Bobby, just as I was going, he said, "Hey, Nick."
I said, "Yeah."
He said, "Don't worry . . . if you get shot, 'cause the President needs a moral issue." [Laughs]
He had a very dry sense—that sounds terrible in print. It was very funny at the time. He had that kind of a sense of humor. . . .

The following year he was in Tuscaloosa to face Wallace at the schoolhouse door, a confrontation which, according to many journalists on the scene, followed a script secretly agreed upon by Wallace and Kennedy.

In Alabama, the situation there, how orchestrated was that?

Not very. We had plenty of communication with Frank Rose* and the university, and they were all, in essence, on our side. We had none with the governor, and Rose wasn't all that sure what the governor was gonna do. I said we had "none" with the governor, none that helped. And whenever you talked to him, he just said, "Now, don't worry, there'll be no violence."

I had a real concern as to, again, whether his people were gonna be disciplined and gonna control that situation.** I had assumed he was gonna stand in the schoolhouse door and refuse admission and that the scenario would go the way it went.

We did make some other plans and did not take Frank Rose in on them, but a couple that pleased me, probably because they were my ideas. One, that once we went on the campus, we would not leave the campus with the students,*** and I'm sure that was not in their scenario anywheres. And the second was that I would not take students up to the schoolhouse door. I would not have *them* refused. He could refuse me, but he couldn't refuse them. It was just a question of dignity, and I didn't want that picture on national television, his turning down two black students. It seemed to me the better confrontation was federal and state authority, not the racial one.

But I deceived the university by getting the keys to their dormitory rooms . . . and then completely without anybody's knowing it, except our own group, after he turned us down, I escorted the young lady, Vivian Malone, and John Doar took the young man to their dormitories. It required me to walk right through the police line, and they didn't know what to do. [Laughs] I just walked right through 'em up to the dormitory where the housemother came down when we went in and looked and saw me and saw Vivian, and she said very warmly, "You must be Vivian." [Laughs]

And then a very nice story followed that, because I told Vivian to go up to her room and come down and go eat by herself in the dining room. Frank Rose just went absolutely crazy. He said, "There's gonna

* The president of the university. He had a reputation for resisting Wallace's efforts to use the school for political purposes.

** At Ole Miss, the previous year, Governor Ross Bar had promised him that the highway patrol would maintain order when James Meredith arrived on campus. But the patrolmen suddenly "just went off the campus," leaving it to a student mob. In the ensuing riot a French journalist and a bystander were shot to death, and twenty-nine U.S. marshals were wounded by gunfire.

*** Vivian Malone and James Hood.

be a riot if you do this." I said, "Look, she's gonna be eating in that dormitory, she might as well start with lunch." She went in all by herself, sat down at a table all by herself, and within thirty seconds, six or eight kids had joined her. And that was that problem, and Rose called me up and said, "You were right."

I couldn't help but notice that you used the term "scenario" about the confrontation. I guess that's the key question. How firm . . .

Well, we knew what we were gonna do. We knew exactly what we were gonna do. We did not know what the governor was gonna do, except we assumed he would turn us down. . . . He did communicate with General Graham. . . . He communicated with General Graham that there'd be no problem, and he said he just wanted an opportunity to say something, and General Graham brought that word [from Wallace], which—I overcame my initial reactions.* [Chuckles]

Which were?

To hell with him. [Laughs] I said, "All right, General, but you tell him it can't be over two minutes long. I don't want a speech."

I remember very distinctly seeing on TV your initial approach to the auditorium . . . my reading of your expression being that it was one of, one, disbelief and, two, disgust.

* That is, the schoolhouse-door confrontation was rigged to the extent that Wallace had sent his pledge of capitulation through General Graham. The general was an ideal go-between. He had come to Tuscaloosa as an Alabama guardsman under Wallace's command. When President Kennedy federalized the Guard, he then became a Regular Army officer under Kennedy's direct command. This account supports the contention of Wallace's home-state critics, who have always maintained that the "stand in the school house door" was nothing more than a face-saving show for the red-necks, more of the same old segregationist sound and fury, signifying nothing.

Television newsman Richard Valeriani remembers talking to Katzenbach and an aide that day in Tuscaloosa: "I was told flatly . . . that a deal had been worked out so that Wallace would be allowed to stand there and make his defiant little speech. And they said, 'Pay attention to what he says.' Because he very carefully did not say, 'I'm not going to allow you to do this. . . .' I mean, the deal was worked out that he would have his day in front of the cameras, in effect, to stand up there and read his statement, and then everything would proceed as though he had not done it."

Heretofore, General Graham's undisclosed role as go-between has been the missing element in speculation about the "deal."

I was disgu—I was awfully tired. I had been up all night, and it was hot as hell out there. Then I'd gone up to pick up Vivian in the car, and I was coming back, got a radio call in the car. Bobby wanted to talk to me, and so I stopped in a supermarket and called Bobby up on the phone, and he said, "What are you gonna say to the governor?" And I said, "Oh, I don't know exactly. . . ."

"Well," he said, "the President says it's important to make him look silly." [Laughs] And I said, "You got any script you want to give me? . . . I think that's pretty hard."

But some of the things that I said, for example, "You know perfectly well what's going to happen," which may have later led people to believe we'd worked it all out, were said to make Wallace look silly. I said, "You know these kids are gonna be registered. You know they're gonna be registered whatever you do. Why do you put on this show?"

From the vantage point of ten years past now, how do you feel when you look back on that period?

Oh, I feel a lot of things were accomplished that were good and that were right, and I think history has proved it to be absolutely right *for* the South. I don't mean to sound pretentious about it, but I think that's true. . . . Every Southern, every *white* Southern politician has been freed by the '64 and '65 Civil Rights Act. You wouldn't have Jimmy Carter running for the Presidency if you didn't have those acts.* He would have had no chance. . . . I think it's been good for the South . . . good for business in the South . . . good for politics in the South.

I guess my biggest satisfaction didn't come from—I thought the whole show in Alabama was ridiculous. In fact, I told Bobby, "Why bother?" I said, "We don't have to go in through the door. Why don't we just go register 'em somewheres else? You don't even have to register 'em. The court's ordered them registered. That's good enough."

And Bobby, I think, made the right decision. He said, "Look, it's too dangerous a situation, and I don't know what that man'll do if he's crossed. He wants his show; you're gonna have to give him his show."

* This interview took place in Atlanta about a month after Jimmy Carter announced his candidacy there. At the time Carter was not considered a serious contender.

ELBERT TUTTLE

The Soldier's Grandson

Chief judge of the U.S. Fifth Circuit Court of Appeals,* which ruled on the South's most important civil rights cases. A Southern newspaper once introduced him to its readers as "the judge who changed your life." He came south by a circuitous route. He grew up in Hawaii, son of a hidebound Republican father and a mother "still very bitter over the Civil War issues." Her father was a Union soldier whose health had been broken in the notorious Confederate prison at Andersonville in south Georgia. "He survived Andersonville just long enough to have married and had a family of three children and died very young, maybe thirty-three or thirty-four years old."

At Cornell he married a Southern girl and in 1923 moved to Atlanta to practice law. ". . . when I came south, I didn't see anything in the Southern scene that made me want to join the Southern Democratic party. . . . It was not really a democratic party." Thus, he remained loyal to his father's party, and in 1954 he became one of "the Eisenhower appointees," Republican federal judges who dispensed a new brand of Southern justice.

A Democrat, to be appointed to the court of appeals, would have had to have the sponsorship of a Democratic senator or the two Democratic

* The Fifth Circuit includes Alabama, Florida, Georgia, Mississippi, Louisiana, Texas, and the Panama Canal Zone.

senators. I did not need the sponsorship of any Democratic political figure to be appointed or to be confirmed. Thus I wasn't in any sense . . . I don't mean to say anybody is "obligated" to a senator once he accepts a judgeship, but at least he doesn't even have to look over his shoulder if he's appointed by the other party. . . .

That's interesting. By and large the Eisenhower appointees to the federal bench in the South performed very well in the civil-rights area.

This is part of the reason, because none of us was identified with the fortunes of the Democratic politicians in the state. To some extent we had opposed them, and therefore we were free of any . . . sense of disappointing "our friend the senator" when we did what we felt was required of us by the Constitution. Of course, the one exception to that is Judge Cameron. . . .*

. . . You were appointed to the Fifth Circuit in '54, an auspicious year for the South. . . . Did you have any presentiment as to what lay ahead for the federal courts?

Yes, I was serving at that time on the planning board of the National Security Council. . . .** And so we thought we were pretty well involved in everything that was going on of importance, and when I told my colleagues good-bye, that I was going down South to become a member of the Fifth Circuit Court of Appeals, the comment was made by one of them, "Well, you think you've had a tough time dealing with the Berlin Airlift, but wait till you start working for the Fifth Circuit in the field of race relations."

---

* The late Judge Ben Cameron of Mississippi, who cooperated with Mississippi authorities to keep James Meredith out of Ole Miss. Four times Tuttle and two colleagues ordered Meredith enrolled, and four times Cameron handed down a staying order. Finally U.S. Supreme Court Justice Hugo Black interceded and set aside Cameron's staying orders.

In 1964 Cameron defied judicial etiquette by publicly denouncing Judges Tuttle, J. Minor Wisdom of Louisiana, Richard Rives of Alabama, and John R. Brown of Texas. Cameron dubbed them The Four and accused Tuttle of using his powers as chief judge of the U.S. Fifth Circuit Court of Appeals to give The Four a rotating majority on the three-judge panels which handled the most important civil-rights cases. As chief judge, Tuttle selected the judges who sat on these panels.

** After Eisenhower's election in 1952 Tuttle left his Atlanta law firm and went to Washington as general counsel to the Department of the Treasury. In that capacity, he represented the treasury secretary on the National Security Council planning board.

He did, in fact, arrive back in the South just in time to greet the flood of civil-rights litigation sparked by the 1954 decision.

You see, the school case dealt with education, and the court said, "Education is somewhat unique, and education is per se unequal if it's segregated." Well, there was the feeling expressed, the clear import, that segregation in any public area must be looked at with great suspicion. But it wasn't said . . . didn't become a precedent that bound anybody, except in school litigation. So when the suits were brought with respect to golf courses and courthouses, voting, jury duty, we faced these problems before the Supreme Court ever reached them.

And the great breakthrough came when Judge Rives and Judge Johnson and Judge Lynne,* all from Alabama . . . sat as a three-judge district court where there was an attack on the constitutionality of the Montgomery ordinance requiring segregated seating in the bus. Judge Rives and Judge Johnson, in the majority opinion written by Judge Rives, applied the same principles that Brown-against-Topeka had applied in the schools to an ordinance requiring segregated seating on the buses. Judge Lynne dissented. From that time on our [Fifth Circuit] court almost without any serious hesitation applied it to courthouses and these other areas of activity.

Of course, the unusually difficult thing about the racial problems during the sixties was that—different from most types of litigation where no lawyer will recommend to a client that he litigate over something that's already been definitively decided by the Supreme Court of the United States—lawyers advised their clients, or clients insisted on litigating over this until there was a judgment of the court affecting that particular body. In other words, *every* county school board considered it was not bound by what the Supreme Court said until there was an order directing that particular county school board to desegregate. So they continued . . . year after year, they would litigate, rather than just recognizing what the law was and comply with it. This is unusual in litigation, because most lawyers don't like to spend their time litigating over a lost cause. But if their important client says, "Well, I want to litigate, and I'll pay to do it," of course, the lawyer is there to litigate. . . .**

* Judge Rives and Judge Frank M. Johnson were from Montgomery. Judge Seybourn H. Lynne was from Birmingham.

** This dilatory strategy, sometimes dignified with the title "massive resistance," was Southwide and carefully planned by segregationist politicians. John Patterson, while attorney general of Alabama, convened meetings of his state's white "constitutional" lawyers. Patterson: ". . . we concluded then that we could never win the legal battle, that you could not square a dual system of that sort under our federal Constitution . . . and that the best thing for us to do would be to never

What you're saying really is that desegregation in the South at that time was almost a schoolhouse-by-schoolhouse . . .

It was, yes, it was. . . . So the courts were faced with the realization that time was running out, and "all deliberate speed" involved more deliberation than it did speed. And we occasionally began to *say* that in our opinions . . . so there wouldn't be any further possibility of delay in the district court.

As an appeals judge, he became well-known for speedy decisions— and for prodding federal district judges to face the inevitable. For instance, in 1960 the federal judge who ordered Hamilton Holmes admitted to the University of Georgia turned around and delayed his own order to give the state of Georgia time to appeal. "Well, it was obvious to me . . . there was nothing to appeal . . . so I vacated the stay immediately." This swift action prevented Holmes from losing another semester—and cost the University of Georgia one final segregated spring.

He moved with equal speed in a 1963 case. On the very night in 1963 that the Birmingham school board permanently expelled hundreds of black student demonstrators, he reversed the school board. "Obviously it was overkill to such an extent that I saw fit to vacate that [expulsion] *order. The children went back to school, and I really think hundreds of children got a high school degree that year who never would have gone back to school."*

You see, we were constantly placed in the position of having to go ahead of what the Supreme Court had done in the field of voting rights of blacks, registering to vote, in the field of service on juries. . . . It was important for us to decide cases if we could in a way that the Supreme Court would merely affirm them. If we didn't take a forward step in each of these new types of cases that came up under the heading of racial cases, the Supreme Court would have been swamped. They would have had to consider every one of these new cases that came up. As it was, our court almost without exception extended the forward-looking view in all three or four of these additional fields, and I do take great pride in the court's having kept ahead of the Supreme Court. Now

admit that, of course, but to fight a delaying action in the courts . . . delay every way we could do it . . . avoid having a decision made in court, if possible, at all costs, anticipating that the decision would be against us . . . in hopes that we could buy a number of years of time for the people to become adjusted to this thing gradually and peaceably. Now this was our approach . . . so that they'd have to take us on, on a broad front, in a multitude of cases. . . ."

we did it only by saying to ourselves, "This is what the Supreme Court will ultimately hold." If we hadn't done it, if we had taken the negative view and said, "Well, this has never been decided by the Supreme Court . . . ," the Supreme Court would have had to face each one of these things itself.

Those sorts of decisions gave rise to a call . . . for "strict constructionists" on the federal bench.

Yes, it is interesting to see what "strict constructionist" means. Actually, it means loose construction. . . . All the Warren Court did was to apply the law strictly, as I see it, or the Constitution. But we know what they mean when they speak of strict construction . . . we all know what it means.

He helped keep a "strict constructionist" off the Supreme Court. When President Nixon nominated Federal Judge G. Harrold Carswell to the Supreme Court, he wrote a letter of endorsement to the Senate committee reviewing Carswell's credentials. But when it was revealed that Carswell had helped draw the membership rules for a segregated country club in Tallahassee, he withdrew his letter. Shortly thereafter the Senate voted not to confirm Carswell. Because of the Fifth Circuit Court's record on civil-rights cases, his withdrawal of support was said to have helped tip the balance against Carswell.

ARTHUR SHORES

For twenty years he was the only black attorney practicing in Alabama. In 1940 he prosecuted a white policeman for brutality against a black union leader and won—before an all-white jury in Birmingham. Immediately after the verdict he was attacked in the courthouse corridor by a black man who "admitted later that he had been paid by the officers. . . . The papers headlined it, and people who didn't know I was practicing law would drop by my office just to see me. . . . So from that day to this, I've never had to want for any legal practice. This same black, being a police informer, sent me numerous cases after that."

He became the NAACP Inc. Fund's counsel in Alabama. He represented Autherine Lucy. He represented the three thousand demonstrators convicted in 1963 of violating Birmingham's parade ordinance and ultimately got the ordinance declared unconstitutional by the Supreme Court. He secured the federal court order for desegregation of the Birmingham schools.

Well . . . early part of September, '63, after the district court entered an order requiring the local schools . . . to integrate, well, that night my house was dynamited. One end was practically blown off. Two weeks later, when the blacks actually enrolled in the schools, I was sitting in my living room and said, "The old saying that lightning doesn't strike twice in the same place may be all right, but I'm goin' sit out on the porch a little while with my double-barreled shotgun and kinda watch out." And the moment I got up out of my seat, my front door was blown in and if I'd been a second or two earlier, it would have caught me full in the face. So that was the other end of my house. Did about eighteen thousand dollars' worth of damage to my home.* But it was covered by the insurance. But I had a hard time getting insurance after that. Even Lloyd's of London wouldn't insure me. But a local company here, unsolicited, an excellent company, came and insured my house and my contents.

Black-owned?

No. No. It was a white-owned company.

As a gesture of—

Yeah, I guess. That's the only reason I could attribute to it.

. . . I've heard that area called Dynamite Hill.** Is that where the appellation came from?

Yeah. Well, not only that. There were several houses dynamited and burned on that hill. You see, here, unlike in the North, we had zoning ordinances that restricted the use and occupancy of land according to race, whereas in the North you had restrictive covenants. And one of my suits was to require the city to issue a certificate of occupancy for a black man who had built a home in property zoned for whites. And immediately after a decree was issued requiring the city to issue this certificate of occupancy, that night his home was completely and totally destroyed by dynamite. Then whites began to move out of the district after the blacks were allowed to move in, and as soon as these houses were emptied and a black would buy 'em, the house would either be bombed with dynamite or burned. The first case was not a class suit. It was directed at this individual home owner. The next case was a class

---

* The bombers in Birmingham could be frighteningly resourceful. Police surmised that one of the bombs in Shores' home was planted by a white man who represented himself as an employee of the exterminating firm which provided termite protection for the house. In the case of the Sixteenth Street Church bombing, it has been speculated that the bomb was planted by men dressed as policemen. No one was ever arrested for any of the Dynamite Hill bombings.

** This is the neighborhood mentioned by Ruby Hurley and Ben Allen.

suit,* and at the end of that decision that house was dynamited. They burned and dynamited several homes up there.

Why did you stay here all those trying years?

Well . . . when I was filing suits to break down certain other segregation laws, zoning and so forth, I had a very wealthy man to offer me, said, "You don't have much here, but I'll give you fifty thousand dollars for what little holdings you have, if you'll pull up stakes and go somewhere else." [Laughs] People thought I was some sort of a nut to begin practice here, but I told 'em if I passed the Alabama bar I was gonna practice like other lawyers. . . .

I'm still not sure that answers the question of why you stayed here all those years.

Oh . . . I say, this was my home. I was born here, and I felt that a black lawyer who was dedicated to practicing here to see if he couldn't ameliorate the conditions of his people, that it offered an excellent opportunity. And I said then that when the race question was fairly settled here to some extent, that this was gonna be one of the garden spots of the country, and my predictions are being vindicated. In 1954 when I took a black down to the University of Alabama after being admitted, they closed the university for three days as a result of riots. And Sunday, the University of Alabama awarded me a degree of Doctor of Humanities.**

Why, in your opinion, did segregation, once the foundations were chipped just a little, why did it crumble so rapidly?

Well, you see we had the law on our side. It was amusing for us to go into courts where these white lawyers were really unprepared. . . .

. . . whenever a case was to be argued before the Supreme Court, the NAACP lawyers would meet at Howard, and the students and professors would serve as the devil advocates. Posing as members of the Supreme Court, they would question you and get you ready for your arguments before the Supreme Court. . . . It was just like being in law school again.

* A class suit seeks a ruling on a broad area of law, in this case the city of Birmingham's zoning ordinances.
** At the 1975 commencement.

I mean we were drilled and with very competent lawyers. There were lawyers from Yale, from Harvard, from UCLA. The N-Double-A-C-P had access to the best legal brains in the country and still has. So when we got into court, we were prepared, and I mean it was ludicrous to see some of these so-called white constitutional lawyers get up and just flail the wind. See, they had been used to their political . . . state courts. They really hadn't been used to practicing too much in the federal courts, and civil rights was unheard of, so far as their having to prepare for or against it. And they were not prepared and none of these cases were lost.

Postscript: He became Birmingham's first black city councilman. In 1973 he won a second term, outpolling some white candidates in their own neighborhoods, but for the first time he was attacked by black opponents as an "Uncle Tom." "I had really represented all the people. . . . I didn't make any distinction. . . . It didn't bother me."

HERBERT JENKINS

In 1932 he joined the Atlanta police force and the Ku Klux Klan, but his citizenship in the Invisible Empire was brief. He was assigned as the driver for Mayor James L. Key, the first of a succession of mayors to owe a political debt to the city's black voters. They had provided Key's margin of victory in a recall election. Officer Jenkins found himself piloting the mayor's 1931 Cadillac to meetings with black leaders.

Well, it was certainly an education for me . . . that was the mayor shaking hands with these people. I never shook hands with a Negro in my life, wouldn't have. But under these conditions, he'd meet the preacher of a church and shake hands with him and turn and introduce him to me, and I'd have no choice. But then after that happened a few times, I took a completely different view of this entire situation, because this was the first time I had ever had an opportunity to meet black people that I recognized as better educated, had traveled more, were better off financially than I was, across the board.

It was at one of these meetings that he met the Reverend Martin Luther King, Sr., the young preacher who had just taken over the pulpit at Ebenezer Baptist. Herb Jenkins went on to become police chief, and in 1948 he hired Atlanta's first black policeman. In 1955 he cooperated with black preachers who asked to be arrested so they could make a test case against Atlanta's bus segregation ordinances. His reputation for cooperating with blacks so galled the Georgia legislature that they passed a special bill aimed at depriving him of his police pension. Through it all, he and Martin Luther King, Sr., stayed in touch.

I talked to him about a lot of things. I sought his advice, because there was times I wanted to know what the blacks was plannin', what they were gonna do next. And I had respect for him and had his cooperation. But as I remember young King as a teenager—just another teenager, and I didn't know much about him until he went to Montgomery. That's when he made his name.

And then as a result of that . . . just to show you how ridiculous it was, I had two captains for the Birmingham state police come to see me and shut the door. Great secrecy. They had [a stage whisper] "confidential information" that young King was not the Kings' child. He'd been smuggled out of the Mideast when he was three weeks old and brought over here, and they adopted him and raised him and all of this. And I said, "Well, I don't know [laughing] . . . I would guess that he was born at Grady Hospital, and I think if you go down there and make inquiries, you can find his record and see when he was born and what time and probably find his footprints. I think they was makin' footprints back then."

And they said, "Well, would you help us with it?" And I said, "Well, I'll call the hospital and tell these people, the people that I know down there, that you are here and you really want to know Martin Luther King, Jr.'s origin, and if they can help you, I'd 'preciate it." So they left and went on over to the hospital . . . but that was one of the things. There was other little things that come up like that durin' that time. . . .

Well, I mentioned these things to King. For I asked King one time later, I said, "Look, they tell me you smuggled Junior out of Jerusalem or somewheres." [Laughs] I mean I didn't have any secrets. I'd tell him whatever I heard or whatever I thought, and I think he did me the same way.

So he comes, and he was disturbed about his son: "They gon' kill my boy." And I said, "I think you're right, with the other things I've seen and heard." He said, "Well, he'll be over here tomorrow, and I'm gon' bring him by here. Will you see him?" I said, "Yeah." . . .

They came in, the two of 'em came in and sat down and talked a little bit, and I told him, "I don't have any ironclad information, but I do pick up these little things, and I think you're in great danger. I think you're a marked man. I think if you don't leave Montgomery and come

back to Atlanta, they gon' *bury* you over there." He said, "You're probably right and I appreciate it. But I want you to know that this is my
job, and if that's the way it ends, well, that's the way it'll have to end. I
wouldn't stay away to prevent it, because I'm gon' do what I know I
must do and let the consequences come."

*After Dr. King, Jr., moved back to Atlanta, . . . did that present
any security problems to the police in terms of protecting him?*

I don't recall any special attention that he ever asked for or that we
ever gave him. Along there at the last, you know, he was under severe
investigation by the FBI after he and Mr. Hoover had an open break.
And on several occasions I'd have a detective come to me and say, "My
friend who is an FBI agent just called me and said, 'Dr. King is in hotel
room so-and-so in such-and-such a hotel with a white woman.'" Didn't
I wanna go out there and raid that hotel? And he said, "I told him I
didn't *think* so." [Laughs] But that he'd come ask me, and he come
asked me.

And I said, "Well, I have great admiration and respect for the FBI,
and they have our *full* cooperation, but don't let 'em push us into doin'
any dirty work they wanna do. And obviously this is some dirty work
they want done, but they don't wanna do it themselves. So tell 'em if
they've got to make a raid, you'll go with them. Let them make the raid
and you'll go to assist 'em if they want you to.

But on one occasion, Baugh . . . now this is Howard Baugh . . .*
some of the agents got ahold of Howard and convinced him that he
oughta do it right then . . . they had had Dr. King under surveillance,
and "Dr. King is now in room so-and-so at the Waluhaje Hotel with a
white woman. I think you oughta raid it."

He said, "Okay. I'll go out there and see." So he went out there and
knocked on the door, and they opened the door, and there was Dr.
King, and there was a white lady, and there was five other people in
there having a meeting, see. And he told them what it was and what had
happened.

---

* Howard Baugh, a boyhood friend of King, was the first black policeman pro-
moted to detective in Atlanta. He was on occasion assigned as King's bodyguard.

Everette Little

Nacirema: Bombings By Contract

He is a captain of detectives in the Atlanta Police Department and a difficult man to interview. After over thirty years on the force, the detective's habit of protecting confidential information is deeply ingrained. However, the story which emerges, bit by bit, is a fascinating one. In the late 1950s, sensing the tenseness of the city, he suggested to Atlanta Police Chief Herbert Jenkins that the department needed a squad to keep tabs on racial terrorists. Jenkins gave him the job. He became one of the South's leading authorities on racial bombings, and in due course, he discovered that many of the bombers belonged to a bizarre secret organization based in Atlanta.

It was an offshoot of the Klan. It was the hard-core group. Most of 'em had at one time been members of the Ku Klux Klan, and they were even too radical for the Klan's thinking, and they developed this outfit called Nacirema. Of course, some of 'em were still Klan members. Some of 'em weren't. . . . We were able to penetrate them. . . . Whenever they would move, why we would happen to be there.

Nacirema. How did they settle on that?

If you analyze that, you'll see that that's "American" spelled backwards. That's what it is. That's what they said was the reason they settled on "Nacirema."

Their notion being that they were somehow protecting . . .

That they were looking out for the interests of the Americans.

What sorts of people were involved? Were they abnormal in any way?

Some were. . . . There were people who were highly educated, people who were influential citizens in the city that became involved in it. And there were, of course, people that had no education hardly, and there were perverts. We had several sexual perverts. There were crippled people involved in it. So it's really not fair to say that any particular type of person was involved, because there were all types.

Did you notice any particularly high incidence of sexual perversion or deformity of one sort or another?

Yes, you could type 'em to that extent. I'd say sixty or seventy percent of those involved were perverted in some manner or crippled in some manner or felt like life had not given them their fair share of good things. . . .

When you say you noticed a high incidence of sexual perversion, are you speaking primarily of homosexuality?

That's correct.

Did Nacirema have a ritual or regalia . . . ?

They had initiation procedure very similar to the Klan. They swore allegiance to the organization.* Their allegiance first was to America and then to the organization and its efforts to protect the American people from this "evil" that was about to be forced upon them.

They made no quibble about being dedicated to violence?

No, among themselves. They were a very secretive group, but in talking among themselves, they planned violence. They thought nothing of

* The oath set death as the penalty for breaking the pledge of secrecy about the organization's acts of violence.

it. They had training schools, sessions where they taught different members how to use explosives and how to set fires, how to use firearms, that sort of thing. They were a very, very radical group.

They actually had "bomb schools"?

Oh, yeah.

Could you tell me what would typically go on at one of those?

They would set up a bomb and timing device and [show] how to manipulate 'em and how to handle 'em and how to set them and so forth—how to make them, how to conceal them. In some instances, they showed 'em how to throw Molotov cocktails and things of that sort into a passing automobile. They burned several cars at one of these [schools], old automobiles. Set 'em on fire to show how effective the weapons were when properly used.

Is there any evidence that this group or individuals in it had any success in "exporting" violence . . . ?

The people that were involved in our investigation were active throughout the Southeast, and they definitely were connected with the bombing of temples throughout the Southeast in that siege in the sixties when the temples were bombed in Birmingham, in Atlanta, and all over the Southeast. . . .

I've heard it suggested that some of the people that did racial bombings in the South during that period actually took "contracts."

I presume you mean that they agreed to do certain types of bombings or certain bombings for certain amounts of money.

Yeah.

Our information was that they did, yes.

You mentioned the synagogue bombings in Birmingham. In your opinion is there any connection with the Birmingham church bombing [in which four children were killed] . . . ?

Yes, very definitely.

Do you think the Nacirema group was involved in the Birmingham church bombing?

[Brusquely, at first] I wouldn't comment on that. . . . Whether Nacirema as an organization participated in the planning, I couldn't say, but we know that people who were very close to Nacirema and who associated with Nacirema members were definitely involved.

He learned from his Nacirema informants that a very small group of fanatics—"I'd say twelve to fifteen people"—was responsible for most of the bombings throughout the Deep South. Since many of them lived in or near Atlanta, he and his squad adopted a policy of overt surveillance and psychological harassment in hopes of sparing the city a rash of bombings. He believes they headed off the most murderously ambitious bomb plot of the Movement years.

This city'll never know how much it owes a group of about twelve to twenty city and federal law-enforcement agents. This city'll never know how much they owe 'em. There's just no way of tellin' 'em. They worked night and day around the clock for six or seven months that I know of, keepin' tabs on these people, knowin' what they were doin', puttin' 'em under psychological pressure where they felt like any move they made might be observed. There was a lot of psychology went into the protection of the city of Atlanta during this particular period of time —and a lotta hard work done.

Psychology in the sense of letting these people know they were under surveillance?

That's right. To a point, we'd let 'em know so much and knock it off. Let 'em think we had relaxed and then when they went to move, we'd be there. . . .

By way of example, this group of people, one of the hard-core group that we know of, had somehow obtained maps of the sewer outlay under the Atlanta University system over there, all underneath there. And they had stolen a vanload of dynamite out of Virginia, and the plans were to blow up that whole Atlanta University housing thing, and they would have done it, had this psychological deterrent not have been in effect.

They were gonna blow up those dormitories?

Yessir! They were gonna blow up the whole area. They had enough dynamite that they were going into that sewer system and place not just sticks of dynamite, but *cases* of dynamite, and set 'em off in a series. This is the type of people you're dealing with.

It could have killed hundreds.

Yeah. By way of example, one of the people who was involved was discharged from the service as mentally deranged. He was an explosives expert. They had the technical knowledge to do the job, and they had the fanaticism to do it.

How close did they come to actually carrying out the Atlanta University plan?

[Softly] Pretty close. Pretty close. Close enough to steal the dynamite and have the plans available and 'long about then we put enough pressure, though. We couldn't let it happen. We would like to have caught [them]. A good law enforcement man likes to let a man commit a crime as long as nobody's gonna get hurt, catch him and get him out of circulation. But you couldn't let that happen. You didn't let that happen.

Too big a risk factor.

Too big a risk factor, yeah. You couldn't even let 'em set it and try to hope to catch 'em doing it. Couldn't go that far. Couldn't do it. Too much involved.

You'd be amazed . . . [Trails off, laughs, indicating he can give no more details] They'll never know how close they came to being caught in Birmingham. [Voice drops] They'll never know how close.

The people that perpetrated it, you mean?

Yes. Had they not committed the act two weeks before they were supposed to have committed it, they would have been caught.

Why'd they jump the gun?

I can't answer that. Some of these people have a sort of an animal shrewdness or cunning, and they're smart enough, if they make a contract to do something, not to do it when they say they're gonna do it. That would be the smart thing to do, and in this instance, I think they were smart. Probably saved 'em from being caught. And we certainly didn't want anything like that to happen in Atlanta, with respect to the Atlanta University setup. We couldn't afford to go along and risk the fact that they might get it in there. They might jump our surveillance some way and get it in there.

The Birmingham situation being an example . . .

Of what happens when your planning goes wrong. When you think you've got everything covered and you let a little sumpin' slip. . . . I feel like there was a timing factor there that kept 'em from being caught.

How long do you think the Birmingham bombing was under planning?

. . . I would think at least thirty days to six weeks. That would be my thinking from information that we received from various sources. See, so often, it's awfully hard to get an informant in this type of organization close enough where he's trusted enough by the hard core that really plan the timing factor, to get him close enough to know exactly when it's gonna be done. You get that it's gonna happen, but you don't know exactly when. And this is the thing: it's almost impossible to know exactly when.

Do you think the Birmingham bombing was a "contract" situation?

I believe it was. [Very, very softly] I believe it was.

LAURIE PRITCHETT

He was police chief of Albany, Georgia, in 1961 when SNCC and SCLC singled the city out for their first major joint effort. He became known as the man who beat Martin Luther King at his own game simply because, before King arrived to lead the demonstrations, he did the obvious thing.

I researched Dr. King. I read about his early days in Montgomery, his methods there. I read that he was a great follower of Gandhi's. . . . He always talked about the march for salt.*

We had planned for mass arrests. We had known that their plan was . . . to overcrowd our jail conditions, thus makin' us have to give in. And this was based on Dr. King's philosophy of the Gandhi march to the sea, which I had read and was fully aware of—of how they had crowded the jails, overrode the British jails and finally had to be turned loose. I had studied this philosophy of his and methods and made preparations that at no time would any be housed in our facilities in Albany

---

* In *Down to Now: Recollections of the Civil Rights Movement,* Pat Watters quotes from a King sermon taped in Albany. "Just a few men started out, but when they got down to the sea, more than a million people had joined in that march. Gandhi and those people reached down in the sea and got a little salt in their hands and broke that law, and the minute that happened, it seemed I could hear the boys at Number Ten Downing Street in London, England, say: 'It's all over now.'"

or Dougherty County. I had made arrangements, and we had it on a map—Lee County, which was ten miles, and then we'd go out twenty-five miles, go out fifty miles, a hundred miles—and all these places had agreed to take the prisoners. So we had buses. When we would book and fingerprint, photograph, they'd come right out and enter the buses and be taken to some other jail. We sent personnel along to see that they were not mistreated . . . stayed with 'em in the jails to see that nobody in the other counties mistreated or mishandled 'em. . . . I think this is one thing that Dr. King was surprised at. This did away with his method of overextending the facilities.

Dr. King was found guilty [parading without a permit] by the recorder's court, and he was kept in jail for a period of time and then made bond . . . I have never divulged where this bail money came from and will not at this time, because of fear of reprisals against people there. A Negro male made his bond. He did it on purpose. Dr. King came out against his objections, and the mass marches continued.

He is talking about the episode of the "mystery bondsman," up until this interview, one of the unsolved riddles of the Movement. King, following the Gandhian tactic, had vowed to stay in jail rather than accept bond. One day an unidentified black man paid King's bond and then disappeared. Segregationists, of course, said the bondsman came from SCLC, and some of King's detractors in the Movement believed he had copped out, too. Journalists speculated that the bondsman might have been sent by the Justice Department, since the Kennedys were known to be unhappy with King's efforts in Albany. They wanted calm to prevail so that a moderate Democrat might win Georgia's gubernatorial election in the spring of 1962. Actually the mystery bondsman was an Albany black man sent by "a coalition . . . between some blacks and some whites that felt that if he was released from custody and left that the mass news media which was there would also leave and Albany would go back to their ways." He attended the meeting at which the white segregationists and conservative blacks hatched their plan to bail King out against his will.

I was not instrumental. . . . I sat and observed. I agreed with what they [proposed], but I said, "I have no intentions of involving myself with this. I will not deceive the people. Now, if this happens, it will be not to my knowledge." And when he come in, I didn't know it until he was gone.

And this caused Dr. King a great deal of concern. . . . I had sympathy for him because it appeared that he went back on his word, see, and this made him lose a lot of respect of the blacks. They said, "Look, this man said he'd stay here forever, and he ups and leaves."

Well, he didn't know who put the bond up. He accused the city . . . this was one of my concerns. I felt that this would cause him to lose respect for me, and I told him just like I've told you, I said, "I will not divulge . . ."

And it did cause him some trouble. You know, it came out in all the news and the television and the newspapers that he had decided to come out and that this was a front, that he had had it done, you know. But he didn't, he didn't have it done.

They brought him to my office, and he thought he was bein' transferred, and when he come in, I had the receipt there, and I gave it to him. I'd had 'em to make a photostat of the city receipt, because we didn't have the original. And I said, "Dr. King, you have been bailed out." And he said, "I don't wanna leave." I said, "Well, I can't keep you." And when he stepped out of my office, there was a mass meetin'. I never will forget, he said, "I been put in jail a lot of times, but I've never been thrown out of one." [Laughs]

His tactics worked. At one point, Attorney General Robert Kennedy infuriated Movement leaders by sending him a telegram of congratulation on keeping the peace.

Dr. King came up with the idea—this was after Attorney General Kennedy had refused to send federal marshals in because there was no violence—Dr. King came upon the idea of a pilgrimage of ministers, clergymen from all over the United States. . . . And this, I think, gave me some of my most tiring times. . . . We had commandeered the downtown motels, hotels. We had lived in there. The men did not go home. They were subject to call at any time, to be available at any time. There were times that we did not go home for weeks and weeks, you know.

And right prior to this pilgrimage of the ministers and clergymen, it so happened that I was in my office with Dr. King and Rev. Abernathy and Holloway* and others in a conference. At that time my secretary rang and came in and had a telegram which I read and must have shown some concern over because Dr. King asked me if it was bad news. I said, "No, it's not bad news, Dr. King. It just so happens this is my twelfth weddin' anniversary, and my wife has sent me a telegram."

---

* Actually Donald Hollowell, the black attorney from Atlanta who sometimes represented King.

And he says—I never will forget this and this shows the understandin'
which we had—he said, "You mean this is your anniversary?" And I
said, "That's right," and I said, "I haven't been home in at least three
weeks." And he said, "Well, Chief Pritchett, you go home tonight, no,
right now. You celebrate your anniversary. I give you my word that
nothing will happen in Albany, Georgia, till tomorrow, and you can go,
take your wife out to dinner, do anything you want to, and tomorrow at
ten o'clock, we'll resume our efforts."

I went home, went out to dinner. Later when we came in, there were
all the news media there, some twenty-five or thirty at my house. They
had heard about it and had come out and brought my wife a nice gift
certificate. And then the next mornin' at ten o'clock we assumed our
confrontation.

*Over fifty preachers, most of them white, did come to Albany. A
news photograph of the period shows him standing with head bowed as
the ministers knelt outside City Hall and prayed. "There were Catholic
priests there, and my religion is Catholic. . . . I gave 'em ample time to
pray. When they finished, I asked 'em to disperse. They refused, and
then I told 'em, I said, 'You apparently came here as law violators, and
my advice is to go back to your various cities, clean your various cities
of the evils of segregation before you come down and throw rocks at
us.'"*

I again asked 'em to disperse in the name of decency . . . it was very
tense. These thousands of people were there. Some had brought their
lunches. You could see in the back of their cars ax handles and things of
this nature. It was very tense and when I gave the order to arrest, there
was a loud roar of approval that went up. . . . I didn't like what I was
havin' to do. But they were arrested. They made bond. I think Wyatt
Tee Walker came in one night with seventy-five hundred dollars and got
half of 'em out. And this is one thing, we accepted nothin' but cash
money . . . this was left up to my discretion. We took cash bonds of
two hundred dollars for every arrest, and this was somethin' that they
didn't expect. And with the mass of people that we had in jail in various
cities at one time, I would estimate we probably had six or eight hundred thousand dollars, and they could not continue to put out this
money. And this is one thing coupled with our nonviolence—the expend-
iture that they were havin' to make—defeated 'em in Albany.

*He helped negotiate the compromise which ended the demon-
strations. It left downtown Albany as segregated as ever. SNCC accused*

King of betraying the Albany blacks who had marched to jail with him. The New York Herald Tribune *called it "one of the most stunning defeats of [King's] career." The* Times *followed a similar theme.* All over the South police wanted to know how he had "met nonviolence with nonviolence." Birmingham, which would be the next city to face King, sent its police chief, Jamie Moore, to study Albany's methods.*

I had known Jamie for years . . . he wanted to follow the same procedure we did. He had told "Bull" Connor about it. "Bull" Connor, Mr. Connor, had invited us over [to Birmingham], and I was expectin' some big robust man. I never will forget, when we entered his office, his back was to us . . . some big executive chair, you know, and when he turned around, there was this little man—you know, in stature. But he had this boomin' voice, and he was tellin' me that they closed the golf course that day. Said, "They can play golf, but we put concrete in the holes. They can't get the ball in the holes." And this give me some indication as to what type of man he was. You know, I think he was an opportunist that could see that if he did this that he could reach political power. We stayed there, I stayed there, briefed Jamie Moore, who wanted to handle it like we did, nonviolently. Dr. King came in. I forget the man, a wealthy black there . . .

Gaston.

Gaston, yeah . . . owned a motel there, and Dr. King and his staff came in and moved into this motel which was close to the church where they were holdin' their mass meetin's. And my advice to Mr. Connor and Jamie was that they should afford him protection. In Albany we had a bodyguard with him at all times. When he would enter the city limits, we'd escort him, take him out of his car, and he would volunteer to leave his car and come into our car. We'd take him everywhere he wanted to go. Where he spent the night, we had people there all the time. We afforded him protection. This caused some criticism that we were payin' tax-payers' money to protect this man, and I felt it was proper. As I told them, if this man was killed in Albany, Georgia, the fires would never cease—if he were ever killed in any city that the fires would be there.

I advised the officials in Birmingham that they should afford him their protection. At that time the Ku Klux Klan was meetin' over in . . . some city close to Birmingham . . . and they were very vocal as to what

---

* See also Andrew Young.

they were gonna do. And I told 'em they should post guards around his motel. They refused to do it. That night they blowed the motel up. . . . They brought out dogs and hoses and all this, and it was in almost eye-sight of the City Hall. Knowin' that they were not followin' my sugges-tions, I felt that I was in the wrong place. I didn't want to be associated with this any way that it could cast a reflection back on me or the city which I represented. So I flew out.

Later, when King was in Selma, I went to Selma. Sheriff Clark was another opportunist, in my opinion. He felt that this was the way he could project himself as the great white leader and impress the people. He made the same mistakes. They came to Montgomery, and I was in Montgomery when they marched there. . . . I never will forget one day there I heard the clap, it sounded like thunder, and we looked up, and it was the sheriff's posse on those horses, and the sparks were flyin' off of the shoes as they come down the street. And they went into the crowd with bull whips, they run up on the porches . . . some of the horses were cut at, which I can't much blame the people.

But this created that problem there, and, as I stated before, Dr. King, when he left Albany, in his own words and in the words of the New York *Herald Tribune,* was a defeated man. In my opinion, right or wrong, if Birmingham had reacted as Albany, Georgia, did . . . they'd never got to Selma. Dr. King, through his efforts, was instrumental in passin' the Public Accommodations [Act] but the people that were most responsible was "Bull" Connor and Sheriff Clark. . . .

IV
REPORTERS

Eugene Patterson

He is editor and president of the St. Petersburg Times, *the first Southern paper to endorse the Supreme Court's 1954 school desegregation decision. From 1960 until 1967 he was editor of the Atlanta* Constitution. *Like his mentor at the* Constitution, *publisher Ralph McGill, he won the Pulitzer Prize for editorials urging racial justice. Together, he and McGill in the sixties made the* Constitution *the Deep South's most courageous—and among segregationists, its most despised—editorial voice.*

A great deal of credit belongs to the *Constitution,* but primarily to Ralph McGill. . . . Going back to the late 1940s, he began in a gingerly way to write about the race issue in the South even before the Supreme Court ruling of '54. But as he said to me in his later years, he went back and read some of that stuff, and it was pretty pale tea. He was not proud of it. He wished that he had been even more forward. But considering the conflicts that beat in on any editor in the South in that period who offended and differed with the majority of his readers, he was an extremely bold man . . . his audacity grew as his outrage grew. . . . As he's told me, "Sometimes you have to walk right straight out in the middle of the ring and hit the other guy right in the nose. You can't pussyfoot and box around anymore." And so by the time of his death McGill had achieved a great reputation for doing that.

Now the *Constitution* offended perhaps the majority of its white readers in those early days, late fifties, early sixties. But by the time Dr. King became the clear leader of the Movement in the South, Mr. McGill was very much on Dr. King's side and was his principal supporter in the press in the South. Now this didn't make many friends for the *Constitution,* but the achievement of McGill was to start a conversation. To know that period of the South is to know that it was frozen in silence. People were not discussing the issue. Neighbor and neighbor were afraid of each other. Conformity was established by precedent. And for a man who might doubt the wisdom of segregation to sit down with his neighbor and say, "Hey, I'm not sure we're right" could have ruined that man in most Southern states. And it could have in Georgia. Therefore nobody discussed the issue. Only the politicians, who were aggravating emotions, were discussing it. McGill suddenly and boldly on the front page of the *Constitution* began to talk openly about the rights and wrongs of segregation, and this led the people to be emboldened to talk about it even if all they did was cuss McGill.

But editors in small and large dailies all across the South suddenly could turn to their segregationist publishers and say, "Look what the Atlanta *Constitution* is saying. I haven't said that much." And you could see it happening all around. People began to discuss the issue, and McGill blazed that trail. Getting the silence broken and getting a public dialogue started was the beginning of the end of segregation. . . .

Were there pressures to report negatively on the Movement . . . ?

Yes . . . most of that pressure came from our readers and for political reasons. They didn't like Dr. King, and they wanted us to hang him. And the FBI . . . an FBI agent was sent to see me with the bugging information that Dr. King had been engaged in extramarital sexual affairs. The FBI agent, obviously under orders of the director, Hoover, because nobody acted without his direction, urged me—he said, "Gene, . . . here you on this paper have raised Dr. King up to be some kind of model American, some kind of saint, some kind of moralist." He said, "Now, here's the information, and why don't you print it?" The FBI, the secret police of this country! And I had to explain to him, "Look, we're not a peephole journal. We don't print this kind of stuff on any man. And we're not going to do it on Dr. King." And I said, "Furthermore, I'm shocked that you would be spying on an American citizen, whether it's Dr. King or some other person because if it can happen to him, it can happen to all of us." And I asked him if he thought this wasn't a misuse of the FBI. But he was highly offended at me, seeing us as an immoral newspaper for not printing back-alley gossip that the secret police of the United States were trying to ruin this man with. . . .

Was this FBI agent that open in explaining his motives for offering you this material?

I've almost quoted him, and he never did understand why we wouldn't print it. Slipping information of that sort around after you've used the apparatus of the FBI to gather it on an individual American citizen is a most dangerous development. And I hope that the current Senate investigations will write legislation that will make it forever impossible in the future.

What was he offering you, tapes or transcripts?

No. He didn't offer me tapes or transcripts. What he offered me was the name of the Florida airport and the time of day that an airplane would be leaving there on a coming weekend when Dr. King was supposedly leaving for a tryst with some girlfriend—perhaps in the Caribbean. He put it to me, "Why don't you have a reporter and a photographer there? Get a picture of this as well as a story on this man and expose him to the South and to the world." And I just said, "Well, that's pretty dangerous stuff, and it's not our kind of journalism." Interestingly enough, that agent called . . . he came to see me a second time. Obviously, he'd checked it back to Washington, and they'd said, "Go back and lean on him." And I showed him the door the second time. A couple of weeks later he called me on the phone. He said, "I'm glad you didn't go ahead and send a reporter and photographer down there because our informant"—which is their name for a bug or a wiretap —"our informant now tells me the trip's been canceled." But that was a seamy side to the period.

Was there . . . anything at the time that would have led you to fit that into a broader picture of FBI activity?

No, not really. I was shocked by this. As a matter of fact, I told John Doar . . . one of Bobby Kennedy's principal assistants at the Justice Department, and Kennedy was ostensibly Hoover's boss. On an airplane one night flying from Washington to Atlanta some months after this incident occurred, I related it to Doar, and I said, "I want you to tell the attorney general about this. He should know what the FBI is up to." Because the more I thought about it, the more worried I'd become about the misuse of secret police powers. And as we flew along in an old four-engine DC-6, I guess, going through the night, Doar listened to me, and it took about ten minutes for me to relate all this to him in detail. He never looked at me; he just stared straight at the seat back ahead of him. And when I had finished, I looked at him for some response: "Yes, I'll tell Bobby Kennedy about it." He just continued to stare at the seat in front of him. He not only did not say one word in reply to me, he never gave any indication he had heard what I was saying to him. And all of a sudden it hit me like a thunderclap that Bobby Kennedy knew about it. And I had made Doar very uncomfortable by relating it to him. Not one expression crossed that deadpan face of his. He just did not respond. It was like talking to a dead man.

You may well have been one of the few people in the United States who had figured out how those pieces fit. . . .

I knew that the FBI was talking to other editors in the South.

How widespread was that practice?

Well, I know of at least one, Lou Harris of the Augusta *Chronicle*. It was for segregation editorially. You'da thought they'da gone right into print with this information. But people who think that don't know the unwritten ethic of the press with respect to the private lives of public men. Taste and horse sense and a common understanding that as long as a man's private life doesn't impinge . . . on the public interest, it's his own business. We don't print that kind of stuff.

So I had a phone call from Lou Harris one day, and he said, "Gene, I had a call from an FBI agent over here, and you'd be amazed at what he told me about Dr. King." And I said, "Lou, you mean sex exploits?" He said, "Yeah." He said, "Have you heard about this?" I said, "Yeah, the FBI has been to see me, too." And I said, "What are you gonna do with it?" He said, "Hell, I wouldn't print that stuff. That's beyond the pale." And this was a segregationist editor talking to me. And I said, "Lou, I'm proud of you. I'm not gonna mess with it either." . . . I'm sure that story was spread to other Southern editors. It's a tribute to the press in the South, the *segregationist* press of that period, that not one word of this ever came into print until after the death of Dr. King. There were certain fences beyond which the press would not go in vilifying and damaging a man, and we didn't do it to Dr. King.

RICHARD VALERIANI

The U.S. State Department Building in Washington, D.C. He is at his desk in a tiny, carpet-lined broadcast studio in the pressroom. He is awaiting the call to a press conference with Secretary of State Henry Kissinger. Waiting, he remembers the night Jimmie Lee Jackson died.

As I recall we were staying in Selma. . . . It looked like a slow night, and Quinn* and I decided we were going to Montgomery and play bridge. We're both bridge players. There was a duplicate tournament in Montgomery, and we figured we'd get a night off. And then we heard about the demonstration in Marion, and we decided to send a crew, and then as long as we were going to send a crew I said we'd better have a correspondent with the crew, so I decided to go up to Marion. And we got there and it was just a very hairy situation. The townspeople were out in force. They harassed anybody trying to cover it, sprayed black paint on the lenses of the cameras, and generally jostled us and intimidated us. So that there was no filming while whatever was going on, was going on.

And at one point, it was fairly quiet. It was *very* quiet, very still, 'cause someone recounted afterwards that he remembered the sound of the . . . of my being hit. Somebody walked up behind me, I forget his

* Charles Quinn, like Valeriani, an NBC News correspondent.

name now, somebody walked up behind me and hit me with an ax handle. Luckily he came with a roundhouse swing rather than with an overhead swing, so that it caught me in the back of the head, where all the bone is, rather than the top of the skull. And there was a loud clunk and a cameraman grabbed me to save me from going down.

An Alabama highway patrolman came over, took the ax handle away from the guy who hit me, threw it up on the steps of City Hall . . . and said, "You've done enough damage with this tonight," but did not arrest him.

I was stunned, put my hand to my head and saw that it was bleeding. Somebody walked up to me, a towns . . . somebody from Marion or I don't know where he was from, but anyway, one of the locals. He walked up to me and said, "Do you need a doctor?" And I, in a daze, looked at my hand and said, "Yes, I think I do. I'm bleeding."

And then he looked at me, he stared me in the face with this ugly look, and he said, "We don't have doctors for people like you."

Tony Heffernan

A New Yorker, he was assigned to Montgomery by United Press International (UPI) in 1961.

I didn't believe that there were people like Wallace. . . . I knew they all took these public postures, but he convinced me he believed it. My first time with him, the first time I ever talked with him—I don't remember the exact date—it was during the Ole Miss riot. . . . And it was like my third day or whatever it was in Montgomery, and Bobby Gordon* messaged me and said, "You might wanna try and get some kind of reaction from Wallace on this." . . . I went looking for Wallace, and sure enough, he was makin' a speech at the Whitley Hotel. . . . I got him afterward, and he said, "I don't want to have any comment on that because"—oh, it was Barnett's speech to the people of Mississippi**—"because I haven't seen anything about it." I suspected that this could happen, so I brought the speech with me . . . and I gave it to him, and he read it. And so he said he didn't want to give me a verbal statement, but he would write one out. And he sat down there, and he started to write on the back, and as he was writing, he was saying things, and I

* A UPI reporter stationed in Birmingham.
** Governor Ross Barnett broadcast a pledge to white Mississippians that he would not allow James Meredith to enroll at Ole Miss.

was taking notes. Aw, he was saying things like, "Stand fast, Governor Barnett, stand tall." And then he went into a tirade about federal judges, and he said to me, "What I really want to call 'em, you can't print." I said, "Well, we'll print it. What do you wanna call them?" He said, "I wanna call 'em sons of bitches." And I said, "Well, I guess we can't print that." [Laughs] . . . that was a hell of an introduction to Alabama at that time.

The general impression that you got from Wallace, Morgan, Trammell . . .* was it your feeling that they viewed segregation as a crusade or a political issue at that point?

In my opinion they were true believers. I remember I went to a Citizens Council rally in Selma that Wallace was to have addressed, but had a cold and could not. . . . Seymour filled in for him, and I drove over there with them in their car. Earl was driving, and Seymour was in the back, and I was sitting next to Earl. They didn't have much to say going over. I can't even remember our conversation going over. So anyway, Seymour made his speech, and—I would like to say this: it's the best barbecue I ever had. [Laughs] It really was. *Fantastic.* I never liked barbecue. I thought, you know, another one of those crappy Southern foods. . . . These people did a fabulous job at that. Oh, boy. I ate and ate and ate.

And of course . . . Dallas County was the only place in the whole state of Alabama where they had a true Citizens Council. It was on a par with anything in Mississippi. You know, the lawyers were members, the bankers were members, the school teachers were members . . . the judges were members. And Seymour made a real, what I would call, demagogic speech . . . he called for social ostracization—is that the word?—of any federal judge that said, "You must mix blood." I remember that, "must mix blood." And I remember on the way back, we were driving through a black section of Selma, and I remember Seymour said, to the effect, "Wherever you go, there's a goddamn nigger town," and he just made a sound, like *RRRRRRRR* and he was in the back seat. [He laughs, demonstrating how he jumped, then looked over his

---

* Earl Morgan, Wallace's executive secretary, was later appointed district attorney of Birmingham by Wallace. Seymour Trammell, who financed Wallace's campaign and served in his cabinet, split with Wallace over how to handle contributions received in Wallace's '68 presidential campaign. He later was convicted of income tax evasion and served a term in federal prison.

shoulder apprehensively.] You know, what the hell? Here I am a poor little boy from New York City.

So I very quickly came to believe that with Wallace and with his closest associates that they were true believers. . . .* I said back then that Wallace is such a political animal that if he had to join the NAACP in order to become president of the United States he would join. But I don't think he would have liked it. . . .

But those days are over. . . . You look at who's there now, politically speaking, and Wallace is the only one [of the old segregationists] left. You go throughout the South, Wallace is the only one left. . . . I think Wallace has moved with the times, to some extent, begrudgingly, because after all, he does have a natural constituency that he can't desert. . . . I don't know, what does he run on now? I mean, it was race—race, race, race—and every time that I was closeted alone with him, that's all that we talked about. Didn't talk about women. We didn't talk about Alabama football. Somehow no matter what you were talking about, the race thing got into the conversation, and he was off and running with it.

I don't really remember the issue, but I went up to interview him in Montgomery . . . this was before he was governor. He was governor-nominate. He was closeted with Walter Givhan, the senator from Selma . . . the most strident in the legislature on race. And I was busy talking to Seymour and Earl about the time of day, you know, and I could overhear the conversation with Givhan and Wallace, and Givhan was talking about an issue . . . a legislative issue totally divorced from race, and before you know it, Wallace's voice started to rise. He was on the race issue. Givhan didn't say a word. I think Givhan was surprised. . . . I don't think people believed that Wallace took himself seriously, and he did. That's, I think, a misjudgment by anybody that he didn't.

* "I don't believe that 'Bull' [Connor] was a true believer, because when Martin Luther King won the Nobel Peace Prize, they asked me in Atlanta please to, you know, get local reaction, naturally. And so, I called 'Bull' at his home, and he said, 'I don't have any comment.' You know, 'What do ya want from me?'

"And I said, 'Well . . . you are who you are and King is who he is and obviously, we'd like to know what your reaction is to his winning the Nobel Peace Prize.'

"He said, 'Just a minute' and there was silence, and he said, 'They's scraping the bottom of the barrel.'

"And he said, 'Okay, is that what you want?'

"I said, 'Yessir, that's what I want.'

"So, he acted like a buffoon, but he knew what he was doing. Very clearly, he knew what he was doing, I think."

What kind of language would he use in relation to blacks?

He called 'em "niggers." I mean . . . he never said anything but Negro in public, which is true. Even at an all-white meeting. There is no question about that. But in personal conversation, they were "niggers." I remember riding with him to a Citizens Council meeting in Mobile, and Joe Langan was the mayor of Mobile at that time, and he was heading up the loyalist Democratic slate for the presidential primary in Alabama. . . . Joe was a Catholic, and his natural constituencies were the Catholics and blacks . . . he made a tough anti-Wallace speech to a black group.

And we were riding, Wallace and I were riding to the Citizens Council meeting at the ballpark in Mobile, and he said, "Where's your mayor today, speaking in niggertown again?" You know, he meant it as a joke. . . . I was in the front seat, and one of the people, one of the boys going to the meeting, saw Wallace, and this guy screamed at the top of his lungs, "There he is!" and jumped as high as a person could jump. I mean, he jumped—his feet went up so high that his arms were below his feet. . . . I said, "Good Lord," and if I didn't understand the tremendous *power* that Wallace had before that, I understood it then. . . .

Favorite Wallace story? You ready? We were flying—this was before he was governor again—we were flying to Biloxi, Mississippi. . . . He was going to Biloxi to talk to the Alabama Farm Bureau,* and he got on, of course, the press and the intellectuals, and he said, "You know, I don't have anything against the intellectuals. . . . The intellectuals do a lot of good, because they're very good at gathering the facts and presenting it to people. Their problem is that they draw the wrong conclusions."

To prove his point, Wallace cited a story on "Papa Doc" Duvalier and Haiti in "the Esquire *magazine," which pointed out that the gross national product was higher in Haiti when the French colonial government was there in the early 1800s than under Duvalier 150 years later. But the author had missed the point, Wallace argued, in blaming the decline on economic factors and government corruption.*

And then Wallace said, "I tell you, any good Alabama dirt farmer can tell you what's really wrong with Haiti."

"What's that?"

* It is quite common for Alabama groups to hold their conventions in Biloxi, a resort town on the Mississippi Gulf Coast.

"They is niggers."

And he lit a cigar, which he very rarely smoked—he just chewed on his cigar—and he looked at me in the most serious way. . . . I was going hmph-hmph-hmph [suppressing a ridiculing laugh] like that, and he was looking at me dead-deadly serious.

WENDELL HOFFMAN

A street corner in Selma. March 7, 1975. He is filming the Selma March tenth-anniversary ceremonies for CBS News.

I was the first cameraman that ever came into this town, and they were lined up around the block trying to register, and James Baldwin was here to kind of give the thing some publicity and so on, and he may have written an article about it. Anyway, they were very resentful of our presence, and of course, James Baldwin especially stirred up a lot of resentment because he's kind of a little wizened man, you know, and it seems that these people resent people that are different. Anyway, we were taking pictures when [Sheriff Jim] Clark was kind of roughing these voter registration people up, and he sent a group of his squirrel shooters over across the street to rough us up. They had sticks in their hands, and they were attempting to hit me in the testicles with their sticks, and I was carrying a camera, and I did this. [He shows how he used the camera to block the sticks.] And the next time I came to Selma, I went to a store and bought one of these jockstraps that baseball catchers use with the aluminum cup on it. So for a long time afterwards, when I came to town, I wore that thing. I was going through a drawer at home there recently and ran on to that thing.

CLAUDE SITTON

That's What I Like About the South

He had worked throughout the Deep South as a wire service reporter before joining the New York Times. *". . . I thought and still think that the job I had, which no longer exists, was the best newspaper job in the world, covering the South. That's eleven states. The* Times *has five men doing that job. When I had it, it was a one-man job. . . . So for six and a half years, from May of 1958 until October of 1964, I worked out of Atlanta and covered everything from the Potomac to the Pedernales. Race, politics. . . ."*

Among journalists covering the Movement, he was the reporter's reporter; his account of a redneck sheriff's invasion of a south-Georgia voter-registration rally is a classic newspaper story. He was also something of an authority on survival tactics for newsmen.

You gotta show people that you've got an open mind, that you're willing to listen to them and that you're not, you know, "the newspaperman from the big city." And it wasn't just the North, it was the big city. I remember I was down in Tylertown, Mississippi, one time talking to a voter registrar who'd gotten in trouble with the federal government because a black civil rights worker had come in there with a Negro to help him register to vote, and this registrar had hit the civil rights worker over the head with a pistol. I was talking with this registrar after the incident, and we talked for a while, and he said, "Say, boy, where you from anyway?" I said, "I'm from Atlanta." He said, "Atlanta?" Said, "That's damn near north of the Mason-Dixon line."

So it's style and manner and just trying to be friendly, you know, and then sometimes it's just standing there keeping your mouth shut. I know, for example, that during the Freedom Rider period, Sim Fentress of *Time* magazine and I were down in McComb, Mississippi, and the Freedom Riders were coming up on Greyhound out of New Orleans, and the first bus station they hit in Mississippi was McComb. . . . Fentress and I were sitting in the café having a cup of coffee when these Freedom Riders walked in, and a full-scale riot ensued right there. I remember one of these Freedom Riders was a track star from one of the schools in New Orleans, and he went up and ran the length of the counter and then table-hopped all the way from the back of the café to the front and through the door. [Laughs] And Fentress and I sat right in the middle of all this hullabaloo, you know, just sat there and drank our coffee—and didn't say a word. The FBI was sittin' down the street in a car. A little later, the FBI came up to us on the street and got a fill-in, wanted to know what had happened. We asked 'em why the hell they weren't there to see for themselves. But there was a local reporter there, and there was a story in the newspaper, the McComb *Enterprise-Journal,* saying that among those present were two FBI agents who sat at a table in the bus waiting room and drank coffee while the violence took place. [Laughs]

What were the roughest places you covered?

Philadelphia was one of 'em. Hell, it was dangerous to walk out on the courthouse square there the second day after the three disappeared. . . . I was walking down the street, and a group got after me. Whites. And I went in a store there. It was operated by a fellow named Turner. Now this fellow Turner was the uncle of Turner Catledge, who was then managing editor of the New York *Times,* or executive editor. And I went in to this Mr. Turner, and I said, "Look . . . these people out there have gotten after me. When I walk back out the door, I suspect they're gonna jump me. Now you don't really wanna have any violence in this town. It's not gonna do the town any good. If they beat me up and send me to the hospital, somebody else just like me is gonna be down here tomorrow. Why don't you go out and speak to those boys, and see if they can't behave themselves?"

And he said, "Look, if you were black and came in here with a question like that, I might do something for you, but you're white, and you're from outa town, and I don't care if they stomp the hell out of you." . . .

Mississippi was bad. Maybe it's a little unfair, and I know the situation in Mississippi has changed radically. Mississippi is no longer the state that it was in that day, and neither is Alabama. But I always felt that Alabama was sorta mean, but Mississippi could be deadly. They'd kill ya over there. And they did . . . two people were killed up there at Oxford when Jim Meredith was admitted. I was there. It was like crossin' no-man's-land to get from a motel off the campus where I was filing my story by telephone, through the rioters, and then up to the administration building where they had Meredith. . . .*

. . . Are there any instances that stand out in your memory of extraordinary physical courage?

Well, yeah . . . there was a fella, a black farmer, who lived on a rural route out of Liberty, Mississippi, in Amite County. That's a, oh, a very rough place. It's cut-over timberland, poor whites and poor blacks. Steptoe** lived right across the road from a white man who had shot down one local civil rights supporter at a cotton gin there in Liberty and a man who was just really violent. Nothing was ever done about this. He was a state legislator, as a matter of fact. And blacks would disappear down there into those swamps and be killed, and nothing was ever done about it.

And yet Steptoe, who lived right across the road from this white man who had killed the black civil rights supporter, Steptoe was very involved in the voter registration situation. He was also president of the Amite County chapter of the N-Double-A-C-P, and I remember Sim Fentress and I went by to see Steptoe one time. . . . I was doing a story on voter registration because Bob Moses—you've run across his name—Bob Moses had been working out of McComb into Amite County and some of those other counties around there in voter registration work, just working by himself . . . which was also a very brave thing to do. But we went by to see Steptoe, Fentress and I, and Steptoe

---

* "One of 'em, a French reporter, was actually executed. I mean, he was shot in the back of the head. He was taken down right off the campus . . . made to kneel behind a tree, and was shot in the back of the head . . . pure out-and-out execution." The Frenchman, Paul Guihard, had been sent by Agence France Presse to give a firsthand account of conditions in Mississippi.

** E.W. Steptoe. In the piney woods of southwest Mississippi, he had a role similar to that of Amzie Moore up in the Delta. He befriended the first SNCC workers who came in the summer of 1961. The killing referred to here is that of Herbert Lee, which was described by Charles Cobb in the Mississippi sequence.

said, "I'm mighty glad to see you folks because as long as y'all are here, I know I got a few more minutes to live." And he really spoke the truth there in Liberty.*

Didn't your wife ever try to get you to quit trafficking around the South?

No, she never did. She was very understanding. Extremely understanding. . . . Gee, I can recall coming into that Atlanta airport on a plane at eleven o'clock at night and taking another one out at three in the morning. I've actually had my wife meet me at the airport for dinner as I was passing through. You know, my wife was wonderful about it. But after six and a half years of it, I just reached the point where it was just too much . . . my family was growing up without me and so forth. So I decided to go to New York. I had sworn that I'd never go back to New York again. But I did. So I stayed four years and this job opened up** and I came down here. I love the South. I wouldn't work anywhere else.

* Steptoe survived, but he is now incapacitated by a stroke.

** He became editorial director of the Raleigh (N.C.) *News & Observer* after serving as national editor of the *Times*.

NEIL MAXWELL

White Humor

He covered the Selma March for the Wall Street Journal.

Everybody talked to Jim Clark or the director of public safety, Wilson Baker. Nobody talked to the police chief, and for some reason, I did. And he was just so gratified to have a reporter come and see him. He had this big cardboard box with a couple of hundred billy clubs in it that he had bought to bust heads with, and the occasion hadn't arisen. The sheriff was doing all the head-busting, so he gave me one of these for a souvenir. . . . I stuck the thing in the top of the briefcase, and it stuck out on either end. I got to the airport, and Joe Smitherman, the mayor—I was leaving, and he was coming in—and he came over and said, "You don't need that in Selma." He said, "We're not going to let anything happen to any of you people." [Laughs]

He also interviewed Judge James A. Hare, the political patriarch of Selma segregationists.

And the judge was the one that was passing sentence on folks at that time. And he was absolutely the most full-blown racist I've ever met in my life. He would tell you that the black people that lived around there were not like black people that lived other places, and he referred to them by their African tribal names, and he said you could tell 'em be-

cause of their [pauses] blue gums. I presume you have to look inside of
their mouth. [Laughs] But he was serious and well-informed on this. He
had a bookcase that had just every racist book that you'd ever heard of
sittin' back there, and it was really appalling to think of a guy that felt
like that putting black people in jail.

There was no attempt to gloss over his racism?

No. No. He was absolutely convinced that he was right and that he
was trying to be helpful, trying to show reporters how to get on the right
track.

I went along on the march. I did not walk, I assure you, but I had a
rented car. And it was a really interesting thing to cover that and then to
read some of the things that were supposed to have taken place there
. . . like the book that Jim Clark wrote, *I Saw Selma Raped,* and stuff
about everybody screwing each other and all that. Hell, after you walk—
what?—fifteen miles, twenty miles, you don't want to do anything except
just sit down and take it easy. [Laughs]

> *When the marchers camped for the first night in a pasture several
> miles out from Selma, he drove out to spend the evening. ". . . I had
> parked my car in the only mud hole in the whole damn place . . .
> there was no chance of getting out of there."*

There were a couple of nuns, as a matter of fact, trying to help push
the car out, and we just couldn't do it. By the time I gave up, everybody
had gone except there was a guy with me from Vancouver, I think,
or Montreal, some Canadian paper, and so he and I had to hitchhike
back. It was this little country road and we were out there about eleven
o'clock at night hitchhiking. And a station wagon drove past and went
about a hundred feet down the road, stopped and backed up. And the
guy said, "Get in," and the seat was folded down in the back so it was
just a flat floor, and we had to crawl in. It was these two drunk red-
necks, and the first thing they said was, "Where y'all from?" And naturally like everybody with any sense, if you had anything to make into
a Southern accent, you did. . . . I said that I was from Atlanta, knowing
that they didn't like Atlanta, but it was better than New York, say.
And this idiot that was with us said, "Oh, I'm from Mahn-tree-ahl,"
and this guy said, "I suppose the goddamn queen sent you down here,"
. . . and *all of a sudden,* he veered off on a little side road down there.

And it really frightened me. It's the only time that I can remember being in fear that something terrible was going to happen, and I thought very seriously about opening the door and getting out of the car, despite the fact that we were going twenty, thirty, miles an hour. Aw, really physically alarmed, you know, and it turned out to be perfectly innocent . . . it was simply another road that went back to Highway 80, and they just wanted to avoid the Army in their drunken condition.

NELSON BENTON

He was the CBS News correspondent in Selma on "Bloody Sunday."

On that Sunday morning there was a meeting there at Brown's Chapel . . . the strategy meeting as to whether the marchers would go or not. Dr. King was in Atlanta. Andy Young heard about it and chartered a plane over to Selma, ostensibly to stop it, was my impression. . . . But there was apparently some sort of power struggle going on between SCLC and SNCC. SNCC wanted to go, and SCLC was saying, "No, now's not the time."* Well, SNCC won. . . .

There was an FBI car in front of the march with two young agents who had become fixtures there. I've forgotten their names; we called them the Katzenjammer Kids. Wilson Baker used to say, "Ain't they the cutest little agents you ever saw." Two real good guys. . . . Well, when the marchers started comin' down the bridge, the camera crew that I was with, we moved on forward to get just ahead of 'em. And the first

---

* According to Ralph Abernathy, he and King sent orders to Hosea Williams not to march that Sunday. "But in spite of the calling off, Hosea claimed that there were large numbers of people who had come, and he just didn't see how they could disappoint the people without having a march, and he asked me to call Dr. King. And I called over to Ebenezer Church and got Dr. King on the phone, and he said, 'Well, whatever you say, Ralph.' And I said, 'Well, if he wanna get beaten up, then go on let him get beaten up.' So I called Hosea back and I told him to proceed."

camera crew that had gone on ahead, guy named Bernie Nudelman, waved us over to where he was and said, "Al Lingo says get right over here, and we'll have a ringside seat."

Well, we did, and you know, it's the most important piece of film that I've ever been associated with, because I think that film . . . had a hell of a lot to do with the passage of the '65 Voting Rights Act.

Those two crews shot the film you see most frequently?

Uh-mm. I've got a print of it in my drawer, as a matter of fact . . . a kinescope of what we put on the air that night. And we shot and there was no effort to prevent us from shooting.

Oh, it was probably two minutes which is a good long time for a fifteen-minute broadcast. In all candor I would have to say that the reason I was pressing for more [on-the-air] time was probably because, under the criteria that we use, it was a hell of a good piece of film. . . . I know I didn't realize its significance at the start. I don't think anybody did till the word started going around, around the statehouse, middle of the week, and the phrase was, "There was too much film." You know, that was the phrase that the governor's people was using. "Just too much film, too much film." And *they* knew the significance. But I don't think we realized it. I know we didn't.

They were saying "too much film" in the sense of too much—

"Too much film" . . . the film was too graphic. And it *was* graphic, God knows. And we had it on two cameras. Had one guy on top of a car, another guy on the ground. As the phrase, the technical phrase [goes], . . . we spent the whole afternoon intercutting violence.

Postscript: Governor Wallace's staff was right; there was, indeed, "too much film" for their purposes. The broadcast film was subpoenaed by the federal court in Montgomery. After examining the film, Judge Frank M. Johnson issued a scathing denunciation of the troopers and enjoined the state of Alabama from further interfering with the Selma-to-Montgomery march.

WILLIAM BRADFORD HUIE

His sprawling, modern house has an incongruous setting—an old-fashioned neighborhood in Hartselle, a sleepy town in the Alabama hills. A widower, he lives alone there, rising before daylight to work on the sequence of World War II novels which he believes will cap his career. His earlier novels, The Revolt of Mamie Stover *and* The Americanization of Emily, *paid for the house and, in fact, made him rich, as writers go. But in the South he is known more widely as an investigator of racial atrocities than as a novelist. His books and articles are required reading for anyone who would understand the mind of the race killer. Yet because those books and articles have been based on information purchased from killers and their accomplices, his detractors have dismissed him as a "checkbook journalist" who has helped criminals profit from their crimes. His argument: "I'm not in the law enforcement business. I'm in the truth business."*

In the first place, the FBI always has used money, and large amounts of it. Other law enforcement agencies have used money and other inducements. Money has to be used for this reason: whenever there has been an atrocity, a racial crime, a racially motivated crime, there aren't any innocent bystanders. You can't get evidence from people who are not guilty. The victims are dead. The only people who know what happened are guilty men. You have to deal with guilty men. Now to deal with guilty men you have to offer them some sort of protection, and if you can't offer protection, money has to serve as a protection. You have to help them in that way, and so I never hesitated to use money where I thought it was justified.

What was the first major case where you used this technique?

The first major case was the Emmett Till murder. This was a young black man from Chicago in 1955, a year after the so-called Black Monday school decision by the Supreme Court. He came down to Mississippi, to Tallahatchie County, Mississippi, and while he was there he became involved in an incident, the so-called wolf-whistle incident, whistling at a white woman, or something. And as a result, two [white men] took him out, and because of what happened when he was with them, they killed him. They killed him, threw his body in the river, and they were subsequently tried. . . . Well, my objective in all such cases is just one, to go to find what happened . . . court trials don't usually establish the truth. It takes a reporter to establish the truth. . . .

I went over to Sumner, Mississippi . . . two months after the trial. The men had already been found not guilty . . . so I went to their attorney, and I told him, "Now . . . the truth has not been established here. The truth should be established for everybody's sake."

And this lawyer said, "Well, I'd like to know what happened. I defended them, but I never asked 'em whether they killed the boy or not. I didn't wanna know, to tell you the truth."

And I said, "Well, I know that. Everybody's been that way, so I'd like to call these men in. You call 'em in, and let 'em just tell us the truth. They're not in jeopardy. They've already been found not guilty. They can't be tried for this murder anymore. . . .

"And," I said, "because . . . for me to publish the fact that they did commit that murder would be what we call 'libel per se,' meaning I am libeling these men when I say they murdered because they had already been tried and found not guilty of murder . . . therefore, I'll in effect pay them for the right to libel them. Moreover, because I think this case means a lot, I would like to make a motion picture of it. I will purchase from them the right to portray them in a film made on this case."

They were called in, and they agreed for the reasons I've said. They didn't think they were guilty. They didn't think they'd done anything wrong. The man who had done the killing . . . told me the truth. They told me.

He interspersed his interview sessions with the two men with field trips to check the accuracy of what they were telling him.

. . . they'd have to tell me the truth at night when I talked to 'em. The next day, I'd go out and *find* the places, *go* to the places they told me to—where they got the weight, the gin fan they put around the victim's neck,* all this sort of thing . . . if I found out that they weren't tellin' me the truth, I wouldn't go through with the deal. . . .

Whenever that story was published, it was tremendously sensational all around the world, published in every major language, and oh, papers and publishers that I had done business with in Italy and France . . . paid me record prices, just to run the *Look* story, to translate and publish the *Look* story. It was very effective. Other people wanted to make a film, but we never got to make the film.**

But I have no regrets. I published the complete truth about a story that certainly the situation demanded the truth. It was good for the country. It was good and right and proper for the truth to be published. So I *published* it. I had to use something like, oh, thirty-six hundred dollars, I think, maybe four thousand dollars, . . . in order to make the story publishable and to make a film possible. All of which was done in that transaction. I don't feel that I did anything wrong and I would do it again. And I would hope that after I'm gone, there'll be other people who will value the truth enough to get it in that way, if necessary.

Were you criticized at the time for profiting from tragedy?

Well . . . no, I wasn't criticized. . . . There have been people who have said, "What about this business of paying murderers?"

All I can say is that if agencies of the United States of America pay murderers and pay other criminals, then I don't see any difference. I don't think that I have done anything immoral or anything of that sort. I'm not claiming that I haven't made mistakes, but I certainly don't feel that I've been guilty of anything unethical or immoral. I've just been effective.

* A joke which made the rounds in the South at that time characterized Emmett Till as the victim of an accidental drowning brought on by his own stupidity. Its punchline: "Crazy nigger stole the fan out of a cotton gin and tried to swim the river with it chained around his neck."

** Under contract with RKO, he wrote a movie script. The producer canceled the film because, given the style of movies at the time, there seemed no way to make a film about two men who casually murder a boy and then escape punishment with the blessing of their peers.

When did you next employ that technique after having proven its success in the Till instance?

The next . . . the most famous case is the three young men who were killed . . . murdered by Ku Klux Klansmen in Neshoba County, Mississippi. I went there very early, three or four days after they were missing, for the New York *Herald Tribune,* and I was involved for a number of weeks in Mississippi, and I was involved in trying to find where the bodies were hidden and in trying to find the truth.

The FBI spent, oh, I think, three million dollars on the Neshoba County case, not all of it in bribes, . . . although they paid lots of money to informers. . . . I didn't use any money in trying to get information. I was able to get some information. I had some idea where the bodies were buried.

In fact, he was believed by many to have told the FBI where to dig.

That story, all of it, hasn't yet been told. . . . I'm not in a position now to start calling names, say "I found this man, I found that," and so forth, but I knew where the bodies were buried before they were exhumed.

At any rate, his snooping—a favorite trick was telephoning Klan wives who, he found, often resented the nights their husbands spent riding to defend racial purity—resulted in the book Three Lives for Mississippi. *Its account of how Chaney, Goodman, and Schwerner died was later confirmed by testimony in the federal court trials of eighteen Mississippi whites charged with conspiring to deny the three dead men "life or liberty without due process." Seven men, including Neshoba County Deputy Sheriff Cecil Price, were convicted on the federal charges, but no one was ever charged with murder under Mississippi law, since state officials declined to prosecute the case. When* Three Lives for Mississippi *was published in 1965, CBS approached Huie about buying the movie rights. However, as in the Till case, there were legal problems involved in making a film about killings in which no murder convictions had been returned.*

So, before the federal trial took place, he secured portrayal rights from Price and from Neshoba County Sheriff Lawrence A. Rainey, who was also indicted. In the 1967 trial, Rainey was not accused of participation in the actual slayings and was acquitted of being part of the conspiracy, but his political career was at an end. Finally in the summer of

1975, over ten years after the three civil rights workers disappeared into the Mississippi night, CBS broadcast the television film "Attack on Terror: the FBI versus the Ku Klux Klan."

I know people in New York and Beverly Hills that didn't think it could ever be done. But I took [release] documents and purchased from Price and Rainey for six thousand dollars each their portrayal rights, the right to portray them in the film. Of course, that remained secret, terribly secret . . . because Price was later tried and had to go to prison and served about three or four years. I lent what little help I could, after he'd served about three years, because of his children, to help him get an early parole. . . .

That film was made possible because of the portrayal rights that I had purchased with CBS money many years ago. When people talk about my using money, the money that I have used has been, first of all, to establish the truth and next to purchase portrayal rights so that a film could be made which can be seen by many, many more people than will ever read about it.

What was the reaction of Price and Rainey when you approached them about buying the rights . . . ?

Remember that these men, as in all these cases . . . the community seems to approve of them during the first few weeks after it. They've got a lot of guys in the community, white men who hate the idea of racial change, who come around and clap them on the back and say, "Old buddy, we'll help ya." Then all that disappears, and they find that they lose their jobs, and then nobody wants to hire them. After a little while, these men really become very sad characters, because all these fair-weather friends they had, all these guys who were glad that they had struck a blow for the "Southern way of life" or something, they all desert them, and they cain't get a dime. They cain't borrow a dime and they cain't get a job. Price and Rainey were both in that position. Both of them were men desperate for money . . . They loved to see me coming. It didn't take any effort on my part, because they regarded me as a lifesaver for them. Believe me, six thousand dollars meant a great deal to them at the time. Oh, no, I was the best friend they had. They hoped that I might want to make another film of some sort.

Why did they settle for so little . . . ?

It depends on . . . your point of view as to whether it's little or not. I can take six thousand dollars in cash and I can buy ninety-five percent of the people in the United States. . . . If you're hungry and hadn't got a job and you've got children to feed, six thousand dollars is an enormous amount of money. Let's say that they weren't settling for a little amount of money. They were settling for what was an enormous amount of money for them at the time.

You mentioned . . . these men who had been politically powerful in Neshoba County were ostracized entirely?

Let's go back to the Till case. Let's go back to the men who killed young Till. Now, remember that after that murder all sorts of money was contributed to their defense, and moreover, white men who had never regarded themselves as their friends, *powerful* men, came around and congratulated them. And remember there were five lawyers in Sumner, Mississippi, and every one of them volunteered to defend these men in their trial without fee, without anything. Everybody's their friend at that time, you see, and they tell me the story because they think that they have the approval of the community.

But remember these men are killers, and even racially motivated, there are not a lot of men who are capable of simply killing an unarmed human being. There just are not many men who are. And therefore after the passage of time, men who have contributed money to the defense of the killers of young Till, they want those killers to get on out of the county. They'll start thinking, "Well, my gosh, if those guys are capable of killing, they just might decide to kill me sometime." So here are men that cain't get a job. "Well, now I—I—I—I put up money to help you in the trial, but now you know, I just—I just—I just haven't got a job for you right now."

And he goes over here and says, "Well, I'm a good farmer. I'll go to the bank. . . . I need four thousand dollars to put in a cotton crop." The banker says, "Well, you know, I'd like to lend you the money, but we're just a little bit short." . . .

Therefore, you find these men right there in that county, they have to go off somewhere else. Yes. They're outcasts. And the same thing is true, happened to Price and Rainey. Oh, they were the heroes of everybody over in Neshoba County. But a year later—well, Price was the deputy and was supposed to be elected sheriff. He runs for sheriff. He doesn't get it. The people don't want him for sheriff. They want him to get on out of the county.

Rainey thinks that he can get a job anywhere. He's an expert mechanic, an automobile mechanic. Hell, he cain't find a place in the county that'll give him a job, even as an automobile mechanic. He goes off up into Kentucky somewhere, gets a job up there, and then people up there, his employers, learn about this business, and they find that they are not happy havin' him around . . . so they find reason [to fire him].*

Yes this is true. You go show me one now. You find me a white man who was in any way linked to an atrocity against a black man back during the Movement days, and I'll show you a man right now who's an outcast. And that happened. That happened to all of them. That's human nature.

For fear or shame?

Both. . . . Take in the Till case. Here's a boy who's big for his age, he could very easily at night be taken for eighteen, which these men did take him to be eighteen. And they kill him for no other reason than he has a white girl's picture in his wallet. . . . They didn't take him out to kill him. They killed him because he had a white girl's picture in his pocket, and he told 'em that she was his girl. It was at the time that they thought that this sorta thing had to be stopped in order to defend the "Southern way of life. . . ." [His voice rises.] But remember that they have shot and killed and thrown in the river a young human being, who's black, but he's a human being. He's not a dog. They have shot him and killed him and thrown him in the river, and he was unarmed, standing there absolutely helpless.

Remember that in the Neshoba County case . . . they grab these three young men who are utter—completely unarmed. They have never seen them. They don't even know them. They kill them because of what they stand for . . . they hate what they're trying to do.

But they're utter—absolutely unarmed and they stand there at night, [speaks in a rush now] helpless, and they shoot them down like dogs. Now, remember that even in the Neshoba County case, while there are six or seven men present, actually there's only one man who's a killer in the crowd. Another man finally comes up and shoots the black boy, but the only man who can actually take a gun and put it to the two white youths, who are unarmed, standing there helpless. . . . There's only

---

* "The FBI set out to break me of everything, and they done it," Rainey was quoted as saying in 1975. "I was acquitted, but I was the big loser." He sold his house to pay legal fees. After losing his job in Kentucky, Rainey returned to Mississippi, where he found work as a guard in a mobile-home lot near Meridian.

one man among those six who's a killer, and if that killer hadn't been there, the others would not have killed those men.

As soon as that's over and months pass, you simply find that people who are glad that they took these civil rights agitators out and killed them . . . they don't want that killer around him. *They're afraid of a man who they suspect is a killer.* A man who can do that. They're just afraid he might get mad at them sometime. So it goes back to the old mark of Cain. The *killer* is a man you don't want around in times of peace.

INTERLUDE

ROY HARRIS AND

MYLES HORTON

The Photograph

Roy Harris: "Mr. Roy." As house speaker and chief strategist for Georgia's gallus-popping demagogue Governor Eugene "Ol' Gene" Talmadge, he was the most powerful back-room man in Georgia politics. When Gene died, he directed son Herman's successful campaign for governor, and with the younger Talmadge's support in 1953 he got the Georgia legislature to establish a new state commission dedicated to preserving segregation. From that time on propaganda, not politics, occupied his attention.

Under his supervision, the commission distributed a photograph which purported to show Martin Luther King, Jr., consorting with "known Communists" at the Highlander Folk School in Monteagle, Tennessee. Segregationists cited the photograph as "proof" that the Civil Rights Movement was directed by Communists, and he and his Atlanta-based commission were hailed as leaders in a new offensive against the integrationists.

The Georgia Education Commission it was, and Ed Friend worked for us, and we sent him up there [to Highlander]. I tell you, I think we published a million copies of that paper at state expense.* And then the States Rights Council** picked it up later, and we scattered it all over the country. And the *Courier* printed that picture of Martin Luther King on the back page. . . .*** I tell you, I have had, I expect, a thousand letters asking if they could reproduce that picture over the years. Even some of 'em the last two years wanted to. And I'm tellin' you, you've got no idea how many of those things were reproduced all over this country and spread out.

Was there any repercussion about the state footing the bill for that?

There wasn't. [Laughs] We had 'em so dead set on that, nobody even said a word about it. [Chuckles, reflects a moment, then speaks softly] That was somethin'. Nobody could defend that.

And as a result of those pictures that we took, Tennessee legislature did away with that thing [the Highlander school]. They absolutely abolished it by an act of the legislature.

How did the Commission find out about the meeting [which King attended at Highlander]?

Some of these darn cranks that's always nosin' around found out about it and I'm not so sure that this photographer, he's the man didn't find it out. I've forgotten now, but anyhow we sent him up there just to attend. He went up there, registered as a delegate [laughs], kept his damn mouth shut, and made pictures, and they posed, and they were tickled to death to get their pictures made.

Myles Horton: A home-grown, East Tennessee hillbilly radical, he founded Highlander Folk School in 1932 to train union organizers for the CIO. In the fifties this rustic retreat in the mountains west of Chattanooga was one of the few places in the Deep South where integrated

---

* An exposé entitled "Highlander Folk School: Communist Training School, Monteagle, Tenn.," in which the photograph first appeared. The Birmingham *News*, biting hook, line, and sinker, then used the Georgia report as the basis for an "investigative" series which answered in the affirmative the question, "Is there a master plan, Soviet-inspired, behind the racial incidents so widespread in America today?"

** He organized the States Rights Council as the Georgia affiliate of the Citizens Council. "The truth of it is, it was the old Talmadge ringleaders, Herman Talmadge and . . . the folks that we depended on, and that was the organization."

*** The Augusta *Courier*, a right-wing tabloid which he published personally until 1974.

meetings were held, and it was this which brought his school to the segregationists' attention. ". . . they thought Highlander was the center of 'this cancerous growth,' and if they could only close Highlander down, they'd stop the spread of the Civil Rights Movement. Only white Southern arrogance could make that kind of analysis."

We had a twenty-fifth anniversary celebration in which Martin Luther King and Aubrey Williams* were among the speakers there, and Mrs. Roosevelt . . . no, it was another time she was there. She was there a year later or a year before. Pete Seeger sang, and we had about a hundred or two hundred visitors came. You know, friends of Highlander, and we had a two-day . . . seminar on the South, talkin' about what was happening in the South.

And . . . it was interesting: Ed Friend came up, and he said he was just passin' by with his wife. They were on a vacation. He was from the sewage-system thing or some sanitation system in Georgia, on vacation. He was a free-lance photographer, and he'd just heard about it, and he'd like to stop by. . . . "Well, you're welcome to the meetings," you know, and he said, "Do you mind if we take some pictures?" I said, "No, there'll be people from the press here. . . . Are you a good photographer?" He said, "Yeah." He showed me some pictures, and I said, "Well, you know, since you are goin' to be takin' pictures . . . maybe you could take some pictures for us. I'll buy some pictures from you. I'll tell you some pictures to take, and we'll buy some from you." He said, "Fine." I didn't pay any attention to him much. . . .

Well, in the meantime, there was a woman we had invited . . . National YMCA board, and the woman couldn't come. She had been a student at Highlander. Her secretary wanted to come. Could she come? We said, "Sure, come ahead. . . ." This was a black woman, brought her husband. He was a free-lance reporter from Texas. . . . He said he might do a story. We said fine and didn't pay much attention.

Well, most of the people knew each other, but this Abner Berry . . . the secretary's husband, and this Friend didn't know anybody there, and so I wasn't surprised when they started talkin' together. They spent a lot of time talkin' together. I just thought, "Well, here's two people that don't know anybody." Thought nothin' of it . . . we're not a very suspicious bunch.

And so I asked Friend later on to take a picture of Martin Luther King and Aubrey Williams, John Thompson, who was the chairman,

* Director of the National Youth Administration under President Franklin D. Roosevelt.

and Rosa Parks and myself. We were sittin' in the front row before they went up to speak. . . . He kept fiddlin' with the camera, and he kept lookin' out of the corner of his eye, and I looked around, and here was Berry . . . bringin' his tape equipment in, and he went down and squatted down right in front of the group. . . . I motioned, told Abner to get away. . . . So he did get away, and Friend took the picture, and then Abner came back and squatted down right in front of this row with his recording equipment. . . . I never thought anything about it.

Well, Friend was still takin'. He took a picture of that, snapped another picture, squattin' down. The reason I'm goin' into such detail with that is when the picture got doctored up, by then they had Abner sittin' in the row, in the chairs. . . . The first picture they circulated was Abner squattin' down in front, and then I guess somebody said, "Hell, we can improve on this."

Anyway, that's how that picture was made. I was rather suspicious of how all that happened. Maybe it's purely accidental, but it's kinda funny, those two characters seemed to be coordinated. I accused Ab—I met Abner Berry later on. He wrote an article for the *Daily Worker,* and two months later he resigned from the Communist party. It was a friendly article, a pro-Highlander article. . . . I was kidding him about it when I saw him. Saw him at the United Nations. He was there one time, and I said, "You know, you really messed us up down there. Do you know that guy Ed Friend?"

He said, "No, he kept buggin' me all the time I was down there. . . . I never understood." I said, "You know what he did?" "Yeah," he said, "I understood what he did . . . I'm sorry, I didn't mean to be used . . ."

I said, "Well, why in hell didn't you tell me you were a reporter for the *Daily Worker?* It wouldn't have made one bit of difference, 'cause our policy is to have anybody there who wants to be. . . . In fact, the Chattanooga *Free Press,* which is a vicious anti-Highlander paper, was there. We didn't try to keep them away. We don't do that." He said, "Well, I just thought it might be embarrassing to you, and I knew I was gonna be friendly."

So, I don't know the story there at all. I just know this was kind of an amusing situation. Anyway, Friend was the one that did all the pictures. I never got my pictures from him. He did all kinds of pictures . . . interracial dancing and interracial swimming and all the things that went on at Highlander all the time. He did a movie while he was there and that movie was used against us in an investigation. I tried to buy the movie. I thought it was a great movie. I thought I'd like to use it to promote Highlander. I had no objections to anything in it. It all looked good to me. It was exactly what we would do. [Laughs] All the things he took, we do. He thought they were terrible. We thought they were good.

The Klan and Citizens Council distributed copies of the photograph throughout the South and, in some cases, had it blown up and plastered on billboards. The "Communist training school" at Monteagle became famous—or infamous in the eyes of the segregationists. All over the South, politicians called for its abolition.

See, we were betrayers. We were white people who were betraying the white people. We were Southerners who were betraying the Southerners. . . . There's no hatred like the hatred of a family that turns on one of the members of the family. That's what we were up against. We were worse than . . . the blacks. We were worse than the Communists. We were worse than outsiders. . . . Their imaginations went wild, and they hated the thing they imagined.

Shortly after the photograph began circulating around the South, the Tennessee legislature appointed a committee to investigate Highlander. Unable to find any basis for punitive legislation, the committee recommended that local law enforcement authorities keep the school under surveillance. Early in 1960 the school was raided, and Myles Horton was tried before a county judge for illegally selling intoxicating beverages (beer, sold at cost on the honor system, was available in the mess hall cooler); operating a school in violation of Tennessee's segregation laws ("We pled guilty to that"); and operating a school for personal gain (IRS audits later failed to support this charge).

We were convicted of those three charges . . . and they used that. See, if you violate the state law, they can void your charter. Never been done before in the history of Tennessee, but they voided our charter, confiscated our property and—and, you know, just took everything we had. . . .

The property that the court confiscated, did you ultimately get it back?

Oh, no, that's all gone, includin' my home and my mother's home, which wasn't part of the school, but was near the school, which they found some way to take.

What did they do with the property?

Sold it at public auction.

That's incredible.

Oh, it's just—people just don't believe it, but it happened.

Was it a jury trial?

Jury trial. . . . Well, the jury was just rulin' on one thing. We had black people there. We had 'em in the courtroom. That was all they were talkin' about, all they were concerned about. You know, the feeling had been whipped up. Now they hadn't bothered about us having black people there all along. In fact, some of the people on the jury had been at Highlander as visitors, eaten with black people. But you know, when they whipped this thing up, and it became a big thing, and they began to revert to their prejudices, and they confused 'em a lot. That was the first trial in the Civil Rights Movement. . . . We were the first victims.

Postscript: Within a week after he had lost the work of thirty years Myles Horton took advantage of a technicality in the Tennessee law to recharter his school as the Highlander Educational Research Center. He rented a house in Knoxville and started from scratch. "We just moved out in the country at New Market two, three, years ago, just beginnin' to build. We got about half as much physical plant as we had at Monteagle. It'll cost us five or six times as much to replace, but it hasn't really crippled our program." Highlander, which fought for the workers in the thirties and forties and blacks in the fifties and sixties, has in the seventies taken up the cause of Horton's own people, the poor whites of Appalachia. Of all its contributions to the Movement, perhaps the most important came by happenstance. It was at a Highlander seminar that the student sit-inners first heard an old union organizing song called "We Shall Overcome."

As for Roy Harris, once he became a crusader for segregation, he never regained his power as a political kingmaker. Nearing eighty now, he still practices law in an Augusta office lined with portraits of Robert E. Lee, Herman Talmadge, and George C. Wallace and, with the indulgence of his wife, still clings to his canny old habit of inviting visiting journalists to his home for drinks and dinner. It is this habit which es-

tablished him as the only segregationist ideologue with a reputation for civility. Mary Harris, a handsome woman some years younger than her husband, has decorated their home around her baby grand piano and her books. "I'm afraid I've not been a very good political wife," she says. "I would never go to Atlanta with Roy and hang out with those people. I preferred to stay home and devote myself to my music and my books and to raising our son." She chats about her enthusiasm for the poetry of Sylvia Plath while he retires to mix the drinks. Shortly, "Mr. Roy" summons everyone to the kitchen where he has mixed giant bourbon highballs in iced-tea glasses. "Wanna hear my favorite toast?" he demands, hoisting his glass. "To the gentlemen. There're damn few of us left."

V
ASSORTED REBELS

Nannie Washburn

A Revolutionary Life

She is old, poor, white—and mad. She went into the textile mills at the age of seven. She has worked twelve-hour days for three dollars a week for a company which refused "to raise the winders to let oxygen in the cotton mill, and they used to haul from eighteen to thirty people out a day." Her first arrest was in 1934 on the picket line at the Exposition Cotton Mill. An Atlanta paper headlined it "Red Women Arrested." Her most recent arrest was in 1975 during a food-stamp protest inside the Georgia capitol. In between, she marched for civil rights, peace, welfare rights. In Atlanta, where she lives in the tough Cabbagetown neighborhood, she is revered by the kids who play at being poor and radical. But she is not playing. The story of her life might have been invented by the young John Dos Passos for USA.

She was born into a West Georgia sharecropper family in 1900. When her parents went to work in the textile mills, her mother fought for the union; her father was a follower of Eugene V. Debs and Tom Watson, the firebrand Georgia Populist who later succumbed to racism. She was recruited into the Communist party in 1932 by Angelo Herndon, a young black man from Alabama who in that Depression year organized an integrated march of one thousand jobless Atlantans on the courthouse. He was promptly jailed for insurrection,* and her first pro-

---

* A celebrated court case ensued. Herndon's twenty-year conviction under the Georgia insurrection law was reversed by the U.S. Supreme Court. For a time,

test marches were in his behalf. Later, her mother gave Herndon a fare-
well supper in their home. Her father, in his dotage and near blind, dis-
appointed her bitterly that night. "He made a remark about the black
people, and he said 'nigger,' and my brother that used to be with IWWs
in the harvest fields—he used to be the organizer—he just went around
and grabbed my father by the seat of his pants and give him a good kick
and kicked him on in the next room. I have to tell it just like it is."

After she joined the Communist party, it was a lifetime on the ram-
parts. She handed out leaflets for the "Scottsboro Boys." Shortly there-*
after the Klan kidnapped her husband and gave him a flogging he
"never did get over." In the fifties she sent her children and grand-
children into the streets with petitions to save the Rosenbergs. She can
still recite the poem Ethel Rosenberg wrote to her sons from the death-
house. In 1965 she was living in Douglasville, the West Georgia town
where she was born, when she turned on the television one Sunday af-
ternoon and saw "the bloody bridge."

I called Dr. Abernathy and he wasn't at home. . . . She answered
the phone, his wife, and I asked her was there anything she could do or
we could do to help. And she said, "Yes, honey, you just don't know
how it is down there and you go down there and you'll learn a lot."
Says, "You'll never believe it."

My daughter was alistenin' in, and she was aworryin' herself to death
about it, because of that bridge . . . So she got the car ready and tuned
up. . . . So my blind son, Joe, and Nellie, my youngest daughter, and I
went to Selma. . . .

How long did it take you to get there?

It was about ten o'clock that night, and we started out fairly early,
but everybody put us off, sent us another route after we got into Alabama. They'd say, "Oh, that's eighty miles from here," and all that kind

---

Elbert Tuttle, then a young Atlanta lawyer and Army Reserve officer, was a member
of the defense team. Tuttle: "I'm quite sure that I have a dossier on me as a Reserve officer by reason of my having represented Angelo Herndon. In fact . . .
a lawyer friend of mine who was in the military, reserve military, told me one
time, said, 'Elbert, I think you oughta know that the people over at Intelligence
. . . are worried about you representing this Communist.' And I said, 'Let 'em
worry . . . he's entitled to a lawyer just like anybody else.' "

* Nine black youths convicted on trumped-up rape charges in a 1931 trial at
Scottsboro, a small town in north Alabama. Eventually the convictions were reversed. An organization affiliated with the Communist party provided defense
lawyers and worked to focus national attention on the case.

of stuff. . . . When we arrived, we got registered at the church, Selma church,* and then the food proposition come up. They had Jim Crow food in the kitchen.

How was that?

Well, . . . my daughter, son, and I refused to eat the Jim Crow food, because there wasn't anybody in the kitchen acookin' except black women that was older than . . . as old as I was and I was sixty-five. . . . I went to Rev. Hollis** and asked him. I said, "I'm not gonna eat . . . we not gonna eat ya Jim Crow food." And he says, "Why?" I said, ". . . My daughter has droved us, my son and I, down here, and I didn't think I'd come to a Jim Crow kitchen." And he said, "You just a guest." I said, "No, I'm not. I just one of 'em." And he said then, "I don't know nothin' we could do about it." I says, "Well, don't you think the black women's been in the kitchen too long cookin' for the white people?" And he commenced studyin', and he said, "The only thing I can do is to let yo'r daughter go in the kitchen. I wouldn't let you." You know, I was sixty-five. . . .

You accused them of having a Jim Crow kitchen in a black church?

Yeah. They didn't have no white people in there cookin', and if I'm a white and comin' in there to eat the food, wouldn't you call it Jim Crow . . . ?

By way of a compromise, her daughter became a cook and she became "hostess" in the dining room there in the basement of Brown's Chapel. ". . . but they didn't know what I was a doin'."

I was a vanguard, but they didn't know it. . . . I know George Wallace. I knew what he was. He was a Klannish sagergationist. So I knew he'd pay any price if he wanted it bad enough to send in somebody in there, Klan or some drunk person come in there and get to fightin', maybe get to shootin'. . . . And I took care of all the dangers. You know what a vanguard is?

No.

Well, it's a detective for the workin'-class people. When I go anyplace, I keep my eyes open, courts or anywhere . . . watch the people,

* Brown Chapel.
** A black minister directing activities at the church.

see that they don't hurt nobody. See that they don't have no weapons to hurt anybody with. . . .

See, I couldn't vote for years 'cause I didn't have a dollar. Used to be I worked on that poll tax years ago. And so I kept my eye open in the office and in the whole church and in the kitchen, too, to protect the workin'-class people, 'cause, we didn't know what might happen . . . they did shoot in at winders.

And it was two weeks before we marched, and they's a lot went on. I know one day we was fixin' to go to City Hall and march to get them to let 'em vote, and we lined up. 'Course, the National Guards was out there, the National Guards. And this man I was standin' by was a big, heavyset black man, and my blind son, and they knocked that big, heavyset man, weighed about two or three hundred pounds, 'bout two hundred and fifty anyhow. Well, when they hit him, you see, when he was agoin' over the line where they told him not to, well, it knocked my blind son and I both down. We was amarchin'. Nellie, my daughter, was in the kitchen acookin'.

They never did let you in the kitchen?

No, they never did let me in the kitchen. [Laughs] I guess they figured I'd cooked enough. [Softly] Naw, that wasn't particular it. Maybe it was. . . .

Did you make the march?

I certainly did make it in good spirits, except my feet. I never did give up. My feet was in bad shape when I got there at Montgomery, had to have 'em treated. I walked the fifty miles . . . and my blind son walked the fifty miles. He was in the *Jet* [magazine] several different times. Then they was a man, Leatheree*, he was a big ballplayer, one-legged. He marched it, too. But Joe made it, but it was *ro-o-ough* trip. You know, Klan was aburnin' crosses and everything like that, even if the airlines was aflyin' over, helicopters or whatever they was.

Why did you feel it was important for y'all to march with these physical ailments that you had?

I didn't feel like I had any. 'Course, my feet hurt a little. I didn't feel like I had any physical ailments. I was only class conscious of my duty.

---

* Jim Leatherer.

That's what I walked for. I walked for freedom, because I knew I'd never be free in white skin as long as the black people was in chains with black skin. See, a white person can't be free . . . poor people, they cain't be free, until the black people's free. Now, I'm not speaking just those two nationalities. I'm aspeakin' about the 'Canos and havin' the Indians on the reservations after takin' their land away from them. I'm angry about that. I'm very angry about 'em chaining the black people and bringin' 'em over here to be chattel slaves. I think it was a awful thing. Against their will. And then black markin' them when they didn't want no more over here, and chainin' five hundred, and sinkin' 'em in the ocean or sea. History'll tell the truth on what the white man's done and I'm ashamed. And I cain't be free in white skin until they free. . . .

You mentioned you met Mrs. Liuzzo. . . .

I certainly did . . . and my daughter and her was 'sposed to be together that night. Anyhow, it didn't happen. She got another assignment some way or 'nother that changed it. . . .

I requested Mrs. Liuzzo, I said, "Mrs. Liuzzo, I'm a lot older'n you and I've had a lot of experience with Jim Crow . . . I wanna give you a little *my* kinda advice." I said, "Don't you git in no car with no black man. If you do, they'd a lot ruther kill you'n a black man, 'cause I've done been through experience of it." And she just shook her head. . . .

She went on anyhow with transportin' people, and my daughter had her car, and she was 'sposed to do the same thing. But my daughter, some other assignment come up that she had to do or use it some way.

But we went on . . . you want me to finish that up? We went on to Montgomery, Alabama. We walked. We slept in cow pastures, unbelievable conditions. But we had the actors and actresses . . . I cain't call all their names. . . .

I would criticize that march: it was too fast. They walked the people to git the march over in, I think, about five days. But I don't think that the marchers shoulda had to walk that fast. Now, that's one of my criticisms.

When we got to Montgomery, of course, they didn't let 'em on the capitol steps, but they was pretty close, and they had a lotta people, and they all had the big meeting, and then we caught a bus to come back. And when we caught a bus to come back, the ambulance that was agoin' to pick up Mrs. Liuzzo passed our bus, but we didn't know what it was. But we learnt later. And we went back to Selma.

I didn't run off quick as the march was over. I stayed around
there. . . . You see, I'm an LPN, licensed nurse, and they picked me to
be on the Medical Committee for Human Rights.* They had a lotta
trouble in Demopolis, Alabama, and wait'll you hear this. The doctors
said would I go to Demopolis, that they was adoin' so much meanness
to the people down there, and I said, "Sure, I'll go," and my daughter
said, "I will, too," and my son, too.

The demonstrations in Demopolis were rough. Her son was arrested.
She set up a makeshift infirmary in a church, treating victims of tear gas
and billy clubs. The police cordoned off the building in an effort to stop
the marches.

But then I stayed in the church, and we slept in there with the black
men. We slept on the benches. I've never been respected as highly by
white men as we were those black men. Now, they was young ones,
from about nineteen to on up. They was one in there forty. He lived in
Alabama, but he was very educated. I would call him . . . I don't know
whether he's still a Communist, but he had been one. Anyhow, we had
to sleep with the lights out, in the dark, 'cause they shot in. They'd
shoot in or one time they throwed a dead snake there, six foot long, rattlesnake. So that was a warnin'. . . .

Now this man, this young man, he . . . they respected us to the
highest, and Nellie and I was all that was in there. You see, I'm far-
sighted and when I'd haveta go to the bathroom, they would . . . this
young man would take me down the steps. And he'd had a little flashlight and he'd take me, where I wouldn't be in any danger of fallin'. And
then he'd come on back upstairs. And they treated me just like a
mother. My sons. And I loved 'em.

So, that just wouldn't do for the white man. They couldn't take it no
longer, and so one day I was cleanin'. Early one mornin' I was cleanin'
. . . havin' everything nice and clean for the first aid . . . the fountain
at the little hall when you go out of the church. And one of those big
guys grabbed me . . . the sheriff. And he liked to have pinched my arm
off, and he drug me out in a car, and he hauled me then to jail, put me
in jail, and they was several black men in there, preachers and so on.

* The Medical Committee for Human Rights, composed mainly of Eastern phy-
sicians and medical students, provided everything from first aid to on-the-spot
psychiatric counseling for civil rights workers. It was especially active in those
areas of Alabama and Mississippi where workers found it difficult to secure reliable treatment at community hospitals.

And I stayed there until they transferred me to another jail . . . The judge sent a doctor down there. We was right in front of the courthouse, and I was aspeakin' of the conditions and so on.

You were shouting out the jail window?

Yeah, I was ahollerin' out the jail window, and they couldn't take it. . . . I went in that second jail on my birthday, the third of May, and this doctor come down and picked me, tryin' to talk to me about the background of my family and so on. So wasn't but just a short time 'til they sent two of the polices down there, and the sheriff come up there and told me to come downstairs. . . . I said, "I don't have my shoes on, let them come up here." It was just a little bitty jail . . . I mean cell. Smallest one I've ever seen. . . . He said, "No, come on." I went downstairs. These two cops, one of them said, "Goddamnit, get them shoes on." Slammed the handcuffs on me, and I didn't know what was agoin' on, you know.

Did you ever find out what charge they had you on?

I didn't have no lawyer . . . they didn't defend me. I mean, I asked 'em what they was gonna do. They said it wasn't "none of my damn business." And I couldn't get no information, or they didn't tell me what. Then when we started out, they says, "We're takin' you to the mental institution where you belong, you bitch, you."

And I went on with 'em and everywhere they said, "You oughta throw ya hands up and pet them niggers." Niggers, niggers, that's all they talked about, niggers. So I had a little incident happened to me. See, they got my pocketbook . . . I didn't have a cigarette and I just said to 'em, I said, "Would you loan me a cigarette?" I says, "I got money to buy 'em, but I just don't have 'em. They took my pocketbook." And he said, "You goddamn bitch, you, I'd throw you in the river." Says, "I wouldn't give you *nothin'*." I just kept quiet, and every time I passed a station, a place where they was black people, I always helt my hand up. They was handcuffed . . . and they taken me to Tuscaloosa mental institution. And oooooh, if they didn't use . . . they cursed me from the time we started, 'fore we started, until we got there. We passed through Scottsboro, Alabama, and I remembered so well aworkin' so hard—we did here in Atlanta—for the "Scottsboro Boys." In fact, all over the country. . . .

And we worked so hard for the "Scottsboro Boys," I'd always longed

to pass through that town, so I did, but it was the wrong direction.*
[Laughs]

How long did they keep you in Tuscaloosa?

They kept me twenty-one days. . . . That's the most ridiculousest
thing in the world. You know, capitalism is the most rottenest thing on
earth. Any country or any society that would give you tranquilizers, and
that's the way they keep all the people down in Milledgeville.** They
keep 'em down all over the country. Now I've done been there, I know.
And those people's eyes is like rattlesnake eyes, they hate you so bad
. . . you see, they knowed I was in Dr. King's march, and they cussed
me all the time.

Did they claim you were mentally ill?

Uh-huh, they sure did. I got the papers here. . . . So they commenced to lock me in a cell the first night, to see that I wasn't gonna kill
nobody. And then from then on, they didn't lock me, they put me in the
ward. And *oh,* how they hated me. Especially a couple of the matrons.
The head matron, oh, how she hated me. You could see the hate in her
face. You can tell a personality of a person when they hate you so bad.
So I stayed there, and the doctor was a Indian doctor, and he wanted to
examine me, and I said, "I don't need no examination, I'm not sick." I
says, "I've got money to have as good a doctor as anybody needs, and I
don't *want* yo' treatment. I don't want yo' examination. I am not sick."

And he said yeah, and he made 'em carry me anyhow, and he examined me. And I shamed him about how the white man, how they had
mistreated the Indians and took all their land and put them on the con-
centration camps. So he—he wasn't no good.

Was this an American Indian doctor?

Uh-mm, down at Tuscaloosa. I got after him one day. He was
apassin', and I said, "Dr. So-and-so, I wanta tell you, I don't see how you
could hardly hold yo' head up, the way they've done yo' race of people,
the white man, takin' their land, stealin' their land, and takin' it away
from 'em, and murderin' 'em and puttin' 'em on the reservation." I said,
"I don't see how you could be a doctor for a place like this."

---

* In all probability, she passed through Greensboro, a small town between Demopolis and Tuscaloosa. Scottsboro is over two hundred miles to the north.

** Location of the state mental hospital in Georgia.

But I stayed there twenty-one days and they wanted to give me shock treatment. Well I'm a out-of-the-state person, and there're certain laws on that, so my daughter in there, my sightless daughter, she got her husband . . . I wouldn't give no name whatever here in Atlanta. But finally I give her name, and her husband called down there and said, "You got the wrong woman." Said, "She's not mentally sick."

HELEN BULLARD

An unabashed civic chauvinist, she once told a visiting reporter, ". . . if anything good spills over into the South, it comes from Atlanta." She is the acknowledged political architect of Atlanta's reputation as The City Too Busy to Hate, managing every successful campaign for mayor from the early forties until 1970. Her success in melding three minorities—blacks, liberals, rich white conservatives—into a bloc capable of outvoting the segs enabled the city to elect mayors who were dedicated to the principle that "you don't 'act up' in Atlanta . . . particularly if you're an elected official." She calls it the Atlanta style, and it was epitomized by the late Bill Hartsfield, mayor from 1943 until 1961 and her favorite among the three mayors she advised.

"Honey, we could have out-Little-Rocked Little Rock easily if it hadn't been for that old man Hartsfield." The turning point for Atlanta came in '61 when the national press flocked to the city for the simultaneous desegregation of its schools and lunch counters. The day ended with Hartsfield guiding the journalists on a Greyline tour of the Atlanta sights as a warm-up for the cocktail party he threw for them that night. A good time, but precious little news, was had by all. ". . . I use taxis all the time and always have, and the drivers that I knew were segregationists. I mean, just red-necks from the beginning. They were so proud. 'Well . . . I guess they didn't get much of a story when they came down here, did they?' You know, people that a week ago had said, 'They ain't

*gonna have mine goin' with no niggers.' But they were pleased that
Atlanta had done well and that we hadn't been like a Birmingham."*

*After a lifetime in politics she is a great storyteller; even so, she gives
up her real "inside" stories only after great deliberation. But she was
quite ill during the winter of 1975—pain sometimes forced her to break
off in mid-sentence—and with the illness came a sense of urgency. One
day she said she wanted to tell a story that only she knew in its entirety
—how the city of Atlanta finally paid tribute in 1965 to its only Nobel
laureate.*

Well, the King dinner was a funny thing. I never see Mrs. King that I
don't think about it. A little group of four people, I guess, met in a
church basement. These were white people. . . . I think that I was the
one who said, "We've got to do sumpin', or somebody's gonna pick it
up that here we've got a Nobel Prize winner and we've never even so
much as acknowledged him." So I asked Ivan* if the city could, and he
said, "Oh, no, nobody would come." So I went to the chamber of commerce, and they said, "Oh, no," they couldn't do that; nobody would
come. . . .

So we'd keep meeting down in this basement of this church . . .
didn't have a penny of money or anything. But then the group got a little larger. You could bring anybody you wanted to, and so we said,
"We're gon' have something even if it's just a box lunch. We're gonna
have something for Martin Luther King, Jr." . . . I guess this is terrible
to tell you this, but we made up a list of about a hundred of the really top
people here in Atlanta, mostly businessmen, and then we sent out invi-
tations to about two hundred people asking them to be sponsors, and to
the letter . . . we attached a list. Now what the list said was, "The following have been *invited* to be sponsors." And I knew good and well
that people were gonna read it, "The following *are* the sponsors," see,
and they did. We just got a tremendous [response] . . . that was the beginning of the yeast working.

Then it began to come together and part of it—now I sure have never
told anybody this. I said something as a joke, and it's the last time I've
ever said anything as a joke, because if there's one thing I've learned,
people take you seriously. I said, "Well, what we gonna do about a present? We have to give him a scroll or something." . . . Finally somebody said, "What do you think we oughta get?" And I said, just being
completely smart ass, I said, "Why don't we give him a Steuben bowl.
That's what heads of state give each other and that's what Truman sent

* Mayor Ivan Allen, who succeeded Hartsfield in 1962.

to Princess Margaret." I said it as a joke, just being smart ass, you know. Well, Miss Priss! . . .

Janice Rothchild* was there, and she said, "Well, I think that's wonderful. . . . Now, we cain't get it from Rich's because Rich's once had him arrested, and somebody would pick that up." So she just called New York, and she said, "I'm Janice Rothchild in Atlanta, and we are planning a dinner for Martin Luther King, Jr., and we'd like to have a bowl." And you know what the man said? "Well, of course, and how lovely for you to have thought of us." The president! She didn't even know his name; she just said, "I want the president."

So she said, "Now, we don't want one of those little finger-bowl things. We want a good-size bowl." He said, "What do you wanna put on it?" And she said, "We'll have to call you back on that." So he said, "Well, yes, and don't worry about the time because we'll drop everything and do this, and if the question of delivery time comes, we'll fly it down in our private plane." She came back and announced it. . . . I thought, *"Well,* there's nothing you can do now. It's already started." [Laughs] The bowl, he was letting her have at wholesale, was eight hundred dollars. Sixteen-hundred-dollar bowl. And there we sat. We didn't even have money for postage, and she had just obligated us. Okay?

Then they had a meeting—where did they have that? I think the Piedmont Driving Club—of the power structure.** And a big executive from First National Bank, good friend of Ivan's, called me and said, "We ain't gonna have no dinner for no nigger." . . . You know, they usually don't meet together, just two or three make a decision, but for the first time they did not have unanimity. . . . Well it was all very hush-hush. Nothing had been in the paper about it. But they left with it unresolved, the power structure did.

Then the next thing that happened, it got to be a *cause célèbre,* and this banker called up Lou Oliver, who was head of Sears at that time,

* A prominent liberal. Her husband, Rabbi Jacob Rothchild, became official co-chairman of the planning committee. In 1958 his synagogue had been bombed by a group calling itself the Confederate Underground, and Ralph McGill's Atlanta *Constitution* column denouncing the bombers won a Pulitzer Prize.

** Taylor Branch, political editor of *Harper's* magazine, once wrote: "Atlanta is the only city I know where everyone speaks openly, and often fondly, of 'the power structure.'" The "power structure" consisted of the city's top white executives; its unofficial headquarters was the Piedmont Driving Club, which was and is rigidly segregated along racial, religious and social lines. At its most powerful during the time of the King dinner, the "power structure" has gone into something of an eclipse with the advent of black political power in Atlanta. But the Piedmont Driving Club, with its unwritten rule barring blacks and Jews, became a center of controversy in 1977, when President Carter appointed club member Griffin Bell attorney general of the United States.

and without giving him a chance to say anything, just read the riot act about "we ain't gonna have no dinner for no nigger." And when Lou Oliver hung up, he turned to his secretary and said, "Well, who does he think he's talking to?" And she said, "What?" And he told her. Well, that night she and her husband went to dinner with another couple, and they were doing "what-has-happened-today," and she told about it. Now, it just so happened that the man of the other couple was a stringer for the New York *Times.*

So here comes a front-page story on the New York *Times . . .* it didn't say who, but it said a banker was leading the fight. Okay. The head of the Tahitian government was negotiating with C&S* here for a twenty-million-dollar loan, so he got the paper at eleven o'clock in the morning and read it and promptly called the Chase Manhattan Bank in New York and said, "Who in the hell is this banker? If it's one of yours, we don't want him coming down here, and we don't wanna have anything to do with him." . . . So then New York called C&S Bank. Now, Mills Lane had not wanted to have it, but he wouldn't tell anybody . . . he spent the next six weeks calling up people and saying, "I was not the one they were talking about. I was not the one they were talking about." You see, after the New York *Times* had it, then the *Constitution* picked it up, and old Granger Hansell,** I never will forget, he wrote a letter and said he would not be a sponsor. The next day we got a letter saying, "I told you I wouldn't be a sponsor, but I've just read the story in the *Constitution* and I will be delighted to be one."

So then the thing began to do like that, and then all of a sudden it was *the* thing to do. And this was the first time Atlanta had ever done anything that they didn't have to do. . . . Everyone started getting tickets, and I oversold two hundred, thinking that nobody will come, and we'll have this room to put people. Then [we] began to get press from the New York *Times* and the *New Yorker,* just everybody wanted to send somebody down. . . . About ten days before the dinner, even my scrambled-egg brain, I realized we couldn't sell any more tickets, you know. [Laughs] Then we got a call from the Ku Klux Klan saying how many people were coming. I said we'd sold fifteen hundred tickets. "Well," he said, "just wanted to tell you, for every person you have coming to that dinner, we're going to have a patrol, a picketing thing, one person, one Ku Kluxer."***

---

* Citizens and Southern Bank. For a time, under chairman Mills B. Lane, it was Atlanta's most progressive bank.

** An Atlanta attorney whose firm represented the *Constitution.*

*** It is interesting to speculate about the origin of this call in light of the Senate Select Committee on Intelligence revelation in 1975 that the FBI attempted to dis-

Of course, I got nervous, and I called Herbert Jenkins, and he said, "Oh, how wonderful." I said, "Herbert, what are you talking about?" He said, "Well, you know"—very apologetically—"I don't have too good a file on the Ku Klux Klan . . . if they wear their masks, what not, they're going to be jerked out and put in the pokey with no questions asked or anything. But if they come without masks, I can have the best file on the Ku Klux Klan of anybody in the whole South." . . . Of course, nothing happened. They didn't come.

It made the national press. . . . I called up WSB* and said, "Call Huntley-Brinkley and tell them that ten days before the dinner, the tickets are all gone." . . . They went on the air and said, "We do have one good thing in Atlanta," and told about it. Okay?

Then the next day, I get a call from the vice-president of First National . . .** I didn't know him . . . he said how was I, and I said I was fine, how was he and he said he was fine. So I said, "What can I do for you? What's the trouble?" And he said, "Well, we want twenty tickets of the Martin Luther King, Jr., dinner." So I said, *"Oh,* you didn't listen to Huntley-Brinkley last night, did you?" And he said [she mimics a lofty, self-important tone], "What has that got to do with it?" "Well," I said, "they just announced that ten days before there were no more tickets." And he said, "Well, now, don't be ridiculous, you can always . . ." I said, "Maybe you could other places, but you cain't do it here." He kept on and on, and I finally said, "Look, I have one ticket, and I don't think I'm gonna eat. I'll be glad to let you have that one ticket if it'll help." "No, I want twenty tickets." So then I said, "Just cain't do it. They're not available."

About thirty minutes later, Rich's, Mr. Dick Rich*** himself called and said how was I, and I said I was fine, how was he, and he said he was fine. I said, "What can I do for you?" And he said, "I want twenty tickets." The magic word was twenty. "Now," I said, "Sir Richard, I'm sorry as I can be but—" He said, "Now, Helen, don't tell me. There're always tickets around." I said, "Yeah, and I've sold 'em." [Laughs] We had this long argument, and I told him, "I have one ticket, I'll give it to you. You can use my ticket." And he said one wouldn't do, he wanted a whole table. And I said, "Look, Sir Richard, ain't nobody gonna have a

---

rupt this dinner as part of its campaign against King. For more on King and the FBI, see the "Black Camelot" sequence.

  * The NBC television affiliate in Atlanta.
  ** Apparently calling on behalf of his superior, who had opposed the dinner.
  *** Who had allowed King to be arrested with the student sit-inners in his store.

table. People gonna sit where they want to—or where they don't want to." [Laughs]

Then Agnes Scott* got in on it, and the night of the dinner, twenty young, pretty things appeared and said they were going to be the hostesses and they would help seat people. Well, by that time I just was —I was numb. I couldn't take it. So then I was trying to figure out how we could do something for Miss Coretta. . . . I just called the florist and ordered two dozen red roses in a big thing tied with ribbon. Then I went to one of these little girls and said, "Now, look, I will understand completely if you don't want to do this." This is an Agnes Scott. "But I want somebody up there when she is introduced just to hand her this. She doesn't have to say anything. . . ." Well, the little girl just lit up, and I said, "Now, you think about this because you're gonna be on television, and you'd better check with your mother and father." "Don't have to check with my mother and father." So that's what we did, and just everything—Ivan came with a scroll. Father—oh, he was the archbishop—Archbishop Hallinan came in on a stretcher from the hospital. He was real sick, but they brought him in and sat him up.

When people walked in that room, in that lobby that night . . . I have never seen people walk with such pride, and they were all dressed beautifully, all kinds of people dressed. They could sit anywhere. So what happened was that without even trying to, it was all mixed up . . . For many people this was the first experience of sitting down and eating with a black person, except at a church meeting or something. So it started off with somebody would say, "Pass me the salt," and then—you know how when Southerners have good manners, they *really* have good manners—somebody would say, "Where do you work? What do you do?" and the man would say, "I'm a chemist. I teach chemistry out at Emory." And then the other man would say, "Isn't that strange? I teach chemistry, too, out at Atlanta University." And then they would start.

Now the reason I know it was such a success was after the thing was over, somebody came up and wanted a program. We had a nicely printed program with all the sponsors on it. And I went in after everybody had gone to find one . . . you know, people just leave those things around. There was not one. I never got a copy of one. They took 'em. And I said to somebody, "Why . . . ?" He said, "Well, everybody got theirs signed by everybody else at their table, and so they just took 'em with 'em." And there was not one left.

But it was a wonderful experience. It was an incredible experience. . . . It was a terribly good thing. And I kept telling Ivan and

* An Atlanta women's college with a traditional Old South ambience.

everybody that would listen to me, which is not too many, that this was important because it was the first thing Atlanta had done that they didn't have to do. Everything else had been the threat of a court order. To me, it was a milestone, and I'm still running into people after all these years who say, "Oh, I saw you the night of the Martin Luther King dinner.". . . I always thought that should somehow be told.

CHARLES R. SIMS

Bogalusa, Louisiana, is a rarity among the small towns of the South in that it has no redeeming touch of grace, beauty, or elegance to surprise the eye or rest the spirit. Originally it was a sawmill town, which accounts for its location on the edge of the Pearl River swamps. Now a dark, hissing chemical plant, which fronts on the main street, dominates the town visually and economically.

A tough town, and he was just the man for it. Here in 1964 he founded the Deacons for Defense and Justice, the South's first organized black vigilantes.

He is to be found in a dim, musty pool hall downtown. Up front, black men watch daytime TV. At the tables, black youngsters, ignoring the No Minors sign, shoot precociously flashy games of rotation and eight ball at a quarter a rack. He collects the quarters. He has the look of a hustler gone to seed. The grip of a pistol peeks from his pocket as he ponders whether he will consent to an interview, after all.

"How'd you find my phone number?"

"I just called information and asked for it."

He seems startled that he could be tracked down so easily.

"Well, I got a million-dollar story to tell. Most of it ain't never been told and ain't nobody knows it but me and one other man."

That man, a black journalist, has soured him on telling his story to anyone. They were going to collaborate on a book about the Deacons, and the journalist made hours of tapes, took all his papers, and hasn't been heard from since.

"When I find him, I'm gonna kill that son of a bitch," he says.

"Well, it might be better just to get your tapes back and write your own book."

"No," he says rather hotly, "I'm gonna kill that son of a bitch."

The prospects for an interview seem dim as he talks on about the book he could write if he takes a mind. He ought to do that instead of giving all this stuff away, he observes. But then:

"You come all the way to Bogalusa just to see me?"

"I wouldn't be here if you didn't live here."

"Well, come on."

We set up the recorder on the backmost pool table, and a ten-year-old black boy named Cotton collects the quarters while he tells the story of the Deacons.

Well, what really made it happen, one afternoon two civil rights workers were attacked by six whites in a black neighborhood. We captured the whites and kept 'em 'til the police arrived, and the police turned 'em aloose. . . . Then we decided since we didn't have protection from the law, by the law, we should organize a group to protect our peoples in the neighborhood. So we organized a group, and by some strange coincidence we started callin' 'em the Deacons. And we took up the job of self-defense. I'd like to explain one thing about the Deacons. We never attacked anyone, but we would defend ourself against *anybody* at any time, anywhere, regardless of the price.

Why did you feel it was necessary to take that position?

When you live in a town and you been in the town all your life and you see the polices enforce the law on blacks for whites but not on whites for blacks, then you know somethin' need to be done. And that's what was happenin' here. The law here, it was on the books, but it was against the black man and nothin' against the white man. We had to equalize that thing. So we organized and let the man know that we meant to protect ourself, and then he start tryin' to do somethin', a little bit of somethin' about it. But not much, until we forced their hand.

How did you do that?

Well, first we cleaned up the neighborhood. All white collectors, white peddlers, and all that stuff in the black neighborhood, we didn't allow nobody in after dark. Caught 'em in after dark, we kinda pepped 'em up a little bit, showed 'em they way out. And in the black Negro neighborhood, we didn't run from the law and nobody else, 'cause we was masters there. Funny thing about it, after the white power structure found out that we meant to defend ourself, they started hanging lights up all over town. We'd been begging for lights ten years, and now we have a light, I think, two to every block. Before we had a light about one every five or six, maybe eight blocks.

What was the Deacons' position on guns?

Oh, we had some of the best weapons. When we organized, we only had the guns that fellas had at their own homes. In Louisiana they call it the Sportsman's Paradise or sumpin' like that, do a lotta huntin' around there. The average dude own a couple of shotguns. Most of us own pistols and all this type of business. We started off, we had that, and I raised a nice sum of money and went to New Orleans, bought a bunch of carbines and some weapons to take care of the work that we had to do. I'd say . . . we was better armed than the police department.

It sounds almost like a state of two armed camps, a state of war.

It looked that way. They brought horses, cattle prods. Of course, we had a *very* smart superintendent in the state then. His name was Colonel Burbank.* I had went over to Plaquemine and saw what happened to the peoples over there. They had some horses stampede through a crowd of people, and I came back here, and I called Burbank in Baton Rouge, and I just told him—we was havin' hell here that day—and I told him to come get these horses out of Bogalusa 'cause if they ride the horses down among our people, we were gon' bury man and the beast, 'cause we were gon' kill both of 'em. In the next couple of hours they were movin' the horses and things out. So we didn't have no problem there.

But we still had problems with some of the state policemen droppin' cigarettes on the girls walkin' the picket lines, tryin' to pull up their dresses. I reported all that. We took pictures of some of it, and every time I found sumpin', I have to admit, Burbank he moved it, 'cause he knew that we meant business.

This was the state trooper superintendent you were dealing with?

Right, but these people here, we couldn't deal with them no kinda way. I believe the Klans had took over the territory. At one time they

* Superintendent of state police.

was havin' meetin's right here in the city. So I had a kinda meetin' with the city council, and I just told the mayor point-blank, "The next time the Klans hold a rally in the city limits of Bogalusa, we gon' have a confrontation right there, 'cause we gonna either break it up or have a war right on the spot. 'Cause this is not what you s'posed to have in the city of Bogalusa, and we not gonna have it." The mayor, he made a smart move. He wouldn't let 'em have any more rallies here, but they went right across the river to Mississippi. But we didn't care anything about that, long as it didn't happen right here in the city.

Was the whole fight here in Bogalusa over the fact that the city was resisting the '64 Civil Rights Act?

Well, just say it this way. The whole city was resistin' the Civil Rights Act, such as public accommodations, the right to set up a picket line picketing merchants for jobs. It's eighteen pickets walkin' the picket line, and you look up, and in fifteen or twenty minutes, you got three, four hundred whites harassin' 'em. That calls the Deacons out automatically and we'd go out.

Now what bugged the man, he didn't know how many of us it was. No one knows now and I hope they will never know. All they know, we had nerve enough to walk among them, and they three or four hundred strong, and didn't give no ground, and if we'da had to, we'd fight right there, in that huddle . . .

See, we had made up our mind on one thing. I know where just about every honkie here live. If he'd attack any my mens, he couldn't go to his house and go to sleep no more, 'cause if he do, I don't know what would have happened to him. I won't say we'da killed him. I got more sense than to use *those* words, but I'm not sure what *would* have happened. And I think they kinda sensed that, because they'd look around, every face that they saw was a Bogalusa born and raised boy. This is a hell of a thing. Here's a cat you've been with all yo' life, and overnight you're on different sides. Now this is the way it actually happened in Bogalusa. Blacks and white got along truly wonderful until they passed the Civil Rights Act, and that white boy found out we didn't have to go to back doors anymore. We could go down front and spend the almighty dollar just like he could. And open up the lines for advancements on jobs, then I don't have to do yo' job anymore. You got to do yo' own job to hold it. Well, this man, he went . . . he went pathetic.

Most of the people that emerged as leaders in the Civil Rights Movement in towns like Bogalusa were preachers . . .

No, that's not true. That's who didn't emerge in the city of Bogalusa.

Well, that's what I'm gettin' at. You don't talk like a man that's ever been a preacher.

No. Nor was I a deacon. I was a party boy, a bachelor, good job makin' a hundred fifty dollars a week when people wasn't makin' much money. I was an insurance agent. Plenty girls. I liked to play. That's all I done, just party and wear pretty clothes. But, when the Civil Rights Movement came about, and we had the day of testing public accommodation, had so much trouble, that day I made up my mind that we was gon' have to fight, whether my people saw it or not. And I made up my mind then that this is where I'll be able to be found, because at least I know what I'm fightin' for. I went to World War Two. I helped train over a thousand men to kill . . . and I didn't know what the hell I was teaching 'em how to kill for. Went in behind the Civil Rights Act, I *knew* what the hell I was fightin': I was fightin' for equal rights that Roosevelt promised us before he died. Didn't do a damn thing about it. Truman, he promised . . . he didn't do a damn thing.

Did the passage of that act change you just that quickly?

Well, it made me think. I was already, I guess you would call it on a militant kick, 'cause I didn't stand no pushin' around by nobody, black or white. I'd been hassled by the police before, but I'd never been *struck* by the law. Had some cats on the police force I was raised up with, and they knew if they hit me they were gon' have to do me in bad, 'cause I was gon' fight back. And I still fight right now, at my age. Don't push me. My time is not long, not put on this earth to stay forever, and the time I'm here, I'm gon' be treated right.

That attitude ran counter to what a lot of the civil rights organizations were preaching at the time. How did they react to you?

Well, it did. . . . I had the privilege of working along with Martin Luther King, spoke on different programs with Stokely Carmichael, Julius Bond, Cleveland Alexander, and Dick Gregory. All the strong boys, you know, and I put it like this, like I told Dr. King, "You got yo' thing, I got mine. It was necessary for us to pick up the gun in Bogalusa. Had I been in Selma when you were marching, I'da organized in Selma. Maybe you wouldn't have lost as many people as you did. And the police certainly wouldn't have stormed me with the horses 'cause we'da stopped 'em or died." I said, "Now you do yo' thing and I'm gonna back you up in doin' you' thing, 'cause this is my job." I said, "Don't you slap me. I will not turn the other cheek, I'll chop your head off if you slap me." And we got along all right. Matters of fact, I spent a hell of a lot of time with all of 'em. McKissick.* I had to guard James Forman every time he came down. He welcomed the Deacons 'cause he happened to come here and King didn't. He knew how dangerous it was here. King didn't. Why, if you were to compare Selma, Alabama, and Bogalusa, Selma wouldn't be a drop in the bucket to this area here.

How did the Deacons spread? How much did it spread?

How did it spread? It spread because I spreaded it. And I don't care who know it. I went and organized black people all over Louisiana. I don't know all the places I didn't go. . . . I went into Mississippi, Natchez, they had problems there. Wherever they had problems just about in the South, I went. Alabama, spent a lot of time over there. And then I got a call from the North . . . I went to Chicago, Detroit, places like New York, Boston. . . .

How big did the Deacons get at its height?

Well, I'll say it this way. When I quit travelin', we had better than fifty-three chapters across the country, and some of those chapters had some branches. I won't tell you how many members we had, but I'll tell you this: if push hada come to shove, we were well covered. . . .

How would you defend it against the charge that it was a KKK in reverse?

Well, the first thing . . . everything we done, we walked like men, and we never done anything 'less we was defendin' ourselves or our people. The Klan, they wear robes and sheets and all that bullshit, and we showed 'em how much we thought of hidin' our faces. We took two Klan uniforms and drug 'em up Columbia Street and burnt 'em on the courthouse steps.

The Deacons' greatest prominence came during James Meredith's ill-fated "march against fear" in 1967. Meredith was wounded by gunfire as he walked down a Mississippi highway. When SNCC and SCLC

---

* Floyd McKissick, who succeeded James Farmer as chairman of CORE.

came in to continue the march in Meredith's behalf, squabbling broke out between the two organizations as to the direction the Movement would take. SNCC's introduction of the Black Power slogan on the march dampened the spirit of biracial camaraderie which had marked the Movement's glory years in the South. During the turmoil he brought a contingent of Deacons into Mississippi to serve as "bodyguards" for the marchers. ". . . I was carryin' two snub-nosed .38s and two boxes of shells and had three men ridin' down the highway with semi-automatic carbines with thirty rounds apiece. . . . See, I didn't believe in that naked shit no way."

A lot of things happened on the Meredith march that was never told, and Dr. King, he was against violence, but when the man fell dead on the Meredith march, marchin' for his freedom, Dr. King was asked to preach his funeral, and that was way up in the Delta. He preached his funeral, but he would not go into the Delta unless I carried him. And he knowed the only way for me to carry him in the Delta, I had to carry him with my gun and my mens, not his. He can let his men trail along at the tail end, but in front and behind, it was gon' be me. And that was the only way he'd go. So, when the chips were down, I won't say the man woulda picked up a gun, but I'll say this, he didn't run one away, 'cause I was with the man. And I respect and admire the man. I think he's a brilliant man. . . .

On that Meredith march, when the Black Power thing came up . . . SNCC, I think, would have been right in tune with you on that, wouldn't it?

No, not the way they done it, no. Look, the Meredith march, it started as a nonviolent march . . . and the slogan Black Power didn't do a damn thing but hurt the Movement. They forgot one thing. They had a lot of white sympathizers was givin' they money to support the black movement 'cause blacks couldn't support it. And when they come up with that Black Power slogan that kilt that support they was gettin' from a lot of places, and even a lot of civil rights volunteer workers *quit* and you can't blame 'em. How can you work with a son of a bitch that every time you look up he's throwin' up his fist talkin' 'bout Black Power. I don't wanna live under Black Power. I don't wanna live under white power. I want *equal* power, and that's what I push. That's what I've fought for, that's what I stand for, and I still believe it. I don't want either one of 'em. Put too much power in any one son bitch's hands, it's too much, and the slogan Black Power, it didn't last. . . . Stokely disappeared, so did the word "Black Power."

That surprised me. I woulda thought that woulda been right down your alley.

Naw, that wasn't down my alley at all, 'cause the cats that was hollerin' Black Power, I was protectin' and guardin' they damn ass. I don't see nothin' they was doin' to even be talkin' 'bout no Black Power. The Black Power, we had it. In them thirty rounds of ammunition on a man's shoulder, we had the Black Power. They didn't have a damn thing but face and ass.

But what?

Face and ass. Face for showin', ass for sittin' on. That's all they had.

VI
BLACK CAMELOT

SCLC IN ATLANTA

ANDREW YOUNG

He was executive director of SCLC. His speciality was negotiation.

I don't know of a single instance where SCLC decided in Atlanta that it was gonna start a movement. In every case it was the local people getting into difficulty and coming to us to help 'em get out. In Albany, Georgia, Dr. Anderson* down there called Martin . . . "Please, just speak for us one night." And so Martin left New Orleans and went to speak in Albany and got to preachin' and going on, and the folk were very excited about it all, and there were two churches packed and people all out in the street, and then Dr. Anderson got up and announced, "Be back in the morning at nine o'clock and bring your marchin' shoes, and Dr. King is gon' march with us." And Martin had no intention of going to jail in Albany when he left here. And it was a little different in Birmingham. In Birmingham Fred Shuttlesworth came over and asked us. He said . . . they just had to do something about Birmingham, and they were gonna do it with or without our help, but they'd like for us to come over and help 'em organize it. The same thing was true with Selma.

See, I'm convinced that Martin never wanted to be a leader. I mean, everything he did, he was pushed into. He went to Montgomery in the first place because . . . he wanted a nice quiet town where he could

---

* Physician W.G. Anderson, a black leader in Albany.

finish his doctoral dissertation and not even have the responsibility of a big church and got trapped into the Montgomery Improvement Association. They literally shamed him into gettin' involved in the Atlanta Movement. He never would get involved in the Freedom Rides. He just refused. He just did not wanna assume the leadership of the entire Southern struggle or of the entire national struggle. And it wasn't until . . . the time of Birmingham that he kinda decided that he wasn't going to be able to escape that, that he was going on.

That notion runs against . . . prevailing conceptions. How sure are you of that?

Oh, I'm almost certain of that. First place, nobody has written a book about the Movement that talked to anybody in depth, except maybe Coretta. You have to separate a sense of destiny and responsibility generally from a specific sense of responsibility for *the* Civil Rights Movement. There's no question that Martin knew he had an important leadership role to fulfill in the nation—he was a natural leader—but he did not ambitiously pursue leadership, say in the sense that Jesse Jackson does now—and I'm not criticizing that—or Hosea.

Hosea's sense of mission is another thing. That's another long story you oughta get into some time. Very briefly, Hosea was in a foxhole in Germany with fourteen other folk or something like that, and a bomb hit directly in the foxhole, and everybody was killed but him. And he laid up there for a couple of days with his guts open almost and spent thirteen months in a veterans' hospital in England. When he got discharged, he was discharged as a forty-percent disabled veteran, still crippled and on crutches and was on his way back to Attapulgus, Georgia. All this time laying up in the hospital, feeling God saved him for something, and on his way back to Attapulgus, Georgia, he stopped in the Macon bus station and drank at the only water fountain he saw, which was the white one. I don't even know whether it had a sign on it. And some folk roughed him up and gave him a hard time about it, and he decided that the Lord saved him to fight segregation.

I mean, Martin never had that kind of messiah complex, see. . . . Almost everybody else had it, though. Bevel had it . . . Wyatt, all of 'em were driven, ambitious sorta guys. Martin never was, and they were always pushin' him, trying to generate ambition for him. He would try to use me to balance them out. He would always expect me to take the conservative side, to sorta neutralize what Bevel and Hosea were trying to do, to give him an excuse to come down the middle. . . . He expected me to go way to the right [laughing] on every question.

That implies a good deal of intricate political maneuvering within the staff.

Always, *constantly.* Oh, Randolph Blackwell entered that staff about '63, too, and it used to be Randolph Blackwell, Dorothy Cotton, and Bevel and myself meeting out at Blackwell's house late at night tryin' to figure out what we oughta do and scheme up on Martin to try to get him to lead it. It was because he really was content being a pastor and lecturer and writin' a book now and then. [Pauses] Even in terms of layin' a strong organizational base for SCLC, Martin really wasn't interested in building an organization to last. He didn't see that as important at all, and I guess I didn't either . . . like we never had the budget to do what we decided to do. We decided to do something and went on out and did it on a kind of faith that the money to do it would come. . . .

Dr. King has been characterized as, after Albany, being hungry for a big win; after Birmingham, being hungry for a victory to match Birmingham. How does that strike you, those characterizations?

Completely wrong. I think after Albany [from 1961 to 1962], he went through a period where he was trying to decide whether to even continue or not. Claude Sitton had written us off: The Movement had failed; Dr. King's leadership had come to an end.* You oughta go back and get some of those New York *Times* stories that Claude wrote. And Martin had just come to Ebenezer Church [in Atlanta], and he got a lot more active in his church. Now . . . somewhere along there, Sol Hurok's agency offered him a guarantee of one hundred thousand dollars just to be a lecturer. . . . I think if he hadn't had to directly turn that offer down, he mighta drifted awhile longer. But because they were pressuring him to become their chief lecturer around the world—as part of Sol Hurok Productions—he had to grapple with it in his mind, and he said "no."

That decision committed King irrevocably to the Movement. It also ushered in the years of triumph—Birmingham in '63, the Nobel Peace Prize in '64, Selma in '65. With the triumphs came an increasing awareness on King's part of FBI surveillance.

He also knew that it wasn't just a matter of them following him around, keeping track on his activities, but that they were really bug-

* Because of King's failure to win a clear victory in Albany.

ging just about every place we went. In fact, we had a kind of running
joke of who all was a member of the "FBI Golden Record Club." . . .
When somebody said something a little fresh or flip, Martin would say,
"Ol' Hoover's gonna have you in the Golden Record Club if you're not
careful."

*King suspected the FBI as the source of an unsigned threatening note
and a tape recording mailed to him at SCLC headquarters late in 1964.**
*The note hinted that he must commit suicide before the Peace Prize
awards ceremony to prevent disclosures which would destroy his reputation. The tape recording was intended to convince him that his enemies
had damaging information in their possession. When the tape was discovered in the heaps of mail at SCLC headquarters on Atlanta's Auburn
Avenue, King invited Young and a few other close advisers to listen to
the tape with him.*

He wanted a group of us to sit down and hear it together, and so we
sat down, and we turned on a tape recorder, and we listened. It was a
very bad quality recording, and by and large was a tape recording made
at the Willard Hotel around the time of the March on Washington. I
don't know exactly when. We were in and out of Washington a lot. And
[it] was basically just a bunch of preachers that were relaxin' after a
meeting. And there were long periods of silence in between, so it was almost like people were comin' and goin'. Toward the end there was a
recording of somebody moanin' and groanin' as though they were in the
act of sexual intercourse, but it didn't sound like anybody I knew, and
certainly not Martin.

You didn't consider it incriminating?

Well, no it wasn't. I think that typifies everything we got from the
FBI. . . . See the reporters said that—well, say John Herbers, the New
York *Times,* said, "The FBI says they have all of this incriminating evidence of stuff, wild parties and stuff like that." And so I'd always ask,
"Well, did *you* see it or did *you* hear it?" And I never yet found anybody to say that they actually saw any pictures of anything or heard any
tape recordings of anything that they consider authentic. They always
said, "But the FBI says they have it." And so we have always assumed

---

* King's suspicions were well founded. In 1975, the Senate Select Committee on
Intelligence established beyond reasonable doubt that FBI harassment of King
had the personal sanction of FBI Director J. Edgar Hoover.

that they *were* trying to smear Martin, to cut down his influence and intimidate us.

The strain between SCLC and the FBI became a public issue after King suggested that Southern FBI agents had been less than zealous in their investigations of civil rights violations. Hoover responded by calling King "the most notorious liar in the country." At that point, SCLC leaders requested a meeting with Hoover to discuss their differences. The meeting took place at FBI headquarters in Washington on December 1, 1964, only a week before King was to leave for Oslo. As soon as the SCLC delegation sat down in the director's office, Hoover took charge of the meeting, steering the discussion away from the problems the civil rights leaders had hoped to explore.

I mean, he took it over and never stopped talking, he was so praising of Martin and the work that he was doing and his winning the Nobel Prize that it really was kinda disarming to us. It looked like the guy was really tryin' to do a job in Mississippi, and he assured us at that meeting that he was about to make an arrest. . . . And so when he was bendin' over backwards tryin' to show us that he was doin' the job, it was kinda hard to bring up another subject when he took up all the time.

But there was never any mention of this "notorious liar" business, and we never mentioned any of the threats. It was a completely—well, the word that DeLoach* used in his write-up on it afterwards was it was sorta like it was a "love feast." And I don't think it was that. I don't like *that* term. But what it was, each person tried to talk about what it was in the other person that they respected. . . . Ralph talked about the respect we had for Hoover as a manager of a massive federal crime-fighting agency. And Hoover really went so far as to congratulate Martin on winning the Nobel Prize and all kinda stuff, and toward the end, we said, "Well, maybe the problem we have is just one of a lack of communication and maybe we oughta stay in touch more." Martin assigned me and Hoover assigned DeLoach and said we oughta talk with each other more regularly. When we got out we had a basic press conference. The press was there waiting, and we had a statement for the press which was very disappointing to them because they were expecting fireworks and a big fight. And so they never believed what went on inside.

---

* Cartha "Deke" DeLoach, Hoover's Georgia-born assistant, sat in on the meeting. With King and Young in the SCLC group were Walter Fauntroy, director of SCLC's Washington office, and Rev. Abernathy, who was the visitors' spokesman. After "the first five minutes when Ralph opened it up—five minutes or less—Hoover talked nonstop for fifty minutes," says Young.

We were disappointed, though, that we didn't face the issue, so Martin decided that I should go back without him to talk to Hoover, and we tried to set up another appointment. The appointment date was set up, but when we got to the FBI agency, we only were able to meet with DeLoach. . . . I just took the lead, and I tried to get them to talk about the rumors that we were getting back from the press. In between that time we had had a meeting with the New York *Times'* Washington bureau where they told us the kind of stuff that they [the FBI sources] were saying . . . that Martin had a Swiss bank account, that we were infiltrated by Communists, and that there was some kind of perverted sensuality or sexuality that predominated in the Movement. I tried to get DeLoach to talk about it and about the fact that the FBI was spreading this kinda information to church leaders, to newspaper people, and the like. And he assured me that the FBI wouldn't do something like that . . .*

I told him that I had actually caught FBI agents following us around and assumed that they were bugging our rooms and things like that and named some of the places. There were a couple of motels that we stayed in around the country, that we stayed in often, and I mean it's not hard to find these little plain green Plymouths [laughs] with two-way radios in them. They're so conspicuous as to be obvious. They're the only cars in the lot that look like that. And so whenever we'd come into a motel and see one of those already parked, we'd know they were there and that the place was bugged. And I'd usually walk around the motel, and you look in the rooms, and the curtain is partially drawn, and you see a guy sitting down with earphones on and a tape recorder, and you know what he's listening to. . . .

It occurs to me that it would have been a logical thing to complain to the attorney general or the President at this point. Did you consider it?

Well, it wasn't . . . First of all, President Kennedy kinda told Martin himself that he was bein' bugged. And in one of the meetings around the March on Washington, when the leaders went to the White House, President Kennedy asked Martin to stay after the other civil rights leaders left, and they walked out in the garden, and President Kennedy asked

---

* The Senate Select Committee on Intelligence established that in a six-year period the FBI made sixteen telephone taps to eavesdrop on King's conversations and bugged eight of his hotel rooms. At one point the FBI published a monograph using information gleaned from its spying and began circulating it around Washington. When President Kennedy learned of this, he ordered Hoover to recall all copies.

about whether or not there was any Communist influence in SCLC, and said that Senator Eastland and the Dixiecrats were trying to use the Communist presence in SCLC to say that the Civil Rights Movement was Communist-inspired and that was what they were gonna use to fight the Civil Rights Bill. And President Kennedy said, in effect, that they were gonna be watchin' us pretty closely, and if we had anybody that was in any way vulnerable that we oughta get rid of 'em very quickly. And Martin came back saying that the President was afraid to talk in his own office, and he said—and he was kinda laughing about it—he said, "I guess Hoover must be buggin' him, too."

By this time, he believes, King had accepted leadership of the Movement as an inescapable burden.

I got the impression, though, that toward the latter years, he took it much too seriously and it was really gettin' him down.

Why do you say that?

It just was. He couldn't relax. He couldn't sleep . . . other than the times that he spent with his family. Even when we were away on trips, he'd wanna talk all night long . . . he talked out ideas. He made his speeches to us before he made 'em publicly. And just physically, I was afraid—in fact, I had had a talk with him shortly before his death saying that he was pushing himself so hard. My feeling was that we had gotten past the Selmas and the dangerous days when we all took it for granted that we might die any day. I said, "Looks like we're gonna be around a little while. You oughta go have a good physical examination . . . start takin' a little better care of yourself."

Postscript: In 1972 Andrew Young became the first black politician elected to the U.S. Congress from the Deep South since Reconstruction. At the time of his election over sixty percent of the voters in his Atlanta district were white. In 1976 his early support of Jimmy Carter's presidential candidacy helped attract the black voters who provided Carter's margin of victory in several important primaries and in the general election. When Carter was asked to list all the people to whom he was politically indebted, he said, "Andy Young." Columnists began referring to him as the most influential black in the new administration. In January, 1977, by appointment from President Carter, he became the first black to serve as United States ambassador to the United Nations.

DOROTHY COTTON

A Woman's Place

She was the highest-ranking woman on SCLC's executive staff and is now an administrator in Atlanta's city government.

I'm conscious of the fact that I did have a decision-making role, but I'm also very conscious of the male chauvinism that existed within the Movement. I was on the executive staff, and that's where a lot of decisions got made, but I'm also aware that like any other place . . . historically, where there was a female sitting, she was always asked to go get the coffee and to take the notes. And interestingly enough, it was a male member of our staff who finally protested that, because I was the education director, I needed to be a part of the deliberations. If we needed someone to take minutes, we needed to bring someone into the meeting, he said, whose job that was . . . There was that kind of role delineation relative to women and men in the Movement.

SCLC was dominated by black preachers . . .

Right.

Do they have a particular problem with male chauvinism?

Oh, I think so. I think they [laughing] are some of the most chauvinistic of them all. . . .

How about Dr. King in terms of women's rights . . . ?

[Laughing] I think that he, too, comes right out of the same society, and he would have had a lot to learn and a lot of growing to do as the Women's Movement took on the momentum that it has taken on. He would have had a lot of growing to do.

Why do you say that?

Well, I don't separate him out at that level from the other Baptist preachers and Methodist preachers that were around our executive staff table, or board table. [Pauses, chuckles] He's probably just turned over in his grave.

Would he have resisted?

No, I don't think he would have resisted. I really don't, because he died saying we've gotta take all oppressed people, and my hope and dream—and maybe it's fantasy—but it is that he would have seen that women are an oppressed class. I don't know how he could have preached what he preached and could not have seen that, too, but it might have been a painful lesson he had to learn. But I think he would have learned it. He would have had to.

He would have been trapped by his own rhetoric.

Yeah, to put it candidly, he would have been. [Laughing] Right. Right.

Her response to the FBI slander campaign:

The man was about love and peace and nonviolence. . . . Nobody can take that away. So what is this need, I ask myself, to allude to anything in his personal life that they may suspect or create or even know? What's it got to do with anything?

J. Edgar Hoover called him the "most notorious liar . . ." I can't even dignify that with a response. I don't want to. Dr. King was a human being, and all that that implies, and I think a marvelous human being, and I loved being in his company, and so did all the people who

worked [in SCLC]. He drew people to him, is what I really wanna say.
He really drew people to him, and someday I'd like to figure out what it
was about him that made people want to be around him, because they
did. We knew him close up, and knowing him close up, I still can feel
the same kind of *awe,* if you will, in his presence and about his whole
person. . . . As well as I knew him, I feel what people felt from a distance, who loved him and cared and almost stood in awe of him. I share
that feeling, too. . . . When I *realized* that, it was almost shocking to
me that I could feel that.

Is there a bond among those of you who were in the inner circle?

Absolutely, that will never be broken. If we live to eighty and not see
each other from now to then, I think that bond will be there. I experienced it a little bit last night. Even those of us who don't see eye-to-eye
on a lot of things. I think of Hosea Williams. I don't see eye-to-eye on a
lot of things with Hosea, but there is a bond I feel with Hosea that will
never be broken. I saw him last night for the first time in a long time,
and I just walked up and hugged him. . . . I mean, I've gotten really
mad at Hosea, really wanna put him in a trunk and shut the door and sit
on it sometimes, but there is a bond. And I told Hosea that I was quoting him very recently in a speech from way back, from his Savannah,
Georgia, days. . . . I remember his saying he would grit his teeth and
say, "One day *my* little boy is gonna sit on that stool at that lunch
counter and *spin* around like this little [white] boy. . . ." It was just a
good feeling. At the moment I saw him I forgot about anything that I
ever disagreed with him on. It was just good. So the bond is there. We
love each other, and I think we always will. It was my family. . . .

Hosea Williams

He was director of the SCLC field staff. His speciality was confrontation.

There was a group that had been with Dr. King for some time . . . Andy and Dorothy and Bernard Lee . . . I'm sure that they were somewhat concerned about others gettin' too close to Dr. King, and I was one of the guys they were concerned about. . . . There were some roadblocks, political roadblocks, thrown in my path in getting closer and closer to King. But I got close to Ralph, who was the *closest* to King, so that gave me a direct inroad to him. There's a lotta politics in the Movement.

But you see, one of the things that was natural about the Movement was the fact that Andy Young . . . was the conservative of the staff and I was the militant, and always there was the debate: Who was right, Andy or myself? And Dr. King usually would take some position in between, sometime extremely close to me, sometime extremely close to Andy.

But you were always ready to keep the pressure on.

Yes, I never believed that any progress can be made other than through confrontation. Andy believed that a lot of things could be ac-

complished around a table, and I just didn't believe it 'cause I think a
mental thing had to take place first in white people's mind. . . . I
thought you really had to take him to some type of physical confrontation and hurt his pocketbook was the main way—boycotts and things
of that sort—to bring him around, really to convince him.

I remember one time . . . there was a big stink about who was going
to now control the SCLC field staff. Awright, James Bevel supposedly
had been over the field staff. There was two cliques in SCLC, the James
Bevel clique, which was pretty much the Andy Young clique, and the
Hosea Williams clique, and they were talkin' 'bout I shouldn't be over
the staff 'cause I was too rough and too gangsterlike, and I shouldn't be
over the staff because I drive people and I dehumanize . . . all kinda
stuff. And we were sitting up in this meetin' and a boy named Willie
Bolden . . . I'm in this meetin' just bein' quiet . . . and Bolden said,
"Well, I just wanna say sumpin'. Dr. King, we love you, but Hosea is
our leader. . . ."
And I said, "Oh, Lord, he done killed me." But you know what Dr.
King said? Dr. King said, he said, "I understand what you saying,
Willie." He said, "Y'all found God through Hosea. Y'all found hope for
the future. You found *yourselves* through Hosea . . . way back in Sa-
vannah 'fore I ever met you."

What attracted Dr. King to me . . . one of his ingeniouses, was his
ability to choose a personality for a given job. And if you look around
him—like James Bevel* was probably the greatest mind in the country
for dealing with young people, Andrew Young probably the greatest
mind in the country for dealing with white people. . . . I was one of
the greatest minds in the country to get people aroused, and my job was
to go into the towns and break the hold that the power structure had on
the people and get them aroused and get them to marchin', picketin',
demonstratin', and goin' to jail. That's how I ended up in jail ninety-six
times, 'cause that was my job. Dr. King saw in me that part of me that I
could arouse others and get others to stand up.

*But the barely contained rage, the roaring voice, the prizefighter build
which served him so well against the cracker sheriffs did, indeed, make*

* Rev. Bevel, who is mentioned in several interviews, was an SCLC tactician
who played a major role in planning the Birmingham and Selma campaigns. He
was particularly adept at getting black high school students involved in demonstrations. After King's death, Bevel drifted away from the Atlanta group of SCLC
veterans and moved to Chicago.

him the maverick of the SCLC staff. They were seminary-trained ministers. He tacked a "Rev." on his name because it helped him organize. To them King was the Movement. He had already led a major campaign in Savannah on his own before he ever met King. The others, like King himself, were products of the black middle class. "I don't know whether the classes ever believed me or not; most of the people in the classes thought I was hustling. But the masses have a knack of believing in me. . . ." For he had shared their experience, and it had formed him.

I was born in poverty. My mother was never married to my father, which was a stigma in the American society. . . . I was reared up in Decatur County, Georgia . . . that's southwest Georgia, and the racism of segregation was so prevalent until it was something that you had to notice, like black farmers couldn't plant tobacco. They didn't allow black men to plant tobacco, 'cause there's a lot of money in it. White people virtually owned black people . . . they'd concoct debts, like you get in jail, all the white man had to do, to come there, and the sheriff would let you out, and the white man tell the sheriff to tell you he paid a hundred dollars for you, but you didn't have to worry 'bout that hundred dollars long as you stay on his farm and work. If you ever left to go to Florida, he'd come get you, arrest you and bring you back . . . There's a white man down there named Wonnie Miller. On the Wonnie Miller farm, all the blacks were born and worked and lived and died in poverty, and they worked like slaves from "cain't to cain't"—say, "Ya cain't see your hand before your face when you go out in the field, and ya cain't see your hand when you come in from the field," because it was dark each time. And Mr. Wonnie used to ride a big horse and never really worked, and he died a millionaire. All his children are rich. . . .

We used to walk two and a half miles to school . . . the white kids always had a bus. No black kids were allowed to ride the bus, and I guess every day of my life—it looked like to me every day, probably just my imagination—those white kids would spit on us or throw rocks at us, holler, and call us "niggers." *Every* day. Pick at us, and I just knew that was not right.

In my early life once whites tried to lynch me about a little white girl that was from a very poor family that lived up there. Her father was a bum, wouldn't work; all he did was fish and hunt all the time, just like some of the black families. The word got around that I was havin' affair with the girl. This was a rumor, and they came to the house to lynch me . . . and my grandfather stood 'em off with a gun. We went over to white man's house, Mr. Wonnie Miller, who took the thing up and stopped the whites. . . .

The vast majority of blacks was reared in the same circumstances I was reared in. It's just hard for me to see how they can go along and take it. Then I educated myself and became a professional person. I thought you could escape black America by being educated and professional and being rich, and you just cain't do it.

He became a chemist with the U.S. Department of Agriculture Bureau of Entomology in Savannah.

I was paid well. I went right up, straight up the ladder. I was accepted, *I thought,* but what I really finally decided, I had hit that "nigger ceiling." They wasn't gonna let me go no higher. . . . I had more publication than all the white guys put together, except an old Ph.D. who had thirty years in the lab. So the assistant chief's job became open, and I thought sure they'd make me the assistant chief, because I thought they had accepted me as a scientist. And they gave the job to a white girl who knew very little chemistry, and that was a very hard pill for me to swallow. But you know the old thing 'bout how Jackie Robinson made it in baseball, the old poem, "Life Ain't Been No Christmas Day," and all this jazz, so I bought it and buckled my bed up: "After all, I'm black and she's white. My day comin'."

I remember one time after I bought this new home and new car. . . . You know, I was a social climbin', middle-class Negro. I guess I was the first black person in Savannah to have a zoysia lawn. I remember buying this grass from Sears and Roebuck, and had sodded my lawn, and I was out there one day tryin' to water it, and my hose would not stretch to sprinkle across the whole lawn. I had a big lot there. And I went back up to this new drugstore . . . gonna buy some hose connectors, an extension to a hose. . . . And I carried my two sons with me. They wasn't but about six and seven, six and eight years old then, and as we walked into this drugstore, it had a long lunch counter and these white kids were sittin' on these stools, spinnin' around, eatin' hot dogs and drinkin' Co-cola.

And my boys started askin' me, "Daddy, let's get a sandwich and a Coke." But I always will believe what they wanted to do was play on those stools, and I said, "Naw, you cain't have a Coke and sandwich." And one of 'em started cryin'. And I said, "Well, you know, I'm gonna take you back home and Momma'll fix you a hot dog and give you a Coke," and then both of 'em started cryin'. And both of them just fell out in the floor, which was very unusual for my kids to do me like that. And I remember stoopin' down and I started cryin', because I realized I couldn't tell 'em the truth. The truth was they was black and they didn't 'low black people to use them lunch counters. So I picked the two kids up and went back to the car and I guess I made 'em a promise that I'd bring 'em back someday. So that really got me involved.

. . . you made yourself one or you verbally made them one?

Well, I verbally made it to 'em. They was probably too young to understand what I meant, but I said, "Someday I'll bring you back." Then I started workin' to integrate public accommodations.

> . . . I started with Mr. W.W. Law* and the NAACP. . . . I heard about Dr. King, and I was very fascinated by him, and I started teaching nonviolence and training students in nonviolence, even though I didn't believe in it. I started using it as a tactic, and I led the first sit-ins in Savannah. . . . I organized and led 'em there for Mr. Law. Mr. Law never did go to jail. I was vice-president of the branch. . . .

I had the largest marches in the history of the Movement there. We started them night marches. I marched eight thousand people at night in Savannah, Georgia, see, and that's what broke 'em up. They'd have so damn many of us, they'd arrest us as long as they could arrest, and just wasn't nowhere to put us. I remember the time they carried a bunch of us out to Tybee and just had a big old fence, about three or four acre land, and put us in there, and we slept out like cattle . . . no bathroom, and they fed us gallons of pork'n beans. They'd cut the top out and set the whole gallon, and you'd stick your hand down there and get you some pork'n beans.

The other weapon, I had a good young boy down there, young boy, Ben Clark, which was my right arm, and I had a lotta young people who would really think. And they did most of the thinkin' and I did the actin'. . . . Ben would march the kids downtown every day. . . .

I'd watch that clock. That's one thing the old supervisor was upset with.** I'd watch that clock. Soon as that clock said *twelve* [claps his hands, speaks rapidly as if narrating a race], I'd have my lunch. I'd take out and jump in the car and take off downtown, eating all the same time. Didn't take but ten minutes to drive downtown, and they got a old

---

* The Savannah NAACP president.

** He was still working as a U.S. Department of Agriculture chemist. Shortly afterward, he secured a leave of absence to devote a year to civil rights work. He never returned to his old job.

rock downtown in that park. They call it the Tomochichi Rock,* and I'd jump on the Tomochichi Rock and speak for ten minutes and jump off the 'Chichi Rock—somebody was drivin' the car about the block—and jump in the car. *Every day* I was doin' that, and I'd take off back, and I'd make it back to that office at twelve-thirty. . . .

You see, here's a significant point. When my boys couldn't eat at that lunch counter, I remember callin' this little group of kids together that worked with me. One of the things that I pride myself in is my ability to relate to young people. I don't ever mess with anybody around my age. My wife's the only friend or companion I have old as I am. I don't mess with old people, 'cause they think too old. They wanna talk about they miseries and all that kinda mess. You hang around young folk, you'll think like young people, see. And I remember calling this meeting of these young guys, and I told 'em what had happened to me, and how it hurt me, and I told those kids, I said, "What way can we break these lunch counters? Time is out for segregation. It's wrong the way these people treat us." And those kids met. The next day they met with me and said, "We got a plan."

Well, Ben Clark was small and short and *black*—typical little small Negro man—but had a voice like a lion. Really, that voice could damn near shatter glasses, and bein' his size, he always tried to act and show up as a big man. Ben was very popular, very popular. . . . Ben said, "I tell you what we gonna do." Ben said, "I'm gon' lead a group to jail." So I said, "You sure you mean it?" Ben said, "You better figure out how to get us out. . . . We got three black high schools. I'm gon' get the captain of each of them football teams, and we goin' someplace and get in jail at one of these lunch counters." Said, "You get us out. . . . The next day I'm gon' get them same captains of them football teams and the *queen* from each school, and I'm gon' carry them to jail. . . . The next time I'm gonna have the captain of the football team, the queen, and the head of the student body." . . . Everything worked dead to Hoyle's letter until 'bout the fourth day, and hell, fourth day they musta arrested four or five hundred kids. We was carryin' all them popular kids to jail, see. The kids was carryin' me faster than I could think and go. To me, this was really revolution. They just was taking over Savannah then. The old police chief 'bout to go crazy. [Laughs]

And how I got into the night march thing was, that night I didn't know *what* to do. We had a church full of people. Honestly we had about a thousand people, and I didn't know what the hell to do. I was frustrated, didn't know what to do, and I was worried about people get-

---

* After a Creek Indian chief who befriended the first settlers.

ting killed and all that, and my name being blasted out the saddle on the radio and TV. "This terrible man tearing up our town." And these boys was back there messing with these girls, and they wanted to take these girls out, and I said, "No, we gon' have night march." . . . And that's the reason we had the night march. Went downtown and the man beat hell outa us and arrested a bunch of us. The next night we had a *ocean* of people. We had more people than any two or three churches around there could hold.

They arrested me at my house that night about two-thirty or three-thirty in the morning, and someone knocked on my door, and I was stupid enough to open the door, and these two white guys had these .38s cocked. And I thought they was Klansmen, 'cause they was dressed just about like you dressed now. Nothing would say they were policemen. And they didn't even show me no badges. They just said, "Let's go. You under arrest." Well, the first thing I said was, "It's the Klans . . . I got a choice. If I don't go with them, they gonna blow my brains out right here, and my wife and my children will forever remember that. But if I go with 'em, they'll probably take me out in the woods and kill me. And if they are gonna kill me, I'd rather for it to happen that way, you know, than blow my brains all over my house, and my wife and children would have that horrible memory."

So I went with them. Well, I found out they made all the right turns . . . heading right toward town. So they made all the right turns, and I got down there, and they said, "Well, we got you for two peace bonds at $2,500 each." I said, "Man, give me a bed." [Laughs] It was a joke to me, you know, and the next morning, my wife came to get me, and they said, "Well, Miz Williams, it's gone up $5,000 more." So she went back and got a $10,000 bond. The first day they ran it up $30,000, and old Mullins* had a stack of them peace bonds 'cause Bobby Kennedy even called him. He really didn't intend for me to get outa jail.** . . . My bond went up $120,000.

But them kids marched every night. They burnt Sears and Roebuck down. They burnt Firestone. Savannah was really in trouble. All right, Mills B. Lane*** called me. To me Mills B. Lane was a legend. The Mills B. Lane family is from Savannah, the Lane family, but he's like a legend down there, Mills B. Lane. And the sheriff came over there and got me out the cell and handcuffed me and carried me up to the jail-

* A municipal judge in Savannah.
** He was to stay in jail for sixty-five days, the longest sentence served by any major figure in the Southern Movement.
*** The C&S bank president. He called as a would-be mediator.

house, up to the sheriff's office, and took the handcuffs off and said, "Answer the phone." I picked up the phone and I said, "Hello." And the fellow on the phone said, "Hey, this is Mills B. Lane, Jr., president of C&S Bank." I knew he was lying; I hung the phone up. So, man, the sheriff went crazy: "Goddamn your soul." [Laughs] And I picked the phone back up, and I dialed the phone, and I said, "Operator, I want to speak to Mr. Mills B. Lane, Jr., in the C&S Bank in Atlanta, Georgia." So sure 'nuff she got him back, and he said, "What happened?" I said, "I hung up." He said, "I don't have time to play." I said, "Well, I'm not playing. I didn't believe it was you." He said, "I wanna make a deal with you. Savannah is my home and I don't wanna see that city burned down. They say you are running that movement from the jailhouse. I want you to stop those demonstrations, and if you stop those demonstrations, I'll make it possible for you to get out."

Meanwhile, his wife and his lawyer had been trying to find enough black property owners to guarantee his bond. They had failed because Judge Mullins insisted that a separate piece of property be used to secure each of the peace bonds.

Well, see, they didn't find but one Negro in Savannah that had enough of them deeds. . . . He was in the faith-healing business, a kind of rootman like,* named Russell Lavender. So my wife and my lawyer came by the jail that morning so happy. "Russell's gonna get you out. . . . Russell decided to put up his property."

And so they was down there verifyin' those deeds, that it was no lien against them, in old Judge Mullins' office. So Russell, just makin' conversation, said, "Judge, how long you think my property be up?"

Old Judge Mullins said, "Oh, about twenty-five years if I have anything to do about it." You know, that guy got his deeds and went home. [Laughs]

And I'm sittin' in the jail so long, just know I'm goin' home. I done got packed up, my little stuff. And they don't let nobody out of jail down there after 4:30 and I kept watchin' that clock down the hall: 4:00, 4:05, 4:10. At 4:30, man, I was settin' up there with water comin' out my eyes, and my wife was 'shamed to come back and let me know that they couldn't get me out.

But Mills B. Lane, what he did, he told Russell Lavender to put the property up, and *he* would put at Lavender's disposal $125,000 at the

---

* A dealer in John-the-Conqueror root, which is used to cast and remove spells in voodoo rites still practiced by a few blacks in remote areas of coastal Georgia. These rites are a holdover from the unique Gullah culture of slavery times.

bank. He could have that much of a draw. See, this guy used his property for wheelin' and dealin' in real estate, so he could go down to the bank and say, "Give me $30,000," or, "Give me $40,000," as long as them deeds was up, see. 'Cause the man's property was worth, hell, several times that much. . . .

So when Mr. Lane said that . . . man, I wanted to get outa jail so bad, 'cause a lotta things happened in my mind in jail. I guess I been very lucky—or it's been the will of God—to go through certain experiences that prepare me for certain other, more tryin' ordeals. Like when I was sittin' in jail, I thought about my wife runnin' around on me, see. I thought about I probably done lost my job, gonna lose my house and my car. What's gonna happen to my children? All kindsa mean things you think about, see. Because a man in jail . . . in confinement by yoself, and the only friends you had was roaches and some bloodstained walls, man. Day after day and night after night, and the only thing you see is them mean, crazy guards. They had some of the *dumbest* guards down there, them jailhouse guards. They wasn't paying the guys 'bout forty dollars a week, so you know what kinda mentality they can hire for forty dollars a week. One just come in there and spit at me, said, "All you want, nigger, is a white woman. You don't want no freedom, nigger. You just tryin' to get to these white women." All that old stuff, day after day after day, you know.

So Mills B. Lane said he would make it possible for me to get outa jail, if I'd call off all the demonstrations, and I never will forget that. That was probably one of the great moments of my life, when I said, "Mr. Lane"—'cause God knows nobody knows how bad I wanted to get outa that jailhouse—I said, "Mr. Lane, if you get me out today, and those lunch counters and restaurants and things are just as segregated, y'all are going to have to put me back in here tomorrow 'cause I'm gonna lead another march." [Laughs] I don't believe I would have if he'da got me out, but I told him that. He said, "Well, uh, we gonna take care of that, too." He sent his lawyer over. The C&S lawyer came over to my cell and we sat down and we drew this thing up, the desegregation plan, and I got outa jail.

The way they did it in Savannah, they formed the Committee of 100, who were the richest and most influential white men and women in that town, this Committee of 100, and they would take blacks and go to the lunch counters to eat. I remember one night, they was picketing a theater, and we went to the theater with the head of the Union Bag, that's the largest plant there, the Union Bag Paper Corporation—one of the head men from Union Bag and myself and my wife and he and his wife and a couple of other people. And the Ku Klux Klan was picketing the filling station, but they worked out at Union Bag, and they saw this man's car and recognized him and *ran,* took the picket signs and ran. [Laughs]

But Dr. King spoke in Savannah, Georgia, in 1963, and Dr. King said, "Savannah, Georgia, is the most integrated city south of the Maxon-Dixon line." So I saw some ready results from my works, and I've always had a lotta faith. I've always respected the Southern white man beyond the Northern white man. The Southern white man has always been more honest about segregation than the Northern white man. The Northern white man claimed the barriers were down, but they were very much up. But the Southern white man let you know in no uncertain terms, "Nigger, I don't want you eatin' in my business." And I've always felt that the Southern white man was much more religious. When he says something, he means it more. So when he tells ya, "You can come on in now," he's 'bout not joking. He pretty much means that you can come on in.

Did you make a point of going back to that . . . lunch counter you took your boys to?

Yeeah . . . That drugstore musta had a lunch counter, I guess it musta been ten or twelve stools. And yeah, man, I carried those boys back there. That was one of the happiest days of my life.

Ah. [Laughs] I remember the first night after I got outa jail, we integrated the DeSoto Hotel. This Committee of 100 arranged all this. We stayed at the hotel. But you know, it's a funny thing about black people. I never will forget how *proud* those waiters were that night. Can you imagine? Well, like me, I tell people, all my life I walked by them lunch counters, and I never thought about sittin' down there. I just know that wasn't for me. It was always a subconscious thing to me, see. So those waiters . . . I remember that night how they tried to wait on us. My wife was raised up a poor girl, but her momma's a maid . . . working for the rich white folk. Some of it rubbed off on them, so my wife was used to silverware. . . . I never will forget how proud. That guy [their waiter] told my wife, said, "I just have to tell you, lady, you sho' can work out with that silverware. [Laughs] You sho' can work out with that silverware." But he was just *proud* of us. Then we left the dining room and sat out in the lobby. Then we just walked around. We was guests of the hotel. We had checked into that hotel, see.

Well, that evenin' before I went out, I carried my boys out to that lunch counter, and we sat there and drank Co-colas and ate hot dogs and spin around them stools. [Laughs] Them white folks was so mad, I tell you [still laughing], they were so mad, man. We sat there. The man finally closed the lunch counter down. We still sat there, spinning on them stools. I said, "It's been long time comin', boys, so let's enjoy it." [Pauses] Yeah, I went back to that drugstore. Old man and I used to laugh about it a lot, old manager.

For a time his star rose rapidly in NAACP. He became a state vice president. In 1962 when the NAACP had its national convention in Atlanta, he ran for the national board of directors.

I was campaignin' for the Mississippi delegation and the South Carolina delegation, and they told me, "You don't have you own state." Well, that was kinda like tellin' a man, "You don't have your own *family*. . . . Your family won't vote for you." So I went back and found out. . . . Roy Wilkins had interceded. He thought I was too militant for the NAACP, and for that reason, Mr. Law was gonna take the delegation against me. So I was pretty much booted out of NAACP, so I kinda needed some place to go, anyway.

But I had been fascinated by King, because the difference in King's leadership and other leaders' leadership—King show you what to do, the others'll tell you what to do. In other words, NAACP sends out a memorandum. I don't know how many times Roy Wilkins been in jail, but Roy Wilkins would write me letters and *tell* me how to get free. And Dr. King, I found him out in the streets leadin' the people, showing them how to get free. So that's what attracted me to him.

I never will forget. It really hurt me. I walked out. . . . Dr. King was right round here on another street down here then, 'bout two blocks over where his office was. And I had never met him really to know him, and I walked out that convention hall cryin', and I went round to his office and asked 'em could I see him. . . . So when I told him my problem, I said, "I wanta work with you. I'd like to work with this organization."

Postscript: In 1974 he was elected to the Georgia House of Representatives, and he is now one of Atlanta's most influential politicians.

Randolph Blackwell

He was a professor at a black college in Huntsville, Alabama, when the sit-ins started. His involvement with the students led to a job with the Voter Education Project in Atlanta. Before long, SCLC, which was notorious for pirating employees from other organizations, had spotted him.

I remember distinctly the interview that led to the hiring, and I gained a great respect for Dr. King because of the way that the interview went. The time that I was invited over, he was in his bedroom resting. Me, Andrew Young and Dorothy Cotton went into his bedroom. He wanted to ask me some questions and I remember the questions. He asked me first how did I feel about nonviolence? I said to him that I was committed to nonviolence, that I didn't arrive at my commitment to nonviolence theologically, that I arrived at it as a social scientist, but that I was firmly committed to nonviolence. The next question he asked me was why did I want to work for SCLC? I said to him that I thought SNCC was philosophically sounder than SCLC, but that I had personally known the agony of having something to say and no platform from which to say it, and that he had the platform. He said, "That's good enough for me," and that was the end of the interview . . . [Laughs] I've reflected on it many times because that was the kind of response that I think could have turned a lot of people off . . . but it didn't disturb him.

Did it present any problems for a social scientist such as yourself coming into an organization that was composed largely of ministers?

No, I came with the attitude that I would lose most of the fights I'll have here. [Laughs] But I'll get more done than I would if I stand on the sideline. I had a conversation with myself that went: "Now, Randolph, now you're gonna lose most of your arguments."

Looking back on it, it was a very strange organization. . . . You had an executive staff of fourteen highly egotistical, stubborn, arrogant people, who were strongly convicted, but willing to lay aside their strong convictions for *a* unity. Hosea is a very strong-willed, strongly convicted person, right or wrong. Certainly C.T. Vivian is a very strong, egotistical person. We all were. . . . The miraculous part of that whole organization was the fact that Martin could hold that kind of team together, and yet I don't say he held it together. There was kind of a commitment to a broader something than any one of us had been involved in. . . . The something, whatever it was to be, could be only through the joint efforts of all of us.

Oh, we used to have terrible staff meetings. [Laughs] I remember we had a retreat once and we had somebody in the retreat from New York. I don't remember who it was . . . but it was kind of a passerby, and we never felt compelled to have private staff meetings. If you passed by and we were having a staff meeting, chances are you could sit right in on the meeting. I remember this person walked out after the first morning session . . . and he said, "Phew, that kinda meeting would tear up any organization I ever belonged to. It's interesting that you guys are still intact." We used to really have some very interesting staff meetings.

Congressman Young mentioned himself being in what he called—in quotes—a conservative branch of the SCLC leadership.

We used to always say of Andy—very much in jest and very affectionately, you understand—that Andy was the Uncle Tom of SCLC, but that's too simple an explanation. Andy had, and possesses even now, the unique capacity to find the avenue to reconcile divergent points of view when the moment comes that all that can be gotten out of a situation has been gotten. The idea was to reconcile and wait for another day. In those instances where we needed to get out of a demonstration, Andy could always find a way to save our face without necessarily completely capitulating. . . .

If he stood at that pole . . .

Competing for the other end would be Hosea and Fred Shuttlesworth.

And where would you fit on that continuum?

I would say I would be found sitting on the sideline borrowing from both, but more inclined to the Hosea-Shuttlesworth end of it. [Laughs]

What did you do during the Selma period . . . ?

What was my job? . . . I had the stay-at-home job. I kept the store. I was not in the field in the sense that the other staff persons were. To a very great extent my job was handling the mobilization, handling the resources for the march, and handling the media from the Atlanta end. By that I mean making certain that all of the organizations that had a history of protest was notified and invited. Say, for example, if you got two thousand trade unions and you can afford from a budget standpoint to send two hundred telegrams, it then becomes a question of which two hundred unions do you wire and say, "Come." If you've got five hundred women's organizations and you can afford to send twenty-five telegrams, which twenty-five out of five hundred do you wire and say, "Come"? And that's a matter of making the distinction between which organizations have a history of protest and which organizations have no history. No need of sending a telegram to the Railroad Machinists. They've never marched in their own defense, so they certainly aren't going to come to Selma to march with you on your issues. You don't send a telegram to the League of Women Voters, 'cause marching ain't their thing, but you send it to the Women's Strike For Peace, 'cause they've been out in the street for the past fifty years. You raise the issue, they'll raise their banner. [Laughs] You follow me? . . .

Further down, as we got closer to the big march, then of course, it was a matter of getting people in there, physically in there. You see, Selma doesn't have a railroad station, didn't have much of a bus station, didn't have an airport. So how do you move ten thousand people in and out? And there were the logistical questions. And then, of course, there were resources to be had on the marches. Where do you get food for three thousand people without buying it?

I don't know. How did you do that?

Well, you pick up the phone and you call the Packinghouse Workers, and you say, "We need food, and the march has already started, and they're gonna bed down in six hours. We need raisins, we need fresh fruit, we need canned fruit, we need gallons of spaghetti, we need gallons of chili beans. Things that you can just take out of the can and heat." See, people forget that there was no food committee and yet there were two and three thousand people to be fed. If a church is gonna entertain two thousand people, they want three or four months to get ready. Then they set up elaborate committees to prepare the food and to serve the food. Well, you might have come into Selma at that time and somebody might have said, "Hey, you wanna work on the food truck?" "Oh, yeah," and at that point you suddenly became a member of the food committee. You follow me? But it went off, and here again, history will record this and say, "That was . . . a great tactical feat." But it wasn't tactical at all. It wasn't planned, it just happened. . . .

At what point did you realize that the march was gonna be a monster event?

May I tell you that, secretly, I knew three weeks in advance? Because I was determined that it would be. Most of the executive committee of SCLC was not too sure how large it should be. As a matter of fact, Hosea said to me, "Randy has messed up the march pumping all these people in here," and he was screaming, "Shut it out, shut it off, shut it off." And I was constantly wiring and telegramming and cabling people to come. It was very interesting. We used to get cables from people like Lord Bertrand Russell. "Lord Bertrand Russell wired today his best wishes," and people on the staff thought Lord Bertrand Russell just saw it in the paper and wired. No, I wired Lord Bertrand Russell. I sent him a cable. I sent about sixty cables, and we were getting all these funny cablegrams from the Dean of Canterbury and Lord Bertrand Russell which helped the Movement psychologically. We were really *somebody* . . . and I remember Dr. King opening his mail, saying, "W-e-e-ell, Brother Ralph is gonna come and march." Ralph Bunche. I had sent Ralph a telegram telling him as a Nobel Peace Prize holder, he had a responsibility to come. [Laughs]

I felt that this was an historical moment. It was very personal with me. I didn't discuss it with anybody. Didn't check it out. I felt that *this* was the moment when it had to be. And that every force that could be rallied should be rallied at this point. I felt we were strong enough in terms of our own integrity to deal with any criticism that we would run into for the lack of preparation. And strangely enough, there was none.

The great fear that Hosea was expressing at that point was that here are all these people pouring in here and we don't have any blankets and we don't have any so-and-so. I remember on one occasion where he was screaming on the phone that he had to have ten thousand dollars for some blankets, and I said, "Hosea, if you just wait, we'll get some blankets." And then we started calling private hospitals and asking if they had blankets in their warehouses that they could lend to us. And somebody in some private hospital, and I don't remember who now, contacted a private hospital in Boston that had closed. And they had something like two thousand blankets. It was a question of how do ya get two thousand blankets out of Boston and into Selma in the space of three hours, because the march was approaching the point where it was to bed down for the first night. Somebody in Boston volunteered a plane, and the blankets were loaded on that plane and flown to Atlanta. I had been soliciting blankets by radio in Atlanta, and we took a truckload of blankets out to the airport. The man opened the back end of the plane, and the plane was stuffed to the brim. We *packed* those that we had into the plane and the plane flew them into Selma . . . and they were there in time for the first bedding down. We did not have those blankets four hours before they bedded down.

WILLIE BOLDEN

He joined SCLC as an organizer at a salary of fifty dollars every two weeks. "I stayed with SCLC from '62 to '70, and I never made seven thousand dollars a year."

We would have retreats every so often. After a very hard and tough movement, Martin would call for what we called a retreat—in the Army they call it R and R—where we would go and analyze whatever movement. Every major movement that we had. At the completion of that movement we would go someplace like Black Mountain, North Carolina. . . . Or we would go to a little Presbyterian place down about forty miles from Atlanta, where we would just play golf, basketball. Martin was an *excellent* athlete. Cat could really play basketball. Moving around the way he did, spending more time in the air than on the ground, he was in great physical shape. . . . I remember once we were playing basketball, and we were gonna play to the point thirty. And of course by point thirty, most of us were, you know, our tongues were hanging out and were really, really exhausted, and Martin said, "Aw, fellas, come on, let's play another ten points." *Excellent, excellent* physical shape.

We would go off into these retreats and he would sit around and that's where he would not have to show the elegant part of himself with the tie. He wore open shirt, slacks, pair of trousers, maybe bedroom shoes if he felt like it, housecoat. And we just sit around, and for a while we would just reminisce about some of the experiences that some of us had in a particular situation, and he would talk about some of the experiences and the very interesting and uninteresting people he met through traveling. And then maybe we'd do that for the first day, just mess around, and of course we would have cocktails. There has been some word that Martin took a hit every now and then, a drink. I am pleased to say I have never, *never*, never seen him take a drink. Or if he did, he did it when I didn't see him.

Then we would get down and really analyze what took place and why it took place and try to understand some of the mistakes and why we made certain mistakes . . . so we wouldn't make those same mistakes again. He was one hell of a Joe. Okay? He never did believe in pulling rank. He did *only* if it was necessary. Always believed in looking out for his staff. By that I mean, he understood that we weren't makin' no money. Okay? If one of us ran into a tight where we really needed to get some bill collectors off of our backs, you had no problem. You didn't feel guilty about it at all, because he would not make you feel guilty. You would just go to him and tell him what you needed and he would get it for you. . . . He made sho' that we did not have to beg nobody for nothin'. He took the position that you cannot work if you're hungry and you cannot think if you're thirsty.

LEON HALL

A self-described "street kid," he was recruited out of a Montgomery high school in 1965 to become one of the youngest SCLC staff members.

I can remember our discovering regularly spies in SCLC, living amongst us, who worked for the government, and these guys, I can remember our chasing these persons away from the house. And Dr. King . . . immediately after Dr. King's coming out against the war in Vietnam . . . there was a spy under every rug.

How would you discover them?

Little things. I can remember one time in our house right after the Selma-to-Montgomery march, in the SCOPE* House we called it—the Freedom House where most of the staff, the field staff, head-quartered. . . . Big Lester,** who was one of the key staff members,

* SCOPE, the Summer Community Organization and Political Education Project, was an SCLC effort modeled on the Mississippi Freedom Summer of 1964. The plan was to bring volunteers into 120 Deep South counties during the summer of 1965.

** Lester Hankerson, who had followed Hosea Williams up from Savannah, was renowned in SCLC for his size and strength.

had some call to go downstairs in the basement for something. And while down there, he heard someone moving around . . . and discovered a guy back up in the hollows of the basement, and he had a tape recorder. And so Lester pulled him out from under there. Some guy kinda like a Texan with cowboy hat and boots . . . just drifted in, and he was one of our recruits, one of our summer recruits, *we thought*. . . . We came to discover that he had a tape recorder back there and had the house wired all up, and he had us so he was taping us. We just started pulling wires from everywhere. They led through where we had one living room where we held meetings, and he had it bugged something awful. And even the bedrooms. So we tore it loose, and Lester was not too gentle with him and intimidated him somewhat, and finally it all come out that he was a spy. He was a plant. We took all the equipment aloose and made him show us where all of his bugs were, where he had mikes stashed, and we took the stuff out. We didn't harm him though . . . we carried him to the interstate. We let him leave walking, leave all his clothes, didn't let him take anything. We then chased him down the interstate.

Did he say who he worked for?

I think he said he was an FBI. I think he said he was working for the FBI. I'm almost certain he said he was working for the FBI.

At another time, we discovered in Hosea's office—Hosea maintained his administrative office in the house—in Hosea's office we discovered by a window a mike about the size of a nickel. It was stuck right under the window ledge on the inside, and his curtain covered it. Very discreetly hidden, and for some reason, accidentally, someone brushed it, knocked it down, and we discovered, here's a mike. For three or four days or about a week, in fact, we kept it. We put it on Hosea's desk, and we'd take it and talk to it. [Laughs]

In fact, the Movement having become so aware of the spying, Rev. Abernathy came out with a slogan in his speeches. He would talk about "doohickey." He would refer to these little mikes we were discovering, "Now, doohickey, now you go tell that. You tell that now, I hope you get it correct."

J.T. JOHNSON

He was working in New Jersey in 1961 when he turned on a newscast and saw his sister marching in a demonstration in his hometown of Albany, Georgia. He came home, joined the Movement and soon signed on as an SCLC field organizer.

The one thing people used to always say about us, you could catch us in any part of the country, but we was all talkin' about the same thing as if we had caucused, but we never did. We was very close people, everybody in SCLC. . . . We used to call ourselves a family, as a matter of fact. And we stayed like that. We really didn't associate with very many other people. During the sixties we didn't have any outside so-called friends. We'd have parties, it would be our parties. We would have dinner at Thanksgiving, it would be us. We'd have Christmas dinner. It would just be us "family" and with our families, and no one else would be there.

And it was a strange thing, with Dr. King you was never afraid of nothin'. It was just no fear nowhere, and that's the kinda feelin' *I* would get when he was around, and you would always feel differently, as if he was a strange person. . . . We was very good friends, I think, and we knew each other. We did everything together. We'd go swimmin', play softball, basketball, and everything . . . It was a different feelin' when

we was relaxin' . . . but whenever we was in crisis, you would always
feel somethin' when Dr. King was on the scene, and I don't really think
it was the fear of him gettin' assassinated. I don't know what it was, but
it was a strange feelin' you would get, motivated in a sense to go on regardless. I don't care what was out there or who was out there. The
nonviolent would come to you and you would march. If that was time to
march, you would march. Even if they had guns, it didn't bother us. We
would just march on, and I began to study and learn nonviolence and
what it meant. It was amazin', because I kinda come up through pool-
rooms and what have you and in the streets myself. My mother died
when I was very young in life and [I] kinda raised myself, so I had been
through the streets and everything else, and the way to survive out
there was to fight. But when I got involved in the Civil Rights Movement, nonviolence became kinda a way of life more or less with me. At
this point now, I still practice it. I try not to be violent. I keep myself
away from those type incidents.

> . . . I kinda left the SCLC . . . I got married, began to build a
> family. Jobs was hard to find, not as plentiful as they used to be. Dur-
> ing the time of the whole crisis, everybody wanted to hire you . . .
> The people who really got those jobs was not the folks who partici-
> pated in the Civil Rights Movement. We caught hell gettin' jobs . . .
> It wouldn'ta happened if Martin King . . . I took a job at Eastern
> Airlines in ramp service . . . I was twenty-three when I joined SCLC
> and was about thirty-three, thirty-four when I left there . . . Folks
> tell me sometimes about it was a waste of time . . . I wasted a whole
> decade . . . They don't realize the work that we've done, they are
> reapin' the results of it, and had we not done that, they never would
> have been where they are today . . . especially the younger genera-
> tion, they don't realize what happened in the sixties . . . nobody
> talks about it. Nobody teaches them what happened . . . I should
> have gotten a job teachin' about the sixties . . . so the kids today
> would understand *how* and *why* . . . It's not because it came on a
> platter, but people worked hard, people even died. . . .

SCLC today is kind of on its deathbed because of the people in the
country, and to let an organization like this die for the reasons that it's
dyin', I think it's ridiculous. Financial reasons. I think that SCLC has
done more for the nation than any other organization in the country.
Now the NAACP, although it might be older . . . personally I don't
think that they have done half the work. And then maybe they have, but
they haven't done the work in the *way* that we've done it. And I think

that SCLC should be an organization that always lives. But here again money is hard to get and nobody seems to care. And that's why I say the people are kind of complacent. And I raise that question because I think black people ought to support it if nobody else will. But they have come to a point where they don't like to. People are very easy to forget. They don't look that way anymore. Used to be a time that SCLC's phones—we didn't have enough in there. People callin' for help, wantin' us to come here, wantin' us to come there. But nowadays things have gotten a little better, and they don't call. You don't ever see 'em. You don't hear from 'em, not even droppin' a dollar into the mail and sendin' it to the organization. They don't get that over there anymore. . . . I don't know. People into their own thing nowadays, people are kinda just doin' their own thing. I don't think people participate very much in nothin'.

Do you miss the spirit of the Movement?

Very much so. I miss not only the spirit. The staff and all of the people that I was around there with . . . it was a close thing with us. We really, I guess the word is, loved each other. It's kinda sad to see us go away into different things.

INTERLUDE

Benjamin Mays

and

Martin Luther King, Sr.

The Old Men: Two Who Knew Him Well

Benjamin Mays was president of Morehouse College when Martin Luther King, Jr., entered as a freshman at fifteen.

It didn't surprise me at all when he was chosen for that role in Montgomery and that he assumed it. It just turned out to be the right choice.

Were you fearful for him?

Yes. I was always fearful for him. I was fearful for my own life for a long time, because I knew that there were certain things that I wasn't gonna take lying down. . . . Of course, I was fearful for him. It was just as dangerous as being in the front of battle. . . . Sure I was afraid for him.

Did you ever discuss that with him?

No, not that I was afraid. He knew it. We didn't have to discuss it.

He knew that his time could come any time. He knew that. He talked with me more about the slanderous things that people were saying about him than . . . "this is going to get me in trouble and I'm going to get killed." He knew that.

What did he express about the slanders?

Well, some guy faked a picture of King with a group of Communists or Communist fellow travelers . . . and spread it all around as if it was King's picture. Then another time they set up some things to try to catch him. For example, he used to go to someplace, some friend's house, to get away to write, and the assumption was that he was over there with women or with a woman. So he talked to me about police comin' over there, and when they found that he was in there writing, of course, they'd go away. He was afraid of those types of things. The FBI was on him all the time. These were the exposures that he was afraid of, that they would ruin his reputation. . . .

Was he aware of their surveillance?

Oh, yeah, sure. Couldn't miss it. Every man was.

. . . was Dr. King's martyrdom, do you think, inevitable?

Inevitable, not that God willed it. Inevitable in that any man who takes the position that King did . . . if he persists in that long enough, he'll get killed. Now. Anytime. That was the chief trouble with Jesus: He was a troublemaker. So anytime you are a troublemaker and you rebel against the wrongs and injustices of society and organize against that, then what may happen to you is inevitable.

. . . didn't you ever feel impelled to try to get him to be aware of that fact, at least?

You know, I—[a long pause] No, you can't do that. Here's a prophet in the line of duty.

MARTIN LUTHER KING, SR.: Well, I was born in the very depths of segregation. I know what it is, I know what it did. I lived when the black man had no right, right or rights, that the white man was bound to respect. He wasn't nothin' but a nigger, a workhorse. He wasn't supposed to have any formal training, wasn't supposed to be bright. I lived in that day. I lived in that day. . . .

I was a sharecropper. My father was a sharecropper, and of course, you know the pattern of a sharecropper. Man owned the land, he owned the mules, he owned everything. You paid for half of the guano that was used to make the cotton grow, and half of some of the seed, plant seed. The rest of that was furnished by the owner of the land, owner of the mule, owner of all everything, and then you worked just for half, and whatever grew on the farm, they'd rob you out of it. Then you wasn't supposed to question them. You just worked and let 'em take from you, and I lived in that.

But I think it did something to me from a child, as I came up in it, and created a hate in my heart against whites. See, I had seen 'em do all these things, wrong, wrong things, saw 'em beat black people up, saw 'em lynch them and hang 'em up by a tree. And I promised to hate every white face I ever saw when I got to be a man. Well, this ain't no more. I don't hate anybody.

At what point did you become able to deal with that hatred . . . ?

Well, I began to deal with it as I felt an urge to preach as a young fellow. I read that book as best I could, the Bible. I read where you don't hate anybody, and I came up then changin' from that. But nobody helped me more than Martin Luther King, Jr. He helped me to rid myself totally of hate, and just before he left and after he left, I wrote *all* hate off for anybody anyway. And I don't—I say, I just do not hate.

Now this is when I really came to grips with it, knowing how dangerous it is. Hate is like sin. When it is finished it brings death. No man can hate and live.

RECESSIONAL

RALPH DAVID ABERNATHY

A Changed Man

He maintains two offices. One is in the old SCLC headquarters down on "Sweet Auburn." It is manned by a skeleton staff these days and so hard-pressed for money that the telephone service is occasionally discontinued until the bill is settled. His other office is in the fancy church his West Hunter Street Baptist congregation purchased from a white congregation which joined the flight to the suburbs when this South Atlanta neighborhood went black. In one of God's sweeter ironies, his new church is next door to the Wren's Nest, the home of Joel Chandler Harris, where the elderly guides still refer to Uncle Remus as "a kindly old nigra."

His office in the church is carpeted, quiet, rather impersonal, his secretary an efficient protectress. Unlike his SCLC office, it contains no photographs of him and King in their denim marching clothes. Something in this room, in his manner, brings to mind what an SCLC functionary had said: "It took him a good while to get over Dr. King's death. We used to travel all over. . . . He was always in a very sad moment. He would sometimes break down and cry."

There is no danger of that on this day; only a time or two does that soothing, deep voice—his trademark among the Movement preachers— grow a bit husky. Yet his telling of the story has about it a ritualistic sadness, as if in telling it so slowly, so meticulously—no detail too small

to be brought out, examined, fitted into its proper place—he will some-
how find the touchstone of those old, good days together.

I do not share the view that Dr. King had any premonitions that he
was going to be killed at that particular time. However, I do share the
view that there were moments in which he was thoroughly convinced
that he was going to be assassinated. He told me in 1965 as we drove
from Montgomery to Selma, Alabama, in our protest there to bring
about the Voting Rights Bill, he said, "Ralph, I thought I would have
been assassinated in Mississippi, but it did not happen. So it will probably come to me over here in Selma, so I want to fix it so that you will
automatically become my successor without having to have a board
meeting or anything. I want you to—as soon as it happens—to take over
the leadership of the organization."

And, of course, number one, I stated that I had no ambitions of being
president of SCLC, and number two, if there was to be an assassination,
I felt that we would be assassinated together because we were together
all the time. I thought that we might go to the car and get in the car and
turn the switch on, and we would be blown up. Or somebody would
bomb the hotel. I just could not imagine living a day without Martin
Luther King, because we were inseparable. It's very, very difficult to
describe that relationship even though we were not *always* with each
other *every* day. But I guess every day we were in contact with one another in one way or the other. Then the third thing, I said to him that I
thought that we were through the rough days and maybe no one would
be assassinated. But there were some very ambitious young people in
our organization—and I did call some names to him—that they should be
his successor if there was ever to be a successor. He said, no, they could
not represent him, he did not want that, because if there was any one
person who could really keep the team together, then it was me. And if
I was able to keep the team together, everything else would fall into
place. . . .

And later in the year in Baltimore while I was out of the room
dealing with the finances as the financial secretary and treasurer of the
organization, he did make that recommendation. . . . I began to hear
his father weeping and I asked what had happened, and a member of
my committee who was counting money with me told me what had happened, that Dr. King had offered my name as his successor and Dr.
King, Sr., just could not take the fact that his son really saw his death,
and he was weeping over it. . . .

Now Dr. King was greatly shaken by the attempted march that we
held in Memphis a week prior to his tragic assassination. On that

march, you remember, violence erupted, and it was the first time that people within our march had actually gone and inflicted violence upon the oppressors. A young group of black men used the line as a means of refuge, and they would go fall out of the line at intervals, certain ones, and smash windows as we marched along. And then would come back and would get right in the line, and say "Oh, yessir, Doc, lead us right on. Lead us right on." We had not workshopped those people. . . .

The disrupters of the march proved to be members of a black youth gang called the Invaders. Memphis police retaliated with tear gas and billy clubs. There was gunfire. Abernathy and King escaped the battle only by jumping into the backseat of a passing car. With a police escort they made their way to a Holiday Inn on the banks of the Mississippi River.

They carried us there, and we checked in, and Dr. King was very, very, very unhappy because a young black man was killed in that demonstration, and it was a very unpleasant thing, and he was so worried that violence broke out. And I couldn't get him to sleep that night. He was worried, worried. He didn't know what to do, and he didn't know what the press was going to say, and it was then that he raised this question with me if those of us who advocated nonviolence should not step back and let the violent forces run their course. . . .

That night, finally—I guess early in the morning—he fell asleep, and the next morning early some representatives from the Invaders came to the hotel to see Dr. King, and I hesitated to wake him up because he had been such a problem that night. . . . When I finally awakened him, he said, "Well, Ralph, you can take care of it. I need to shave," because he had called a press conference that morning. They said they wanted to see Dr. King, and so finally, once he had finished shaving, he agreed to give them about two or three minutes, and they admitted that they were the ones who had committed the violence. . . .

He didn't spend very much time with them. He went right on to the press briefing, and it was there that he really came forth like a lion. He just had so much—I don't know what it is. Normally he would sit quietly until Rev. Bernard Lee, his assistant, had introduced him to the press and laid down the ground rules for the press conference. But Dr. King walked right in and ignored Rev. Lee and myself and everybody else and just took over his own press conference, and said, "Ladies and Gentlemen, I'm most apologetic for being late, but this is not a press conference as such. We can have any question on the record or off the record, so please feel free to ask whatever you want to ask." And he was just—he was so beautiful until once we got upstairs, I just really had to hug him. I had never seen the lion in him come forth like that. After that terrible and dreadful night, you can see the contrast. He just met the challenge.

Then he said, "Ralph, I want to get out of Memphis. Get me out of Memphis as soon as possible." This was on Friday, and he said, "You've got to get me out of Memphis." And I got him to agree that once we got to Atlanta that we would go to a movie, because I had never seen him so upset. He had this obsession—I had gone on a trip around the world and this had taken me for about thirty days away from him, and once I got back Dr. King had begun, as we would travel, to do what he had never done before, and that was to preach his sermon over and over again to me. While I was away he preached some sermons. He preached "The Drum Major,"* and he preached that sermon sitting on a plane to me. You would not understand; it's kind of common among some black Baptist preachers, every time you see them, they're preaching sermons. They're giving you their sermons that they preached last Sunday and their points. Well, you don't find this in the circle of high-class preachers. You know, you preach it and you're through with it and you go on to something else. But he had begun—he wanted me to know all of these sermons and illustrations that he had given. . . . I had noticed all of these things, but I paid them not very much attention.

Once we were back in Atlanta on Friday, he then wanted me to drop him off because my car was at the airport, and then he wanted me to go to the health club. We always had one form of recreation, and that was to go to the Butler Street YMCA health club where we would take the exercise, swim, and the steam baths, and get a good rubdown. Of course, he just didn't want to give that up and I thought that was good for him, but I told him I needed to go home and let my wife see that I was really alive after all that had taken place in Memphis. He called me from the Y and said to me that he wanted to cancel the movie engagement because he didn't want to be with anybody that night. He only wanted to be in the presence of myself and Mrs. King and Mrs. Abernathy, my wife. He said those were the only people he wanted to be around. He had ordered some fish, and he wanted our wives to prepare it, and I told him that he didn't have to bring the fish to my house. I could provide the food. He said, "Well, David, you understand I've already ordered it and my drivers'll pick it up."

And so sure enough they came, and we were up all night long, until

---

* A prophetic sermon in which King asked that whoever preached his funeral characterize him as a "drum major for justice." A recording of the sermon was played at King's funeral service at Ebenezer Baptist Church later that same year.

finally he went to sleep in our new house—we had a new house then—on our little love seat, after teasing us about the love seat. It's made only for two. He cuddled up on it. There were two love seats, and he said, "You aren't even able to have a decent sofa." It wasn't a long one . . . you couldn't stretch out on it. Then I finally got over on the other love seat, and I fell asleep, and my wife fell asleep at the counter in the family room around the stove. And Mrs. King, who had recently undergone surgery, went back to the bedroom, and she fell asleep on the bed. When we knew anything, it was eight o'clock the next morning, and we had a staff meeting scheduled at nine at Ebenezer Church. Of course, they got up and went home, and I got up and went on to the meeting.

And we just couldn't get anything right in that staff meeting. The question of whether to go to Washington—Dr. King and Rev. Bevel and Rev. Jesse Jackson began to raise that same old question of whether we ought to go or not. We had been discussing it for about a year that we *were* going, but in every meeting they would say, "We shouldn't go," and finally Dr. King just got up and left—once he got there. He was very late getting there. When he went out, I went out behind him, and I asked him where was he going, and he said that he was going to take his daughter to a music lesson. But I found out later that this was not so. He was just going to get away. And I said, "Martin, what is wrong with you? Tell me." And he said, "I'm going to the country, and I'm going to stay with one of my members. I need to go to the farm, and I'm going down there." I said, "Well, tell me what is bugging you." And he said, "All I'll say is, Ralph, I'll—I'll snap out of it. Didn't I snap out of it yesterday? You said I did yesterday at the press conference. I'll pull through it." And I told him to call me and let me know where he was.

While he was away the staff really rallied and got itself together, and Hosea Williams insisted that I not relate to Dr. King what they had decided as a staff to do—that was to go to Washington, but to go first by way of Memphis and straighten out Memphis—but that I was to have Dr. King to come, and I was asked to produce him. . . . He came to the church, but he stayed downstairs talking with his daddy and kept us waiting for three or four hours before he came upstairs. And they said they had the Holy Spirit and all. If it was the Holy Spirit, by the time he got upstairs, it was all gone.

We persuaded him, however, to go on to Washington that night and preach at the Washington Cathedral the next morning. And Jesse Jackson and Hosea Williams and others would go into Memphis on Sunday evening. Andrew Young was to go on in on Monday, and I was to come in on Tuesday. I waited, waited, and waited Tuesday for that call, and I never did get it until real late, and I wanted to know what time we were leaving, and he said, "Aw, I decided we wouldn't go today. Let's don't go today. We'll go tomorrow." So Wednesday we found ourselves on a plane for Memphis, and the plane sat there at the airport for about an hour after we had boarded, and we had no contact whatsoever with the pilot. He didn't say anything. And finally he came on and said, "Ladies and gentlemen, please forgive us for this delay, but we have a distinguished person on this plane today. Dr. Martin Luther King, Jr., is on this plane, and we had to have this plane guarded all night last night, and then we had to check every piece of luggage to make sure that there were no bombs on board." And Dr. King laughed, "Well, isn't that something, Ralph? If they're going to get me, why would he tell it to me and tell it to me out over the speaker like that?"

Now, we flew on into Memphis, and he acted very, very well. He didn't want to go to the mass meeting that night, Wednesday night, when he made that great speech, "I've been to the mountaintop," because tornado warnings were out and maybe a tornado had come to Memphis because it was really raining. He didn't want to go . . . because he liked big crowds.

He went to speak in King's place, and found a crowd of only one thousand in an auditorium which seats ten thousand. But the crowd was so enthusiastic that he placed a call to King at the Lorraine Motel and talked him into coming to the meeting. Once there, King gave the great speech in which he seemed to predict his own death. King likened himself to Moses who had been to the mountaintop and looked over into a promised land which he would not be allowed to enter with his people.

After that, we went down to dinner, and went back to the motel, and he was very happy and relaxed. On Thursday, we had a staff meeting, and then he and I had lunch. Neither of us ate breakfast, but we had lunch, and the waitress couldn't get the order right, and we ate it from the same platter. We had catfish. He loved catfish and so do I, and we ate from the same platter. Then he visited with his brother, A.D., who happened to have been there. And finally, he called me, because I had had an afternoon nap, and asked me to come down to the room, and when I went down to the room, he said, "We have just talked with Mother, and we have talked for more than an hour. You know, she's always so happy when A.D. is with me. I wish you had been here where you could have talked with her."

We were preparing to go to dinner, and there was no sign that he had any fear or any premonition that anything was going to happen at that time, because we were going to a soul dinner, and he wanted to know what the lady had for dinner because he really was not interested in just eating steaks. He loved soul food. He talked me into calling her to find out what her menu was. I did call Mrs. Kyles* and she told me, and I repeated it so he could hear. She had roast beef, but then she had chitlins and she had pig feet and potato pie and everything he liked. He was ready to go, and then we went back to our room where we stayed, and he took a shave, and I told him some problems I was having of going to Washington for the first phase of the Poor People's Campaign. I could not go because of a revival service, and he began to try and help me get the minister for the service, because he said he wouldn't think of going to Washington without me. I would not relate this in the meeting earlier that day because I didn't want to dampen the spirit of the meeting. . . . He made a special call to New Orleans, and we couldn't get that minister because he was out in the rural [area] at a conference with his bishop. And he said, "Then you will have to go to West Hunter and tell them that you have a greater revival, a revival to revive the soul of this nation, and they'll understand."

Naturally I agreed that I would do that and he said, "Are you ready?" And I said, "Yes, wait just a minute, though, let me put some after-shave lotion on." He said, "I'll be standing here on the balcony," and as he walked out on the balcony, he saw Jesse Jackson, who had been very objectionable to our going to Washington for the Poor People's Campaign. Dr. King was really trying to build a bridge there, because Dr. King had kind of lost his patience at that point, and he said, "Jesse, I want you to come and go to dinner with me and have your band play for me tonight 'Precious Lord, Take My Hand.'" This was not his favorite song, but it was a song that the band played very well. And so I told him, "Tell Jesse not to bring too many people," because we didn't want the food to give out, and Dr. King said, "Ralph said don't bring too many, Jesse, now," and then the driver said, "Dr. King you better go back and put your coat on. It's kind of chilly out here."

And I was going up with my after-shave lotion to my face, and before I could put it on, I heard what sounded to be a firecracker, and I heard the groans, and I looked and he had fallen right back. Had he fallen right straight back, he would have fallen right on me because I was standing right in the door. I immediately rushed out, and they were saying, "Take cover," but I had no concern for any cover. My concern was for my friend. I really—I think he knew it was coming, and one of the first questions Andrew Young asked me once I had gotten back from the hospital and from the morgue. He carried me in the room, in the

* Wife of Rev. Samuel B. Kyles, the minister who had invited King to Memphis.

bathroom, and he asked me, "Ralph, I *know* Martin would tell you anything. Did Martin know anything? Did the FBI or anybody inform him
or tell him, or were they harassing him? Was anybody bothering him?"*
And I had to tell him in all honesty, "No, not to my knowledge." If so,
he had not said one word to me. All I know is that once I was back
from my trip to India and around the world, he was kinda a different
man, as I look back on it now. . . .

Was he conscious after the shooting?

I felt that he was. In fact, I'm certain that he was. I would say that he
was. I didn't have very far to run. It was just a few steps that I really
had to make when I rushed to his side. He appeared to be terribly
frightened, and it was the left jaw that I patted and said to him over and
over again, "Martin, this is me, this is Ralph, this is Ralph, and you
have nothing to worry about. Don't—don't worry. It's going to be all
right. This is Ralph." And he—his lips quivered, but no sound came, and
then he gave me a straight look in the eyes, right straight in the eyes, as
though he was trying to communicate through his eyes, and then of
course, he relaxed his eyes. He was conscious.

The first person to get up where we were was Rev. Young, and Rev.
Young came up and saw: "Oh, my God, my God, it's all over, it's all
over." And I said, "Oh, *no.*" I became furious and angry, and I said,
"No, no, Andy, don't you say that, don't say that, don't say that." And
then there were some other people from the Human Relations Commission, a young man who kept down low, and he brought me a pillow to
put under his head and another—everybody was keeping down—a blan-
ket to put over him and to keep him warm. And then Rev. Kyles, who
was our host in whose home we were going to eat, came back up the

* Andrew Young's suspicions about the FBI, first voiced that day in Memphis,
have persisted and were reinforced by the Senate Intelligence Committee's findings
on "the paranoia that we know now existed in Hoover's mind and . . . some of
the agents in the FBI." Young continued: "See, we were confronted by a black
community that was losing faith in nonviolence, saying nonviolence couldn't
deal with the economic problems, nonviolence wouldn't work in the North. And
our answer was, well, maybe the kind of marches that we had in the South would
not work, but that massive civil disobedience would work. And so we had
escalated the rhetoric of nonviolence, not Martin himself, but me and Bevel and
Hosea and everybody else, so that there was a real fear of Martin comin' to
Washington with thousands of people to disrupt the life of the government. And
some of the kinds of things that were in the newspapers and in the Congressional
Record around that time lead me to think that there would possibly have been
people in the federal government somewhere that made a decision that Martin had
to be stopped."

steps and I told him to get a ambulance. And he went in and he just fell across the bed and started screaming, and I told him there was no time to scream and cry, that we had to get him to the hospital. And in a little while—he never did get the switchboard, but policemen were in the area —and in a little while an ambulance come, and I don't know where the ambulance came from. I rode with him in the ambulance, and I helped the attendant to give him oxygen, and I could hear them. The attendant told me that he was conscious and that they were taking his blood pressure. And then once we went in the operating room, I could hear them talking saying what his pressure was and what the pulse beat was and so forth. So he was conscious, and he lived, really, about an hour.

Was there no opposition to your going into the operating room?

No, the only thing was once we—I helped them to take the stretcher out of the ambulance, and I went right in the operating room. Rev. Bernard Lee was with me, also. And once we put him on the table, then the nurses were first there, and they said that everybody had to get out now, and everybody left except me and Rev. Lee. And we removed ourselves out of their way, because we didn't want to be in their way or interfere with their work. And they went out and came back in again and said, "Now, you must all get out. You all must leave." And we just made it very clear that we were not going to leave, that we were going to stay with him and who we were. When the doctors came, they began to work, and I guess they knew who we were, and they didn't bother us.

At what point during this series of events did you give up hope of his life?

Only when the neurosurgeon . . . shook his head. I saw him. I saw the little doctor come in dressed in a green uniform. Several doctors had been in—and they had cut aloose the shirt and the suit and everything, and the wound was actually seen, and he came in, and he stayed for just a few minutes, not long, and when he looked, he shook his head, and he went out. And I knew then that—that Andy was right, that it was really all over. I didn't know who this doctor was until later. I guess the attending physician, or it may have been the doctor in charge at the hospital, I don't know what his name was, came over and said to me, "You're Rev. Abernathy?" And I said, "Yes." And he said, "Well, I'm afraid that it's—it's—it's over, and it will be an act of God if it is, because if he lives, he will be a vegetable the rest of his life, for he will be paralyzed from his neck down." He said, "You saw the little doctor that was in here and left out?" And I said, "Yes," and he said, "Well, that's the little neurosurgeon, and there has been terribly bad brain damage, and he would only be a vegetable if he lived, and I don't see how he can make it." He constantly from then on kept me informed. A little later he came back over and said, "Well, that's about it." They were giving him some air, pumping something into him or over his mouth or something at that point, and this doctor came over and said that, "It's about over." He said, "What they are doing now is what they always do for important people," and then he interrupted and said, "Well, you know, all people are important. I don't mean that. But for people on the basis of their position." He said, "But it's really over."

Is it true that you and Rev. Lee then stayed through the whole post-mortem process?

No, not through the postmortem process. You mean, after death? No. We went to the airport as soon as the doctor told me that it was really over and he was pronounced dead, and that he would tell the press only the time, the exact time of Dr. King's demise, and any other statements, I would make them. I went over and took from out of his pocket some of his personal effects. Then I went out and talked with the press and from there to the airport to meet Mrs. King. But while I was at the airport, looking for this flight, I was paged and informed that Mrs. King was not arriving on that flight, because she had found out in Atlanta before boarding the plane that he had passed, so she was not coming. So then in lieu of press conferences, I wanted to go to the morgue. This was my wish that I would go to the morgue. And when I went to the morgue, the coroner was there and he welcomed my coming, because he said the body had to be officially identified and didn't anyone go in, I don't think, but myself. I went in the morgue, and I picked up this piece of brown paper that covered the body of my friend and my buddy, and I told him that it was he.

T